0014749

DATE DUE

MAY 4   19

SHAPSCR99

THE PRIMAL SCREEN

Also by Bob Shanks

NONFICTION
The Name's The Game, *with Ann Shanks*
The Cool Fire

FICTION
Love Is Not Enough

SCREENPLAYS
Love Is Not Enough
Drop-Out Father
Once Upon a Beverly Hills
He's Fired, She's Hired
Drop-Out Mother

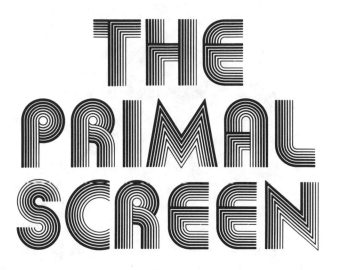

THE PRIMAL SCREEN

How to Write, Sell, and Produce
Movies for Television

with complete script of

Drop-Out Father

BOB SHANKS

W · W · NORTON & COMPANY

New York   London

ACKNOWLEDGMENTS

The poems "Don't" (page 384) and "The Pure Idea" (page 89) by E. E. Spitzer are reprinted by permission of the author.

The letter from Irv Wilson written on behalf of NBC (page 181) is reprinted by permission of Irv Wilson and NBC.

The screenplay for *Drop-Out Father* (pages 186–300) is reprinted by permission of CBS, Inc. © 1982 CBS, Inc. All rights reserved. Other CBC materials are reprinted courtesy of CBS, Inc.

Published simultaneously in Canada by Penguin Books Canada Ltd, 2801 John Street, Markham, Ontario L3R 1B4
Printed in the United States of America.

The text of this book is composed in Meridien, with display type set in AKI Lines & Benguiat. Composition and manufacturing by the Maple-Vail Book Manufacturing Group.
Book design by Jacques Chazaud.

First Edition

Library of Congress Cataloging in Publication Data

Shanks, Bob.
  The primal screen.

  Includes index.
  1. Television authorship.   2. Moving-picture
authorship.   I. Shanks, Bob.   Drop-out father. 1986.
II. Title.
PN1992.7.S5   1986   808'.066791   85–8807

ISBN 0-393-01993-4

W. W. Norton & Company, Inc., 500 Fifth Avenue, New York, N. Y. 10110
W. W. Norton & Company Ltd., 37 Great Russell Street, London WC1B 3NU

1 2 3 4 5 6 7 8 9 0

For Ann, because I love her,
And because she never thinks it's hopeless.

For writers, because I admire them,
And because they mostly think it is.

Contents

ACKNOWLEDGMENTS 9

PREFACE 11

Chapter 1 *Movies for Television* 19

Chapter 2 *How to Sell One* 50

Chapter 3 *How to Write One* 88

Chapter 4 *Drop-Out Father* 178

Chapter 5 *How to Produce One* 301

SUMMARY 384

APPENDIX 387

INDEX 407

Acknowledgments

I thank Ann Shanks for being wife, partner, and friend; for her love, her dedication to work and to laughter, all of which have contributed so richly to my life and to this book. I thank my father, W. Glenn Shanks, who encouraged every wholesome aim. I thank Ed Barber, the editor of this book, for his friendship, patience, and steadfastness; and for his sagacious ways with written weeds.

I am grateful to the following: Susan Holliday of CBS, CBS Entertainment, and the Writers Guild of America for their generous permission to use certain materials; to Michael C. Conley, CBS Press Information; Richard Connelly and Tom Mackin, ABC Press Information; Gene Walsh, NBC Press Information; the A. C. Nielsen Company; and the National Center for Health Statistics, Washington, D.C.

I received assistance and information from *The Hollywood Reporter, Daily Variety,* and *Variety,* for which I thank them.

I recommend the following publications, which have been useful and enlightening: *Adventures in the Screen Trade,* William Goldman, Warner Books, Inc., 1983; *American History/American Television, Interpreting the Video Past,* edited by John E. O'Connor, Frederick Ungar Publishing Co., 1983; *Film Comment,* "Family Plots—Writing and the Mankiewicz Clan," Stephen Farber and Marc Green, August 1984; *Screenplay, The Foundations of Screenwriting,* Syd Field, A Delta Book, Dell Publications Co., Inc., 1982; *The Inside Story of Roots,* David L. Wolper with Quincy Troupe, Warner Books, Inc., 1978; *The New York Times Encyclopedia of Television,* Les Brown, Times Books, Inc., 1977; *The TV Schedule Book,* Harry Castleman and Walter J. Podrazik, McGraw-Hill Book Company, 1984; and *Word into Image, Portraits of American Screenwriters,* American Film Foundation, 1981.

I thank Ed Spitzer for permission to reprint his poems, *The Pure Idea* and *Don't,* and for his enduring sensibility and comradeship.

There are five teachers in particular whose instruction and lives have helped shape my life: at Indiana University, Dr. Lee Norvelle and Professor William Kinzer; at Lebanon High School, Lebanon, Indiana, Mr. Paul Neuman, Ms. Jane Ward, and Ms. Mary Ann Tauer. They taught me to see, to listen, to talk, to write, and to respect.

Continuing thanks to all of the executives, artists, technicians, and craftspeople in the thousands who have contributed to the television shows with which I have been associated and who have eased so many dreams into reality for all of us.

And to writers, who preserve our tiny clearing in the universal brush.

Preface

There is oxygen, our animal appetites, and then, there is television. Viewing has become a primal human need. We ape its values, attitudes, language, and dress. Its haste. The shallows. We covet its merchandise, needed or not. We surrender the outdoors, alternate activity indoors, action and time. We give it our senses. Our brains. Goodness and evil, sublime and mundane wash us amain and we are blurred in our retention of the differences. There will never be a bald-headed president again. Television is a kind of destiny now. Like climate or topography or the color of your skin. We live secondhand.

Personalities and fictional characters on television become more real or cherished than friends or members of the family. There is birth or death. And down the hall or in the next-door room, relatives are watching television. People make love with the set on. Or use it not to. They abandon their babies to it. In the Al Pacino movie *Scarface,* a woman sits watching television while in an adjoining room a man is being murdered; and you know it has happened in life. A condemned murderer in Texas, James Autry, requested on the 1984 day before his execution by lethal injection that the occasion be televised. "It's not real—all that real—to the public if they don't see the execution," he said.

There is in my own life a small incident that I cannot forget. At the Aspen Institute, Ann Shanks (my wife and business partner) and I were members of an American Film Institute panel devoted to television. The panel included the Reverend Donald Wildmon, a minister from a small town in Mississippi. Wildmon had been denouncing network programming—an open-season sport—and trying to organize an economic boycott of it. He had achieved Andy Warhohl's didacticism that everyone in the country should get the chance to be famous for fifteen minutes. (Presidential assassins have a standing invitation.)

After a lot of hours and a lot of talk, all the people on the panel had had their say and had been won over by their own words to a firm belief in what they had believed before they got there. We no more exchanged ideas than we did suitcases, but the mood was tolerant and affable and gave a passable imitation of scholarly. Our deeper fires were banked.

Then, Reverend Wildmon, with scorching sincerity and barely restrained rage—he was nearly in tears—unburdened himself in a choked near-whisper: "When I come in at noon at home to sit and have some lunch with my son, I keep flipping around the dial, and there's never anything fit on the TV for a parent and child to watch together."

At first, there was silence, then the panel roused itself defensively to deal with the "filth-in-television" issue. But we ignored completely the more arresting point that a father and son could not better spend their lunchtime together than watching television. Here was potent testimony to television's primal power in our lives. We may know that like the air we breathe it is polluted, but it is no longer thinkable to do without it.

Viewing in the American home (or at least having a set turned on) now consumes an average of seven hours and two minutes a day in an estimated 84,900,000 households, according to figures used by the A. C. Nielsen Television Index for the broadcast season of 1984–85. And, as sure as Third World debt, these numbers grow annually. (The figure in 1983–84 was 83,800,000.) They are for households only, mind you. No figures are available for dormitories, clubs, offices, hospitals, bars, brothels, and the back seats of limousines; nor for the agate-eyed legions who now stare daily at the television screens of computers.

For good or ill then, and a lot of low-level radiation, you are likely in a lifetime to spend more hours watching a television screen than you will spend in school or working or sleeping. Only the hours you will spend dead hold an unassailable quantitative edge over the hours you will commit to watching television; some would argue that it is a standoff between death and television when it comes to unconsciousness.

There is even the terrible possibility that you may write for television. And, that you may write a movie for television.

That is what this cautionary volume is about: writing, selling, and producing movies for television. (I will touch on directing, but not in detail. I see that as another book.)

If you are a television dramatist or aspire to be, you may already be questioning why you have to bother your muse about the grubby business of selling and producing what you write. Aren't those separate functions? Can't others on your behalf sully themselves in the Agora? Of course, they can and do. There are writers, period. Sellers, period. Producers, period.

If your aggression level is about that of "Mister Rogers Neighborhood" you will be uncomfortable with selling and producing and you are well-advised to stick to the storyteller role. Or, you may simply decide that selling and producing are time- and energy-eaters better left to others. Either way, you can make a successful career in television movies with writing as your sole occupation. This does not mean that you should now stop reading and use this book to balance a chest of drawers. At the least, if writing television drama is your single career interest, you will learn something about that here, and, in following the wider thesis of this book, you will understand what happens to your work and why.

You will certainly be a more effective television dramatist, if not necessarily a better one, if you will sell and produce your scripts. If you can combine these divisible and often divisive functions, you will be in a position to maintain the maximal achievable control over your work. That, for me, is the point—control over the work. Not total control. In television that is impossible. But maximal achievable control. (Of course, you will also make more money.)

There are multiple forces contending in television that will often improve, but just as often erode, appropriate, reassign, and mangle your original work. Mabe you don't or won't care. Lots of writers turn in their scripts and never look back. Malibu and Mercedes are more important than their material. Or, their television writing may be only the money-means to support what they perceive to be their more serious books and plays and poems. Many of them contend, though I never believe them, that they don't care if their scripts get made—and many don't—as long as they continue to get assignments.

But most of us do care about what we write for television, in and of itself, and, while it may be a depressing consideration to some, we write as well as we can. We want our scripts turned into movies and we want those movies when they finally reach the screen to come as close as possible to our original visions of them. Anything less is cynical or silly.

All television dramatists, but especially new ones, must respond to the forces of the television marketplace. I will try to make you understand these rules of the game and why they exist and how to use them—and when and how to challenge them. Finally, it is your individual talent, character, personality, experience, persuasiveness, cunning, and ratings success that will combine to determine your placement—never a fixed position—on the power scale of affecting final results.

This volume is meant to be immediately useful to aspiring television movie writers, then to writer-producers, then to producers and executives who will never write but need to work with writers. I hope also that it will prove valuable to every thoughtful person in our society who must be interested in television and its processes because of its powerful presence in our lives.

My own life in television has taken me from shows on French Impressionist paintings and Thomas Jefferson's Monticello to the ridiculousness of taping a wet T-shirt contest. Though I am now mostly writing and co-producing movies for television, I have, over the years, been producer, director, writer, executive of drama, comedy, variety, documentary, news, talk, sports on NBC, CBS, ABC, PBS, and Group W—Westinghouse over the air and cable. I have received awards and critical praise; calumny and scorn. I have been rewarded with mega-dollars and in my psyche. I have also been fired, canceled, unemployed, underemployed, and bruised to the emotional bone. Some of my shows have been number one in the prime-time Nielsen ratings, and one was fifth from the bottom.

Through all of it, I have wrestled with my ambivalence about the medium and my role in it. I was made sharply aware of that in 1979, when, for my work in television, I was named distinguished alumnus of Indiana University, along with Dr. Joseph Mueller, who was being honored because he had invented fluoride toothpaste and had put a near-end to human tooth decay. The horrifying thought came to me that night that while he was strengthening enamel, I might be softening brain tissue. Now, our societal rewards were equal. More than equal. Following the ceremony, the crowd clustered, not around Dr. Mueller, but around me—for news of "Good Morning America" and Barbara Walters. Even the good doctor and his son—who asked my help in getting him a job in television. What hath Vladimir Zworykin* wrought? What is this blue-eyed monster?

I am exhilarated by television's force for good and proud of some of my good work in it, but I am suspicious of it always and disturbed by its powerful corrosions. Its massive falsities and mediocrities. Dejected by its torrent of waste. It is not so much my fear that television has destroyed American culture as it is my belief that it has now created it. An actor is president. "Dallas," "Dynasty," and Richard Dawson weigh more heavily in the collective American consciousness than our libraries, laboratories, and Lincoln Centers. More citizens know the rules for playing "Family Feud" than know the meaning of $E = MC^2$, or "A rose is a rose is a rose." Millions know that Carl Lewis won four Olympic gold medals in August of 1984. Anybody here know the names of the two doctors who announced a cure for malaria that same week? Television paid little attention. Does Michael Jackson's video "Thriller" really speak to or for our aspirations as individuals and as a society? To and for our souls?

Relax. I am not going to shoot down any geosyncronous satellites. I am not a revolutionist but at best a middling upwardly-mobile subversive who will willingly do most of the work in television's current system, though I do try to keep in mind that conscience should not come in decorator colors.

As you may have guessed already, this book is not an academic treatment of its subjects. It is not an outsider's research, pocked with footnotes and sources, or chunky lifts from others' oral or written views. No distance

---

*Russian-born U.S. inventor of the electronic camera and picture tube.

14

separates you or me from this. I make my living doing what I talk about here. These are bulletins from the operating room, from one who feels he is both patient and practitioner. I am, mostly, talking about my own personal experiences and work, and I will tell you as much as I know how to.

THE PRIMAL SCREEN

1

Movies
for Television

In the beginning, there were no movies on network television.

Then, there was one. *The Wizard of Oz* on CBS. That started in the season of 1956–57 and became an annual special.

Soon, there were many. The first regularly scheduled movies slot came on NBC in the autumn of 1961. The series was called "NBC Saturday Night at the Movies," and the first film, which premiered on September 23, was *How to Marry a Millionaire,* starring Marilyn Monroe, which probably is more information than you think you need on the subject, until you get zapped by it someday playing Trivial Pursuit.

While it was inevitable that all the major film studios would sell their pictures to the networks, as these became the dominant entertainment force, all of the titles in the NBC series that first year came from Twentieth Century Fox, which needed the cash. Elizabeth Taylor and Richard Burton were filming *Cleopatra* for Fox in Rome, where there had not been such heated fiddling around since Nero. As Burton and Taylor's passions soared, so did the movie's budget, until Fox had to sell off most of its studio backlot in Los Angeles to the Alcoa Company, which turned the property into Century City; and thirty-one of its films to NBC, which turned them into formidable primetime ratings competition for CBS and ABC. Movies on primetime had come to stay.

ABC followed the leader in April of 1962 with its "Sunday Night Movies," which is still on the schedule. A few weeks into the 1962–63 season, NBC quickly had to add a second movie umbrella, "NBC Monday Night at the Movies," when two of its back-to-back one-hour series, "It's A Man's World" and "Saints & Sinners," folded.

CBS, with the most hit series, did not add a movie night until 1965. Three years later, though, you could watch a movie on one of the three networks every night of the week. Soon, if you were truly dedicated, and you didn't mind your friends thinking of you as an eggplant, you could watch *ten* network movie showings in every seven primetime evenings, as the networks started going head-to-head against each other with movie "nights."

In this period, all the movies shown on all the networks in primetime were "theatrical" motion pictures; that is, motion pictures made originally for exhibition in movie theaters. The massive television use of this material soon made it clear that, despite the thousands of feature films that Hollywood and the rest of the world had turned out in the previous fifty years, the entire output was rapidly being consumed and the choicest titles were even then becoming prohibitively expensive. The growth of color television proscribed the use of black-and-white films, especially on NBC, the parent company of which is RCA, a color television manufacturer. This further reduced the available and desirable films.

A couple of other problems arose: For one, fewer theatrical movies were getting made. By the mid-1960s, television itself, an exploding pop music record industry, live pop concerts, and the ills of our inner cities had turned a lot of the nation's large cinemas into office buildings, parking lots, or echoing cavities of urban decay; a lot of the smaller houses went "X."

For another, the few theatrical films that did get made were trying to compete for audiences with television. They were increasingly provocative, explicit in language, and full of good old gratuitous sex and violence, far beyond what the networks could then air.

Television executives saw their movie golden goose running out of eggs just at a time when the audience had become ravenous. So, they invented a new goose. Somebody got the bright idea to make movies especially for television, movies that could be exhibited afterward in American movie houses and in foreign markets as well. "Made-fors" never made it in American theaters and have limited appeal in movie houses overseas, but there was and is a vast and lucrative secondary television market for these films in domestic syndication and foreign outlets. As we know now, almost all old movies, even the bad ones, can play forever on television somewhere, since our tolerance for them seems as boundless as it is frequently incomprehensible, and a new American audience is born every seven or eight years.

Again NBC led the way. That network contracted with Universal Studios to supply a series of two-hour made-for-television movies under the umbrella title of "World Premiere." The first such picture was called *Fame Is the Name of the Game*, and it "premiered" in November of 1966.

These movies each cost between 750 and 800 thousand dollars to make. The money was supplied by the network, which, in return, got the right to air each picture twice over a period of three years. After that, Universal was free to sell them wherever it could.

In 1969, ABC, which then always got the table leavings when it came to stars and series, and which was jokingly described as running fourth in a three-network race, scheduled—in self-defense no doubt—a made-for-television movie slot that, to everyone's surprise, hit a ratings jackpot: "ABC's Tuesday Movie of the Week." These ABC originals were first made by M-G-M and then by various studios and independent suppliers. The films were ninety minutes in length and cost just 400 thousand dollars each. They were, of necessity, aimed at a young, urban audience, since latecomer ABC had nearly all of its affiliated stations in big cities—the multistation markets—and none of the older, established stars. NBC and CBS as the older, more entrenched networks were, of course, in these major cities as well, but they also had scores of affiliates in two-station or one-station small towns and rural areas, where ABC was shut out. These smaller markets forced NBC and CBS to program more conservatively.

By the television season of 1971–72, ABC, with its more daring and youth-oriented subject matter, reached critical mass with its made-for-television movies. "Tuesday Movie of the Week" moved into fifth place in the ratings among all programs in the season-to-date averages. One of the films, *Brian's Song*, achieved a stunning 32.9 rating and a 48 share. (More about numbers and ratings later.) This placed *Brian's Song* in the top ten highest-rated movies—all movies—ever shown on television. When you consider that *The Wizard of Oz* held five of these top-ten rankings, the result is even more impressive. Not surprisingly, ABC added a second made-for-television movie package the following season: "Wednesday Movie of the Week."

Barry Diller, now chairman of the board of Twentieth Century Fox, was in charge of the ABC movie operation. Bachelor Diller, small and compact, bald before thirty, his clothing always a fastidious casing, icy and aloof (he has been known to buy two first-class tickets when he flies so that no one will be seated next to him), then explosive off a hair-trigger temperament, is, with it all, one of the very best. He is a tough businessman but also a showman, an enthusiast for the business and the creative people in it. He is, I believe, simply, a fan. Of established people, though he will not tolerate their excesses, and of newcomers and fresh ideas. I like that he has maintained the spirit of a poor kid being locked in overnight in F.A.O. Schwarz on Christmas Eve. And, it comforts me to know that he smokes even more than I do.

Whether by design or accident, ABC and Diller had with their movies tapped into a gusher: the Baby Boom generation, that most mammoth of American generations, which had been born by the unprecedented millions in the happy years between 1946 and 1963, following World War II and Korea.* This generation and its free-spending parents were determined to put the Great Depression and one and a quarter ghastly wars

---

*In the years 1946 through 1963, there were 70,817,723 Americans born. For comparison, in the preceding seventeen years, 1928–45: 40,179,571, and in the following seventeen years, 1964–81, 57,579,968, est.

behind them. They who gave to their own kids everything they thought they had missed themselves were who the advertisers wanted most to reach, and, suddenly, ABC had them.

It is fascinating to track this Baby Boom generation as it moves along its time line in our society and to trace its affects on our culture. Not only fascinating, but required homework if you want to work successfully in television. Because the generation is so massive in number, and because it was raised as the most affluent in human history, it has a penchant for spending as though every day were one in Yuletide season. Its influence in America will be foremost until it dies. Its interests and wants per force become the dominant national interests and wants. You will have to write and produce programs to satisfy its members.

In network television this generation has taken us from "Leave It to Beaver" and "The Wonderful World of Disney" in their childhoods to "Shindig," "Bewitched," and "Batman" in their early teens, to "That Girl," "The Dating Game," and "Laugh-In" in their late teens; and, in their rebellious and idealistic early twenties to "relevant" programs, rock'n'roll, and made-for-television movies with bold themes. We even got to see black people! Then, in their late twenties, as they searched for something to replace their exhausted rebellion and battered ideals, they were served the past, the innocence of yesterday—"all my troubles seemed so far away"—as expressed in "Happy Days," "Laverne & Shirley," "Little House On The Praire," and "The Waltons"—and they rushed to it; until, in the ripening 1970s, when they got tagged "The *Me* Generation," which probably they had been all along, they turned their lingering adolescence toward the avaricious toys of grownups and made hits of "Dallas" and "Dynasty," "Hotel" and "Falcon Crest," those make-a-buck-any-way-you-can-and-always-look-out-for-number-one shows, which, along with the hedonistic puerility of Magnum on "Magnum, P.I." and Sam on "Cheers" (ain't nobody poor on "The Love Boat" either), is rather where we are today.

Another aspect of this generational phenomenon in television is the recent emergence of people over forty, many of whom dare to show wrinkles and gray hair. Larry Hagman, John Forsythe, Joan Collins, Linda Evans, Brian Keith, Donna Reed. Even Jane Wyman and Barbara Stanwyck! Such ancient creatures previously had been virtually against the law on television unless they were nasty, senile, or selling denture cement. But, ah, the Baby Boomers are aging, so their icons must age as well. It is not surprising that Reagan is their president.

As this generation moves into its sixties and beyond in the twenty-first century, becoming the world's oldest teen-agers, will television provide it with a hundred ripped-off versions of *King Lear* and *On Golden Pond?* I can hear the programming meetings now: "Give us a "Gin Game"—but sexy. Maybe she's a retired hooker—and he's afraid of commitment."

Even now, for instance, with the Baby Boom generation in its thirties, you have probably noticed that feature films and television are exchanging roles. Television, that traitional angler after the acne set, now offers made-for-television movies that treat more serious "adult" subjects and in longer forms, while the movie houses, playing mostly to the base instincts of its base audience, fourteen- to twenty-four-year-olds (a shrinking market pool, given the declining birth rate), now are glutted with the ninety-minute likes of *Porky's, Fast Times at Ridgemont High, Valley Girls, Risky Business, Splash, Ghostbusters, Gremlins* (and other terrors), *Police Academy* I & II, *The Karate Kid* (one of a score of *Rocky* rip offs), the megabuck-inflated comic book memories of Lucas and Spielberg, and the umpteenth dance film. Yes, there are exceptions, on both television and in the movies, but the point remains. If I were scheduling a network's programming today, I would continue to aim straight at the Baby Boomers and their concerns.

While the 400-thousand-dollar made-for-television movie was flexing million-dollar muscles in the autumn of 1971, another programming phenomenon had made its civilized bow the summer before. On CBS. In what most network executives at the time viewed as the program equivalent of tithing in religion, CBS ran a six-hour BBC drama with a lot of people standing around in costumes, talking in funny English accents in one-hour installments that played over six weeks. The program was called *Six Wives of Henry VIII,* and, despite its exotica and languorous pacing, it performed surprisingly well in the ratings. No one knew it yet—the term hadn't even been coined—but the mini-series had arrived.

PBS moved quickly—or its corporate underwriters did—to bring in other British mini-series, or limited series, as they are sometimes called: *Elizabeth the Queen, The Forsyte Saga.* This kind of material became institutionalized in the series called "Masterpiece Theatre" on PBS, which some wag said stands for *Principally British Shows.**

The commercial networks were slower to respond to the mini-series form. They thought *Six Wives* had been a summer fluke against weak competition and that, despite PBS's success with the form, their own mass audience would not in sufficient numbers watch a closed-end story that would require a viewing commitment of several nights or weeks running. Especially if the material was British, the only model at first.

But, in the autumn of 1973, NBC, with faltering weekly series, having decided to give the form a try, presented its adaptation of *The Blue Knight,* a best-selling American novel about cops, written by Joseph Wambaugh,

---

*My wife, Ann, started a one-woman war against Mobil Oil because it spends millions on these safe, artsy shows with a nineteenth century colonial sensibility, while flipping only an occasional quarter into the blind-man's cup of original America productions. All of the creative and craft unions supported her at first but lost energy when it came to maintaining the pressure. Ann's point, by the way, was not to deny us British product of the quality of Olivier's *King Lear* and other splendid productions but to encouage these companies occasionally to put their money where their pumps are. We buy ARCO now, which does support American production.

the ex-cop from Los Angeles. The program was four hours long and played in one-hour episodes over four consecutive nights.

ABC presented its first attempt at a mini-series a few months later—a low-risk three and a half hours—in April 1974, safely out of the primary ratings season. This was an adaptation of Leon Uris's best-selling novel, *QB VII*.

What *The Blue Knight* and *QB VII* had in common, besides actress Lee Remick, were mostly critical acclaim and, even more important, success in the ratings.

While the networks did not stampede to the form, other mini-series were now put into production. In January 1976 ABC presented, in two consecutive nights, four hours of *Eleanor and Franklin*, based on Joseph Lash's book of the same name; and, in February and March of 1976, ABC made a quantum jump in the form by programming twelve hours of *Rich Man, Poor Man*, an adaptation of the novel by Irwin Shaw, which ran once a week in one-hour episodes. *Rich Man, Poor Man* was such an enormous hit (making stars of Nick Nolte and Peter Strauss), that it set ABC on the high road to first place in the ratings among the networks, a spot held for twenty-odd years previously, and mostly since, by CBS. (*Eleanor and Franklin*, also a success, spawned two sequels: *Eleanor and Franklin: The White House Years*, 1977, and *Eleanor: The Years Alone*, 1978. When NBC tried to capture the numbers magic of the mini-series form on a steady basis with a regularly scheduled weekly series called "Best Sellers," it fell flat. Much of the material in this latter series was wanting, and perhaps the saturation factor robbed the better material of the rarity and importance— and extra promotional possibilities—of a legitimate limited series.)

And then, there was *Roots*.

This production of Alex Haley's semiautobiographical novel by David Wolper (the same David Wolper who received such lavish praise for his production of the opening and closing ceremonies of the 1984 Los Angeles Summer Olympic Games) remains the single most powerful event in the history of American television, subsequent claims to that title notwithstanding (from *The Winds of War* and *The Day After* in 1983 and, in 1984, the Summer Olympics, all of which had sizable impact).

There is a lot to learn from a study of how *Roots* came to television.

It aired first in the winter of 1977. The commitment to produce it came a full year before that historic January week, and, before that, the preliminary steps had begun as early as April 1974. This is your first lesson.

While a project from idea to completion and airing may not always take that long, although some take even longer, all television movies have long periods of gestation. That is the reality and you must be prepared for it, financially and psychologically. It is a battle all of us fight every day, and a lot of good and talented people fall by the wayside because they cannot take it emotionally or survive it economically.

Exceptions that come to mind of movies made quickly are *Raid at Entebee* and the first use of the Jean Harris story.* These movies got on fast (three to four months from "go") to take advantage of the headline heat associated with their stories and because more than one network at a time was preparing a picture on each of the subjects. Even so, these exceptions would not be likely to involve you, unless you were a well-known, experienced writer and producer with a track record of creating similar kinds of pictures—someone who has easy access to the networks and holds the networks' trust.

The *Roots* producer, David Wolper—and I know firsthand because I have made a program for him—is a gentleman, thoughtful, soft-spoken, and measured, gray as a naval base in his persona and as tough and smart in television as they come. In a business too often dominated by producer-salesmen who will sell anything or anybody and "give good meeting," as we say, but then cannot deliver the program or, too frequently, do not even seem to care about the actual program, Wolper is the antithesis of that type, but he is also a superb salesman-producer. As a salesman—and you must be one in television—Wolper has no jokes, snappy patter, gifts-as-bribes or any of the psychological selling gimmicks. Instead, he has belief in what he is selling.

He is a complete producer. He is involved in and committed to a project from the first, when the idea is a seedling, through to making sure that the log line in the newspaper listings is effective. And along the way he insures that there is oxygen for everyone else working on the project.

Wolper would disavow the label "intellectual." He is openly scornful of the tea-sipping kind who hold their noses as they contemplate anything in our society that is popular. Yet, he is, if intellectual means using your mind and using it professionally, an intellectual in the truest sense. He *thinks* about television, seriously and respectfully. He knows its uses and users. He knows first—and you must never forget it—that it is a mass medium. To be effective, you must have millions upon millions of people watching a program. Wolper finds this no more deplorable or constrictive than McEnroe does a tennis court that has boundry lines and a net. That is the game. Its drama and reality. For too many television players this becomes an excuse for hand-wringing, then contempt, and finally, cheap goods.

Wolper respects the mass audience. He likes the mass audience. He dares to believe that television—popular television—can educate, and likes

---

* *Raid at Entebee* told the story of the hijacked El Al plane and passengers held captive by Moslem terrorists at Entebbe Airport, Uganda, in July 1976, and of their subsequent rescue by Israeli Defense Forces. Jean Harris is the ex-headmistress of an exclusive girls' school in Virginia who drove to Westchester County, New York State, in March 1980 and shot dead her lover, Dr. Herman Tarnower, best known for his best-selling book, *The Scarsdale Diet*, who apparently had not been able to curb his own appetite for other women. Ms. Harris claimed the shooting was an accident. A jury decided otherwise. She was sentenced to prison, where she remains.

to call himself a "visual historian." He dares to take an audience to the better parts of itself.

The audience may not always know that it wants these better things from television, since they are mostly absent, as it sleepwalks or sleepsits through "The A Team" and "The Dukes of Hazzard" and all the other preponderant drivel. (The set is always on to something, now that television has become primal.) But if you make this kind of larger television and you are not pretentious, arcane, or—especially—if you are not boring, the audience will rouse itself and come with you by the tens of millions. What gets 35, 40, 50, and 60 percent shares of the audience? Not the garbage. Mostly quality. By quality I mean relative commercial television quality. Mass-appeal quality. Not Beckett and Barthelme and other intellectual boutiques. When you want that kind of television on the commercial networks, I suspect that you really want to exclude the audience, to succor your sense that you are better than everybody else. I mean quality television that *includes* the audience, without pandering.

In television movies, I mean *The Autobiography of Miss Jane Pittman*, *The Missiles of October*, *Pueblo*, *The Gathering*, *Friendly Fire*, *Golda*, *Jesus of Nazareth*, *The Divorce Wars*, *The Holocaust*, *Shògun*, *Special Bulletin*, *A Streetcar Named Desire*, *Something about Amelia*, even *The Blue & the Gray* and *George Washington*. Each of these programs had at least a 35 percent share of the audience and most had 40 percent or better.

These movies had scope and substance. Big ideas. They taught. They are, with all their warts and flaws and commerical disciplines, serious television entertainment, and audiences responded to them seriously. *Roots* was the fullest, finest expression of this kind of lasting television.

Roots was a novel-in-progress when David Wolper first heard about it in 1972 from actress Ruby Dee, who was having dinner at Wolper's home, along with her husband, actor-director-writer Ossie Davis. Wolper was intrigued at once. When he pursued the book, however, he found that Columbia Pictures already had it under option.

This happens often. Long before they are published or produced, or even finished, books and plays are optioned for feature films or television. Networks and the larger production companies have staff people, readers and scouts, who are in daily contact with agents, with publishers and theater companies all over the country, thus assuring them access to material long before the public hears about it. An option simply means that you have paid for the right to hold a project exclusively for a period of time in which to try to sell it and get it written. Sometimes, projects are financed up front for publication or stage production by networks and by film and television companies, since they know that success in one of these forms first enhances movie value.

Wolper had to forget about *Roots* and go on to other projects. I asked him once about this common occurrence. "What do you do—how do you deal with the loss—or the rejection—of a project you love?" He shrugged and said, "I go on to the next one. That's how it is." (Boundaries and nets.)

This is another lesson that may need pointing out. Do not rely on one or even two or three projects, no matter how much you love one. The process is too precarious, too stretched-out in television, even with success, to commit yourself totally to one idea. You have to have lots of ideas in development at the same time. Ann Shanks and I had twenty-seven various ideas in different stages of development in 1985, including two possible Broadway shows. Only two of these went to production and one to script. While some have carried over into the next year, others have had to be abandoned. As small as our company is, we keep an internal "Status Report." We update it weekly. I will show you a sample in the chapter on selling. When one of many ideas is rejected or abandoned, it hurts, but you do not break.

In April 1974, over two years after having first heard about *Roots*, Wolper, who lives in the Bel Air section of Los Angeles, was having lunch in New York City when two young black women entered the restaurant. Wolper knew one of them, a William Morris agent named Cynthia Robinson. Since all the tables were taken, Wolper invited Robinson and her friend to join him at his table. The other woman turned out to be Pat Alexander, who was at the time Alex Haley's secretary. Wolper remembered. Alex Haley. *Roots*. He told Ms. Alexander that he had tried a couple of years ago to get the rights but that Columbia pictures had them. Ms. Alexander told Wolper she believed the option had run out. She thought the rights were available. Right away, Wolper tracked down Haley's lawyer, Lou Blau, a man whom Wolper already knew, and opened negotiations.

In May, while he was still in negotiations and before he had secured the rights to *Roots*, Wolper pitched the idea to Barry Diller at ABC.

This may seem questionable, trying to sell something you do not own, but it is a common practice in television and essential to survival, especially for independents. There are only three places—maybe five or six these days—where you can sell a television project. If these pass—say "no," that is—and the odds are that they will, you have nowhere else to go. Option money can run as high as 250 thousand dollars or higher for a hit book or play.

The proper ethics of the situation dictate that you tell the potential buyer that you do not have the rights yet but that they are available and that you are in negotiations, if you are. Only if they want to go forward do you tell them what those rights will cost. They will expect you to pass along the cost as part of the project's budget.

Speaking of ethics, or the lack of them, once, when I was a buyer, I had three different producers in two days pitch Doris Kern's book about Lyndon Johnson, each claiming he held the rights. I called the publisher, got the name of the author's agent, called the agent, and found out that only one of the three had even said he wanted to begin negotiations.

Dealing with the rights owner or his representative is trickier, if you want to be honest and not get stuck having to pay a huge option price for a project no one wants. You should also get used to calling a project a "property," since that is the term most often used in the business, as in "I have this property—*Ecclesiastes.*"

If the book or play is really hot, its representative is going to make you pay the price—and quickly. There will be stiff competition, and reps know that producers are likely to "shop"—try to sell—a property before they have acquired it. Also, they will negotiate only with established producers, networks, and studios, unless you are an established multimillionaire willing to pay a ridiculous premium.

If the property is a good one but was overlooked on the first wave of its publication or staging (we will talk later about properties other than books and plays), the option price and all other pricing will be lower. Even here, if you are a beginning producer and / or writer, the price is likely to be beyond your reach. Sometimes, however, you can acquire a property for a low option price—$500, $2,500, $5,000—if you shorten the option period or offer larger than usual inducements if and when you sell the property and / or it goes into production.

You can propose a two-tier option structure. Tier one, at a low price, would allow you a short period of time—three months, six months— in which to sell the property up to the scripting stage. Tier two would allow you a year, eighteen months, or two years—for which you would pay a more equitable price that can be passed along to the buyer, permitting you to hold the property while everyone involved is waiting for the script to be written and to be "picked up"—meaning that it goes into production—at which time you would have to pay *the purchase price.* The purchase price must also be considered as a cost of the picture that will be charged to the buyer. The purchase price pays for the absolute rights to a property to make a film (and usually to secure other uses as well—merchandising or a series spinoff, for instance) forever or for a long, extended period of time. It almost always grants you the copyright in the film work, rather than that being kept by the first author. It is said that James Michener got as much as one million dollars as the purchase price for the rights to his book *Space,* the basis for the thirteen-hour mini-series presented on CBS and produced and considerably written by my friend Dick Berg, who is not the man who told me that figure. (Dick Berg was the executive producer on the project and holds equity in the film property. He hired veteran producer Martin Manulis to be the on-line producer.)

As a fledgling producer-writer, you will almost certainly have to pay some kind of premium other than up-front hard cash to get a position on a book or play or other property owned by someone else, but you cannot give away the store. If you do, expecting to get this later from a network or studio, you may have given away so much that the property is financially unproducible, even if the material is attractive to someone. What you can always do, of course, is give away as large a part of your own potential piece as you wish. This is a way sometimes to "get into the game," but don't ever give away your work fees or more than 50 percent of your profit interest. Instead, find another property. Go on to the next one.

There is Wolper in May 1974, at ABC, pitching *Roots* in Barry Diller's office. Diller showed some interest in the project but turned it over for more detailed examination to his then-assistant, Lou Rudolph, who is now an independent producer-writer. Rudolph, ignited by Wolper, caught fire about *Roots*. He began to think of it as his project.

A network programming executive can and must get a proprietary feeling about the projects he likes or is assigned. If you are in a network and supervising a project, it is spoken of as yours by others in the network. They look to you as the party responsible for that project. If it fails, it will be yours for certain. If it succeeds, you will share the credit with those above you, since it is a truth, as President Kennedy said, that "failure is an orphan, but success has many parents." (Lou Rudolph was to get a promotion as a direct result of *Roots*'s triumph.)

To get someone inside enthusiastic about a project is an outside producer-writer's dream, and you should encourage that executive, even at the lowest level, to form a sense of parenthood or authorship about your project. That executive then is in there every day selling for you. That executive has access not only to the formal programming meetings but to casual encounters as well, where a lot of decisions are made.

Lou Rudolph persuaded Diller and Brandon Stoddard, who is a diminutive Yalie and Connecticut blueblood who would make George Bush feel like an ethnic, that they should move ahead with *Roots,* subject to approval by upper management and the board of directors. Stoddard, by the by, was then vice-president of novels for ABC, reporting to Diller, and is currently the president of ABC Motion Pictures, Inc.

At this stage in the story, *Roots* was being contemplated as a six-hour limited series. This meant then a potential investment by ABC of roughly three million dollars through production. That kind of money commitment then required approval at the top.

Network executives at various levels have varying power. The lower ranks—program executives, managers, supervisors—and zonk, they are even called directors and executive producers, titles that mean something in production—have, aside from their persuasive abilities with those higher up, negative power only. That is, they can choose not to see you, and, if they do, they can say no. I do not have much respect for those executives who serve only as conduits for bringing projects into the weekly programming meetings. I admire those who are definite about properties and ideas, even if the answer is no, and who select some they really love and believe in and will fight for. In my experience, it is these young risk-taker executives who will rise. It is absolutely astonishing when you are inside how much you can push around a big company and get things done.

Vice-presidents, of course, begin to have some positive power. Some can commit to script at least. And now, these days, we have the titles senior vice-president and executive vice-president. These, like new areas codes in the phone system, were added because of an overload of vice-presidents. Senior and executive vice-presidents, no doubt you have figured out, have more power, and some can commit to production, though even here some senior and executive vice-presidents are more senior and executive than others. At one network, CBS, only Harvey Shephard, the senior vice-president, programs, CBS Entertainment, can commit movies and mini-series to production.

I would guess that in 1974 Barry Diller had the authority, granted on an annual basis, to make x number of movies—I have forgotten how many, but let's say forty. He had a development fund that allowed him to commission perhaps an additional ten scripts that could go bust or be abandoned for any number of reasons. Given the vagaries of scheduling, a volatile competitive marketplace, a fickle audience, some bad executive judgments, and / or faltering creative talents, every network or studio has a budget for failures. For "development," they prefer to call it. "Failure" is such an unpoolside word. While it would seem a lot of failures get aired, there are worse ones that have been shot and shelved or that never got up off the pages—and, as I think about it, some better ones.

When I was vice-president of specials for ABC and, among other duties, was responsible for "ABC Theatre," the network's premier showcase for dramatic material, I had one of these busted scripts. Only one, fortunately. I was always underspending my development fund, which is a bureaucratic no-no. How can you get a bigger allocation the next year if you do not spend everything this year?

Anyway, in walks this producer with Liv Ullman's best-selling book of autobiographical musings called *Changing*. Not much of a book, but these often make the best movies, and besides, Ullman and the women's movement were very hot that season and Ullman's candor in the book about her life intrigued me. There was also the attractive possibility of Ullman portraying herself. I thought the producer's initial approach to the material was all wrong, however, and I said so in several testy meetings. I believed I had an approach to the material that would work and, further, suggested an experienced writer whom I felt confident could make that kind of an adaptation. When the producer, still pouting, finally agreed to do it my way, I commissioned a script. Sounds arbitrary, right? Probably, but a network has the right of approval over casting, producer, director, writer, composer, director of photography, art director, and all other creative elements of a project, including, first and foremost, the script, and I was, in this case, the network. The dumbest thing to do when you have power is not to exercise it. (These network controls have increased in recent seasons, and, of course, now that I am outisde, they chafe.)

So, eight weeks after my last meeting with the producer, the script arrived on my desk. Guess what? It was written exactly the way the producer had suggested initially. *Cute*. Look, I was not going to be spiteful just because I did not get my way. If the script and the approach had worked, fine. I am not fool enough to throw away forty thousand dollars of ABC's money on personal pique. (Forty was the top rate for a two-hour script in those days.) But, simply, the approach and the script were awful. Forseeably bad, I thought. And uncorrectable. I abandoned the property for ABC, and, as far as I know, it never got on anywhere else. But the really unpardonable sin in this story, in case you missed it, is the producer's deceit. Of agreeing to one approach and pursuing another. Never, never, *never* do that to a network. I am not saying you cannot fight for your vision of a project. You must, if you believe in it and want to put your name on it. I don't want you to be the producer or writer (and I know several) who says, "I want it to be orange," and, when the network says, "I like blue," immediately says, "Blue, yes, blue is perfect. I like blue. I *meant* blue." But if a network overrules you, you can either take the project somewhere else if it is not committed contractually, or you can do it the network's way. The fight is finished and honorable. If you want to build a reputation for personal dependability, not to mention continuing to get work, keep your word.

Wolper secured the rights to *Roots* in August of 1974. He was to pay Haley 50 thousand dollars as the option price, against 250 thousand dollars for the purchase price if the project went to production, plus 15 percent of all future profits.

Three days after Wolper got the rights, ABC, with its upper management's approval, called him to say it was now able to commit to *Roots* in a step deal. Three days after that, Wolper and ABC signed a deal memo to that effect. The first payment was 50 thousand dollars, the exact amount that Wolper had to pay Haley for the option.

Had Wolper gambled and won? Maybe, but I doubt it. I am sure he and Rudolph were talking frequently. I am sure he knew the temperature readings of ABC's management. He would know from experience that once an executive at Diller's level wants a project and has the enthusiastic support of his boss—at that time, Martin Starger,* the president of ABC Entertainment, the division responsible for programming the network—the board goes along almost without fail. (Though, of course, *Roots*, with black protagonists and white villains, may have caused some hiccups in the ayes, not to mention moans in the sales department.) I would guess Wolper knew the exact date of the approval meeting. It is very likely more than coincidence that he locked up the rights only three days before being notified officially that ABC would proceed.

Let's back up a bit. A "deal letter" or "deal memo" is usually a one or

---

*Starger is now partnered in an independent production company, Rule-Starger, which is based in Universal City, California, with Elton Rule, an unruffable man of good looks and the former president of ABC Companies, Inc. Both are good television company, sensible and witty.

two-page document initiated by the network or buyer that spells out in headlines, so to speak, the major provisions of an agreement between the parties. It will set forth the understanding about the monies, the steps, the time frame, bind the executive producer and producer to the project, and establish the network's controls. This allows everyone securely to start work on the project immediately, rather than wait for the full contract, which may take months to prepare and which may extend to fifty or a hundred pages, anticipating everything but the sex, height, and weight of your great-great-grandchildren. (I have had at least one program, a series, go on and *off* the air before the full contract got signed, though all parties performed smoothly under the provisions of the initial agreement.)

A "step deal" means the agreement between the parties goes forward in steps. It means the network or buyer, not the producer or seller, can end the agreement after each step in the arrangement. For a regular series the steps are, at the maximum, 1) an outline or "bible" and x number of story lines; 2) a script; 3) x number of scripts; 4) a pilot—sample program; and 5) an order of x number of programs. For a mini-series, the steps might be the same, though outlines and bible are usually folded into a script commitment. If the mini-series is contemplated as six or more hours, a step might be writing a bible and two hours of script before further commitment. Usually, however, the major steps are 1) a script or scripts (with bible) and 2) production. There are only two steps for two-hour movies: script and production. You should know that a deal or agreement always contemplates success. That is, the contract from the start covers all aspects of the project from step one through to completion. You do not negotiate anew after each step.

A "bible" is a manuscript that details characters, relationships, settings, and the narrative thrust of the story broken down into scenes and acts and hours. Networks require it to see if they like the characters and to see where the story is headed. Even if there is verbal understanding about the material, a network wants it in writing in this form before a script is written. They do not want to be locked to a finished script that may surprise. Writers are perverse animals, writing is a perverse act. The writer and the story, left alone, may go off on their own in some untoward direction. The writer and story may do this in any case, but there is recourse for everyone involved to the bible or blueprint, and the writer is supposed to follow it in detail. A network or other buyer is allowed by WGA rules (the Writers Guild of America, and more about it in chapter 2) to get two drafts and a polish on a script for the money laid out to any one writer (or writing team). If the writer has gone off in his own direction, the network or buyer is down to one draft and a polish owing due, which is seldom enough to get a script right. A "polish" means small rewrites of a draft as opposed to a complete rewrite or a new draft.

In the real world, most conscientious writers will work beyond the "two drafts and a polish" rule when there is good faith on both sides. But the rule is in place and valuable to protect writers from arbitrary and ignorant changes and excesses.

There is another compelling reason for a bible on a mini-series (or series or soap opera): More than one writer may be assigned to the project. The bible sets a style, character understanding and language, and the plot or story line for all the writers to adhere to.

Wolper had a one-year option on *Roots* with the right to renew. With ABC's approval, Wolper assigned Stan Margulies to be the on-line producer. Margulies, a man of vast television and feature film experience, was already working in Wolper's company. Wolper offered the scripting job to several well-known writers, only to find that they were unavailable. Finally, at ABC's recommendation, he hired Bill Blinn in late November of 1974. Blinn, a veteran television writer, had written *Brian's Song*, for one. (He also co-scripted the 1984 feature film *Purple Rain*, starring Prince.)

Before the work began, Wolper bound the ABC executives even more tightly to the project, increasing their sense of personal commitment, by hosting a luncheon for Brandon Stoddard and Lou Rudolph to meet Alex Haley, who is said to be a gifted verbal storyteller. Rudolph reported afterward that he cried openly and that there were tears all around as Haley described his journey to his *Roots*. This was a subtle asset, but one that Wolper used to good effect.

The author of a book or play that is purchased for film, unless he is signed to adapt it, and frequently even then, is not very welcome at any subsequent stage of the process. As Samuel Goldwyn is said to have said, "Let me make you a rule: No writers at story conferences." Or as Mae West put it, "My writers should be obscene but not heard." Irving Thalberg said, fatalistically, "Writers are a necessary evil." That will give you some idea of how producers and stars (and directors) usually feel about writers. The feelings have not changed, though the current crop of picture-powers is not as quotable.

But Wolper seems to have admired Haley from their first meeting, and while he did not involve him in any of the details of the movie-making craft beyond consultation on scripting and was not bound to do so contractually, he did always include Haley, seeming to be nourished by Haley's spirit and deep sense of what *Roots* meant. Margulies and Blinn shared this feeling.

By January of 1975, Blinn had written a 200-page bible. Three additional writers were hired: Max Cohen, Ernest Kinoy, and James Lee. All three were experienced television dramatists—and white. That latter fact bothered Wolper, but there were few black television writers; in fact, none with this kind of experience (how could there be with so few opportunities over the years?), and ABC was insisting on top, tested writers.

After a false start, Blinn had had to rework the bible. Initially, he had the story begin in the present and frequently intercut the present with past events. Haley, as a character in the drama, was the central figure throughout. This approach kept stopping the narrative flow and breaking off the emotional impact. On a second pass, at ABC's urging, Blinn took out Haley and structured the story in chronological order, eliminating some other characters as well and expanding still others. Kunta Kinte became *the* leading character until he had to die, but as a much older man, deep into the story. This is a good rule for a mini-series or even a two-hour movie for that matter: Hold a likable, empathetic character as long as possible through the story. For God's sake, and Neilsen's, do not kill him or her off early. Haley as a character on screen (James Earl Jones) did not finally enter the *Roots* story until toward the end of the television sequel, *Roots, Book II,* in chronological sequence.

All four writers worked into the summer of 1975 on their parts of the six-hour script. Blinn became the head writer, a kind of writer-editor, making sure that the others' work was compatible, and was to get a "developed for television" credit as well as writing credit.

Stoddard and Rudolph remained on the project for ABC, but Barry Diller, having been promoted to ABC vice-president of programming, fashioned a lackluster primetime schedule in the fall of 1974. (It was so bad that all we vice-presidents had to start flying economy class. But let me be fair. ABC Records also dropped a bundle that year.) Before he could be fired, which seemed likely, Diller moved on to chairman of Paramount Pictures. Nearly everyone was surprised but admired this nimble corporate somersault. In the business it is called "failing upward."* Or, at some companies, "the son-in-law also rises."

By the following spring Starger was rumored to be in trouble himself, and by summer he was gone. Because everyone in television blabs so much and thrives on one another's failures, I put great credence in rumors in our business. Within a few months at most, I find, they are nearly always confirmed as fact. The business rumors, that is; not so much the bedroom ones, which are fewer and farther between these days. In an age of avarice, the board room beats the boudoir for titillation.

Fred Pierce replaced Wally Schwartz as president of ABC Television and in June of 1975 brought in Fred Silverman to replace Starger as president of ABC Entertainment. (We are getting a lot of presidents, too, have you noticed? Soon, perhaps, we will have senior and executive presidents.)

Silverman, a kind of programming Icarus, took off from early success at CBS, soared at ABC, then crashed when his wings melted as president of NBC. He is now in California developing, among other projects, animated cartoons for Hanna-Barbera, a division of Taft Broadcasting.

I was at ABC as vice-president of late-night when Silverman arrived.

---

*Diller had, however, immense and continuing success in his ten years at Paramount, as he had had with making movies for ABC. He moved to Twentieth Century Fox as chairman in October 1984.

My only prior experience of him had come when he was at CBS and I was producing "The Merv Griffin Show" for that network. We never met, but when the ratings showed that the audience preferred Johnny Carson to Merv, it was Silverman who caused me to be fired as an interim balm for that smarting reality. Not surprising, as you will find. Getting fired is a fact of life that producers share with baseball managers.

At ABC, Silverman was a chain-smoker who had grayed early, wore good suits carelessly, and was built like a refugee's suitcase. He lived and breathed programming night and day and owned a gutty genius about television in all its aspects. He is said to have taken a television set onto the beach with him during a vacation in Hawaii—and this was long before Sony Watchman. I liked his street-fan fervor for talent, especially new talent, and I enjoyed his acidic humor. His glee was genuine and extravagant when he liked something, even to a minor character's voice in a Saturday morning animated cartoon; but his dejections were equally intense when he was disappointed or had been crossed. He seemed to take every obstacle or human shortfall in others as an intentional personal affront.

I had enormous professional respect for Silverman, and our thoughts about shows connected more often than not. A month after he arrived, I was promoted and charged with the task of creating a new morning show to compete with "Today" and to replace ABC's first effort in that arena, the stumbling "AM America." My new title was vice-president, early morning and late night. It brought to mind an obscure apparatchik in a bureau of weather in the USSR. (Ann Shanks's favorite funny word became what we called at the network our "dayparts.")

Fred Pierce prompted my getting the opportunity to create "Good Morning America,"* but Silverman probably could have stopped the assignment. (I think Pierce, currently president of ABC Companies, Inc., a tall, dark, intelligent man, who is laconic and reserved in his outward manner but whom I know to be equally warm and amusing, is the ablest executive in television.)

Silverman did everything in his considerable power to back me in making "Good Morning America" a success. Also, after he (and Pierce?) had promoted me to vice-president of specials, Silverman was my only ally in 1977 when Barbra Streisand, having been turned down by all the movie studios, was ready to do *Yentl* as an "ABC Theatre" presentation. He and I both got shot down on that one.

Silverman and I got along okay socially, too, but we proved by nature to be ill-proportioned to work well together for long and our relationship became increasingly sulphurous. But that's another story. I moved over to ABC News and to Roone Arledge, where I developed "20/20." That, too, is another story.

---

*Pat Weaver, Frank Magid, and Woody Fraser did *not* create "Good Morning America," though they are often quoted, perhaps misquoted, as saying otherwise.

When Silverman arrived at ABC and learned about the *Roots* project, he was so enthusiastic about it that he ordered an additional six hours. A very gutsy decision. That fixed it at a total of twelve hours, which is what eventually would be shot and aired.

The four writers on *Roots* now kept writing. A lot. The budget was doubled to six million dollars or thereabouts. Finally, in January of 1976, the scripts were finished and ABC made the commitment to go to film. Shooting was set to begin in April. Before we leave *Roots,* there are a few more lessons to be learned, and I will tell you a story about its scheduling that I witnessed.

In dealing with this epic story of blacks in America, Wolper and company knew that everything hinged on getting and holding the audience the first night. Getting and holding the audience is the challenge for any television program, of course, but it posed a particularly difficult problem with *Roots.* The stuff of the first two hours took place in Africa, then on a slave ship. While it was highly dramatic material, it was also very rough and, it was feared, unpalatable for the majority white audience. Not only might the white audience have difficulty identifying with the central characters in the drama, they were likely to be openly hostile to being reminded of the sins of their fathers. If every black in America watched, that still represented only about 12 to 15 percent of the available audience. Would whites tune in and stay tuned in for such downbeat material and for seeing their kind portrayed as villains? And what would draw people to their sets to watch this program in the first place? The major parts were to be played by black actors. How many "name" blacks were there? Especially for these African hours, where blacks had to be black-black, since there was none of the miscegenation that would come when blacks got to America.

The question of attracting people to the program in the first place would be addressed by major promotion, imaginatively conceived, which we'll come to. The question of casting was handled by beefing up two white parts from what the characters had been in the book and by signing Ed Asner and Ralph Waite to play them. Ed Asner was the lovable Lou Grant figure off "The Mary Tyler Moore Show" and a principal player in the popular *Rich Man, Poor Man* mini-series. Ralph Waite was the lovable father on "The Waltons." A small part was written in for the nonactor-great-athlete O. J. Simpson, who was one of the most popular people in the country that year. In the business, this latter kind of casting is one aspect of what is called "stunting." As in a stunt or trick. Cicely Tyson was encouraged by the importance of the project to take a small part. These four made for powerful casting for the first night. These were popular, respected, and comfortable personalities. This allowed Wolper and the network to go with an unknown in the key role of Kunta Kinte, which turned out to be good show business as well. LaVar Burton, as a totally new face, gained instant sympathy and credibility, with no history to overcome. You believed him the more as Kunta Kinte because you had never seen him as an actor. Reviewers and critics are likely to be more receptive to newcomers as well. They like to "discover" people.

Assuming you already have other names in a cast—and I mean likable names—and you are faced with a key part for which there can be a choice between a talented unknown performer and an established name, though an established name you do not think is right for the part and one whom you know from his or her last few times out the audience has rejected, I recommend going for the unknown everytime. At least you start even. At least the audience won't see the name in the listings and say, "Uck—him again? Let's watch something else."

Once, in an "ABC Theatre" presentation called "Mary White," when Gregory Peck was not available for the part of William Allen White, the great Emporia, Kansas, newspaper editor, and all the next "names" felt like audience turnoffs, I let the producer, Robert Radnitz, go with Ed Flanders (now on "St. Elsewhere"), who is a hell of an actor, though nobody knew it then. Another unknown named Katherine Bellin played Mary. There were *no* names in that production. That was really foolhardy—but it was wonderful. And, carefully promoted, it got a 36 percent share of the audience. Don't risk that too often, or you will be out selling wallets on a street corner.

The principle of casting familiar and likable television names was followed as often as possible throughout *Roots:* John Amos, Lawrence-Hilton Jacobs (hot off "Welcome Back, Kotter"), Leslie Uggams, Ben Vereen, Richard Roundtree, Lou Gossett, and George Stanford Brown (hot off "The Rookies"); Lorne Greene, Robert Reed, George Hamilton, Chuck Conners, Vic Morrow, MacDonald Carey, Sandy Duncan, Linda Day George, and others. Remember the lesson. Name casting helps you get rating points. Another rule, the David O. Selznick rule: If you cannot get one or two really big names, get lots of medium names.

Wolper—and here is a stand worth taking with a network—got his way by getting at least one black director—Gilber Moses (two hours)—among the four who were hired to direct *Roots.* It was not an easy battle. For the record, the other directors were David Greene (three hours), John Erman (one hour), and Marvin J. Chomsky (six hours). Wolper also persuaded ABC to let him hire a black director of photography, Joseph Wilcots—the first one ever in television—who DP'd the last eight hours of *Roots.* Steve Larner was the DP for the first four hours of the program, since ABC had insisted on someone with "experience" to get the thing going. I do not mean to demean Larner's ability—he is very experienced—nor do I mean to make ABC the villain here. In fact, after viewing Wilcots's first rushes, the executives there were as enthusiastic about his work as Wolper and Margulies (Wilcots was particularly adept at lighting black actors, who because of a simple law of physics, are harder to light, especially in scenes with whites. He had, I am sure, given the problem much more thought than white directors of photography). It is simply that millions of dollars and lots of careers ride on these movies and finally on the two extremely critical jobs of director and director of photography. Two-hour television movies are shot in eighteen to twenty-one normal working days (overtime is a sin), which means shooting seven to nine pages and forty to fifty setups a day. A setup is everytime you have to move the camera to a different location and change the lighting, even in the same scene. In a feature film, you may shoot as few as five setups a day and only one to three pages. As one television movie director said about his job, "Art, my ass—it's survival."

All of us, producers, directors, writers, actors, and so on, face the "track record" problem in television. I wrote in another book* about how readily you get pigeonholed in television. If you have done tape it is tough to be allowed to do film, and the reverse is true. I did variety early in my career and could not sell a documentary when I wanted to. When I had done some rather good documentaries, I could not get variety assignments since now I was a "documentarian"—and I certainly could not get a drama I wanted. Now, recently, I have written and with Ann Shanks co-produced movies for television. All of these have been contemporary comedies, so, of course, we cannot yet get a serious drama. We are trying to break into primetime series, too.

"But, you've never done a series," people say.

"No," I say, "I've never done anything before I've done it the first time. And, I know Ann was born a woman—sorry about that—and without a track record. She, too, before she did it, had never written three books, taught photography at The Museum of Modern Art, directed or produced a movie for television, or won the twenty or more film festival awards she has. Or, for that matter, had three children." (Ann says having children is the best possible training to become a producer.)

I don't mean to say here that just anybody can or should be allowed to jump into highly complicated professional situations. Sadly, untrained, inexperienced people do sometimes get thrown in over their heads. I only mean to say that when you have demonstrated skills that are transferable from related shows and circumstances, there is still a bias about taking you on in a new specific category. I know why. As a buyer, I have been guilty of the bias myself. Because, even in the best of circumstances, television success is so perilous and mercurial, buyers grab on to whatever certitude they can find or manufacture. "Doing project Y? Charlie was a big hit doing project Ys. Let's get Charlie. If Y fails, we can't be blamed, because we got the best. In fact, we only went with Y as an idea in the first place because Ys have been so successful."

If the rest of us face the difficulty of "track record," blacks and women and other minorities face it in extremis. How do you build a track record if

---

The Cool Fire: How to Make It in Television (hardcover, New York: W. W. Norton, 1976; paperback, New York: Vintage, 1977 and 1983).

you cannot get on to the track or into the arena? (Wilcots had been given the chance to learn his craft in the navy and to develop it in civilian life by two of only a few influential industry blacks, Barry Gordy of Motown on *Lady Sings the Blues* and Gordon Parks, a former *Life* magazine photographer, on *The Learning Tree*.)

There is one female director of photography in television. Maybe there are others by now, but she was *the one* for so long that you still think of her alone. Her name is Brianne Murphy. Again, one need not be a racist nor a chauvinist pig in the pressure cooker of television to be wary of hiring people who have not had the specific experience you are looking for, but it helps, and for that kind of bias that so afflicts our industry and society, Ms. Murphy gave the best retort I ever heard. When she was a news camera"person" covering a politician's press conference, the politician looked down and, seeing the hand-held camera that Ms. Murphy was cradling on her shoulder, said, "Isn't that thing kind of heavy, little lady?" She shot back, "No more than a kid."

While we are at it, the director of photography directs the camera crew. He makes possible the shots that the director wants or, in some cases, tells the director a shot will not work and suggests an alternative. He oversees the technical quality of the filmmaking. With the director, he visits locations and sets to forsee shooting requirements, chooses the appropriate lenses and the film stock, and involves himself in the effects to be used. First and foremost, aesthetically, he lights the scenes for the camera—that is, designs and supervises the lighting. The job is artistic-technical, always in support of the director's vision.

While many directors are very able technically, ideally, once the shot is blocked, directors should be focusing on interpreting the script and on enriching the actors' performances. Next, they should concentrate on the overall look of the scene: composition of the shot, wardrobe, makeup, setting, props, and coverage for editing. Coverage means shooting the same scene from enough different angles—for simple instance, wide shot, medium, closeups—so that you have enough material later in the cutting room to make the scene come alive or "play." You have "covered" the scene.

Too often in television, directors fail to direct performers. You will hear such perfunctory instructions as "Give me a little more," "Take it down a peg," "More energy," "A little sexier," and so on. Even if directors are good with actors, and many are not, often they are simply preoccupied with banging out the setups that they are required to get each day.

Because directors have so little time in television movies and cannot afford to spend much of it on performances, or are technically oriented and have little to offer the actors, you tend to get the same actors over and over. These actors may not be great, but they are safe. You know what to expect. You know they will be there on time, know their lines, prepare their own approach to the problems of the role, which means mostly that they will give the same performances they gave the last time out, since they probably have been type-cast and will in no way impede the time schedule bulldozer.

There is almost no place in television for actors who want to "work" on their parts. I know a fine actress—a star—who worked with a director in a television film and occasionally asked for help by questioning scenes. The director was so put off by this that he refused to hire her for his next film for a part that she fitted perfectly. "She's too much trouble," he said. "Motivation and all that crap."

Now how was Wolper going to get the audience to tune in to *Roots*? Promotion. As we have seen he had already used the easiest, most immediate way to promote a program: He had cast familiar and likable names in as many parts as he could.

We have also seen how Wolper promoted *Roots* within the network. He had made sure that the appropriate executives came to share his true believer's zeal about the project. He had thrown the solid rock of Haley himself into the placid pool, and the network executives had responded by becoming the first of the waves that were to reverberate throughout the nation, creating a mystique about *Roots* before the television series even hit the air. Wolper knew these convinced executives would convince other executives and would fight for priority attention in the network and especially from the network's own advertising and promotion department. This is critical. Long before your project faces outside competition for a restless audience, the battle for attention must be won within the network.

As in most large organizations, there are small fiefdoms within a television network. Each area of programming, sales, affiliate relations, business affairs, engineering, broadcast standards, and advertising and promotion has its vested interests and territorial prerogatives. Any one of these departmental warlords can help or harm your project. I am sure the ABC executives supervising *Roots* wooed these other executives with formal briefings, lunches, and other more casual one-to-one get-togethers in person and on the phone. They may have even brought in Wolper or Haley to speak in person and to stir up the sales department. I know that Stan Margulies flew Haley in to make his *Roots* speech to the cast when shooting began on location in Savannah, Georgia. I am sure the vice-president of advertising and promotion was handled carefully. Imagine him being hostile or indifferent to your project.

Of course, with the potent backing of Silverman, a *Roots* convert and a demon for promotion, the vice-president of advertising and promotion would not be allowed to act on his own. Wolper was assured of what is called a saturation on-air campaign and more than usual expenditures for newspaper, magazine, and radio advertising.

Anyone over two years old in this country knows what an on-air promotion spot is. In toto, they are a kind of mental Love Canal, and we are so bombarded with them that it is surprising that our brains are not fried. Of course, an educator could make a pretty good case that they are. Still, if you think these on-air promos are bad, think about *my* idea of hell: Sitting for eternity through a public television station fund-raising drive.

Anyway, an on-air promo spot is that three-second (do you believe it?), ten-second, seventeen-second, thirty-second juiced-up ad for an upcoming program, which, in the longer versions, show the most provocative moments from the production. Different ones are cut to appeal to the different audiences watching at different times of the day: male macho emphasis for inclusion in sports programs, romantic ones to put into women's-appeal shows, and so on. Silverman agonized over these on-air promo spots as much, it seemed to me, as he did over the programs. Wisely.

A saturation campaign means that a preponderance of these available spots is given to one program. As ubiquitous as these spots may seem to you, there is a finite number of them available, and producers and executives fight for them as though they were golden nuggets—or Olympic pins. And for good reason. Experience shows they work. On-air promos are, far and away, the most effective means of advertising a program.

A good producer will work to make sure that he gets not only his share but yours, and will work with the programming executives and the advertising and promotion people on the content as well. Usually, on-air promos for a program are scheduled to run only the week or ten days before the program is to air. For *Roots*, the on-air campaign began a full month before.

Networks do not like to take newspaper and magazine ads. These are expensive and, according to conventional wisdom, not particularly effective. Networks do take them, of course. One does it because the other networks do it. One does it for an advertiser, as part of a sales contract. One does it for prestigious programs. For a season kickoff. For the debut of a new series that everyone is high on. To impress Washington, D.C. And, to please the stars and production company and personnel of a show. It is hard for them to make a poster of an on-air promo, or glue one into a scrapbook. These "vanity" ads will be placed only in New York and Los Angeles newspapers and in the show business trade papers, *Variety* and *Hollywood Reporter*, where stars and company are going to be sure to see them. The next tier out from these two towns for newspaper ads would be a network's O & O markets—those cities in which it *O*wns & *O*perates a station.* Almost never will a network buy newspaper ads beyond the top fourteen-to-twenty-five markets. The magazine that gets the most network advertising is, of course, *TV Guide.*

Then, there is the free editorial space to be had in *TV Guide,* the Sunday newspaper television supplements, and the daily newspapers. There is lobbying from "televisionists" that goes on with the *Guide* to get a cover story and a "Close-Up" that is as intense as any in the corridors of Congress or the fifty state houses. These two items are considered second in importance

_____

*Each network is now allowed to own seven VHF stations and five UHF stations for a maximum of twelve.

only to on-air promotion for attracting audiences.

To be considered for a *TV Guide* cover, you need to have your program and promotional materials ready five to seven weeks ahead of publication date in the week of your air date. A "Close-Up"—that sizable print description boxed with an accompanying photo about your program published among the listings for the day you are on—requires three to four weeks advance submission of material, as do a detailed program listing and log lines.

Log lines are those short blurbs next to the listing that are meant to say something to grab the reader and turn him into a viewer. You know: 8:00. Happy Days. "The Fonz has to choose between jail and marriage—some choice, but hilarious—and gets out of both." That kind of thing. Wolper used these log lines in a fresh way for *Roots*. He used them without hype to outline the story of each episode in considerable detail. The impression was one of dignity and importance. He took a chance on their being too long and drier than most log line blurbs, but editors ran them in full. There are services—*TV Log*, for one—that you pay to get your listing and log lines starred and in bolder black ink, so that your program stands out from the others listed for the same hour.

Sometimes, when the film or tape of your program is not available for screening by *TV Guide* staff members to meet its deadlines—and this happens often—the magazine will consider giving a cover or Close-Up based on your submission of casting, good photography, and an honest script. By honest, I mean an "as-to-be-aired" script. Never submit an earlier draft or an earlier cut of your film that contains material that will not air. *TV Guide* will never trust you again.

There is a lot more to tell you about how to get print and television space, but I will come to that in the chapter on how to produce, since promotion is such an important part of a producer's function.

In addition to the efforts of ABC's very able press people, Wolper put on an outside press representative who was assigned to *Roots* full time. Whenever you can, make sure this is an item in your budget. Network press people do a good job, but each is assigned to a number of projects and never has time to devote fully to yours.

During the long months of shooting *Roots* in the spring and summer of 1976, reams of written information and bundles of still photographs poured forth from the set to print, radio, and television outlets all over the country. This before any air date was set. For years, as he researched and wrote the book, Haley had been touring the country speaking about the saga of *Roots* to any group who would have him. This too had started a groundswell of curiosity and anticipation about the book well in advance of the television program or, for that matter, the book's publication.

Talk shows and print interviewers in America thrive—survive—on stars. Wolper did not have one or two stars. He had twenty. As the air date neared, this kind of coverage became a flood. And, a fascinating thing was happening to actors who worked on *Roots*. Their emotions were genuinely stirred. Chords in them had been struck that had not been sounded in years. This made them even more compelling than usual in public. A kind of fraternity, a religiosity about it developed in all those associated with *Roots*.

As early as October 1975 Wolper had met with ABC people and Doubleday, Haley's publisher, to coordinate everyone's promotional and advertising efforts. By educating them to the power of television, he convinced Doubleday to double its print run of the book from 50 to 100 thousand copies. He knew that, having done this, they would also increase their advertising budget to protect their investment. With Haley having finally finished the book (it took him twelve years in all), Wolper got Doubleday to agree to an October 1976 publication date, which, knowing ABC's scheduling plan, would give a four-month headstart on the television airing. Close enough to keep the book fresh; far enough away to build an audience.

Everyone involved had a great promotional weapon in Haley. Some authors are terrible on television, radio, and in person and hate the idea of having to promote a book personally. Haley loved to travel the nation, loved the people he met, and was absolutely charismatic on the tube and person-to-person. Again he set out and was indefatigable in criss-crossing the country on behalf of *Roots*.

Of course, you can have all these professionals, all this money, and other resources, and still give birth to an Edsel. As much as everyone involved was devoted to *Roots*, no one could be sure of the final effect of all their efforts. One thing no one foresaw was how deeply the book would hit the nation's emotions. It became an immediate and profound best seller, nearly a million copies by Christmas. Haley became a national celebrity, respected, beloved.

By October of 1976 the filming of *Roots* was completed and the post-production begun. It was time to schedule *Roots*. It had been talked about for January and February of 1977. February is a key ratings month every year for a network. It is known as a "sweep period." That is, the ratings services—Nielsen and Arbitron, or ARB—in addition to their normal samplings, "sweep" the nation, undertaking special audience surveys market by market, individual station by station. The major sweeps take place three times a year—roughly, in November, February, and May. The ratings that a station gets during a sweep determines what it can charge for advertising spots until the results of the next sweep period are in. The most important sweeps are the ones in November and February, when sets-in-use* numbers are highest (you watch more television in autumn and winter than in spring and summer) and stations can charge their highest rates. Nationally

---

*Sets-in-use is a figure that represents the number of television sets turned on in relation to the total number of household sets available to be turned on.

as well as locally, then, hundreds of millions of dollars swing on the numbers in the sweeps. This is why networks, to help their affiliated stations as well as themselves, schedule what they perceive to be their most potent audience-grabbing shows in these months. It is why you pull your hair out trying to decide which of two or three special shows to watch that are crashing head-to-head-to-head on the same nights during these periods. It is why during these same periods you see a lot of prostitute segments on your local news. Hookers get good ratings.

Everyone who counted at ABC knew that *Roots* was something extraordinary, perhaps unique in television programming history, long before it aired. The more closely you were involved with the project, the deeper this sensation ran. But even with this genuine excitement and the momentum coming off the success of the book—what's a few hundred thousand copies to a television executive for whom fifteen million viewers in primetime is a failure?—there were serious and ulcerous second thoughts about the program. Every vice-president in every department, each a stockholder, was nervous.

The original scheduling plan for *Roots* was to follow the model of *Rich Man, Poor Man,* the previous season's big mini-series winner; that is, to air the programs in one-hour episodes over an extended period, in this case, eight weeks. But *Rich Man, Poor Man* on a rising but still lowly regarded network had caught the competition by surprise and had caught the coattails of the 1976 Winter Olympics, which had been a real eye-opener in the high ratings it achieved. This was unprecedented. Winter Olympics had always been ho-hum in the numbers, as they were again in 1984. And, *Rich Man, Poor Man* had been about white people.

Now, the competition would be more sophisticated in its counterprogramming. There was no Olympics lead-in or buildup. And, heaven help ABC, *Roots* was about black people. These concerns were not illusory. Would the white majority audience watch? Would the ABC affiliated stations in the South even carry the program? Would advertisers buy it? (It was being sold on the basis of a projected audience in the 28 to 31 percent share range.) Even if it got out of the gate strongly at the start, couldn't the competition chip away at it hour by hour with hotshot specials, assuming the story held?

If it ran over a period of eight weeks and got low or modest numbers, ABC was sure to lose its hard-won first place among the networks and millions of dollars in revenue. And, in February—a sweep period? Failure here could be disastrous! But a decision as to how to air it could no longer be avoided. The post-production and promotion deadlines were coming due.

In October of 1976 I sat in on the critical meeting in which the final decision had to be made. Honestly, I don't know why I was there, having had nothing to do with the development of *Roots.* Perhaps, it was simply a need for in-gathering. Security in numbers.

The meeting took place adjacent to Fred Silverman's office, in the conference room on the thirty-seventh floor of ABC's Sixth Avenue headquarters building in New York. Fred Pierce was there. Along with three of his key administrative vice-presidents, Tony Thomopoulos (heir apparent), Mark Cohen (money), and Sy Amlen (research). Jim Duffy was there— the president of the network, which had him in close touch with the affiliates. Jim Shaw, head of sales at that time. Ed Vane, the vice-president to whom reported the vice-presidents of daytime, children's, late-night, early-morning, and specials programming. Al Schneider, the VP of broadcast standards and practices. Jack Curry, VP of advertising and promotion. There may have been others. And, of course, Fred Silverman.

Silverman led the meeting, pacing up and down the room, his head wreathed in a movable cloud of cigarette smoke. Silverman praised *Roots* and reviewed the original airing schedule. He asked Duffy about the Southern affiliates. Duffy said that all were nervous, and anxious to see the program, but none had defected yet. From what they had heard about the show, some of them feared it might cause black riots.

"Terrific," Silverman said, sarcastically.

Schneider thought the content was too rough for early evening scheduling.

Shaw reported that no one advertiser or select group of quality advertisers was buying yet. Not so much that these were balking at the theme or the potential controversy. Simply, twelve hours was a big-money bite for so few sponsors—and our audience projection was low compared to the cost. He did feel confident that "participating" advertisers would fill the "avails"—the available commercial spots. "Participating" means a lot of sponsors in the show but none that has program identification. It also means lots of hard sell, low-cost products from cat food to toothpaste, rather than automotives or Xerox or IBM and General Electric. This point bothered Silverman. "How the hell can you cut to a deodorant commercial after Kunta Kinte's just been sold into slavery—and whipped?"

The tone of the meeting—of Silverman—was very defensive. He emphasized all the potential pitfalls of airing the program over eight weeks. Then, he dropped his bombshell.

"What if we ran it every night for a week? The whole twelve hours. I think it would have a hell of an impact that way. Either way, it only screws up a week."

Everyone laughed, nervously. No one had ever run such a program every night in one week. Silverman made a good case that if the program did bomb, only a week would be lost and there would be no damage to the February sweep, because that was another thing: He wanted to air *Roots* in January. Because everyone shared his anxiety about the show, no one resisted the idea and that is how it happened. In self-defense, with no surety that it would score in this form. As a further defensive move, the single-hour episodes were scheduled at 10:00 P.M., so, if they failed, they could not pull down the ratings of the other programs on those same nights.

This description is not a criticism of Silverman's plan. I think it was a masterstroke. I believe to this day that *Roots*'s impact over eight weeks would have been dissipated seriously and its lessons for America diminished. The numbers would have been lower.

As it was, in its one-week airing—eight nights, actually—from January 23 through January 30, 1977—it captured the nation.

I need not dwell on the well-documented and tremendous impact of *Roots*. Only to share with you the unbelieving glee that came from Silverman and every other executive at ABC as we got the overnight ratings each morning. When the high 40s, low 50 percent shares came in following the first night, everyone was ecstatic but holding his breath. That had been an unprecedented promotional buildup to the program. Probably, you could have gotten an initial 40 percent share of audience by showing color bars. But the encouraging evidence was that the numbers grew through each fifteen minutes of that first night's two hours. Far from tuning in and then, in disappointment, deserting, the audience kept getting larger. The second night produced 50 + percent shares, and as the week progressed, the number crept into the 60s and 70s. It was a triumph in every way. It went in the national numbers from 28 million homes viewing the first night to 36,380,000 homes in the final night. That's 85,000,000 viewers for the final episode. It averaged over the eight nights a 44.9 rating and a 66 percent share. A total of 130 million Americans saw all or part of *Roots*. It captured, up to that time, eight of thirteen spots of the highest-rated television programs of all time. (The other five spots belonged to three different Super Bowls and two nights of *Gone with the Wind*.) All the Southern stations carried it, though some affiliates did complain, "Why didn't you run it in February—in the sweep?"

It is perilous in American life to say "we will never see its like again," but chances are about *Roots* that you can chisel that in stone and not be wrong before weather or the vandals take it away.

To this day, it makes me, who had nothing to do with it, feel proud to be part of a television that can be that good and that lastingly important. It is a standard by which to measure your own more modest attempts.

Where are we now with movies made for television and mini-series?

As early as the 1971–72 season, at least one network, ABC, was airing more made-for-television movies than theatrical films, and it has been that way for all three networks ever since; but, though increasingly disturbed about the high cost, the networks had continued for a few more years to bid on feature films. Today, they don't much bother. The emergence in the mid-1970s of pay-cable television services, whose primary attraction was theatrical films, uncut and uninterrupted, that had their first television runs on the cable channels, meant that by the time the networks took their runs of the same films, a good 20 to 30 percent of the potential audience had already seen them. Accordingly, network ratings of theatrical films have nosedived. Major film companies, led by M-G-M / UA, are trying to launch independent over-the-air "networks" on an occasional basis to replace the income from this traditional network market for those films that have been seen first in theaters and then on cable. This cable inroad has increased the number of made-fors and minis on the established networks.

These pay cable services also have increased the number of market-places for original or newly made films. While the number of originals they commission is relatively small now—perhaps one a month—it has to grow. Like the networks before them, these services—Homebox Office, or HBO, and Cinemax (owned by Time-Life) and Showtime-Movie Channel (owned jointly by Viacom and Warner-Amex) face an increasingly expensive and diminishing supply of theatrical films. Another problem with these feature films, as we have seen, is the crossing demographic curves of the movie theater audience (14- to 24-year-olds) and the television audience (over thirty) that subscribes to these services. So, it is inevitable that HBO and Showtime/Movie Channel (the latter had been separate entities but merged in 1983) will have to make more original films (and series). You are aware, no doubt, of HBO's *Sakharov* and *The Far Pavillions,* the latter a pay-cable mini-series first televised in 1984. These were not made for the bubble-gum or galleria set.

Pay cable is a tangible market now. So, in a smaller way, is "American Playhouse" on PBS. There is also O.P.T., or Operation Prime Time, which is a conglomerate of independent over-the-air stations that pool money to purchase once or twice a year an outside-produced, newly made film for airing on an ad hoc "fourth network." The big man here is Al Mancini, who works out of Tele-Rep in New York. Recent examples: *Golda, Sadat, Blood Feud,* and *A Woman of Substance.*

But the gleam in every televisionist's eye is home video. That is, the production of movies directly for video cassettes aimed at the home con-sumer. No middle network, no over-the-air, and no cable. The fastest-selling toy in the country right now is not the home personal computer but the video cassette recorder in half-inch format, either VHS or Betamax. Six million new homes a year. This is already a major secondary market (2.5-billion dollars in 1984) for theatrical films and a primary one for other material, such as *Jane Fonda's Workout.* It is also of grievous concern for advertisers on traditional television. The latter have a problem because they know millions of people are now recording shows as they air for playback at a more personally convenient time, and, when these people do watch the delayed programs, they "fast forward" through the commercials. This is eventually going to bring network advertising pricing down. Who wants to pay for commercials nobody sees?

The advantages of home video original movies are that people can watch the movies they want to watch when they want to watch and, if they buy the cassettes rather than rent, can watch as often as they want. You can build your own video library, and it is happening now.

A major problem for this marketplace is promotion and advertising. How do people know which of these movies they want to see? Where are the on-air promos? The pre-sell of feature film advertising and media reviews?

Book publishers have faced these problems for years. Some of their solutions spring to mind for home video and should prove to be effective, because more people than read books are going to "read" movies: Video stores, of course, like book stores; and video-of-the-month clubs, like the Book-of-the-Month Club. For instance, there is the CBS Video Club, which charges from $39.95 to $79.95 per cassette, per title, which are mailed to your home. There is a monthly guide also for ordering the CBS Video Club Program. There will be the usual critics and reviewers specializing in commentary on home video originals. Interviews and articles. Ads in all the video and arts and leisure publications. TV ads à la some romance novels. In-store trailers and teasers of available films. Nearly all of this is happening now.

I foresee someone soon, if it has not already been done, buying a mailing list of videocassette recorder owners and sending them a monthly video magazine called *Previews* or something, which will highlight all of the films being made and marketed. Who will pay for such a venture? You, in some kind of subscription price, and, you guessed it, commercial advertisers.

I think by 1990 pay cable will have plateaued as an entertainment deliverer and that this home video market will be the dominant outlet for original television movies.

In the meantime, your present-best hope remains the traditional networks, ABC, CBS, and NBC, who of course, will also be large in home video movies, since each of them already has a movie-making company in place. In the 1984–85 over-the-air season, the three networks programmed over a hundred new original films in the two-hour form to fill six scheduled movie nights*—Monday (two), Tuesday, Wednesday, Sunday (two), plus roughly seventy-five hours of mini-series. (And put this in the American Time Capsule while you are at it: out of sixty-nine other regularly scheduled series at the start of the season, twenty-three were cop and detective shows.)

While there has been an unsettling trend lately to trash the mini-series form—and I look for this to get worse before it gets better—clearly seen in 1983–84 in *The Last Days of Pompeii, Lace,* and *Master of The Game,* and in 1984–85's *Mistral's Daughter, Lace II, A.D.,* and *Hollywood Wives,* the networks did come through with *Space, Christopher Columbus, The Atlanta Child Murders,* and *Fatal Vision.*

All of these latter programs, (some were better, some were worse) continued to have nobler ambitions. They sought to educate, provoke thought,

---

*ABC's regular series failed early in the season of 1984–85, and it had to go temporarily with movies on Thursdays from 8:00 to 10:00 P.M. (Eastern and Pacific).

and challenge sleepy beliefs. To hit deeper emotionally.

(The British, once more, showed everybody how it is really done with *Jewel in the Crown* presented on PBS.)

In the two-hour form, the networks offered serious treatments of wife beating, children's suicides, sexual compulsions, child abuse, homosexuality, and other shadowed caverns of the human experience. There were biographies of Raoul Wallenberg, the Swedish diplomat who helped thousands of Jews survive in World War II, and Florence Nightingale, the founder of modern nursing, plus Martha Weinman Lear's wrenching story of her husband's heart disease. There were new interpretations of literary classics (not all of them successful or skillful): *The Sun Also Rises, Camille, The Arch of Triumph, Anna Karenina, Death of a Salesman,* and *A Christmas Carol.*

(And, of course, Ann and Bob did *He's Fired, She's Hired,* a comedy about the serious subject of what happens when a husband gets fired and the traditional housewife has to go to work.)

That's some pretty good stuff for one season. Grownup. Upper-middle-brow. Can this be the much-abused commercial television system that presented all of this? Oh sure, there was a lot of exploitation, trivialization, and a lot of junk, but there is some hope here. An invigorating possibility. It makes it worthwhile to be a part of it. Let's get on to the next chapter and see how you go about that.

2

How to Sell One

I don't know how to sell a movie for television. Not the way you would reproduce a science experiment anyway. Nobody does. Or all of us who try to would be even more successful at it than we are. But there are some things that the rest of them and Ann and I have tried that seem to work some of the time. First, the turf.

Each network's programming comes through one of three divisions, Entertainment, News, and Sports. News and Sports actually produce and own the programs they supply. Entertainment does some of the time but is restricted by law to the number of primetime hours it can own and mostly licenses its programs from outside suppliers.

It is the Entertainment division that we are interested in here and more specifically the department within that division that is responsible for getting movies and mini-series made for the network. At all three networks, this department is a separate operation from primetime series, drama and comedy, which have their own departments. As do the other programming areas: Specials, children's, variety, daytime, early morning, and so on.

So, the first thing you have to do is be where these movie and mini-series departments and the people who staff them are. That means two places, New York City and Los Angeles.

You can't be serious. One is a human zoo. The other's a cancerous urban growth. Wouldn't I have to learn some Spanish as well as Yiddish?

Look, do you want to write these movies or not? Sell them? Produce them?

Sure, but what about the mail or Federal Express or the telephone and computer terminal? Alvin Toffler promised me I was going to be able to live anywhere. Society was expanding like the universe and cities were in decline, he said.

Well, he was wrong. These people I am talking about like to go out, mingle. They want to have lunch. They go to charity dinners and awards banquets. They *own* tuxedos. Didn't you ever take a meeting?

Why? Is one missing?

These people have to take meeting or die. They have decorated offices so if you do not go there how are you going to know from the windows and the corners and the square footage and the size of their plants who is important and who is not?

The size of their plants?

Get real here, okay? Even if you are Arthur Miller, who lives in Connecticut, these people do not go to see him when he does television. He comes to them in New York.

I can't. I just can't.

Okay, okay, skip New York. I happen to love it, but it's not for everybody, and the networks have cut back on their programming staffs there. For movies and minis, they don't even have specifically assigned vice-presidents there.

Did you say you love New York? Did you actually live there?

Sure, are you kidding? Ann and I raised our children there.

You raised children in Manhattan?

Sure, three. A girl and two boys.

Are they—dead?

Don't be ridiculous. Well, they did get mugged a couple of times, but— okay, okay, I know New York is dangerous and dirty and the streets are full of mental deficients and you pay $800 a month rent for a closet. More if it's a walk-in. Don't tell me. When I was starting out there, I didn't have to get up to go to the refrigerator! My bed was in the kitchen! But Los Angeles. You want to know about Los Angeles? Remember that book *When Bad Things Happen to Good People?* A friend of mine's writing one called *Los Angeles: Where Good Things Happen to Bad People.* But one of these two places is where you have to be. These are where the action is. Where the buyers are. Now make up your mind.

Well, New York is rich, culturally—but there's garbage in the streets and winos in the vestibules. Well-dressed women wear jogging shoes.

Look, are you the New York type or not? You've got to know these things about yourself. You've seen Woody Allen's movies. And Martin Scorcese's. Can you relate to that or not? If you are really serious as a writer, maybe a developing novelist or playwright, and are masochistic about getting your laundry done and do not care if your tomatoes have any taste and raspberries cost twelve dollars apiece and love the theater and great bookstores and serious music and museums and a twenty-four-hour-a-day street circus and a full *New York Times,* not that wimpy little national edition that is always a day late with the ball scores, which is what you will get in Los Angeles, then you will be all right in New York. You can sell from there and work. A lot of people do. Though a lot of them are established names who made it in television when there was still a lot of television being made in New York. Or they get to be known from writing plays and books. New York has a few network buyers and some production companies and good agents. The other thing New York has is lots of daily nonstop jets to Los Angeles. If you think you cannot afford it, give up something else to fly first-class always, since that is where the buyers sit.

Tell me about Los Angeles.

You want Los Angeles? Safe, right? James Garner, *a leading man*, got punched out at an intersection after a fender-bender by two guys who wouldn't even get "under 5" parts on "The Rockford Files," and Penny Marshall—Laverne—was assaulted in her own home. Two months after Ann and I moved here there was a triple murder across the street two houses up. There was a SWAT team in our shrubbery. In Beverly Hills. *Above* Sunset. But look at the bright side. As the Baby Boomers age, crime is down. Seven percent last year. What else? Okay, it has no center. You know that. There is a crack in the basement, which if there is ever a seven-point-plus on the Richter Scale (and it's coming) will make Phoenix, Arizona, the film capital of the world. You know that too. You know it has the Pacific Ocean that every couple of years eats a few houses in Malibu that cost a million bucks apiece, which are then rebuilt at two million bucks apiece and freeways that look like a barium scan of a very sick person and air that most days looks like a bad bouillabaisse and is "unhealthful for sensitive people." What? You're sensitive people? You're a writer? Boy, have we got a lot of work to do.

But, there are no two ways about it. If you are serious about writing television movies, you almost have to come to Los Angeles. (Would you like to buy our house? Michael Landon lived here. Everybody has to live somewhere where somebody famous lived.) You have to come here because Los Angeles has television vice-presidents and senior vice-presidents and executive vice-presidents and they all know how to drive German cars and they have reserved parking places with their own names stenciled on the concrete stoppers and they get waved through by uniformed guards at gates where you cannot back up or the one-way spikes will make rubber slaw out of your tires and they never pay to see a movie (or know how an average audience reacts) because they are on everybody's free screening lists and they get their issues of *Daily Variety* and *The Hollywood Reporter* on the same day as the date on the masthead, which you cannot do in New York, and they wear sports clothes to the office—cotton—all year round and they eat alfalfa shoots and raw fish and kiwi fruit. We are talking perks, power, and a sybaritic life-style. (It *is* much easier to live here. When we first arrived, Ann rushed into Bonwit Teller's early one day, exclaiming to a clerk, "I'm next, I'm next." "Of course you are, dear," the clerk said. "You're the only one here.")

We're talking networks, pay cable, studios, production companies. Buyers, baby, buyers. By the score. And producers and directors and actors. On the outside, it may seem all Foster Grants and suntans and palm trees and Bougainvillea and swimming pools and tennis and have-your-answering-machine-call-my-answering-machine, but inside the modish manufacturing plants, it all comes down to a blank piece of paper—110 blank pieces of paper, give or take a few, for a two-hour television movie—and the whole industry closes down if you do not fill them. You or one of us like you. THEY HAVE TO HAVE SCRIPTS.

That is the truth, even if you do not think so when you get here. When you get here you will think everybody from San Bernardino to Santa Barbara has a script for sale and nobody is going to read yours or pay you for it or produce it and relatively you are right. (Ann Shanks, attending a film seminar at a downtown Variety Arts building, crossed the street against the light. She is from New York, but that's no excuse. When the cop stopped her—and jaywalking is serious—he found out that she was a producer. How? She told him, naturally and quickly. He did *not* give her a ticket. Instead, he took down her home address so he could send her a movie script he had written.)

But most people here who call themselves writers cannot write, and the other ones, the ones who can, will keep you company. You will need company, because writing is lonely, which is perhaps one of the things you like about it, and you will, I guarantee it, be lonely in Los Angeles, but at least not as lonely as in Terre Haute, at least not as lonely as a writer. You know your brother-in-law back there thinks you are weird for wanting to be a writer in the first place and wonders why you don't get *a real* job. This middle-class mindset is why I put off full-time writing for twenty years—that and the tuitions, etc. But people in Los Angeles will understand. Some of them, anyway. Maybe you are weird, but they will be weird in the same way, which helps you feel not so bad about your own weirdness, and that makes the possibility of pursuing happiness and having a nice day better already. Then, of course, you will find that when you do get to be friends with other writers, you will wear the enamel off your molars trying to hold the smile on your face while they tell you about some assignments they got that you know you should have had. But, company loves misery in plumbing too.

Okay, now I have you in Los Angeles. I hope you got here with a college degree or a prison record—something from somewhere where they taught you something about putting words down on paper. Now what?

First, have some money. Or be willing to earn some legally to feed yourself and pay your rent. Wait tables, type or word-process, park cars, pump gas, deliver pizzas. One very fine young writer I know supports himself by writing questions for a game show. You will have to be prepared to do something like this for quite a while. If you think you are suited to producing as well as writing, you should look less for the kinds of jobs above and concentrate more on working in an established production company. As a production assistant or secretary or gofer. These jobs are highly cherished and hard to come by. A lot of other young writers will be after them, naturally, but so will all those producers-in-training who cannot write. This does not mean you should not go after them. Test your resolve. Meet people. Get out there. In one of these entry-level jobs, you should have the opportunity in detail to observe more experienced professionals and, with little personal risk, learn a lot that you have to know. Dealing in actual situations, you will be able to second-guess how you would handle what your management is handling. In a production company job, you will also be positioned, after a prudent time interval, to show your writing to someone there who is higher up and who may be able to sell your script on the strength of his or her name. Or, at the least, to tell you what is wrong with your work and help you fix it.

Oh, yes, make sure you know how to drive, then get a California license and buy a car. Even if it is a junker without fenders or a trunk door. M-G-M in Culver City is twenty-one miles from Disney Studios in Burbank, and it would cost you $34 by cab or take you the better part of a week to go between them by bus, which are the only forms of public transportation. Everything in Los Angeles is physically half an hour away, at least, from everything else; even your closest friend. Emotionally is even farther, according to Ann.

Next, you have got to have more guts than a tennis racquet factory to survive psychologically. I am not kidding. This is not *42nd Street* or Kansas, Toto. They need us, sure, but they do not need us either. You will be ignored, kept waiting, put on hold with music you do not like, rejected and humiliated. Regularly. It happens to the biggest and the best. One of the most successful producers out here told me, "I learned a long time ago to put my pride in my back pocket. I'll get on my knees to make a sale."

Once, the American Film Institute was having a fund-raiser evening built around what they had voted as the best films of all time. One of the top ten was *All about Eve*. Joseph Mankiewicz—who wrote and directed *All about Eve* and won Oscars—got a mimeographed invitation to the event. For $350, it said, he could "come and mingle with the men who had made those films."

Wait. Pre-*Julia* (and another film to come that will be based in part on the material), Lillian Hellman took her brilliant auto-biographical work, *Pentimento*, into a television network to offer it as a dramatic special. She had to go to the office like everybody else, and the kid she had to meet with did not even read the book. He sent it to the reading department for a "reader's report." These reading reports are also called "coverage," for some strange reason. All networks, studios, and larger independent production companies have full-time readers who provide "coverage." These people can reduce *War and Peace* to a few pages and, God help us, give you a fairly accurate summary of what it is about. Plus a highly-opinionated view as to whether it will make a decent movie or not. (Hellman herself, as a young woman in Hollywood, had been a reader for M-G-M.) When the coverage came back, *Pentimento* was rejected as being "too soft for television."

That kid executive was not unique. Nobody important or demi-important in Hollywood reads. Another writer friend, Tommy Thompson, whose book *Celebrity* became a successful mini-series, told me about something that happened to him shortly after that book came out. He was at a Hollywood party—Tommy loved the Hollywood parties the way Margaret Mead loved Samoa—and ran into a *big* producer—Macro. He came up to Tommy and said, "Tommy, your new book is just terrific. I haven't finished it yet, but I'm halfway through the coverage."

Nobody important in Hollywood writes either. A longtime acquaintance is Alan Landsburg, a very capable and successful producer who used to write. When Ann and I came out to Los Angeles, he met with us about having us join his company. During the meeting I did say, "I want to write, Alan." He looked at me—we were in the Polo Lounge of the Beverly Hills Hotel, where else?—as though I had just committed a felony. "Bob, please," he said. "Don't write. You're much too valuable for that." Within the year I knew what he meant. I was a producer-executive who could have ideas and concepts—high concepts—and properties. I could talk-sell, *deal* ten movies in the time it took me to write one. See, that's how it's done. If you are smart in Hollywood, you "create" projects, but writing is something you hire someone else to do. Strange. But I go on writing anyway.

Well, what do you say? Ask yourself, "Self, am I strong enough to handle all that?"

All right. You have looked deep into your soul, which may be the last time you will be asked to do that, and you have decided that you have the heart of a lion and the stomach of a sewage purification plant. You're the write stuff. Now. How do you get started?

Surely, unless you arrived on this planet with E.T., you must know somebody in Los Angeles who has something to do with television. Maybe somebody your own age—somebody from your home town or somebody you went to school with, or camp. Or met on vacation. Maybe you have the phone number of your mother's old boyfriend who is now a security guard at SkinFlick Pictures. None of these may lead anywhere, but explore them all. Think some more. Think about every other even slimmest possibility in your life.

Let me tell you about mine. When I first went to New York, from Indiana and the army, I knew two people and had the names of two others. The two I knew, whom I had met in the army, were Howard Rayfiel, a show business attorney, and John Corry, who now writes for the *New York Times*. John, who was trying to get started in journalism, did not know anybody in those days, so he was no help, except to commiserate, which was a help. Howard was just beginning a practice and was struggling—his biggest client was a Rockette who had broken an ankle at Radio City Music Hall—but his brother, David Rayfiel, now a screenwriter and playwright, was dating Maureen Stapleton, who used to room with Janice Mars in the same building where Wally Cox and Marlon Brando were also roommates. Janice was a wonderful Edith Piaf kind of singer, and all those friends and some others bankrolled her in her own saloon called the Baq Room, which was on Sixth Avenue between Fifty-third and Fifty-fourth streets. Howard recommended me not only to the Rockette (I was not married then) but to David, who recommended me to Maureen, who recommended me to Janice, who hired me as her only waiter. The Baq Room was located in a brownstone where the ABC Building is now. Irony, Irony. That is where I later worked for six years as a programming vice-president.

When I was working there—the Baq Room, not ABC—if you served liquor in New York State, you also had to serve food. We did not have a kitchen and we could not afford a cook. In those days, the Sixth Avenue Delicatessen was next door and the adjoining buildings had back doors opening into a common fire alley. I made up a menu with fancy-name sandwiches—I think some of these were in French—all of which corresponded to sandwiches on the delicatessen's menu. Not many of the people who came to the Baq Room came for food, but when they did order something off my menu, I would write it down on my check pad, walk to the back as though on my way to our kitchen, then run into the alley and into the deli and order the corresponding sandwich—to go. Then I would run back—nobody ever questioned why I was wet on those nights it rained— unwrap it, put it on one of the plates I had bought, and serve it, with a cloth napkin and all. And I would up the deli's price by a dollar-fifty.

Earlier, David Rayfiel had held a staff writing job on an NBC show called *America after Dark* and had helped me to get the job of coffee boy there. (I took my fifty-cup urn with me to the Baq Room.) That's where I met John Carsey, who, when that show folded, moved on to the new "Jack Paar Tonight Show." A year and a half later, thanks to Carsey, who is a writer and the only leprechaun in Los Angeles, I was able to get a job with Paar as a talent coordinator. Everything after in my career flowed from that.

Howard Rayfiel also introduced me to George Kirgo. George, who now lives in Los Angeles and is a wonderful television dramatist and playwright and a steadfast friend, worked on "The Arlene Francis Show" in those days. The show used audience contestants from time to time and I was really starving, so George would book me every couple of months as a civilian in the audience. (It was legal then, or, at least, not yet illegal.) I always won some small cash or usually a gift—a wristwatch once—which I would pawn for spending money. Later, because he wrote two books and is very, very funny, I was able to book George on the Paar show, where he became a regular.

The two other names I had came from my family. My dad was in the retail oil business in Indiana; a small business that they sold to a major oil company. He gave me the name of the big company's internal advertising director, whom he had met once, and I went to see the man. Wow, in Wall Street. He did not know much about show business, but he was interested in my writing interest. We got on to the oil business, which I knew a little about from my father. I said why do big companies like yours spend a hundred thousand dollars and up to build filling stations and then lease them to people who have no training and end up bankrupt. He sat up. He agreed. What would I do about that? Train them, for one thing, I said. For another, in the meantime, I would provide them with a manual about how to manage their business. Insurance, taxes, the works. We agreed I should try my hand at such a document. I didn't know anything about insurance and taxes, but I knew a lot about libraries, and so within a month—for no pay, mind you—I had finished the manual. Guess what? I could not get through to the man, but his secretary said why don't you send your work in and I'll be sure he gets it. I never spoke to the man again, but I am sure the secretary kept her word. A few months later my dad received a beautifully printed manual called "How to Run a Filling Station." You bet, I recognized the writing style. But everything in life is a lesson, right? As Nietzsche said, "That which does not kill you, makes you stronger." (*Never* quote a philosopher in a network meeting. Unless it's Groucho Marx.)

The other name was given to me by my dad's brother, my Uncle Herb. Herb lived in St. Louis, where he knew a man at Ralston Purina who gave Herb the name of a man in their advertising agency in New York, Roland Martini. He was a good man. He gave me the name of a kind show business manager named Robert Coe, who, despite my lack of talent, got me several jobs as an actor in television shows and commercials. I thought I was pretty hot stuff for about a year, until I saw Warren Beatty do some scenes in the acting class we took together conducted by Stella Adler.

All of this is just to get you thinking about your own life and to show you where it can lead. People will help you. Some people. And maybe someday you can pass the favor on. I know your parents probably want you to be an astronaut or accountant or something—even a lawyer—before they want you to be a writer. But chances are they will help too if you ask them. Or maybe you know a sympathetic teacher. Maybe they know the local movie exhibitor or somebody at the local television station. These people will know people who know people who are in the business in Los Angeles. Or how about politicians? Your mayor or councilperson or state representative or state senator or your congressperson? Networks and studios are very attentive to people in Congress. A politician can get you in to see someone. And someone will lead you to someone who will lead you to someone who will lead you to someone who may lead you to a show business lawyer or agent.

Sooner or later, you are going to need one or both.

Agents always get a bad rap. Overheard at the screening of *Jaws:* "Did you notice Joe? (An agent.) He cried when the shark died." Or, "Charlie's not so bad. He came through that time I needed blood donors." "He did— an agent?" "Sure, came to the hospital, waited till the sun went down, and bit six nurses." A lot of agents deserve the bad rap. A larger number do not. They serve a critical middleman, middleperson, function in our business, and perform the task with skill and ardor. Some are even creative. I do not mean that they write or direct, but they do come up with ideas. Still, the negative reputation clings. This mark on the profession is one reason so many agents finally become producers or executives themselves, roles that carry more prestige.

Why do agents bear this stigma in the first place? Some of them, as I have said, deserve it, but overall the fault, Dear Brutus, lies not in our stars nor in our agents but in ourselves. It is our own immaturity. The immaturity of the creators—and the buyers. We resent our dependency on agents. On buyers. If we were grown up enough to handle our own affairs and confront our rejections directly, we would need agents less or not at all. But dealing directly hurts. Raw emotions get involved, even with success. When you work, it is bad enough that you have to contest over the scene you wrote that ends Act 4, but if you have also been hassling earlier about money and terms, you and the buyer will have an even rougher time working together. Agents buffer. They absorb a lot of this heat and hostility, frustration and resentment. They serve as a conduit for the truth as well, and, unless you are a seven-minute egg, you will learn from that.

If you are selling, buyers will be more open with agents as to why they don't buy your ideas than they will with you.

If you are working, a buyer will seldom be able to tell you face to face, "You're a two-week-old fish. This script stinks and so do you. You call this writing? I call this a rape of our forests. I could have the Sierra Club make a citizen's arrest." Your agent will tell you. Somehow. Chances are that he will soften the blow to help you save face and protect your tottering ego. "You stink" will become "They want to go in another direction. Well, they did mention you've got to work harder on the dialogue and structure." Something like that. If he believes in you, he will also know that that buyer could be wrong. He will take your stinking script to other buyers.

There are any number of other practical reasons for having an agent.

Some buyers will not see you or read you if you do not have an agent (or a production company tie-in).

Agents will be better at the business in show business than you are. Some creators can handle the work and the business side equally well, but they are the exceptions.

Agents can tell the world how wonderful you are much more graciously than you can, though they always leave something out.

Agents can be the villains, while you stay Alan Alda or Mary Tyler Moore.

Then, even when you are working, while you are in the midst of writing, producing, whatever, that great American television movie—or delivering pizzas—you will not have time to keep up with the buyers in hopes of selling a next project. Agents will. And they have access. They are dealing with buyers all the time. They socialize with them. They know day to day if NBC wants a "Beaver Molests Gidget's Granddaughter" or that ABC has a three-picture commitment to John Ritter and cannot find a "high concept" for him. A high concept is an idea that has a great gimmick and can be described in one sentence: A great white shark terrorizes a summer community, which is saved from the shark and its greedy mayor by a lone hero, the local sheriff; a wet *High Noon*. Or, a rich man buys Richard Pryor as a toy for his son. That is a high concept.

Agents can save you endless time and energy by telling you the kinds of materials the buyers are looking for and where the deals are. Agents have information. And the bigger the agency they are in, the more they have. Loads of it. If William Morris had had offices in Iran or Beirut, the CIA and American government would not have been surprised by what went down there. Figure it out. If William Morris, the biggest agency, has two hundred actors on its client roster, say, and fifty or so producers and fifty directors and fifty writers, the agents there know through these clients alone about almost every project in town. That is why William Morris agents have two internal meetings a week, to share information.

They know the salaries, the profit percentages, the stage of development of a project, the clout and talent of individuals on it. They know which series stars and companies have movie-of-the-week commitments. They know more about all three networks combined than any one person in any one network knows.

If your agent, again, is an agent in a big company—William Morris, ICM, CAA—he will be able to "package" you with some of the agency's other clients—production companies, directors, and star actors, for instance. This gives you synergistic power. If the network or production company will not hire you as an individual, but the agent can package you with Tom Sellick, who is his client and whom he has convinced that you are the next Robert Towne, then you are going to get the job. If the agency has a literary department and a theater department, it can alert you to properties that are developing out of those areas. You will not be surprised to learn that the aforementioned Dick Berg, who got *Space* for television, and James Michener, who wrote the book, are both William Morris clients.

The trick is to get your agent to package *you*, to share the information he has with *you*. Most agents will have other clients in your speciality. Going against these other clients is your first challenge. You have to convince your own agent by being more persistent, more appealing, more productive, and potentially more profitable than the others. Secondly, keep in mind that the agent is these days more often part of an organization of agents. He works first for the organization, then for you. In his view, the agency will remain and the networks go on forever, relatively, as do the studios and larger production companies. You are an individual. You may leave your agent. Or you may bomb. Cool. Get leprosy—which is defined as two back-to-back sub-20 share ratings. This equation does not necessarily mean that your agent will subvene your interests to these ongoing entities, but, to put it politely, be aware that you and your agent will not always share common goals. He may, to meet the organization's profit projections for the year, stick you quickly into a project that will make him a fast buck but that just is not right for you. When you need a fast buck, you may insist your agent do this to you. On the other hand, I have known agents who have fought the buyers suicidally in the interests of their clients and have been seminal in shaping their clients' careers.

None of the above is a knock against agents. It is the reality. Agents no less than a gaggle of writers will measure out some venal, some virtuous, some sage, some foolish, some effective, some incompetent. In any case, an agent is not a savior or guru or daddy or mommy, though some will play at these roles and some clients will demand that they do. The point is that you have no right in the relationship to assume that you can abandon your adult responsibilities. You must contribute to the relationship. You must work with the agent. You have to share information with him so that you may expect to get it in return. You must stay informed yourself about the business. You cannot sit in your room or on the beach doing nothing. You have to continue to make your own calls, read the trades, develop your own contacts and projects as well as relying on your agent. You have to listen to his advice measured against his experience and success, but you have to know in your own character when it is right or wrong for you. If, after everything, you and your agent can become friends, and that does happen, so much the better, but that is not what the relationship is about. Finally, you have to demonstrate talent that he can make money on. He has to pay his shrink too, remember. And, having you as a client, he probably goes oftener. What? No, Ann and I do not have agents for television. Owen Laster of William Morris does represent me for books.

Here, if you are just starting out, is the worst news of all: You will not be able to get an agent. Oh, maybe some of you will. But rarely will an agent take the time to nurture a newcomer or even read his material. The agent does not have the time to take. He has x hours and has to make x dollars. A good agent can be a mentor, certainly, but that is not his primary mission. Still, you should not be dissuaded from trying to get one. If you do not know anybody who knows anybody, try writing an intelligent, arresting letter—you are a writer, yes—and send an example of your work along with a synopsis of it. Send only one script. Your best one. If you have more than one, say so in the letter. If the material you send and the letter (keep it to one page) show promise, some agent may want to meet you. May want to read more. May take a chance on handling you. Send your material to lots of agents at the same time. Do not wait to hear back from one before approaching others. Follow up these mailings with phone calls, polite but persistent.

There are smaller agencies and individual agents who will be more receptive to unestablished writers. This is always a shifting reality in terms of who they are, so you will have to ask around when you get to Los Angeles. The Writers Guild of America, even if you are not a member, will be helpful in telling you which agents are legitimate.*

In its present structure, the Writers Guild of America was formed as recently as 1973, in a consolidation of various radio, television, and motion picture organizations representing writers, all of which could trace their histories to the founding of the Authors Guild in 1912, the first association of scriveners in America to look after writers' interests.

The Authors Guild continues to be concerned with the interests of book writers but lacks the punch of being able to strike collective bargaining agreements with publishers. Its counterpart for the stage, the Dramatists Guild, does have muscle in representing playwrights' interests and established long ago terms and conditions under which writers work in the theater, where the writer has more power than in any other area of the bought and sold word. These two organizations, the Authors Guild and the Dramatists Guild, both located in New York City, are linked in the umbrella organization called the Authors League, with a combined membership of roughly 12,000.

The Writers Guild of America, which is not affiliated with the Authors League, has two constituent parts: the Writers Guild of America, East, which has jurisdiction east from the Mississippi River, with its headquarters in New York City at 555 West Fifty-seventh Street, New York, NY 10019, telephone 212-245-6180; and the Writers Guild of America, West, which has jurisdiction west of the Mississippi and is headquartered in Los Angeles at 8955 Beverly Boulevard, Los Angeles, CA 90048, telephone 213-550-1000.

The Writers Guild has roughly 7,900 members with a ratio of five to two west to east. As a labor union, it represents the membership in radio, television, and motion pictures through collective bargaining agreements with the commercial networks, PBS, all the major studios and independent producers, and a number of local stations. Thus far, the pay cable companies, HBO, Cinemax, and Showtime/Movie Channel, have refused to acknowledge the Guild's jurisdiction and have no agreements with it. As of this writing, the Guild has not challenged this situation aggressively. Many Guild members, through pseudonyms and second- and third-party entities, do pay cable work. It is a rancorous reality that must come to eventual confrontation.

You do not join the Writers Guild of America as you might some sort of industry club. You do not join with the intention of writing. You must have proven, applicable writing credentials. In order to qualify, you must fill out a detailed application; pay the initiation fee of $1,500, plus annual dues of $100 and 1 percent of your gross income as a writer in the covered areas of radio, television, and motion pictures; and show proof (a signed contract, for instance) of a writing deal with a signatory company. In regard to this latter provision, there are more complicated rules. When you are

---

*The complete list of WGA signatory agents is in the appendix.

ready, contact the Guild for more detailed and current information.

In its areas of coverage, the Guild has been a powerful protector of writers, who, otherwise, as individuals, would be as cold-bloodedly exploited as they were before its founding. The Guild, in addition to settling minimum wage rates in all categories ($28,506 for network primetime two-hour movies—$10,959 for the story and $18,720 for the teleplay),* vigorously enforces rules defining all aspects of a writer's services. It further provides generous and humane medical, retirement, and death benefit plans.

I am a member of the Writers Guild of America West (and the Authors Guild), and our production company, Comco Productions, Inc., is a signatory to its contract, which is called the Minimum Basic Agreement, or MBA. In the appendix of this book you will find the Writers Guild Code of Working Rules, its areas of functions and services, its standard contract forms for free-lance television writers' employment, and a writer's flat deal.

Here are some other things you should try when you get to Los Angeles. Join the National Academy of Television Arts & Sciences, which is not a labor union and not restrictive in membership to work performance. It is an industrywide association of people in all categories who work in television or are interested in it. Go to the general membership meetings of the Academy and to the social and educational functions it sponsors. Do the dirty work on the committees. You will meet lots of people and gather lots of information. For women, join Women in Film and ditto advice.

If you have a play, try to get it produced by one of Los Angeles's small theater companies. It is almost always easier to get an agent or a buyer to look at a piece of your work than it is to get one to read it. Plus, the fact that you have gotten a production—a vote of confidence from somebody else—gives the agent or buyer more confidence in you.

If you look like Sam Shepard or Christie Brinkley, try acting or modeling. This will draw attention to your writing.

Get to be a reader. You will learn a lot about craft as you go through other writers' material, and you will have access to some buyers. Especially if they like your style in your reports.

Go to writers' and producers' workshops. There must be at least fifty of these a year in Los Angeles. It is astonishing how candid and accessible the biggest people in our business are when they are on the panels of these seminars. People who normally block you out with a phalanx of secretaries and assistants and who would not tell you a trade secret if you put a burning cigarette to their bare feet will talk to you courteously after these sessions and will blurt out truth after truth after truth during them.

At some point, you will need a show business lawyer. For one thing, you should have one to look over the contract that you sign with an agent,

---

*This is the figure for 1985 according to the Minimum Basic Agreement of 1985. It will increase in March 1986 to $30,644 and in March 1987 to $34,628. Few working writers get paid only the minimum.

since these are subject to negotiation. There are several excellent, influential entertainment law firms in Los Angeles and New York. Ours in Los Angeles is Weissman, Wolfe, Bergman, Coleman & Schulman. In New York it is Paul, Weiss, Rifkind, Wharton & Garrison. Again, when you get to Los Angeles or New York, you will get to know who some of the other good entertainment law firms are. Go through your personal life to see if anybody you know knows anybody in these firms. At the beginning, perhaps, one of these lawyers will carry you for free or for reduced fees. Some good men early in my career did that for me.

Why do you need an entertainment lawyer? Well, first, as Samuel Goldwyn said, "a verbal agreement isn't worth the paper it's written on." If it is a written agreement, it will be complex. You will need an experienced professional to steer you through the potential dangers and civilized larcenies. Too, if your lawyer is one of repute in the business, having him says to buyers that you are serious about the business, and, though you may be just starting out, that you know the machinery of the business and are not to be trifled with. Since you are not likely to have an agent, you will probably sell your first project or projects on your own, in which case you will definitely need a knowing lawyer to negotiate your deal. (Even with an agent, you will sell projects on your own.) While entertainment lawyers do not function as agents, and are barred by law from soliciting work for you, many have splendid contacts in the business and can put you in the way of an assignment by saying the right word here and there.

If a lawyer does negotiate a deal for you, he will charge you a one-time fee for the service, not 10 percent of your earnings forever on that project as an agent will. Do not be shy about asking the lawyer up front what his fee (and estimated expenses) will be.

Let's get to the networks. Each network's movie and mini-series department is set up somewhat differently, but each serves the same purposes and carries out similar functions.

At CBS in Los Angeles, the department is located in a modern concrete and glass building, cum state university, on Radford Street near Ventura Boulevard in Studio City in a refurbished complex that used to be the Republic Pictures lot and is now called the CBS/Fox Studios. (Twentieth Century Fox shares ownership.) The overall complex contains a number of soundstages—"Hill Street Blues" is shot in one of these—exterior sets, production offices and support services, editing facilities, and the inevitable studio commissary. It is fun to go onto this lot. You feel as though you are truly connected to movie-making.

In the department here is a vice-president for movies and mini-series, who reports to the president of CBS Entertainment, whose office is across the hills in Los Angeles at Fairfax and Beverly Boulevard in a CBS facility called Television City.

Reporting to this vice-president of motion pictures for television and mini-series are three vice-presidents: one for mini-series and two for motion pictures for television (one for movies that are licensed from outside suppliers and one for "in-house" movies that are totally financed and owned by CBS Entertainment).

To "license" a film means that an outside production entity will own the film but that a network will have paid to have the film exclusively for a given number of "plays," "runs," or "airings" over a given period of time. Today, this is usually two runs over four years, a standard procedure at all three networks. In such a licensing situation CBS, say, will pay a gross amount—roughly a million-plus per hour or two million-plus for a movie of the week as the license fee. The network will maintain its creative controls over the project, but the outside supplier will be responsible for delivering the film for that price, or under, since the supplier will try to make a profit. Or over. Often, going in, without any disasters, these outside pictures will be budgeted to cost more than the network has paid. In some cases, this over-the-license production money will be an inducement to the network to go ahead with a picture. The outside supplier, however, is not Santa Claus, though all studios claim to lose money on mini-series and to go into deficit on movies as well. The outside supplier will expect to get his money back and make a profit from subsequent or additional sales of the film. He will make money by selling it in domestic syndication eventually or by getting up-front money from foreign theatrical and/or television distributors. Say you want to make *Napoleon's Retreat from Russia* and your budget says it will cost five million dollars, only two-plus of which you can get from a network. You will have to make up the difference (and any profit) by selling it to American syndicators and overseas buyers. If you can make the numbers come out, a network will be delighted to have a rich-looking production for under half its cost.

A network will always demand a "deficit financier"—an entity the network knows has money to pay for any costs above the license fee—"overruns" or "overages"—an entity that can guarantee completion and delivery of the film as contracted. This is usually a major studio—Universal, Warner's, and so on—or a major independent. As a small independent or individual, you will have to make a co-production deal with such a dificit financier. To protect itself further, a network will pay out the license fee money only against certain stipulated actions: so much on the signing of the contract, so much on completion of the script and the second draft, at the beginning of pre-production (typically six to eight weeks ahead of the first shooting date on a two-hour film), the completion of principal photography and delivery of the acceptable answer print.* You never get the two mil in a lump sum.

---

*The "answer print" is the color-corrected and exposure-corrected print of the film. When sound is combined on the same print it is called a "composite print." A final composite print is the one that will be used for airing or, more accurately these days, will be used to make the transfer to one-inch videotape, which is what

The mini-series vice-president has a person reporting to him who is called a director. He also has a couple of lower-level executives or assistants reporting to him.

The two motion-pictures-for-television vice-presidents at CBS have four to five directors reporting to them. One of these directors is based in New York. The directors will report to one of the two vice-presidents depending on whether the project in question is an in-house or outside production. Commonly referred to as in-house and out-house.

There are four to six assistant directors and program executives at the next level down. These do a lot of grind administrative work—preparing status reports, competetive reports (tracking what the other networks are doing), script expediting, intra-network coordination with sales, broadcast standards, business affairs, research, and advertising and promotion. (The higher-level executives also do a lot of administrative work and coordinating with their counterparts in these other departments.) The lower-level people do get to sit in on meetings with sellers—as witnesses for later potential "he said, she said, I said, you said" conflicts; a second opinion; administrative follow-through; to mitigate against a seller bribing a single buyer; and to learn with the possibility of moving up.

The director-level people are the front line for presentation meetings, or as we call them "pitch" meetings, or pitches. In which you "pitch" (present) an idea for a movie. These director executives are also the day-to-day contacts once you have made a sale. They will give the first notes on the outline and subsequent drafts of the script before passing the material higher. They will work with you on interdepartmental considerations. On casting possibilities—in conjunction with CBS Casting, a separate department housed over at Television City (and in New York) that is very powerful. It has casting veto power over you and the movie programming people as well. The directors will work with you on selecting the other creative elements as well—the director and composer, for example.

None of these movie and mini-series department executives will negotiate your deal, however. That is handled by business affairs, which at CBS is a very autonomous department.

Though the policy at CBS is for directors to take the initial meetings,

---

will air. The first answer print almost always needs correcting. Scenes may be too green or blue or red, for instance, or the exposures—the amount of light—may be too dark or too light. These scenes will then be "timed." A "one-light" print or a "work print" is struck from the exposed negative at a single setting, a standard median exposure and color formula, so certain scenes will need more specific settings. When you "time" scenes, you stop at those scenes and reset exposures and colors, letting those scenes have the specific time in the process they need to get them correct. A work print, by the way, is what you "work" with when you are editing the film. Why is the later print called an "answer" print? Because it accurately "answers" the corrected internegative from which it is struck or made. All television movies, incidentally, are shot on 35mm film.

the first level of vice-presidents will also hold pitch meetings with the more important suppliers around town, being sure to include a director in the meeting as well, in order to preserve the form and to carry out any followup steps that may be required. This applies to the top vice-president as well. Everybody in the department reads every script that is in development, and weekly there are two key meetings of the department. One to share information about the status of committed projects; another to discuss new pitches. I will go through the process in more detail in the chapter on producing.

At ABC, as of this writing, there is a vice-president, novels, limited series, and motion pictures for TV. Under this slot come a vice-president, novels and limited series, and a vice-president, motion pictures for television. Next down are a number of executive producers for each category. It is awkward setting the number because the chart is fluid. (You will find, as you go, that my facts may be wrong by the time you read them, since television is so mercurial, but you can depend on the truths.)

As at CBS, the entire pitch community is allocated among these executives. Each will be assigned a certain number of studios, independents, and so on and will work with these exclusively as they deal with the network.

Here too there are additional support people and everybody at least through the first two executive levels has his or her own secretary. The administrative functions are the same at all three networks.

ABC's movie department has its offices in the ABC Entertainment Center in Century City, which is in West Los Angeles, cheek by expensive jowl to Beverly Hills, on a street called Avenue Of The Stars. ABC also makes in-house movies through a company called Circle Films. As far as I can tell, there is no ABC television movie executive based in New York. Everything in the ABC movie setup reports finally to Brandon Stoddard, President, ABC Motion Pictures, Inc.

NBC has a vice-president, mini-series and novels for television, and a vice-president, motion pictures for television. The mini-series VP has assistants. The movie VP has two directors and support-level people. The two VPs report to the senior vice-president, programs and talent. The NBC movie offices are located in the NBC office/studio/local station complex located on Alameda Street in Burbank. The building was erected in the thirties and is a rather good example of art moderne architecture, which shows more dramatically in its new beige color than it did in its former bilious aquamarine. The procedures followed at NBC parallel those that I have described at the other networks.

HBO and Showtime/Movie Channel have executive structures based on the network models, as are the executive alignments at all the major studios and independent production companies. HBO and Showtime/Movie Channel have executives in New York who can take pitches.

One very valuable resource that will help you through the maze of all of this in Los Angeles and will give you the titles and names of the players of the moment, within a year, is *The Hollywood Reporter Studio Blu-book Directory,* which is published annually. It costs $25 but is worth it. It has additional listings and information on all aspects of the business.

Okay, let's say you have an agent and let's say he has set up a pitch meeting for you at one of the networks. Let's say at CBS with a director, motion pictures for television. What do you pitch? How do your prepare?

First, you will have found out from your agent or another source if the network is looking for any particular type of movie at the time you are going in. Each network usually develops a range of types. ABC with its urban-young outlook (and NBC because Brandon Tartikoff, the president of NBC Entertainment, and Steve White, vice-president, motion pictures for television, were trained at ABC) lean to glitzier, sexier material. They are high on high concept. On controversy, CBS, generally speaking, is more conservative and family-oriented. But all three will have some mysteries, some car crash chases, some horror, some love stories, some true stories out of the papers or off "60 Minutes," some biographies of famous people, that sort of thing. In 1984–85 all three networks got a taste for social issue movies. "Trauma drama," these have been dubbed. As their development develops or bombs or as the society is perceived to have shifted moods, the networks will decide that they are short in a particular category. One time it may be comedy, another it will be what they call "affliction pictures" or "sick pix." Disease, palatable death, that sort of thing.

You mean *Who Will Love My Children? Bill?*

Yes, that's the idea. Or, they will be faced with a competitive situation that needs counterprogramming. In 1984–85 CBS was looking for male macho action ideas to go on Wednesday night against "Hotel" and "Dynasty," soap programs that have strong female appeal, which did not work. In 1985–86, as you see, it is more trauma drama and "true" stories. Faction.

They will buy a stunting idea. Example: Olivia Newton-John has a big hit record called *Physical.* And a music video of same. The country is in the throes of a fitness madness. And music video madness. So somebody pitches the bright idea of a movie using the title *Physical* (you cannot copyright titles) * and centers it on a dishy-looking girl who has a great body to begin with. But at first she hides it in a lot of fat-looking clothing. So we can be told she needs to shape up to feel good about herself and hold her man, etc. We will see her wet and sweating and sexy and moving to pop music— music video. The picture gets made. And the audience loves it, right?

Wrong. The audience yawns and changes channels, because it watches

---

*Producers can join the title registration bureau, through which members agree to respect prior claims to titles. The law itself recognizes that titles may take on unique secondary meaning and importance. You would, for instance, be barred from calling a play *The Odd Couple.*

a lot of television and sees right away the kid is a looker from the start and maybe somebody is trying to manipulate it and there is not a lot of story or soul and the audience knows that it is an audience that watches television movies, which is not the same audience that watches music video. Besides, who needs that sweat? We got our home cassette of Jane Fonda.

In any case, you should know what they are looking for. This does not mean that you cannot come in with a story that is off that type. As the cliché goes, "A good story is always in fashion."

You should have your story written down on a few pages. Not too many. Not too much print on any one page. Lots of white space, as *Cool Fire* readers know. This presentation is what you will leave behind and is sometimes called a "leave-behind." It should be bound in one of those inexpensive binders you can find in stationery and drug and dime stores. I like the kind that has a solid back and a transparent front. Do not bring in presentations that are stapled together or paper-clipped. Pages get lost. Paper clips catch on other presentations in the stack. There will be a stack. Buyers get pitched lots of ideas. Present two copies of your presentation. One for the buyer and one for the buyer to send along to script and idea registration, a function usually performed by the broadcast standards department. Production companies have their own specially designed binders. All pitches are registered for later reference in case of conflict as to whose idea an idea is and to establish the chronology of its submission; and in case of legal action.

You can protect your own ideas, presentations, treatments, scenarios, formats, synopses, and completed scripts in three ways. In the case of completed works only, you can apply for federal copyright through the United States Copyright Office, Washington, D.C. 20599. With all of the above variations, you can send yourself a dated copy of the material by registered letter. If you will leave this unopened until such time as a dispute arises and can show your registered receipt as well, you are not guaranteed legal protection of the material, but you will have clear proof of the date of your finished authorship of such material. A third means of protection is available to members and nonmenbers alike through The Writers Guild of America's Manuscript Registration Service. Again, this service does not provide absolute protection under the law but only establishes proof of a completion date for the material submitted. You may submit for registration finished work, formats, outlines, synopses, treatments, senarios, and presentations of ideas. I suppose it may seem odd, but I have never used any of these services.

When you are in the pitch meeting do not give this written presentation to the buyer until after you have talked the idea. If you give the buyer the written presentation while you are talking, the buyer will be half-listening, half-reading and will miss the idea both ways. Here is the original presentation we submitted for *Drop-Out Father*, the full script of which follows in chapter 4:

DROP—OUT FATHER

a movie for television
2 hours

from
ANN SHANKS
BOB SHANKS

to be written
by
BOB SHANKS

COMCO PRODUCTIONS, INC.
address
Los Angeles, CA
phone

<u>LOG LINE</u>

''Caught in the rat race and think the rats are winning? Find out what happens to one family when an upper—middle, upward—manic father drops out. A comedy.''

DROP-OUT FATHER

This is a comedy.

The idea starts to form for 47-year-old Ed McCall when he is driving his battered Ford station wagon on a Monday morning through
the cold January rain to the commuter train station in Stamford,
Connecticut, for the ride into New York.

The car breaks down. Looking under the hood at the enigmatic maze
of parts and wires, with the rain dripping off of him, McCall begins
thinking about his life. His 22-year-old son, an unemployed college drop-out--''sensitive and trying to find himself''--drives
a TR7 and lives in Greenwich Village in an apartment Ed McCall
pays for. His 20-year-old daughter, limping through Vassar,
drives a Volkswagon convertible. His 18-year-old son, who is a
senior in high school and plays guitar, drives a Datsun 280Z--
and McCall crazy--with the amp he keeps in his room which has to
be the loudest in the free world. McCall's wife, who uses it mostly
to get to her shrink's and to the country club, drives a new
Seville.

McCall begins adding up the payments on these cars and wonders
why it is that he, who pays, drives the wreck. This leads him to
thinking about all the other expenses: the mortgage, insurance,
monthly allowances to unproductive children. Shrinks. Taxes to
a looney-tune government. His chest tightens. He has trouble
breathing. What is he working for? What's it all about?

McCall slams down the hood, pushes the car to the side of the road,
and walks to the station. This is not too bad, since the rain has
turned to snow. He has missed the 7:05, his regular train, of
course, and gets the 7:50 instead, which arrives New York at 8:20.
At least, that's what the schedule says. There is no heat in the
train and no available seat, but it does break down. We are dealing with a man on the brink.

As creative supervisor at an advertising agency, McCall makes
$100,000 a year. He has $1,000 in a savings account, $480 in
checking. His investments lose money. Still, he is thought to be
successful and talented.

When McCall arrives late for work, his boss rejects his new campaign for Starteeth, a new nonbrushing tooth cleanser, and makes
threats that his job is on the line.

That night at home at dinner, McCall sees his family, who pays no attention to him, as vultures pecking away at his body. His life has lost meaning. The idea to do something about it grows stronger.

Maybe he's not well. He goes for a physical. The doctor tells him he is a wreck. A sure candidate for a heart attack, a stroke, or cancer. Maybe all three.

Then Ed McCall's friend and colleague, Adam, age 45, dies of a heart attack. McCall, mourning his own life as well as his friend's, slips on a patch of ice on the steps of the funeral home. He breaks his ankle. That does it!

Ed McCall summons his four children and his wife (''Why can't you get a job, get liberated? Other women do.'') to a family meeting--at his bedside.

He announces that he is tired, disgusted, taken for granted, and that he has had it. Here is his idea: He is quitting his job, firing the maid and gardner, selling the house and the cars, canceling all but his GI insurance. He makes a ceremony of burning their credit cards. He is dropping out.

He will buy a loft in New York, furnish it at thrift shops and get a chauffer's license. ''I'm going to take French, learn to play the piano, and read thick, important books. I will go to museums and improve my tennis. Maybe I will get to know a black person. You're welcome to join me--I love all of you--or did--maybe can again--but from now on you make your own way.'' Carrie, the 12-year-old, thinks her Dad's idea is great and wants to go with him.

The wife and Vassar daughter are in shock. What will friends and family say--his boss? The ''sensitive'' son knows this will end the checks from home. He threatens to go back to college to hold Dad to his promise that he would pay for school. Ed says the offer is no longer open. The boy can go to school on his own. Maybe then he will appreciate it.

Ed moves to the city with Carrie, the 12-year-old ''overachiever,'' who at first loves the adventure but then misses her mother.

The rest of the family is furious. They refuse to go along and, at first, refuse to talk to Ed or have anything to do with him.

Ed's boss thinks the whole thing is a ploy to get out of his contract and go to another agency. The boss offers a raise. He is dumbfounded when Ed refuses.

Ed's wife retains a lawyer, who charges Ed with desertion.

The wife gets a job eventually––as a secretary. She does well. She likes it. She works her way up to administrative assistant to the president.

The oldest son, relieved of his silly rebellion about not going to college, opens a ceramics shop in Boston. He makes his own pottery––what he has always wanted to do. The shop succeeds.

The Vassar daughter, a C–minus student, only going to college for men and to extend her adolescence, dares to study and go for a law degree.

The wife finally joins Ed in the city.

The 18–year–old also comes to the city. At first, he is terrified of blacks and foreigners in the inner–city school he attends, but with Carrie's help, makes friends with two black guys who let him join their rock band.

By Christmas of the following year, everyone is functioning, wholesome, and happy. They come together Christmas Eve. They realize that before they had only been living halfway, trying to fulfill other people's expectations.

It is a wonderful Christmas. The family is now grateful for the gift Ed has given them––their own self–sufficient lives. He is the happiest of men to have his family again, and his new, saner life. He toasts the family in his newly acquired French, ''Joyeux Noël.''

THE END

Here, as I promised you in chapter 1, is that internal status report that Ann and I maintain about our various projects. One page from it, at least. Because *Drop-Out Father* got on eventually, there were many subsequent pages for it tracing its course. This example is an early version, done when the project was new. As you can see, I had the idea for the movie in January of 1979 when I was under contract to MCA-Universal to develop projects. We pitched it first at ABC, where it was rejected immediately in the pitch meeting, then to NBC, which developed the script. Of course, as often happens, the movie ended up being made by CBS. Without Universal's involvement. I will go into *Drop-Out's* history in more detail in chapter 4. For now, the point is to urge you to give yourself some kind of system for keeping track of your ideas. Here is how we do it, listing each project on a separate page with the projects in alphabetical order by title, with a cover page that reads:

<u>COMCO PRODUCTIONS</u>
<u>PROJECTS</u>
<u>STATUS REPORT</u>

Date:

We find it is a very useful reference and a prod to discipline. It forces you to keep coming up with projects and to keep them moving.

<u>PROJECT</u>	<u>DISPOSITION</u>	<u>STATUS</u>
Drop-Out Father	Len Hill, ABC 2/16/79 Rejected, ABC 2/16/79	Presentation 2/4/79
<u>EXECUTIVE PRODUCERS</u>	Deanne Barkley, NBC 2/20/79 seemed to like Recommended to Klein 2/26/79	John Schulman Negot. — Steve Mayer — NBC 7/2
	Barkley meeting 3/13/79 script deal.	Script due 12/1
<u>PRODUCER</u>	Jane Deknatel — Robert Harris — Universal 2/22	
	Al Rush meeting 5/31. Will push NBC for paper.	
<u>DIRECTOR</u>	Notified 7/12 — going ahead! by Irwin Moss & Jane Deknatel	

<u>WRITER</u>

<u>OTHER PRINCIPALS</u>

When you read *Drop-Out Father* you will see, as I did to my amazement in rereading the presentation, that its spirit and structure are contained in this brief original presentation. That probably makes it a good presentation, an effective one. It set forth a workable idea. The spine of the story and several major incidents were there from the start. You could see scenes playing, although I got very hung up early on the cars, which would not play easily as I described it in the presentation. I did use the cars in the movie eventually as something *seen* but not talked about. The presentation had—good, bad, or indifferent—a beginning, a middle, and an ending. Too, the story had appropriate television values: a likable, identifiable family in a comprehensible conflict, and a happy resolution.

Now, look at the cover page again. It provides a title for the movie. It tells you who is presenting the project, as well as the essential information as to the name of the producing company, its address, and phone number. If you have an agent, the agent's name should appear on this page also, along with an address and phone number. Elementary, but you would be astonished at how frequently this information is left off.

In this case, of course, the cover page gives the name of the person who will write the script. If you are pitching as a writer only or as a writer-producer, certainly you will include your name as the potential writer.

If you are a producer only, you may have a writer committed ahead of time to the project, but do it only if you know that writer is one the network likes. That writer's name should be on the cover page. As a producer only, if you cannot interest a specific writer in your project or you have doubt about a writer's status at a network, it is better then on a separate inside page to have a list of "suggested, possible writers." Or, you can, safely and simply, avoid naming a particular writer or set of writers at this initial step. If the network likes your idea, the executives there will have ideas of their own about who should write it.

Each network movie department has, as opposed to a blacklist, a "whitelist." That is, a list of stars, directors, writers, and producers whom the department likes. "Likes" in this case means not affection but past and current performance. Track record. Try to know which of the people in these categories a network is high on. This is certainly the kind of information an agent should know.

If there is a director on the network whitelist who will commit to your project up front, this should not hurt your chances for a sale and may gain a more respectful hearing, though a director attached to a project in television does not carry the same weight as having the commitment of a hot director in theatrical motion pictures.

If you know your idea is a good one for a certain star and if you know that the network has that star under contract to make a movie, you are certainly going to point out that your idea is right for, say, Kate Jackson or Robert Guillaume. When you cannot know whom a network has under contract, it is safe to assume that the network has movie-of-the week commitments to its major weekly series stars. Many producer-writers specifically mold ideas for stars who have movie deals.

Without an agent or inside access of some kind, you can get this information cumulatively by reading the trade papers, *Daily Variety* and the *Hollywood Reporter*, every day. It is there in abundance. Hard facts about who has deals where. Reading the trades also gives you an over-all feel for the business. You will begin to know who the key executive players are and will be able to follow their musical-chair comings and goings. You will see the interconnections among networks and suppliers and who the consistently working directors and writers are. All kinds of patterns will emerge.

The hard part of reading the trades everyday is the sense you get of how successful everyone else is but you. A friend, a very accomplished playwright-screenwriter, went to London for the opening of one of his films there. Months later, on a visit of my own, I ran into him still there.

"Aren't you ever coming home?" I asked him. "Why are you here all this time?"

"I like not having to read everyday what I'm not doing," he said.

But the impression you get from the trades about other people's successes is illusory. Some of it is out-and-out hype and most of it is about different people every day. Besides, why should you be spared the anxiety all the rest of us feel? I suppose the true mark of maturity comes with being able to ignore the successes of your peers and to compete only against your measure of your own abilities. By that standard, I would say I am about 14.

Star casting beyond the stars under contract to a network can also help you sell a picture. One producer friend sold a mini-series idea to one network by coming in with a commitment from a big star in a series on another network. The property in question was a book that the star could read and judge, and the star had a production company which was to co-produce (co-own) the project. This made the up-front commitment possible. Keep this in mind. Most stars do have their own production corporations. Many of these "companies" are for tax protection first and to accommodate personal vehicles for the star-owners second. Only a few have ambitions to produce projects whether there is a good role for the stars in question or not. Howsoever, these stars are looking for projects. Usually, they are drawn to published books, produced plays, or completed scripts. Rarely will a star commit to an idea or treatment only.

If you have been able to get access to a star and have that star's commitment up front, be sure to bring the star to the network meeting. This will get you the meeting faster and will immediately increase your "sell" strength. There is a good chance such a meeting will turn into a lunch! Buyers, despite rumors, are human. They too like to be able to say guess who I had lunch with today. Again, be sure that you have not mentioned or made a commitment with a star who is not on the network's approved list, or who has a bad history at the network.

Okay, there you are in the meeting. How do you handle it? I think I am the last person to ask. I can tell you about the setting and the dynamics, but since I hate these meetings I am no good at them, or I am no good at them because I hate them. I go to as few of them as possible. The rush for me—it is a physical exhilaration—comes with the formulation of an idea. The thinking it through and writing it down. Solving the problems of an idea. By the time I get to the pitch meeting, I have been through this process and believe the idea's merit is transparent. If the buyer does not share this vision right away, I get depressed and angry (the same thing, right?). In truth, in a kind of self-fulfilling prophecy, I get depressed and angry on the drive to the meeting. Not good.

How do I think like that and survive in a business built around these meetings? Apparently, from the reports of others, I am better in these meetings than I think I am, but more importantly for me, there is Ann. She goes to the meetings. It's her meeting, even if I am there. She loves the meetings. She loves the people. She is genuinely interested in them individually, rather like a botanist turned loose in a rain forest. She has made *friends* with major buyers.

I was not much better off as the buyer, truth to tell. I guess I simply do not like the situation. All of this is meant to get you thinking about yourself. Your strengths and weaknesses. You must sell. If you are not good at it, you will have to get better, and you can by forcing yourself; and you will have to develop an alternate way to accomplish the end—an agent, a partner, something.

Now for a startling bit of news, if you think of yourself as a writer: The true pitch is not written but verbal. As both buyer and seller, I have experienced repeatedly in these meetings that writing is secondary. It is talking that counts. You have got to be able to talk your movie idea. If you can say it in one sentence, so much the better: "I want to do the love story of Prince Charles and Princess Diana." "Ed Asner to play Knute Rockne." This will not be enough if you are new; still, something like it is a very effective start. The more experienced you are and the more the buyer knows your track record or has worked with you before, the more you will succeed with this simple pitch. Sometimes you will not even need a written presentation. Just rush in and yell "sperm bank" or some other hot category.

Take a moment longer to think about those two one-line ideas, Prince Charles and Knute Rockne. If you are a beginner, forget about the first one and other ideas like it. When something like Charles/Diana bubbles up in the news, at least fifty professionals are on the phone to the network buyers they know and from whom they can get a quick response. It will take you weeks, perhaps months to get your network meeting. By then, Charles/Diana will be gone. Maybe not so on something like Rockne. He is no longer "hot" but is still a powerful American icon. No network ever went broke doing remakes, and a contemporary star of status could reenliven Rockne. This latter, in fact, is an idea I did pitch to a network and one that got me very close. Asner was hot on *Lou Grant*, the fiftieth anniversary of Rockne's death was coming up, and "The Gipper," Ronald Reagan, was in the White House. Also, I took it to a buyer whom I knew loved sports stories.

Why didn't the idea go? Ed Asner came out publicly involved in the politics of El Salvador and the ratings on *Lou Grant* softened. The show was canceled and Asner was no longer a marbleized American hero. An instant ice age hit my idea. I told you it was perilous. But, the point is, look for these kinds of connections and combinations. They do hit. Think of this past season's *Anna Karenina* with Jacqueline Bisset. Nobody would buy that book alone, but with a movie star in her first television appearance, the project took on new luster and became salable.

It helps to know who Knute Rockne is or what *Anna Karenina* is. It has just occurred to me that some of the buyers may not know. One network buyer, for instance, is reported from a meeting to have thought that Eugene O'Neill was an agent at William Morris.

In a meeting of our own, Ann and I were trying to sell *The Birth of Israel*, for the 1987–88 season, which would mark the fortieth anniversary of that nation. A rich and heroic, uplifting reality, we thought, with enough blood and sex and combat to satiate the dullest-witted Java Man with a Nielsen box. No. We were wrong. We were told it was "foreign." "Americans don't like anything foreign." I heard myself averring something silly like, "But Jews have always gotten good numbers. *Golda, QBVII, Exodus, The Holocaust*." "*Exodus* was a movie," I was interrupted (I didn't think we were there to sell a coloring book), "and, sure, as long as it's Jews in Germany. Nazis are numbers." I was speechless, but so was Ann, no easy feat. The buyer finally intruded on our reflective stillness, which had been interpreted as needing a defense. "*We* do history. We're doing three nurses on Bataan. We'll even show the Death March—but not horrendous." And then, gaining confidence, "It's sort of "Charlie's Angels" goes to war." Now proudly. "An *American* war." I felt like crying after that meeting.

In yet another meeting, Ann and I pitched *Hiroshima*, John Hersey's searing journalistic account of what happened in the lives of six people who lived through this overture to Doomsday. Hersey's book is not some tricked-up flash-forward disaster movie but the real thing. (We did not have the rights nor did we claim to, but they were available per our inquiry, although Hersey is suspicious of television and wisely (if not commercially) would prefer the Japanese to make a film if it were to be made.) Anyway, the buyer's stunning, unironic response was, "We already have an atom bomb picture."

After I'd related these stories, a friend tried to cheer me up by telling me about a meeting in which he pitched an Oscar Wilde biography. The young buyer seemed interested, came forward in his chair on "Reading Gaol," and interrupted, "Tell me—does this Oscar Wilde fella come with the package."

All the more reason then to make sure, without being condescending, that you inform the potential buyer of a project on a comfortable level. "You ever see Garbo in *Anna Karenina?*" Great love story. Timeless. Sexy, tragic. Big success the first time. A classic. I've got Jackie Bisset—her first—*first*—television commitment. She'll do it. The remake. I can get extra production money with that. Isn't that great?" Or, "After the Olympics and with the new spirit in the country, I think it's time for a really solid football picture. They do well, you know—*Brian's Song, Something for Joey*. One of the biggest pictures Hollywood ever made was *Knute Rockne, All-American* with Ronald Reagan—maybe we can get him to host a White House screening—and Pat O'Brien as Rockne—the great Notre Dame coach. The guy was funny too. Once, when he didn't like the way his team was playing, he went and sat in the stands. Kind of a Bobby Knight—with warmth. You like Ed Asner? Rockne sort of looked like Ed Asner, who'd be perfect. It's got all the right values. God, patriotism, a love story, family, underdogs who win." Pitching like this, it does not matter whether the buyer knows the specific projects or not. You have given him a range of comprehensible television values that he does understand. You have not embarrassed him or her in a practical sense (though you may have embarrassed yourself). But look, as Will Rogers said, "We're all ignorant—just on different subjects."

If your project is an original, good luck. That is the toughest sell of all. There is no certitude from another source. Especially if you are new, you will really have to work hard and in a very narrow commercial range. Increasingly, for any project short of a hot package/high concept, networks want storylines in considerable detail. You must have a beginning, a middle, and an ending. You must have rich detail in incidents and characterizations. Your chances are enhanced if you have a hook or a gimmick. Even so, be sure to have the one-line description as well. It is a working cliché that buyers want to know the idea in a log line. Many will say openly, "What's the *TV Guide* log line?"

How many projects should you pitch in a meeting? There is no rule and much depends on your experience and your relationship with the buyer. For two-hour movies, pitching one project only is fine. Mandatory if you are there with a star. On your own, pitching two or three ideas is okay, too. Be wary of pitching more than three—four, if you must—since the buyer's sensitivity will dull with each no or mildly interested reaction. Right or wrong, these buyers have heard all the ideas, or variations of them, and are accustomed to making quick judgments. How does your idea shape up, not only on its own merits but in terms of the kinds of projects already in development? Who are you compared to another producer? Even if your idea is a good one, can you produce it, write it, bring it off, bring it in? Who is coming in tomorrow, the day after, next week, who may be more experienced or politically connected and may have better ideas or leverage to fill those finite number of spots remaining? Who will help the executive's own career? Who can hire me, the executive may be thinking, if I get fired here? Or get me to the "A list" parties? All of these are questions a buyer/executive will be asking himself even before he hears you out. (I know a considerable number of buyers are women, so I am not unmindful here of saying "himself" and "he," to the syntactical detriment of women, but the majority of buyers remain male, so please regard my usage as a reflection of that reality and as a less cumbersome piece of linguistic luggage, rather than any semiotic sexism on my part.) One network buyer admitted openly, "Why should I buy from you when I can buy from X (a major independent)? He can give me a job someday. Can you?" This is the Pentagon syndrome of generals and admirals leaving the services to join corporations that they have been buying from. It is odoriferous but true. People also still sleep their way in and up. Out-and-out bribes are not much in fashion but gifts, Raiders tickets and such, can still work wonders.

If you get excitement from the first idea you pitch, although you are prepared with two, three, or four ideas, I suggest you hold back on the others. If the buyer asks for more ideas, then go for it.

If number one is considered okay by the buyer, but the buyer says they have that or something close to it in the works, move quickly to the second. Do not challenge the fact that they already have the idea in the works, or an idea close to it, and do not get paranoic about it. It is, no doubt, true. They are not trying to steal your idea. How many are there really? With an entire community playing this hard game, it is certain that ideas are going to overlap or even be the same.

Unless you have Ann-Margret in *A Streetcar Named Desire*, I think it is a waste of these meetings to pitch only one idea. Take your shot, but remember the buyer will be thinking that you played your best shot first so will believe the subsequent ideas are of decreasing importance even to you and may start tuning out. The buyer will also begin to doubt your earnestness about any one idea as you pitch an increasing number. On the other hand, your number two or three may just be the bell-ringer. Depending on your personality and chemistry with the buyer, you may be able to convince him that you are a creative cornucopia. You may walk in and say, "I have four fantastic ideas for movies and I love them all equally. They all have special meaning to me and these pictures must be made. I don't know which one to start with."

On the other hand, never project the emotion (or the reality) in the song from *A Chorus Line:* "I need this job." The buyers themselves are desperate enough without the smell of your desperation. Remember that it is a law of nature to run from the wounded member of the herd.

As to the dynamics of these meetings, remember that you will be kept waiting. Do not let the surroundings intimidate. Study them. Break things into details. See specifics. This calms the nerves as well as sharpening your powers of observation. Be alert to exchange amenities with the receptionist or secretary or people passing through. This may lead to extended conversation and to information about the operation. But, guys, cool it. Do not "come on." If you are kept waiting a half-hour, try to reset the appointment while you are there, nicely, and leave. Reset it from home later if you have to. This is respect for yourself, but, in a more practical sense, you will not be facing an indifferent or harassed buyer half-listening because of something that pressed him to be that late.

When you do get into the office, do not settle in for a social occasion and do not be misled. It will be polite, for the most part, but this is cold-hearted business. Precious time. If you are offered coffee or a soft drink, know right off that the buyer has planned more time for the meeting than you are going to get if such an offer is not made. Buyers usually allot at least a half-hour for a pitch meeting but will be greedy to recapture extra minutes if the full time does not seem warranted.

You never have to go right to the idea, unless you are asked to. Every buyer, enough to make it true, will expect some chat before getting to the reason for the meeting. I call this phase "foreplay." The warmup. Tricky, but a chance to connect. If you can and can honestly mean it, comment about the décor, a picture on the wall, a striking blouse, or an unusual necktie. Be sure to admire a framed movie ad if you saw the movie. "Hey, *Little Red Riding Hood*. I loved that movie. Did you do that?" You can be damned sure the ad will not be on the wall unless the buyer had something to do with getting the picture on and unless the movie succeeded. If you can remember, refer to something specific you liked in the movie.

Only get more personal if there is a prior friendship or an opportunity of the moment, such as the buyer getting a call from his mechanic (cars are very personal in Los Angeles) telling him his car needs a new MacPherson strut, which I just recently learned is not a dance step. If you can relate knowingly to something like that, do it. Ann once helped a buyer think of a suitable gift for his girlfriend when he realized in a panic late in the day that it was her birthday. Incidentally, she learned a lot about the girlfriend and, consequently, a lot about the buyer.

If a must-take telephone call comes in for the buyer, offer to leave the room for the moment. It is both courteous and it shows a certain presence of mind and a sophistication about the buyer's reality. It is also flattering. You have inferred his importance.

Take the standard good manners with you. As to dress, it is strictly your personal choice these days. New York is more formal and no one is quite sure what California is. Certainly more informal than New York. Do what is comfortable, though I would not go in like Dolly Parton or Boy George, unless, of course, you are.

Finally, since you are yourself, there will be no escaping being yourself. Trust it. And, probably ignore all the other foregoing advice.

All right. You are early in your career, so, as you have not been able to get an agent, you have not gotten this network meeting either. Are there options? Other places you can go? Yes. The studios and the major independents. Each of these has a programming department, set up along the lines of the models I have described for the networks, whose jobs are to call on network buyers. The three commercial networks, the pay cable channels, and, to a considerably lesser degree, PBS remain the ultimate purchasers, but the studios and independents represent additional avenues leading to these cores. The major studios are MCA-Universal, Warner's, Columbia, Disney, Twentieth Century Fox, Paramount, and M-G-M/UA. The major independents are Charles Fries, Lorimar, Telepictures, Aaron Spelling, MTM, Embassy, David Wolper, EMI, Dick Clark, Leonard Goldberg, ITC, Landsburg Productions, Orion, Metromedia, Carson Productions, and Group W-Westinghouse. There are even more smaller independents who have access to the networks: our company, for instance, Comco Productions, Inc.

You will, starting out, have to approach these entities. The same general conditions that obtain with the networks apply here. They too will be reluctant to meet with newcomers and to consider treatments or ideas. Your best approach is to begin with a letter and follow this with phone calls. Yes, calls, plural. Even biggies seldom get each other on the first call. If you are not called back—and do not expect to be—keep calling. You are the one who wants something. And keep your cool. Be polite. Never say, "So and so's harder to reach than the president." It is not true, and you will alienate the secretary. Befriend this harassed soul. Tell the secretary in some detail why you are calling. If you persist and remain courteous that secretary will subconsciously or consciously become your ally. "Oh, call so-and-so back. He or she is so nice—and bright." At the worst, this secretary will refer you to an executive who is likely to talk to you.

When you do make contact, ask to be able to submit *finished work*. We have not discussed your talent yet and your work efforts. If you are a writer, write. And then write again. After that, write some more. There was a time when writers wrote because they had to write as they had to breathe. The word came first, then the deal. Nowadays, it is just the opposite—and once you are established that system makes arguable sense—but nothing will move you along faster at the start than finished work. It is tangible. Buyers can deal with it. You will get coverage! You will also find out if you can write. There may be only two times in your life when you can know the luxury of writing without a marketplace commitment. When you are young with a low overhead and when you are old and rich enough.

Even if it is adjudged that your finished work needs work, and all buyers will think it does, it should demonstrate your gifts for plot, dialogue, character, humor, and so on. Buyers may be encouraged to talk to you and to work with you. Finishing work will also help you hone your craft.

What should you do when your idea is rejected? The first thing, of course, is pitch it somewhere else. The other thing is never to question or argue about why you got a no.

While at ABC, I had wanted to do Garson Kanin's deeply moving play about a loving, long-married couple, called *A Gift of Time*, in which the husband is dying of cancer. My upper management rejected my proposal—

"it's a downer, a 12 share—" and I dropped Kanin a short note saying no.

Sometime later, having lunch, I apologized to Kanin for not explaining in detail why I could not do the play as an *ABC Theatre*.

"No need, Robert," he said. "Let me tell you a story. Do you know who Julius Rosenwald was?"

I nodded. "One of the founders of Sears Roebuck, wasn't he?"

"That's right. And a major philanthropist." Kanin went ahead to tell me about a charitable organization in Chicago that came every year to solicit Rosenwald. In preceding years he had been very generous to the organization, but, finally, one year when its executives arrived to make their pitch, Rosenwald turned them down.

"But why? Why, Mr. Rosenwald, after so many years do you now say no?" Rosenwald was silent. The charity executives persisted. They would not leave without an explanation. Finally, Rosenwald said, "I don't like artichokes."

"You don't like *artichokes?* But what has that got to do with our charity?"

"Not a thing. But you have demanded a reason. When the answer is no, one reason's as good as another, and, therefore, I don't like artichokes."

That story has been my comfort for unexplained rejection ever since.

What happens if a studio or independent *is* interested in your project? The question involves a lacery of response. If you have started with one of these entities, you may get some option money for the idea. If the project sells, and you are the writer (and producer), you will get the fees for performing these tasks. You may get "housekeeping"—an office, a secretary, and a phone. You may get certain royalties and you may get a percentage of net profits—or fees and profits on any spinout uses of your idea—i.e., series, sequel, book, musical, play, cartoon, T-shirts, and so on. I should point out that hardly anyone ever sees any money from net profits. Lesson? Get as much up front as you can. You will not own your project or get gross profit percentage points.

If you have made the sale to a network yourself, in "laying off" the project to a deficit financier, you are in a stronger negotiating position. You may now get a cash guarantee, a better housekeeping deal, and perhaps some equity or ownership in the project. You certainly will get a better royalties deal and additional points of net profit. By the way, if a network offers you an in-house deal when you are starting out, take it. The network will own your picture, but you will have gotten your work fees and the credit, which is essential to building a career.

As your work becomes more attractive, you may be able to make what is called an umbrella deal with a studio or major independent. This gives you an annual cash guarantee from 50 thousand to 500 thousand, depending on your clout. Shared ownership, probably. An investment tax credit. Additional staff aid in the housekeeping area, such as a development person—a reader or scout for projects.

All monies that you earn during the contract period of an umbrella deal are applied against your annual cash guarantee. If your income exceeds your guarantee, you keep 100 percent of the additional monies. These umbrella deals can be exclusive, semiexclusive, in which case you expose all ideas to the umbrella company, but if they say no in a stipulated time—sixty or nintey days say—you have the right to try to sell the rejected ideas elsewhere—or nonexclusive, which may mean that you are committed on only certain specific projects. All of these variations are subject to different pricings and conditions.

These umbrella deals can help you to sleep soundly. There is regular money coming in while you (and the studio) are in development and trying to make sales. Your office, clerical, and administrative needs are being met—and paid for. You have the support of the entity's business affairs and legal and sales forces. These are likely to have more combined network clout than you as an individual. A studio will be able to find projects beyond your personal reach. Or, if they or you find a project that needs money to develop, this entity pays for it. Option money, that sort of cost.

While all of this is a gamble on the part of a studio or independent, the people running these companies are not compulsive Las Vegas types. They only "bet" on experienced, successful producers and writers and stars. These days, they seldom wager very much without your having a network commitment. Even so, many will refuse to get involved. Except for Warner's and Columbia, the major studios have begun to shy away from made-for-television movies and mini-series. They contend that these provide dubious profits. In the 1983–84 season, out of 472 hours of movie and mini-series programming on the three networks—originals and reruns—only 128 hours came from the major studios. Just over one-fourth. The rest came from major and smaller independents.

The studio reasoning is that on a two-hour movie for television, they are paid from 2.3 million to 2.5 million by the network, which ties up the picture for two runs over a period as long as four years. The studios assert that the pictures actually cost them from 2.8 million to 3 million to make. Then, when, finally, they are able to sell the movie in foreign markets or syndication, a title may be dated and will earn no more than 300 thousand, minus residuals, and usually closer to 150 thousand on average. If you accept these studio figures, you can see that it is a losing proposition for them.

Individual independent critics, however, contend that a 30 percent studio markup on each picture gives the illusion of unprofitability, a charge the studios deny.

There is no question that studios are making fewer movies made for television and mini-series, which gives credence to their argument; and, certainly, a studio can make more on a regular series, which is why they concentrate their efforts in that area. "Magnum, P.I.," for instance, has already brought in over 200 million dollars from domestic syndication alone.

Most studios are interested in made-for-television movies only if they serve as "backdoor" pilots for series; that is, movies that work as sample programs for becoming regular weekly series. These are called "backdoor" pilots because they are out of the regular pilot-making process, which calls for a half-hour or one-hour sample program to be made that may or may not air as an individual unit and has little or no subsequent value, if the series does not get on. The backdoor movie pilot will air on its own merits whether it becomes a regular series or not and can be exploited as a single entity down the line in syndication or foreign markets. Recent examples of backdoor pilots are *Mickey Spillane's Mike Hammer* and *Cagney & Lacey*, both of which were initially two-hour movies made for television.

Whether a studio charges each movie with a 30 percent overhead markup or not, a major studio does have major overhead. Independents and individual producers do not, or have less, so movies made for television and miniseries remain attractive and profitable for these. These entities are very disciplined in producing movies at or very near the price the network will pay. (We were 35 thousand dollars under budget on *Drop-Out Father*.)

If a producer gets his fee—from 60 to 100 thousand for a two-hour movie (and another 30 to 60 thousand for writing it) and gets the 6.5% investment tax credit on, say a 2 million dollar picture (130 thousand dollars), he will earn from 220 thousand to 290 thousand on one television movie. If you add the minimum 150 thousand from foreign and domestic syndication sales, he earns from 370 to 440 thousand. Is it any wonder that there are so many eager independent players in this game?

Withal, studios and major independents will continue to wager on smaller independent and individual producers and writers. The owners and managers of these companies are, for the most part, executives, businessmen, not creators, but they know that to have product—movies—they must invest in the services of those people who can create the programs. The views expressed by the heads of the corporate parents of at least two studios—Columbia and Paramount—are disquieting in this regard. It was reported in *Variety* that Martin Davis, chairman of Gulf & Western, which owns Paramount, thought Barry Diller and Michael Eisner, the most successful executive team in Hollywood for the decade 1974–1984, got too much credit for Paramount's success. This contributed to their exodus, Diller to Fox, Eisner* to Disney. Roberto C. Goizueta, chairman of Coca-Cola, which owns Columbia, has been quoted as saying that "special creative skills are overrated." These non-show business people may be in for a rude shock,

---

*Eisner is my favorite biggie. With geothermal energy and Ensign Pulver ingenuousness, his verifiable smarts are tempered with a shirt collar that is always askew and with a quality Camus refers to when he says, "There is no love without a little innocence." This kernel of childhood in an intelligent, savvy, moral grownup, who loves the business with a passion few of us can sustain, makes Eisner at Disney a kind of destiny fulfilled. I predict big things from that union.

as was Transamerica when it let the five key show business executives who successfully ran its United Artists subsidiary get away. Without them, Transamerica's next film was the forty-million-dollar H-bomb, *Heaven's Gate*, which precipitated Transamerica's exit from the entertainment business. (It sold the mortally bleeding United Artists to M-G-M.) In my own experience, I remember trying to persuade Don McGannon, then head of Group W-Westinghouse Broadcasting, to keep Merv Griffin, who was asking for an additional one million dollars a year to do the Westinghouse "Merv Griffin Show." From Merv's point of view (and from that of any knowing show business person) the request was not unreasonable. The show was netting thirteen million dollars a year, and, despite my pride in my own contributions as producer, Merv was the show. But for a corporate type the request was outrageous. McGannon refused to grant it, Merv left for CBS, and his Westinghouse replacement failed within the year. A million saved was thirteen million lost. More, since Merv has been on the air all these years since. Guys who build ships, bottle pop, sell insurance, and manufacture light bulbs have trouble relating to the valences of talent.

All of the elements of these housekeeping and umbrella deals are, of course, subject to negotiations, negotiations that get as arcane as a colloquy of medieval theologians. Certainly, you will need a knowing agent or entertainment lawyer to guide you through the undergrowth of this kind of agreement.

Yes, we do, if you are asking yourself. Ann and I, through our Comco Productions, Inc., have an umbrella deal with Charles Fries Entertainment, Inc.

Now, what do you pitch?

I have mentioned trying to find out specifically what a buyer is looking for. I have mentioned published books, produced plays, and true stories from "60 Minutes." I have described, for you starting out, the difficulties of acquiring this kind of material in competition with more experienced writers and producers. The same goes for true stories in all national publications such as *People* and the newsweeklies and the *New York Times*. It does not apply so forcefully to your hometown paper or stories coming up through publications that are not mass-popular. True stories, factual phenomena coming from these sources, give you a better chance. Not everyone reads the *New England Journal of Medicine*—it will be in your library—or the Grover's Corners *Gazette*.

Do not forego your education. Has anyone done that classic you loved as a student? Well, maybe Norman Rosemont, who specializes in pop-classic literature, has—*The Prisoner of Zenda, A Tale of Two Cities, Captains Courageous, All Quiet on the Western Front*, and so on. (One wag said, "I know how to put Norman out of business. Steal his library card.") But Rosemont and others cannot do or have done them all. Think of the books and plays that you have read and loved. Even if they are not classics. Think public domain. That is, works on which the copyrights have run out. You will not have to pay. Think of magazine stories that stuck in your mind. Think of social trends. Think of pop records or commercials. The movie *Harper Valley PTA* came from the record; the Mean Joe Green Coca-Cola commercial became an after-school special on ABC.

I was not being facetious at the beginning of this chapter when I said to use ideas from your home or background or personal experience, especially if you are interested in writing original dramas, as I am. Each of us has experienced something that is close to us that likely will make a movie. You must not overlook your own life or the lives around you that you know about. These are not as ordinary as you may view them as being.

There are two ideas for movies, both of them right out of my life, that I thought were very good. I should have thought of those movies. I should have sold those ideas. One was *My Favorite Year*, a picture about a young man working on a television show who was responsible for nurse-maiding a drunken Errol Flynn-type movie star (played by Peter O'Toole) who was to be a guest on the show. I was a young man. I was working on a television show ("The Jack Paar Tonight Show"). I booked Errol Flynn himself! He was swacked! I was responsible for getting him to the stage! Why the hell didn't I "see" that story? The other was *Breaking Away*, the picture about the townie kids in Bloomington, Indiana, who feel inferior to or resentful of the kids at Indiana University and who, at the end of the picture, triumph by winning The Little 500 bike race held each spring at the school.* I went to Indiana University. We used to fight with townie kids. I swam in the limestone quarries. I did the play-by-play broadcast of The Little 500 on the university radio station, WFIU-FM. All of that seemed so normal and mundane to me—and of no possible interest to anyone else. It took Steve Tesich, a Yugoslav émigré who went to Indiana University, to see it for the colorful and dramatic situation that it was. And to win a writing Oscar for *Breaking Away*. See what I mean? Rethink your own experiences.

Okay. You have the idea and you are ready to write a television movie. Let's go to the next chapter and talk about that.

---

*In reality, no nonuniversity teams are allowed in The Little 500; Tesich took a liberty in the script.

3

How to
Write One

Before we get to how, you had better think about why. Why do you want to write and why do you want to write movies and why do you want to write movies for television? Glamour? Fame? Riches? The spiritual need to express yourself? To leave a little personal graffiti on the face of the globe? Power? Something of all of these motivates you, no doubt, and something of all of these is possible.

There is a glamour—if you compare the work to unloading trucks at the supermarket. But writing does not come close to being a Beverly Hills hairdresser.

Fame? Quick—name ten television movie writers. Five? One? You may have struggled and come up with a name or two, though you would certainly have an easier time naming novelists or playwrights. I have just stopped a moment to do the same thing, limiting the selection to living Americans. The novelists came to mind very quickly, the playwrights moderately fast. It has taken me a while to come up with the television movie writers, even though I work in the field and know some. I listed all of the writers as I thought of them. Since I could name another thirty easily, I see an aesthetic bias on behalf of novels, and it would seem that a white male bias clouds the entire list, but this is a test of fame that should be held to a rigid standard of spontaneity. As a rough equivalent of TV-Q, a service that measures fame by rating performers' "likability" and the public's "familiarity" with them, I give you my list to test your familiarity with the names on it.

Novelists	*Playwrights*	*TV Movie Writers*
Saul Bellow	Arthur Miller	Bill Blinn
Norman Mailer	David Mamet	Abby Mann
Gore Vidal	Neil Simon	John Gay

James Michener	Garson Kanin	William Hanley
Philip Roth	Edward Albee	Stanley Greenburg
John Updike	David Rabe	James Costigan
Issac Bashevis Singer	Wendy Wasserstein	Faye Kanin
Kurt Vonnegut	Harvey Fierstein	John McGreevy
Herman Wouk	Christopher Durang	Loring Mandel
Joseph Heller	Sam Shepard	Ed Anhalt

See what I mean? I do suspect that by writing television movies, you will be more famous than your mailperson or even your doctor, but you will not achieve the fame attainable for writers in other areas. Another spot test. Who of you remembers from chapter 1 even the names of the writers of *Roots*?

Riches? If you make a hundred thousand dollars a year, you will be in the top 2 percent of American taxpayers, and a lot of television movie writers qualify. You will take it, right? But television writers do not make money in the way an actor, director, producer, or television executive can with comparable success. And, only about 6 percent of the membership of the Writers Guild of America make this hundred grand or more in any given year. You could probably do better with a good liquor store. Or a McDonald's franchise.

The need to express yourself? Before you write FADE IN, you yourself, because you want to make a sale, will have limited what you can say and what you can say it about because you will be aware of television's commercial and middlebrow inhibitions. Next, a nice gang of buyer-executives, a director, usually more than one producer, and a few stars and their agents will be altering what you do write. Even if a script survives with your name on it (and your name alone), there is every likelihood that the final version to the original will be something like a bad facelift. When you finish a first draft, you will come to learn that THE END are the saddest words. Following these, the world takes over the little world that you have fashioned and furnished. Someone is bound to move your favorite chair. Alter the way your heroine walks into a room and touches at her hair. Your hero's voice will change. An inflection will be wrong. The music alien. Someone will have blacked a tooth in the picture. A word will be— different. A poet friend, Ed Spitzer, expressed this condition for me forever in a poem called "The Pure Idea," which begins, "Say, you will to split an apple or an atom—delicious—the pure idea—one infinite instant before one mouth speaks against it, one hand raises for it; that infinite instant before the drudging doing."

A personal mark? Maybe. We know a film can reach an audience fifty years later. Will one hold for a hundred? Five hundred? A millennium? Think of your ten favorite movies. Here is my list:

Casablanca	*Annie Hall*
Gone with the Wind	*The Grapes of Wrath*

On the Waterfront	*The Best Years of Our Lives*
All about Eve	*Sunset Boulevard*
8½	*The Bridge on the River Kwai*

Let's make it a dozen with *Paths of Glory* and *Dr. Strangelove*. Fifteen: *A Lion in Winter*, *High Noon*, and *The Wizard of Oz*. Oh, and *Citizen Kane*, of course. This is fun, isn't it? Okay, you know the question, and if you remember that Joseph L. Mankiewicz wrote *All about Eve* and know, because he is also the star and the director, that Woody Allen co-wrote *Annie Hall*, you have two out of the sixteen. How about the others?* You will recognize some of the names when you read the list—as novelists and playwrights. Or directors.

Of course, we dealt with fame earlier, so you could argue that, even though they are anonymous, the writers of these films (and the ones on your list) have left their marks nonetheless. They have with their work, I suppose, but which of them is identified with it? Which of them towers as a maker of motion pictures? The American Film Institute has thus far given its annual live achievement award to:

1973—John Ford	1979—Alfred Hitchcock
1974—James Cagney	1980—James Stewart
1975—Orson Welles	1981—Fred Astaire
1976—William Wyler	1982—Frank Capra
1977—Bette Davis	1983—John Houston
1978—Henry Fonda	1984—Gene Kelly

Counting Orson Welles and Gene Kelly as both, I come up with seven directors and seven actors. Zero writers.

Here for the record, is my television list (with writers):

Marty	Paddy Chayefsky
12 Angry Men	Reginald Rose

---

*Casablanca: Julian and Phillip Epstein, Howard Koch; *Gone with the Wind:* mostly Sidney Howard (and Ben Hecht, Jo Swerling, Oliver H. P. Garrett, F. Scott Fitzgerald, Donald Ogden Stewart, John Balderston, Michael Foster, Winston Miller, John Van Druten, Edwin Justus Mayer, John Lee Mahin, and maybe some others); *On the Waterfront:* Budd Schulberg; *All about Eve:* Joseph L. Mankiewicz; *8½:* Federico Fellini, Tullio Pinelli, Ennio Flaiano, Brunello Rondi; *Annie Hall:* Woody Allen, Marshall Brickman; *The Grapes of Wrath:* Nunnally Johnson; *The Best Years of Our Lives:* Robert E. Sherwood; *Sunset Boulevard:* Billy Wilder, Charles Brackett, D. M. Marsham, Jr.; *The Bridge on the River Kwai:* Carl Foreman, Michael Wilson; *Paths of Glory:* Calder Willingham, Jim Thompson; *High Noon:* Carl Foreman; *Dr. Strangelove:* Stanley Kurbrick, Terry Southern, Peter George; *A Lion in Winter:* James Goldman; *The Wizard of Oz:* Noel Langley, Florence Ryerson, Edgar Allan Wolfe, with music by Harold Arlen and lyrics by E. Y. Harburg; *Citizen Kane:* Herman Mankiewicz.

Patterns	Rod Serling
The Missiles of October	Stanley Greenburg
The Autobiography of Miss Jane Pittman	Tracy Keenan Wynn
Roots	Bill Blinn, James Lee, Ernest Kinoy, Max Cohen
Brian's Song	Bill Blinn
That Certain Summer	Richard Levinson, William Link
Eleanor & Franklin	James Costigan
Friendly Fire	Faye Kanin

This television list is harder to come by and not so deeply satisfying as my movie list. (The first three titles were "live" television dramas later made into theatrical motion pictures.) I could not have the same heated arguments with you in its defense as I could and would relish with the movie list. I wonder why that is? Perhaps movies in the more formal setting of a darkened theater have more impact organically than movies received on television screens. Perhaps, when I saw some of the movie-movies, I was younger and more impressionable, although young people today seem to react to these same movies with equal caring. Two observations about both lists. Of twenty-six titles, only eleven are originals and only three (or four if you include *8½*) are comedies. (I know I have left out Chaplin and that is regrettable, but I stand by my list, except to say that Chaplin as Hitler in *The Great Dictator* in his pas de deux with the balloon-world globe may be the single finest scene on film ever.)

Power? What is that? Altering the course of a river? Making jobs? War? Peace? Creating wealth? Social change? Expanding or contracting human rights? Who has it in America? Billionaires. Bankers. Legislators. Institutional investors. Key executive branch officials in the federal government, including the president. Foundations. Corporate heads. Bureaucrats. Some governors, judges, and mayors. A few union leaders, teachers, scientists, and journalists. Sheriffs. Do television movie writers? You would think they have a little with so many millions watching their work, at least in the realm of ideas, but it is so subtle and indirect, I think, as to be unmeasurable. Rather like, at best, the itch of an occasional minor rash on the body politic.

Oh yes, *The Day After* caused a stir. It forced the Secretary of State to bring his wingback chair and fireplace with him to television to make a warm milk defense of the administration's nuclear build-up policy. It drank a lot of ink and ate a lot of videotape. It achieved for Ted Koppel and his distinguished panel who followed the airing of the drama the highest rating ever for a television news discussion program. It may even have traumatized a few kids, though I wonder, since most have been watching the local news and attendant entertainment horrors since birth. Did it affect nuclear policy? Not a tick. If you accept the figure that 600 nuclear weapons are made every year in America alone, 11.5 got made the week of the broadcast and 2.3 that day, which assumes they do not fabricate on Saturdays and Sundays. Richard Perle, in the Department of Defense, whom a primetime television audience has never seen and who has never been elected to any office by anybody, continued his exercise of true power in nuclear policy.

As someone said, even staring, you never look at the same river twice; so it is with the endless flow of television. *The Day After* becomes the program before. Its true effect? A few more goods moved off the shelf and the showroom floor.

Then, why write at all and why, especially, write movies for television? Despite whatever strand of amino acids makes you do it, here, I offer, is reason enough, even for the lowly television movie writer:

A blank page?

Yes. When you have filled it, the human world awakes, thinks, acts, takes over. Everyone else now has an opinion. Everyone else now becomes a writer. Or editor. Blank, they wait. Suspended. Helpless. The executive, the director, the star, the audience. The American Film Institute's list of life achievers. Everybody. Nobody can do a thing until that page is filled by the writer. Delicious. The pure idea. If that is not fame, riches, glamour, immortality, or power, it is better than all of these. It is you against blankness. Against the wonders of your own being. Your will. Your choices. The universe. It is primal. Creation. Everyone else is an interpreter.

It is never writers who climb Everest or reach the Pole or jig-walk the moon. Why should they? The blank page is fierce firstness enough. Every day I can riffle through a ream of Everests resting on my desk.

Hey, wait a minute. That's pretty big stuff. From this we get "The Dukes of Hazzard" and all that other drivel? Yes. But that is one of the choices to make. Nobody is coerced into writing "The Dukes." If that is your level, so be it. I won't write shows like "The Dukes." I am not even sure I could if I tried. I wish garbage would not get on and I wish writers would not write it. But it does, and they do. Maybe you can't wait to get a crack at it. To live in Beverly Hills and not look back. Even so, the most cynical, sunken scribbler shares in the force of the blank page.

Now that I have you feeling pretty important about yourself as a writer, let me tell you how the rest of the business feels about you. Over forty years ago, F. Scott Fitzgerald said it carefully, "Writers are the women of Hollywood." It is true today. Both sides of the equation. While women have made visible strides in our business, fewer than twenty television movies in thirty years (three of them by Ida Lupino) have been directed by women. (One by Ann Shanks.) The better news is that many, many more women get opportunities to produce and/or to write, but the business is still heavily dominated by men in both numbers and power. Writers, even the best, even white, even male, are also a low caste. While it is not always the case, most often, once the script is finished, writers are fogotten—forbidden—in the rest of the movie-making process. In the six "ABC Theatre" movies I developed, I met only one of the writers—by accident—at an answer print screening when the picture was finished. None ever came to a network meeting in which I met with the producers and directors, to whom I gave my script notes. I never saw one on location or on the set. No one questioned it. Maybe some writers prefer it that way. I do not. That is why I urge you to get to a position in which you can produce what you write. As a producer-writer I invite myself to the meetings and to the set. I can intercede.

On one of our projects, *He's Fired, She's Hired,* I was interceding when I thought certain lines were not being felt right and read right. After a while, I sensed that maybe I was going too far and apologized to the director. Marc Daniels, wise and kind, a television director for nearly forty years, nodded and smiled. He said, "I'll tell you if it gets too much. But it's okay. I wasn't there when the page was blank." I think Mark, who is theater-trained, would always welcome the writer on the set, but most directors (and actors) do not. As the producer also, you need not ask their permission.

Let's get to how.

Let's begin with the basics. The mechanics. Or, as some say, the grammar.

First things first. Movie scripts are nearly impossible to read. If not impossible, at least a pain. They are a pain for the very reasons that I am about to set forth—and insist that you learn as second nature. It is all those damnable terms, shot numbers, and the muddled structure of the page. But these items of form have become customary over the years, so you must know them and know them well for a number of sensible reasons. First, they will discipline you to think filmically. Force you to "see" what you are writing. Buyers and other readers, including actors and directors, will expect your script to be set up in the usual manner, so even if it is not a masterpiece, the script will be recognized as professional and will not be thrown away unread. Buyers and all the other people whom you want to read your script read hundreds of them. They think reading them is impossible also and they hate to do it, so to speed things up, they have developed a number of harsh standards. Two things most professionals will do when picking up a script are 1) check the number of total pages and 2) check the form and neatness. If the script for a two-hour movie is longer than 125 pages or fewer than 95, they are likely to cast it aside immediately. If the script pages are messy, at an angle, unbound, fuzzily reproduced, or lack movie script structure, this also usually provides a fast one-way ticket to the reject pile. (By the way, make lots of copies of your script. They are seldom returned.) If the script is clean, bound, set up in form, and runs right around 110 pages, the reader will start to read. This may be your finest moment. Since a reader reads so many lousy scripts, it is at this point when he begins that he says the silent prayer, "Oh, Lord, let this one be fresh, entertaining, and wonderful." He reads. The first ten pages. That is all the time you have to grab him. If you can get him in five pages, so much the better. Never mind how many great scenes you have written deeper in. If there isn't some arresting quality in the beginning, you are finished.

You don't have to open with an earthquake, a man and woman making passionate love, a car crash, a bomb going off, or with a knife at your hero's throat, although many television movies fall lazily into the cliché trap—and many succeed. You can start quietly if the moments build one on another. You can establish place and mood, and of course the beginning is your only real chance to establish or introduce character. To let us get to know your people—your hero. And to like him. He can be a nudnik or a social outcast, but he must be likable. Someone we would want to know or care about and will allow to come into our homes. If he is an antihero, there must a trait or deed of redemption. We must be able to empathize with his circumstances and behavior.

I consider the opening of *Drop-Out Father*, by design, to be low-key, ordinary, but one that grabs you nevertheless. Within the first five minutes, you know that Ed McCall is an upper middle-class, recognizable, real person. (Another tip: Get your star on early.) You know Ed is anxious, worried about aging and his empty life. With a steadily mounting series of mishaps, he is on the trigger of a crisis. You see his home, his wife on pills and Phil Donahue, three of his children in vapid rebellion, the balancing, wholesome relationship with the youngest child, the centricity of money, and the shallowness of his work. All of this is revealed with increasing pressure on Ed until the Act One ending of his having his wallet lifted by a pickpocket.

Within the first five minutes, I think I also get the reader to laugh. From the movie's history, I would say I succeeded in placing the hook. The reader will be thinking, "I want to find out what happens to this likable man whose problems I recognize."

To comfort the buyer, he sees almost right away that nothing in the picture is exotic in terms of sets, casting, or locations that make the script impossibly expensive to produce.

Some other fundamentals. Most of us count a minute of playing time on screen as one page on paper. It is a rule that seems to work out (in theater and theatrical movies as well). By this reckoning, you would think 110 pages is too long for a 2-hour television movie, if you realize that a network hour is never more than 58:30 and that there are, by the time you subtract commercials (3 network minutes in each primetime half-hour— 6 in syndication), news briefs, local commercials, and promos, only about 24 minutes of playing time per half-hour, or, roughly, a total of 96 minutes of program time in the 2-hour block. (In the business, we call "60 Minutes" "48:30.") Still, with your camera directions and character descriptions and the page structure of the movie form, 110 pages for a script is right. While you may have several full pages of dialogue that take a minute or under to play, you may also have a direction that says "Hair-raising car chase" that only consumes one line on one page but takes 90 seconds to 2 minutes of screen time. Some scripts may play to time at 98 or 100 pages; others at 120 or even 125. It depends entirely on the material and the pacing.

I tend to overwrite always, so my movies never come in short. I do try to build in at least twice in every script what I call "accordion" scenes: dancing, a musical situation, my hero overhearing slice-of-life joke lines from minor characters, which can play longer or shorter depending on the time needs of the overall picture. I really like any picture of mine to be at least 5 minutes over in the rough cut. This gives me the opportunity to have some choices and to make really tight cuts on all scenes.

Being a word man, I am comforted to know that the picture is long, so

I can eliminate all those driving shots, all those slow establishing shots, all those zooms and pans that directors seem to favor. They call these shots "opening up" the picture. I call them "closing it down."

In one movie, after the director's cut, I was told we were 20 minutes too long, even after the director had eliminated several critcal scenes. When Ann and I got our producer's cut, we restored all the lost scenes and came in 30 seconds short! That is how much judgments can differ on pacing—especially in comedy.

In television movies, the director, by DGA rules (Directors Guild of America), gets the first cut. That is, he gets first crack at editing the picture. Then, the producer gets his chance to edit the film. The network always has final approval—and cut. As the writer only, I would not have been allowed any legal opportunity to cut the movie and, in the case mentioned, would have had to accept the director's (or producer's) languorous version of my script. As the writer *and* producer, I got my innings. Oftentimes, the producer and director will work together on the cut of a picture. Ann and I prefer to let the director work alone—then to work alone ourselves after that.

A network will accept without penalty a picture that is a minute or less short. It can fill the time with promos or public service announcements. If a picture is more than a minute short, the network can withhold some of your production money. Never will a network accept delivery of a picture that is longer than the proscribed length.

Every 2-hour movie is divided into seven acts. Remember that in Act One you must allow for MAIN TITLE CREDITS and that 40 to 45 seconds of an epilogue or coda must be given over to END CREDITS. These are also called OPENING CREDITS and CLOSING CREDITS. Your main title credits may have as many as eighteen "pages"—that is, information on eighteen different full-frame cards—"in the clear," as we say. That really means that only one name will appear on the screen at a time. These main title or opening credits include the title of the picture—hence the "main title"—and star names in the cast, which may come to as many as eight or ten separate listings. Also included will be the names of the executive producer, the producer, editor, composer, director of photography, art director, writer, and director. One nice WGA rule: the writer's name must come adjacent to the director's name, which comes just before the picture begins in earnest.

The closing credits, as you have seen, or not seen, since they go by so fast, unless you are a loving mother, need not be "in the clear" or on separate pages. These credits are bunched together in smaller type and are either "punched in"—several names on a page, cutting from page to page (frame to frame)—or will appear on a "crawl." On a crawl, the names are mounted on a continuous black strip that moves on rollers, and the effect is that the names "crawl" up the screen "supered" (superimposed—put over some visual material) from bottom to top in a steady flow. For these always-bunched credits, I prefer a crawl, as it allows the eye somewhat more opportunity to catch the names, which earns the gratitude of at least the families of the people involved. In the closing or end credits are listed the names of additional cast members and the crew, as well as rights entities, union approvals, acknowledgments, and the film's copyright notice. End credits customarily end with the logo or trademark of the producing company.

If you are the writer only, you need not concern yourself with the details of the closing credits except to write at the end of your script END CREDITS & COPYRIGHT. You *will* have to keep in mind that you must allow time for them. I also think it is the writer's responsibility to have some thoughts about what appears visually behind them.

As to the opening credits, your involvement is more complex. Some movies on television handle the main title credits simply by playing them over black, but this is rare. All of us in television are quite properly nervous about the restless, fickle audience. It is mandatory to get the story going immediately in order to hold the audience and to find a way to integrate the opening credits while the story is in progress.

All of you have seen the attempts. The picture opens instantly with action. The boy-hero says, "Ma, I'm goin' to the city to find Joey." "Oh, no, Billy, you can't. The city's a jungle. It destroyed your brother. Joey's as good as dead. I don't want you, my baby, dead too." "A man's got to do what a man's got to do, Ma." This plays in the clear. Then Billy guns away in his 4x4 pickup truck, as Willie Nelson, voiceover, sings the title theme song, "A man's got to do what a man's got to do," and the opening credits come up supered over our hero in traffic. (Endless driving and traffic shots appear beneath opening credits.) The last credit—always the director's— fades out just as our boy-hero reaches the city, pulls up in front of his brother's last known address (and miraculously finds a parking place right in front). He gets out of the truck, stares up the façade of the building, and watches as his brother's body comes hurtling down to go splat on the sidewalk. We knew that Ma's dark warnings about the city and the brother's terrible fate there meant that the kid brother was in for some hot times too. All hell was going to break loose, just as soon as we could get through these credits that these unions and agents have stuck us with by contract. In this example, we are amply rewarded for our patience by the brother's demise. Did he jump? Was he pushed? We know the hero will find out. We are hooked. Just as we were by that first dishy babe in the water in *Jaws* who got eaten, Jantzen and all, as part of the main title sequence. Just in case none of this seems adequate to hold the audience, in televsion movies we are shown a minute of highlights of the film before the film begins.

Script pages are the standard 8½" by 11" in size. I set my pages up with a lefthand margin at 15. This assures that, when the script is bound, nothing is hidden or cut off on the left side. I number the pages sequentially, start to finish, in the upper righthand corner. Scenes and acts are not there indicated, as they are in theater scripts. Acts—ACT ONE—are in caps, underlined and centered from 44. The same with act endings—END OF ACT ONE. I begin a new act on a new page. Each scene is numbered as a shot in numerical sequence, and there is no scene label from one to the next.

I put these shot numbers at 15. As they get into two and three digits, there is no problem, because I begin directions at 20. This leaves four spaces on shots 1 through 9, three spaces on shots 10 through 99 and two spaces on shots over 100. I put the shot number only on the lefthand side. Some prefer to put the shot number left and right. The long camera directions and character descriptions begin at 20 and continue across the page in a full line. If these get to be too large in mass for the eye to read easily, I break them into the equivalent of paragraphs by spacing but always starting at 20 and without indentation.

I start characters' names at 40, then under this, single-spaced, I start the dialogue at 30. If I have short, internal directions, these are in parentheses beginning at 35.

If a speech of one character has to carry over to a next page, I indicate this on the outgoing page with (MORE), which I start at 40 single-spaced under the last line of dialogue; on the incoming page, I type the character's name again, with an abbreviated "continued" next to it in parentheses: CHARLES (CONT'D). A scene that carries over from one page to the next is indicated at the bottom of the out-going page by (CONTINUED), which I start at 60, double-spaced after the last page line; on the incoming page, I write the same shot number—say, 15, and CONTINUED: in caps, no parentheses, but with a colon. I do add in parentheses the number of pages the scene has been running, for instance: 15 CONTINUED: (3).

If you are not soundly asleep by now, let me agree that all of this is better understood looking at it rather than trying to make sense of it in a written description. It is, I see, rather like the instructions for the assembly of a child's toy. Here, in picture fact, is what I am driving at.

Following are the first ten pages of my script *Once Upon a Beverly Hills*, which is a comedy about an innocent family from Indiana who must move to Beverly Hills and deal with its sophistries, because the seventeen-year-old daughter in the family has become the sex symbol sensation of this year's hot-hit television show, "The Chick from Chickasaw County."

This idea, inflated and exaggerated, grew out of my own experience. When we moved to California, our youngest child, John, finished his high-school days at Beverly Hills High School. The school is rich—it has oil wells on the property—and many of the students have famous parents. John's recounting of stories about the kids there, and the excesses brought on by fame and money and the pursuit of these, were very funny—and sad. (This script was at first called *Rodeo High*, since I named the high school Rodeo after Beverly Hills's famed shopping street Rodeo Drive, which is pronounced ROW-DAÝ-O rather than ROẂ-DEE-OH as in bronco-busting. This potential confusion of pronunciation is one reason I changed the title.)

Further, I am from Indiana originally and hold to the idea that I have not been totally corrupted by my adult life in New York and Los Angeles. And, of course, I am very familiar with television and all the players in it. I gleefully satirized the worst people and aspects of our business.

I believe these pages will show clearly most of the movie "grammar" elements which you will have to know. Then, when we have gone over these, I will try to set forth my reasons for appoaching the story as I did. The first ten pages will permit us to evaluate the idea of grabbing the audience early and get into the difficult technique of exposition. You will have to be the judge of whether I succeeded in what I sought to accomplish.

ONCE UPON A BEVERLY HILLS

ACT 1

We are in Darwin, Indiana, a county seat farm town of 10,000 people, located 25 miles from Indianapolis.

FADE IN:

1   EXT. HIGHWAY—HIGH CORN ALL AROUND—EARLY MORNING

We see a large, 18-wheel rig, a moving van, with lettering on the side, ''AMERICAN VAN LINES,'' and in smaller letters beneath, ''Moving Coast-to-Coast,'' as it travels along the highway. We ESTABLISH, then the truck goes past the CAMERA which then COMES TO SETTLE on a sign by the side of the highway which reads, ''WELCOME TO DARWIN, INDIANA, POP. 10,000, AN ALL-AMERICAN TOWN.'' A new sign has been added at the bottom: ''HOME OF SAMANTHA THAYER.''

2   EXT. THAYER RESIDENCE IN DARWIN—EARLY MORNING

WIDE SHOT of a large, inviting, but unpretentious two-story white frame house with a porch running the length of the front. Parked at the curb are four mobile TV mini-vans with their identifying signs: ''SHOW BIZ NIGHTLY,'' ''WCRN-TV, INDIANAPOLIS,'' ''WIDY-TV, INDIANAPOLIS,'' and WERC-TV, INDIANAPOLIS.'' There is also a Darwin police car. COP and TV PEOPLE stand about idly.

3   INT. THAYER RESIDENCE—MASTER BEDROOM—EARLY MORNING

We are in a tasteful, middle-class bedroom. Double bed. There are several packed cardboard wardrobes in the room. In the scene are EUNICE and HAROLD THAYER. Eunice, age 44, is attractive, but not at all glamorous. She is very Midwest, a small-town woman devoted totally to her family. Harold is good-looking enough, with a full head of hair, flecked with gray. He is 46. He is sober, responsible, a solid citizen, devoted to his family, Eunice especially. Both are in bed in nightclothes. Eunice gets up and puts on a robe. She looks back at Harold. Harold's pajamas are beige—with little brown trout on them.

                    EUNICE
          You awake?

                    HAROLD
               (into the pillow)
          It's not even me.

                              (CONTINUED)

3   CONTINUED: (2)

>   EUNICE
>   (going to the window,
>   she raises the blind)
>   Today's the day.

>   HAROLD
>   California's not America.

>   EUNICE
>   (looking back a him)
>   Harold --

>   HAROLD
>   This is America.

>   EUNICE
>   Then what's California?

>   HAROLD
>   Forest Lawn -- for outpatients.

Eunice looks out the window and sees the TV News People and
JAMIE as he comes off the front porch.

4   EXT. THAYER RESIDENCE—EARLY MORNING

Jamie Thayer, age 15, comes from off the front porch with his
bicycle. He is handsome, lanky, terrific -- a well-adjusted
kid. A young Henry Fonda. He reaches the TV People and the
Cop.

>   TV PEOPLE, VARIOUS
>   Hey, Jamie. Hi.
>   (one sings ''California,
>   Here I Come -- '')
>   How you doin', kid?

>   JAMIE
>   Hi.

>   TV MAN #1
>   Samantha up yet?

>   JAMIE
>   (shrugs)
>   She always liked her beauty sleep.

>   TV WOMAN #1
>   (ruefully)
>   Coals to Newcastle.

>   (CONTINUED)

4   CONTINUED: (2)

> TV MAN #2
> My wife could use a little beauty
> sleep--about twenty years.

> TV MAN #1
> (to Jamie)
> See yourself last night? We had
> you on the news.

> JAMIE
> (nods, smiles)
> I was--behind the mayor, I guess.
> I saw my ear.

> TV MAN #2
> You know politicians and TV, kid.
> Your guy Mayor Breedlove's a real
> hamhog.

> JAMIE
> I don't mind. It's Samantha they
> want.

> TV WOMAN #1
> We'll make it up to you at the
> gala.

> JAMIE
> (nods)
> Gotta go. I'm late for my paper
> route.

5   INT. THAYER MASTER BEDROOM--EARLY MORNING

> EUNICE
> (looking out the window)
> There goes Jamie. This'll be the
> biggest day in the history of
> Darwin, Indiana.

> HAROLD
> (still in bed)
> What about the State Fair? When
> Herschel Buckner won the calf-
> lifting contest?

> EUNICE
> This is bigger.

> HAROLD
> At least no hernia.

(CONTINUED)

5   CONTINUED: (2)

Loud SOUND OF MOVING VAN HORN.

                         EUNICE
               Oh, no. The movers're here.
               They're early.

6   INT. DARWIN MESSENGER PRESS ROOM—EARLY MORNING

We SEE a high-speed press printing the morning paper ESTAB-
LISH, with good sound bite. An older male printer picks up
one of the papers coming off the conveyor belt and looks at
the front page. We see it: A full banner headline says,
''SAMANTHA THAYER DAY!'' Second line: ''GALA TO MARK
EVENT.'' Beneath this is a huge portrait of Samantha Thayer
(she is beautiful) with a caption below that reads, ''TV STAR
IS DARWIN'S OWN.''

7   INT. DARWIN MESSENGER DELIVERY BOYS' ROOM—EARLY MORNING

TIGHT CLOSEUP of Jamie, who is wearing a pair of out-sized,
novelty store sunglasses, a gift just given him by his fellow delivery boys.

                         DELIVERY BOY #1 (O.S.)
               All right!

                         DELIVERY BOY #2 (O.S.)
               Okay!

                         DELIVERY BOY #3 (O.S.)
               They're great!

                         DELIVERY BOY #4 (O.S.)
               Really wild!

8   INT. DELIVERY ROOM—EARLY MORNING

We now SEE the DELIVERY BOYS, aged 12 to 15. The room itself
is piled high with freshly-printed papers, many of them
folded and already in their canvas bags.

                         JAMIE
                    (really touched)
               They're terrific. Honest.
               Thanks a lot.

                         DELIVERY BOY #1
               Hey––can't let our old buddy move
               to California without sunglasses.

                                        (CONTINUED)

8   CONTINUED: (2)

> DELIVERY BOY #2
> (falling apart)
> Hollywood! I still can't believe
> he's gonna live in Hollywood.

> DELIVERY BOY #3
> Dummy--will you get it straight?
> Beverly Hills--with a swimming pool.

> DELIVERY BOY #4
> (picking up newspaper with
> Samantha's photo)
> And America's sex goddess--Samantha Thayer!

> JAMIE
> Come on, guys--she's my sister.

Boy #4 buries his face in the paper and makes animal noises
and kisses the photo. Delivery Boys all go crazy.

(NOTE: WE SHOULD BE FINISHED WITH MAIN TITLES.)

9   INT. THAYER RESIDENCE—MASTER BEDROOM—EARLY MORNING

Harold is still in bed. Eunice is dressed now.

> EUNICE
> She's only seventeen.
> Samantha needs us out there. And it's a
> wonderful opportunity for Jamie.

> HAROLD
> He can be a doctor in Indiana.

> EUNICE
> There's a lot more for him there.

> HAROLD
> I thought everyone in California
> was a health nut.

> EUNICE
> You know what I mean. You're just
> being--I don't know what.

> HAROLD
> Scared.

> EUNICE
> Yes, scared and--scared?

(CONTINUED)

9   CONTINUED: (2)   6.

                         HAROLD
         A little. A lot.
                         EUNICE
              (coming to him, sitting on the bed)
         You are?
                         HAROLD
         Darwin's my home, Eunice.
         My whole life. Boy and man. Born
         and raised. You too. We don't
         belong in Beverly Hills--wearing
         sunglasses and living off our daughter.
                         EUNICE
         We're not liv--she wants us to
         come. it was her idea. She's got
         the money and--we'll each have
         our own bathroom.
                         HAROLD
         I'd forgotten that was the true
         meaning of life.
              (warmly)
         Besides--I've always liked you
         in my bathroom.
                         EUNICE
              (gets up)
         Well--I have to say it. I've
         gotten very used to such things
         this past year--living out
         there with Samantha. Why shouldn't
         we live well? God certainly can't
         mean Arabs and athletes to be the
         only ones.
                         HAROLD
              (mildly shocked)
         Eunice.
                         EUNICE
         Well, I'm serious. We've worked
         hard--over twenty years and,
         well, we've done all right--with
         the drugstore--but your daughter
         is rich. Her TV show is a big
         success.
                         HAROLD
         And stupid. ''The Chick From
         Chickasaw County?'' I can't even
         watch the dumb thing.

                                    (CONTINUED)

9   CONTINUED: (3)

Harold gets out of bed and goes to the window.

> EUNICE
> Harold, you can't back out now.
> The house is rented. You've sold
> the drugstore. You can't--

> HAROLD
> (looking out the window)
> The moving van crushed our lilac
> bush.

10   P.O.V. OF SCENE IN FRONT OF THE HOUSE

We SEE the van mangling bushes; the TV People and Cop drink coffee, etc.

> HAROLD (V.O.)
> I can't go to the bathroom
> without being televised.

11   INT. THAYER RESIDENCE–MASTER BEDROOM–EARLY MORNING

> EUNICE
> (coming to him)
> Now, Harold, please. Try. For
> my sake. You know we can't keep
> living--you and Jamie here, and
> me and Samantha in California.
> It's been a terrible year without
> you. For me, anyway.

> HAROLD
> (nodding)All the time you been gone--
> all I did was ache.

> EUNICE
> (they embrace)
> Oh, my dearest dear--I love you
> so much.

> HAROLD
> (after a beat)
> I am not gonna drive a foreign car.

12   EXT. DARWIN MOTOR LODGE–DAY

We are out by the Interstate. We START on the identifying motel sign which, a la Holiday Inn, carries the message:

(CONTINUED)

12   CONTINUED: (2)

''WELCOME SAMANTHA THAYER GROUP.'' We PAN off the sign to
SEE four black limousines parked in front, the motors run-
ning. A Darwin police car is at the head of the line, with the
CHIEF standing by it.

MAYOR CLIFFORD BREEDLOVE stands by the first limo. He is in
his mid 30s, chubby, balding, cheerful. He wears white shoes
and light blue trousers--too short--with a white plastic
belt. His jacket is plaid and his shirt is red and his tie is
white. He is approached by a CLUSTER OF PEOPLE headed by MAX
TABER, Samantha's agent. Taber is perhaps 42, but tanned and
toned. His clothes are expensive Beverly Hills. We will soon
meet the others, THE ENTOURAGE.

                    MAX
          You have got to be Mayor Breedlove.

                    BREEDLOVE
               (with a vigorous handshake)
          None other--Welcome to Darwin.

                    MAX
               (disdainful)
          Defeats his theory, doesn't it?
          I'm Max Taber, Samantha Thayer's
          agent. You know Paige Turner--her press rep.

                    BREEDLOVE
               (pulling out namecards
               from plastic hoder)
          How was your flight, Mr. Taber?

13   CLOSEUP OF CARD: ''MAYOR BREEDLOVE, MORTICIAN, ADDRESS.''

                    MAX (V.O.)
          No movie and a stewardess with
          hairy legs.

14   EXT. DARWIN MOTOR LODGE--DAY

                    BREEDLOVE
          Isn't that nice? My card.

Breedlove gives a card to each person now as he is introduced.

                    MAX
          This is Samantha's personal
          manager, Ira Lunt; her accountant,
               (MORE)

                              (CONTINUED)

14   CONTINUED: (2)

> MAX
> (continued)
> Sidney Pincus; her lawyer, Bergen
> Sedwick; her California pastor,
> Bobby Joe Good——

> BREEDLOVE
> I've seen you on the TV, Reverend.

> BOBBY JOE
> God bless electronics.

> BREEDLOVE
> It's good in my business, too.

> MAX
> This is make-up, Candida Majelski.

> AMADEUS
> (waving a hair brush)
> I'm hair——and a barrel of fun.

> MAX
> Amadeus Portman. This is Astrid
> McBride——Samantha's psychic
> slash astrologer.

> ASTRID
> Beware the City Council on the 13th.

> BREEDLOVE
> (impressed)
> I will, I will.

> MAX
> Okay, everybody——into the cars.
> We're going to Samantha's house
> first, then to the gala.

The Entourage turns and starts to get into the limos.

> REEDLOVE
> (pulling pages from suit
> pocket)
> Max, I'd like you to take a look
> at something.

15   EXT. DARWIN MOTOR LODGE—DAY

Favor Entourage.

(CONTINUED)

15   CONTINUED: (2)

> BERGEN
> (looking at Breedlove's
> card)
> Mayor--and funeral director?

> IRA
> It's eerie--I haven't seen a
> single Mercedes since we got here.

16   EXT. DARWIN MOTOR LODGE–DAY

Back on Max and Breedlove.

> BREEDLOVE
> Well, what do you think? It's
> my speech for the gala.

> MAX
> (reading from pages
> Breedlove gave him)
> 'One score minus three years ago,
> our Harold and Eunice Thayer
> brought forth on this continent
> a new person named Samantha,
> conceived in beauty and dedicated
> to stardom?'

> BREEDLOVE
> It's good, isn't it? I wrote it
> myself.

Max winces, as--

> AMADEUS
> (coming up)
> Max, I've got to call the Coast.
> What's the time difference here to L.A.?

> MAX
> A hundred years. Call from
> Samantha's. We gotta get going.
> Everybody in?

> PAIGE
> Lance Loren is missing.

LANCE LOREN, Samantha's vocal coach, who is black, comes
running out of the motel.

> LANCE
> (stops, big arms
> gesture, sings)
> 'Oh, What A Beautiful Morning.'

> (CONTINUED)

On page one of the script I have no idea why I put first, "We are in Darwin, Indiana, a county-seat farm town of 10,000 people, located 5 miles from Indianapolis." This properly belongs after FADE IN, which should be the first direction in every script. It was, probably, a vestige from an early first-first draft before I put in the film grammar. I think it was the first image or set of images in my mind. I think almost no movie writer begins with the mechanics of form. I always start writing about the characters, the locales, then snatches of dialogue, then a complete outline, before I go to script and put in shot numbers and camera directions.

FADE IN: always come first after the centered title and <u>ACT 1</u> or <u>ACT ONE.</u> It means that we are coming from a blank or black screen, gradually—one or two seconds—into an image, a picture. I set this at a margin of 20 in on the left and follow the words with a colon. Almost always the instruction opens each act, as FADE OUT. (with a period) closes each act.

Then, I space after FADE IN: and give my first shot number and description, starting it at 15 in from the left:

1 EXT. HIGHWAY – HIGH CORN ALL AROUND – EARLY MORNING

This is a rather typical description. The first direction following the shot number is always either EXT. or INT., which means "Exterior" or "Interior," which indicates whether the shot takes place outdoors or indoors. Cumulatively, this instruction is essential to the director and ADs (assistant directors) in planning their shooting days, to the art director in determining location looks and sets required, and to the producer and his people in compiling a budget. It sooner or later affects everyone—wardrobe, makeup, actors, director of photography, sound, lighting, and the entire crew.

The next description—in this case, HIGHWAY – HIGH CORN ALL AROUND—describes the more specific location and in this one gives an added indication of farm country and time of year (late August).

Next, I have written EARLY MORNING. Typically, this time-of-day instruction is given only as DAY or NIGHT. I like to be more specific to guide the director in the particular kind of light I seek for the scene. Also, this kind of specificity helps me "see" the look of the film and more clearly to keep in mind my time frame as one of the tangible elements in a movie. It helps me define the movie's logic.

These headline instructions following each shot number are always in CAPS and must be kept brief. If you must go to two lines, the second line should begin under EXT. or INT., always keeping the shot number clear. Remember, all you are saying here is simply the shot number, indoors or out, place, and time of day. If you need to describe the scene in more detail, you space a line and, starting at 20, begin the further description in upper and lower case.

In this extended description, all character names, camera instructions, and significant objects should be in CAPS the first time they are introduced. In my example, under shot 1, WE SEE should have been in CAPS, because WE SEE is the CAMERA SEES, (as MOVING VAN should have been). Everything else in that description seems correct. Notice that in this very first shot we have established where we are and that someone famous is or has lived there. We have the action of the moving van. We are not sure yet of the van's significance, but with our attention being drawn to it, we will be assuming that someone soon to be introduced is either arriving in Darwin or departing. Who? Which? Our attention is engaged.

Shot 2 increases our information and our curiosity. TV crews certainly signal an event or someone famous. Seeing the house after seeing DARWIN, INDIANA and SAMANTHA THAYER in the first shot, we know where the house is and are pretty certain who lives there. Who is she? Why is she important?

By shot 3, we are in the house and are meeting two of our principal characters. We learn quickly that today is a special day and begin to tie the moving van together with the talk of California. Also, the conflict is introduced. Harold is torn about going to California. This by the fourth sparse line.

I should have indicated in the script that MAIN TITLES begin in shot 1. I did on the middle of page 5 say (WE SHOULD BE FINISHED WITH MAIN TITLES), so experienced readers will know at that point how I have intended to have the MAIN TITLES integrated with the action. By the way, never specifically "spot" individual titles in the script. You will not know how many will actually be required eventually, but, more important, it will be a cumbersome intrusion in the script, obstructing the reader's easy access into the story.

You see on page one the use of short directions in Harold's speech at the bottom of the page:

                    HAROLD
               (into the pillow)
          It's not even me.

And you see the indication of the scene carrying over to the next page with (CONTINUED) at the bottom of page one. At the top of page two, you see the example of CONTINUED: (2). The 2 in parentheses means this is the second page of this shot.

On page four, we see a new symbol: O.S. This stands for "off-stage," which may also be indicated by O.C., which means "off-camera." What it tells us is that the person speaking is in the scene and will be seen or has been seen, but not at this point nor during this speech. It is a device to be used when you want these lines spoken but want the visual attention on something or someone else. In this case, I wanted you to be looking at Jamie in the outsized sunglasses, before knowing the circumstances of where and why he is wearing them. That I come to in the next shot—shot 8. I think this manner of introducing the key element first, followed by additional picture information, heightens the visual interest and keeps the audience stimulated with successive introductions of information. The sunglasses and our star—in fact, the entire circumstance—would be blunted if I came to the scene immediately in the wide shot. This off-stage or off-camera voice sometimes is handled thusly:

DELIVERY BOY #1'S VOICE

Sometimes you will see the letters V.O. following a character's name. This means VOICE OVER. You could see the character on screen and hear his inner thoughts, for example, VOICE OVER. Or it can be a narrator's voice, someone you will never see in the movie. Or it can be a character's voice giving information about other characters while the speaking character may or may not be on screen.

In *Once Upon a Beverly Hills* we have, by the end of the MAIN TITLES, met three of our principal characters in HAROLD, EUNICE and JAMIE. We know quite a lot quickly about their current lives and how these are about to be altered. We have heard a lot about SAMANTHA. We know she is beautiful and sexy. We know she is an important television star. We have met her entourage. By now we are very eager to get a look at her and to see what all the fuss is about. This creates high and suspended interest but is a risk in that when you do see her, she must have an impact equal to our builtup expectation. Since this is a comedy, her first line must also get a laugh. I think it works. She comes in two pages later on page 12, like so:

```
18   INT. THAYER RESIDENCE–SAMANTHA'S ROOM–DAY

         ''Girlish'' room. SAMANTHA THAYER is seated before a the-
         atrical-type makeup table and mirror. Samantha is 17, going
         on 18. She is an absolue confection of a girl. Her body makes
         grown men cry. She is mega-blond, beautiful in a 50s-Miss
         America, apple-pie-innocent kind of way. Just finishing
         fussing over her are makeup woman Candida Mojeleski and
         hairdresser Amadeus Portman. The rest of the Entourage is
         grouped around.
                       SAMANTHA
                   (into the mirror)
            Am I okay? I don't want to look too 17.

                       EVERYBODY
                  (Lance always sings)
                       Perfect.

                       SAMANTHA
            Is my hair okay?
```

                         EVERYBODY
          Perfect.

                         SAMANTHA
          I slept in the neckbrace.

    As you can see, I keep my character descriptions and camera directions as terse as possible. I will use known symbols: Jamie is "a young Henry Fonda." Samantha is "mega-blond beautiful in a 50s-Miss America, apple-pie-innocent kind of way." This saves a lot of time and creates an instant image in the reader's mind. I would, however, not use this technique for adult star parts. Stars do not want to be compared to other stars. Stars see themselves as unique. Usually, I am not so specific about grownup star part ages either. Saying exactly that Eunice is forty-four and Harold is forty-six lacks star tact. It is enough to say the children's ages. The stars reading the script will decide how old they have to be—or how young they can get away with. Every star character should be at least "attractive" or "handsome enough." Nobody, man or woman, wants to play a bow-wow or even plain. I think the positive characteristics with which I have endowed Harold and Eunice will please stars who would be reading the script. They see that they will be playing that most desirable part of all—a likable character.

    Never be too specific in your physical descriptions of star parts—or any part, unless some physical characteristic is essential to the plot or mood. The star reading knows what he looks like or how he wants to look. If you miss that in your description, or go against it, the star will read on with discomfort and may not even be conscious of why he does not like your script. Furthermore, it is likely that more than one star will read the role. While you could probably right now make a list of ten stars who could play Harold and another ten for Eunice, each of these stars, quite properly, will see no one for the part but himself or herself.

    Besides, finally, you are not writing a novel. These descriptive passages will never be seen on the screen. Again, keep them short, which does not mean that they have to be dull. I work hard to make them clear and to make them entertaining. On props and action I am as specific as I can be. I want to get the director and everyone else involved to see the picture as much as possible in the way that I am seeing it. The more general I am, the more specifically it will become someone else's vision. He who sets the agenda usually gets the most out of it. In our Constitutional Convention, for instance, in Philadelphia in 1787, it was the Virginia Plan, drawn up ahead of the convention by James Madison that was used as the working document. Madison shrewdly knew that he would get much of what he wanted if it was his plan they discussed and debated—and, of course, he did. He did not get everything he wanted but more of what he wanted than if he had allowed someone else's plan to be the paper of departure. That is one way you get to be the Father of The Constitution—and, in this case, the protector of your script and of your vision.

Throughout, the directions I give for both the camera and the actor are minimal. They are there only when I believe a specific look, article, gesture, or emotion is essential for creating a mood or motivation—or a laugh—or in heightening the viewer's (and the director's and the actor's) understanding of character and story. I do not and should not break the script into every single shot that the director will shoot. Take shot 5 for example. It consists of five dialogue lines, two small internal physical directions, and one sound effect. My message to the director is simply that I would like Harold to be in bed still (he is resisting the day and the event of moving to California, which is central to the story), and for Eunice to be at the window. Eunice is excited about events; her being at the window expresses this and allows her to see for us the arriving moving van (signaled by the moving van horn blast) and it creates physical distance between this couple and, therefore, conflict or potential conflict. All the rest of how the scene is to be shot I leave to the director.

Chances are that the director will shoot the scene in at least three set-ups: a medium wide shot or two-shot (two people) of Harold and Eunice, a medium closeup or closeup of Harold, and then a similar medium closeup or closeup of Eunice.

Because I direct from time to time (as does Ann), I see the scenes as I write them. If I were shooting this one, I would begin with Eunice's POINT OF VIEW or P.O.V., out the window, seeing Jamie on the sidewalk below. I would then DOLLY BACK to REVEAL Eunice, probably before she speaks. With her back to us, I would have her say, "There goes Jamie." (This line could also come O.C. before we see Eunice.) Now I would have her turn to the camera and say, "This'll be the biggest day in the history of Darwin, Indiana." For Harold's line—"What about the State Fair? When Herschel Buckner won the calf-lifting contest?"—I would shoot it as a two-shot of Harold and Eunice to establish or clarify where they are and where they are in relationship to each other. Furthermore, I would compose the two-shot with Harold in the foreground and Eunice in the background. Harold's line must be understood clearly, since it sets up the laugh punchline to come from him next. I would cut to Eunice for her next line, "This is bigger," in a medium close-up. Then, I would come to Harold in a medium close-up before he speaks—even let him pause or, as we say, take a beat. "At least no hernia." Need I say, that is the line that should get the laugh? And does. I would go back then to my two-shot for Eunice's last speech, "Oh, no, the movers are here. They're early." Maybe walk her forward on "They're early," past the camera, as though she were on her way downstairs to greet them. Or, simply cut away with Harold and Eunice in position.

A director would shoot this entire scene from each of the angles I have chosen so that he will have "coverage" of the scene. That means the actors, even if they are off-camera, will say all their lines for each other during each take. All of the five shots I have selected—four setups—are cuts. I am sure you must see that if you put in this much shot detail, your script will run to several hundred pages and no self-respecting director will want to touch it. Still, it is important for you to "see" how scenes can be shot as your write them. Joseph L. Mankiewicz said it emphatically: "Every screen writer worthy of the name has already directed his film when he has written his script."

As you see, I have asked for no specific camera directions. The scene is short and straightforward. I have not even indicated wide shot, since we have already established these characters and the room. And, because there is nothing portentous—no hidden thoughts or meanings in either of my characters, I have not asked for an extreme closeup, or "choker" as it is sometimes called. Such an instruction would communicate something too extreme, too dire or ominous in the scene. Extreme closeups, or sharply acute angles up or down, or the use of special lenses and lighting create tension on the screen, best saved for deeply emotional drama, psychodrama, horror, mystery, suspense or melodrama. Avoid these in comedy—unless, of course, they work as in *Young Frankenstein*.

Unless you want specific effects, it is always better simply to set the scene and the characters, leaving to the director the choices of angles, lighting, and lenses.

It is likewise advisable to keep internal directions to the actors to a minimum. Mostly, the context and the characters' dialogue, if it is true, will convey the emotional meaning of a scene without a lot of annoying "(coyly)," "(angrily)," "(flippantly)," and so on cluttering up your script. In Shakespeare, there is never a direction to the actor other than the content of the spoken lines, except to enter and to exit.

While we are on this, let's define some more of the terms that you will have to use, including even those we have been using thus far. Indeed, let's jump into it and define all of them at this point:

> **FADE IN:**—Coming from nothing on the screen to an image. 1 or 2 seconds. Can be longer.
>
> **FADE OUT:**—Going from an image to a blank or black screen. 1 or 2 seconds. Can be longer.

Both FADE IN and FADE OUT can be used internally in a picture to indicate time change and locale change, as well as being used to open and close acts.

> **CUT or CUT TO:**—Going from one image to the next one immediately. Literally, cutting from one piece of film to another. This is the standard means of going from shot to shot or scene to scene and is understood to be used when no other direction is given.

This is why I do not bother in a script to write CUT TO:, though it is perfectly acceptable to do so.

DISSOLVE TO:—This is an optical effect that allows an in-coming scene to be superimposed over an outgoing scene. It can be a fast dissolve—1 or 2 seconds—or a really slow dissolve—4 to 6 seconds. It is used most effectively to show a time lapse. It can also be used to create a change of mood or locale or as an entrance in memory to a flashback. Good for a romantic montage.

RIPPLE DISSOLVE TO:—An optical effect that makes the outgoing and incoming images ripple as standing water might when disturbed. Use this rarely. Only when a character's thoughts are to go back in time. Or when a character in the present begins narrating past events that are then to be enacted. These circumstances can, however, be achieved with a simple dissolve. Ripple is usable for dreams or hallucinations as well.

MATCH DISSOLVE TO:—An optical effect in the dissolve that is like our other dissolves, but in this case the camera must shoot something so that it frames in the outgoing shot in an exact match with the incoming image. For example, you are telling the story of a person and showing him both as a man and a boy. You may have as your outgoing shot a medium closeup of the character as a boy. In a matched dissolve, you will come to the character as a man in a frame that "matches" the one you have left. You are duplicating frames but changing the content. Another example: You could go from a statue of a person to the real person.

PAN TO:—The camera base remains in a static position but the camera itself moves either left or right on a horizontal axis. If you are shooting an actor and he walks left and you wish to follow him, your direction would read PAN LEFT or PAN WITH. Panning is side-to-side movement. You can PAN OFF an actor or object to another object or actor.

SWISH PAN—A panning move made so rapidly that the images blur to the human eye.

TILT—The camera base remains in a static position but the camera itself moves up or down in a vertical plane. If you are starting on the entrance to a building and then want to show the building's top or some elevation, your direction will read TILT UP the building. Or, if you are on an actor's face and want to see something in his hand that is out of the frame, you will write TILT DOWN to actor's hand. It is up-and-down fulcrum movement.

CRANE—This is vertical movement where the camera base moves to a new elevation, either higher—CRANE UP—or lower—CRANE DOWN. In an open-faced set that shows two floors connected by a stairway, you could CRANE UP as an actor climbs from one floor to the next above, all the while holding the actor in the frame, or CRANE DOWN to see the actor descending the stairs. The most powerful crane shot I ever saw was in *Gone with the Wind,* when the camera starts close on a few wounded Confederate soldiers and CRANES UP (and in this case DOLLYS BACK) to REVEAL a multitude of wounded soldiers at the train station in Atlanta. The immensity of the tragedy of the Confederacy is emblazoned on the viewer in a single moving and expanding shot. The camera is mounted on a crane arm that is counterweighted to rise or fall smoothly. The cameraman rides along with the camera. A crane is always on wheels so that the base can DOLLY or TRUCK as well. If a professional crane is not available, sometimes the effect can be achieved with a CHERRY PICKER, an implement used to pick fruit or by power companies to work on high lines and street lamps. Professional cranes are noiseless and move smoothly; cherry pickers usually make noise and jerk.

DOLLY—The base of the camera moves on wheels toward or away from the subject being photographed. If my camera base is ten feet away from an actor and I want the camera to move toward the actor—to, say, five feet—I will write DOLLY IN. The converse is DOLLY OUT or DOLLY BACK. This latter instruction can be used also to maintain the same distance. If an actor is walking toward us and we want to keep the frame we have, the camera will DOLLY BACK as the actor walks towards the camera. If this kind of shot lasts for any length of time, it is a DOLLY TRACKING SHOT, usually written TRACK WITH or TRACK BACK. The crew lays down tracks on which are mounted the wheels of the dolly, so that it can ride smoothly and give a jiggle-free image.

TRUCK—The base of the camera moves on wheels on a line parallel to the subject. If the subject is an actor and he walks to the left and you wish to keep the same picture relationship, you will write TRUCK LEFT or TRUCK WITH. Interesting effects can be achieved by the subject and camera moving in opposite directions in a parallel horizontal plane. An actor may walk left and the camera TRUCK RIGHT at the same time. Try this with a friend. You be the camera moving right while your friend walks left. You will see a startling angle change, with dynamic camera movement. This is a good technique for introducing new or surprising situations on the screen while holding your actor in the frame. The most memorable trucking shot for me is in Jean-Luc Godard's *Week-End,* in which he has the camera "truck" parallel to a long line of stationary automobiles stuck in traffic. The trucking shot feels as though it covers miles and certainly achieves a stunning emotional impact about this aspect of crowded urban life and the contemporary pain of seeking pleasure. Actually, in this *Week-End* example, it is a TRUCK TRACKING SHOT, usually written as TRACKING WITH or TRACK along.

EXT.—Exterior, or out-of-doors.

INT.—Interior, or indoors.

SUPER—Superimpose.

C.U.—Closeup, usually meaning a bust shot or from the collar bones up.

M.C.U.—Medium closeup, usually meaning chest-high on a person.

E.C.U.—Extreme closeup, usually meaning a person's face, seen hairline to chin. Can be even closer, such as just mouth, nose, and eyes. All of these "closeup" directions can refer to objects as well as people. E.C.U. is sometimes written as CHOKER.

WIDE—Means that you want to see in full frame what there is to be seen.

EXTREME WIDE—Not very effective on television, but you might want it to show New York City, Los Angeles at night, or a battlefield. EXTREME WIDE is also sometimes indicated as PANORAMA or PANORAMIC.

ZOOM—Meant to indicate movement in the zoom lense that can go from a closer shot to a wider shot or vice versa. The direction of movement is indicated by ZOOM IN or ZOOM OUT. Pace is usually indicated, as in SLOW ZOOM IN or QUICK ZOOM OUT.

RACK FOCUS—This indicates a zoom movement from one end of the zoom lens's capability to the other, done quickly so that the interior images blur to the eye. Overused in music videos

2-SHOT—Showing two people at once in the same frame. Or, if specified, it could be a person and another animal—2-SHOT—JOE & HIS DOG—or a person and an object—2-SHOT—JOE & THE VIETNAM SCULPTURE.

3-SHOT—Same, only 3, and so on to GROUP SHOT.

AERIAL—Various shots from above. Can be as low as a second-story view or as high as from a helicopter or an airplane or blimp. Static camera base or moving.

ELEVATED—Shot from above, but not so high a point of view as from a plane or helicopter. Not a moving shot.

DAY FOR NIGHT—Should never appear in a writer's script. If a writer wants night he writes NIGHT. DAY FOR NIGHT is a director's note or the producer's to indicate that the shot will be made in daylight to save lighting and money but must look like night on the screen. This is achieved by filters on the lens, stopping down the apperture either in shooting or later in the lab.

ESTABLISH—Showing whatever is indicated for long enough to "establish" it in a viewer's mind.

MONTAGE—Various scenes cut or dissolved quickly back-to-back. I called for two different montages in *Drop-Out Father*, which I believe are good examples. The first is a series of shots of Ed McCall and his young, sympatico daughter, Elizabeth, touring New York City when they have first arrived there to live. It shows them in quick sequence at the United Nations, various museums, touring the theater district, shopping, and coming out of the Plaza Hotel to get into a horse-drawn cab. A montage is perfect for showing varied but separate activities in compressed time. (Easy and overused to show courtships in love stories.)

The second montage in *Drop-Out* is a juxtaposition or inter-cut of Ed's activities in his new life in New York and Katherine's, his wife's, as she undoes her old life in Connecticut. Montages allow for quick and dramatic contrasts. The great Russian film director Serge Eisenstein was the first to use the montage for contrast and irony. I remember one gripping intercut of his scenes of animals being slaughtered in an abatoir with scenes of soldiers being slaughtered on the battlefield. A montage can also be a series of still photos as well as live action scenes.

COLLAGE—Multiple, overlapping images in the same frame.

SPLIT SCREEN—Two images in the same frame, dividing it. These can be vertical or horizontal and when desired should be so indicated: VERTICAL SPLIT SCREEN or HORIZONTAL SPLIT SCREEN.

QUAD SPLIT—The frame is divided into four equal boxes, each box showing a different image.

3 SPLIT—The frame is marked off for three different images, which can be arranged horizontally or vertically.

GRID—The frame is divided into multiple boxes—more than four—which contain individual images, which do not overlap. Usually in multiples of four—eight, twelve, sixteen, twenty, twenty-four, twenty-eight, or thirty-two.

WIPE—An optical effect that erases an outgoing scene without super-ing, as a new scene comes on to fill the frame.

NATURAL WIPE—A wipe in which something in the scene itself "wipes" out the outgoing scene. Example: a person walking toward the camera who comes so close to the lens as to wipe out the image. A train running over a camera buried in a pit between the tracks. Or: a big bus or truck passing between the camera and the subject.

P.O.V. or POINT OF VIEW—This shot always follows a shot of an actor looking at someone or something. It is a shot of the person or object being looked at as seen from the first actor's point of view. Seen as though our actor sees it.

REVERSE—This shot is a 180-degree reset of the camera from the preceding shot. If you are shooting my front from the waist up, your REVERSE shot would be the very next shot showing by back from the waist up.

JUMP CUT—Usually a mistake, this jarring cut in which people or objects in the two connected pieces of film "jump" or shift position in the frame can be used to good effect to show chaos or a confused mental state in a character.

JUMP SOUND—Harsh audio cut from one sound (or silence) to another sound, without blending or fading the previous sound elements. Jet engines, machinery, jackhammers, gun shots, or squealing cats are all good sounds to jump to from relative calm in the preceding cuts. These will jolt the viewers and add energy to your sound track.

SFX—SOUND EFFECTS.

BLACKOUT—Going from an image on screen to blank or black screen on a straight cut.

FREEZE or FREEZE FRAME—Holding a frame as a still photo. You can go along in live action and at one point "freeze" the frame— and the action. Or, you can begin on a freeze frame, then release it and continue in live action. This freeze effect is done optically. For my money, woefully overused.

V.O. or VOICEOVER—A voice speaking over picture, without lip sync. The character speaking may be in the film but not talking on screen at the point of voiceover. It is a good technique to use for a character's internal thoughts or for his narration of events. Also, the voiceover need not belong to an actor we will see in the film. It may be an unidentified, disembodied announcer or narrator, as was the case in *Winds of War*, to compress time and to declare large hunks of historic information or exposition. This latter use of voiceover is always a good crutch for sagas, though I feel it is something of a cheat.

O.C. or OFF-CAMERA—A voice heard from a person not seen. The person may have just appeared on screen or may be about to appear. It is the voice of a person who is in the scene.

O.S. or OFF-STAGE—Same as above.

REVEAL—Camera starts on some detail or less important subject, then pulls back to "reveal" in the same shot the truly important subject of the shot.

Now a consideration that seems to cause considerable confusion: camera position, left and right.

CAMERA LEFT—This describes the area of the frame that is on the left as seen through the camera or from behind the camera. Left as you look at the scene.

CAMERA RIGHT—This describes the area of the frame that is on the right as seen through the camera or from behind the camera. Right as you look at the scene.

Okay, that seems simple enough to understand, you say. Wait. Now there is stage position, left and right.

STAGE LEFT—The left side of the playing area from the actor's position as he faces the camera. Left as you look at the camera lens.

STAGE RIGHT—The right side of the playing area from the actor's position as he faces the camera. Right as you look at the camera lens.

The tricky part is that CAMERA LEFT is for the actor STAGE RIGHT and CAMERA RIGHT is for the actor STAGE LEFT. This really does not affect the writer but gives fits to directors and actors. *All writers' directions in a script should be from the camera's position,* so that if you want an actor to move to his right or stage right, you will indicate this by writing "actor moves CAMERA LEFT."

S.O.F—Sound on film.

M.O.S.—No sound on the film. This phrase was coined when a European editor said, "Mitt out sound."

DOWNSTAGE—In film it means that part of the playing area that is closest to the camera.

UPSTAGE—That part of the playing area farthest from the camera.

F.G. or FOREGROUND—Objects or persons in the frame that are closest to the lens.

B.G. or BACKGROUND—Objects or persons in the frame that are farthest from the lens.

SOUNDTRACK—The audio part of the film. What you hear.

LIP SYNC—A person's lips on screen are syncronous with the words being said in the sound track.

LIP FLAP—A person's lips on screen are *not* syncronous with the words being said in the sound track. A no-no.

OPTICAL—A special visual effect shot on an animation camera or processed in a lab.

MAIN TITLE SEQUENCE—That which is on the screen while the credits appear at the beginning of a picture.

MAIN TITLE—The name of the movie.

That should see us through for now. There will be some more definitions—production and editing terms—in the chapter on producing.

About this business of naming a movie: While the insider arguments are endless, no one knows for certain the true effect of a title on a picture, whether it can help make a picture a hit. If the script or the production is poor, a title cannot save it. On the other hand, without much supporting evidence, I do believe that a good title can help a good picture. Even, at the start, a bad picture. At least, it can hook the viewer's interest and pull him in. An obscure, silly, or repugnant title can, likewise, keep a good picture from being sampled. I go on faith that coming up with the right title will help my movie find an audience. I believe also that it is an essential element of the writer's craft. Besides, I find simple pleasure in coming up with titles—for movies, books, name it (no pun intended).

When I begin a script I do not always have the title in mind, but I like to have it. I will stall the writing for days in the hopes of finding the title before I have to begin. When I do not have the title, I am always slightly uneasy about the project and find the writing comes harder. If the title is right, and it comes early in the project, it defines the essence of the piece, which gives me great confidence. It is very important for me that the title say what the picture is about.

For instance, I am very proud of my titles "Good Morning America" and "20/20." I think they wear very well, "talk" in everyday converstaion, and, most importantly, reflect the spirit, or at least the goals, of those two programs. "Good Morning America," which I stole from a volume of Carl Sandburg's poetry, sounds friendly and communicates personally and immediately. Not unlike its father, Sandburg. This warm and human feeling was what I wanted the program to have, to counter a then rather austere, gray, authoritarian, self-serious "Today" show. "20/20," of course, means perfect human vision. Not that the program always has it, but the title defines the attempt of the program to try to put in focus all of the complicated stories it treats in our perplexing world. In the beginning, "Good Morning America" was scoffed at by all the wiseguys as being frivolous and a bit democratically patronizing. There were a lot of "20/20" hindsight jokes as well. But, very quickly, the two titles settled into everyday acceptance and easy usage. The titles were true to the programs, and I believe the programs have remained true to their titles.

One movie, which I adapted from an unpublished novel by Judy Rand, was referred to throughout the writing and the shooting by the name of the novel, *Paper Castle*. From the start I had wanted to change it. While *Paper Castle* was pleasing enough, I thought it was amorphous and, for television, downright dangerous. There was the negative "paper tiger" in the language, George Plimpton's *Paper Lion*—a nice takeoff—and *Paper Chase*, though currently on Showtime, a failure in its run on CBS, where our movie would play. Any confusion of this latter program with our movie was sure to harm. Seeing it listed, a casual viewer, and many of them are, might think he had already seen it. Also, castle has been overworked in titles.

The network agreed that we should have a title change, but no one could agree on what it should be. Early on, I had come up with *He's Fired,*

She's Hired, but it went unloved by anyone else. From among our own production unit and the CBS executives, another thirty or forty titles were proposed. Several of them by me, though I kept coming back to *He's Fired, She's Hired.*

The chief argument voiced against this new title was that it "gave away what the story's about." I said, "That's exactly why it's good. You know immediately the subject area, but not the story. You don't know who he is or she, or the circumstances. You just know a man gets fired and a woman gets hired. Does he get fired because of her? Does she take his job? Are they married? Not married? Do they get married? *He's Fired, She's Hired* these days ought to grab attention on several levels. And the rhyme in the title says comedy."

"Too frontal," people continued to say. Ann said, "What about *Mutiny on the Bounty?*" That got attention, but still no approval. We were at an impasse. New suggestions got worse. From my own network days, I knew each network had a service for testing titles. I am not sure of the details. I think ten or fifteen civilians from Long Island or the San Fernando Valley (the contemporary versions of "But will it play in Peoria?") sit in a room and a tester throws out a batch of titles on which they vote. I am not sure whether the testees are given a summary of the storyline.

There is also what is called "concept testing," which networks do a lot of. Testees are given a paragraph defining a program concept and are asked whether they would be likely to watch such a program. For instance: "A boy prince talks to his father's ghost and gets the idea that the father was murdered by a brother of the father so the brother could be king and marry the dead man's widow, the boy prince's mother. The boy prince's girlfriend kills herself and all the leading characters get murdered at the end." Would you be *very* likely to watch? Would you be likely to watch? Would you be likely not to watch? Would you be *very* likely not to watch? You can imagine the results of such a test, which is why you will never see *Hamlet* on a commercial network. "Hart to Hart," by the way, came as a direct result of concept testing. The idea of a loving husband and wife as crime fighters consistently scored high in a number of ABC concept test situations over a period of three years.

Anyway, Ann and I made up a list of our ten favorite titles (or the ten least offensive) from the gaggle that had been talked about, took the list to the network and said, with democratic fortitude and trepidation, "Why don't we let the people decide?" CBS agreed and sent the titles for testing. Two weeks later we had the results, and *He's Fired, She's Hired* came in first. Following the test, some other CBS executives came up with additional titles, none of which Ann and I liked. Again, we turned to the people. These new titles, along with *He's Fired, She's Hired* and the number two choice from the first batch, which I have forgotten, were submitted. *He's Fired, She's Hired* won again, and that became the name of the movie, which had its first airing on Tuesday, December 18, 1984. It starred Wayne

Rogers, Karen Valentine, Elizabeth Ashley, and Howard Rollins. John O'Connor, reviewing it for the *New York Times,* hated the title.

Drop-Out Father was *Drop-Out Father* from the beginning. It certainly satisfied my standard for saying what the movie was about. Perhaps with books and theatrical motion pictures this kind of specificity is not so necessary, but in television, I think it is essential. So much is competing for our attention constantly. We all make very quick, intuitive judgments about our choices. I think if you zero in on what it's about, and what it's about has appeal, the viewer will come to you. At least, he will be able to find you. Still, in this case, I kept fussing with other titles. I liked it, but somehow I felt *Drop-Out Father* sounded old-fashioned. It felt like a dozen sitcoms from the fifties with a very dog-eared sixties word thrown in. But nothing else ever said it as clearly, so I stayed with the title, which CBS also liked. My other small tests for titles include saying them out loud in all the ways I know they will be used on air: "*He's Fired, She's Hired* will continue after these messages." "We'll return to *He's Fired, She's Hired* following station identification." "We now return to the CBS Tuesday Night Movie, *Drop-Out Father.*"

I like *Once Upon a Beverly Hills.* It says fairy tale and comedy and clearly tells you where you are—in a place most of the world is curious about. I was never too happy with *Love Is Not Enough,* which is a novel and screenplay adaptation I wrote about a marriage and one woman's liberation within the marriage. It started out being called *I Can Make It without You.* I thought/think *Love Is Not Enough* smacks of a cheap romance or soap opera, which is not at all the tone of the story. But, I lost to the publisher, relenting to the false myth that anything with love in the title does well. In any case, I cannot disclaim it. I am the one who came up with *Love Is Not Enough,* which apparently it is not—as a novel. After a couple of good reviews, the book sank like a rock.

I like very much the names of Ann Shanks's three children's books: the one on recycling is called *About Garbage & Stuff,* the one on aging is called *Old Is What You Get,* and the one about teen-agers in prison is called *Busted Lives.* I am also rather fond of *The Cool Fire,* which are words I see now from time to time in lower case in articles about television, which I suppose means the title has become part of the language.

I like *Primal Screen* because I believe it is accurate, but it does border on something I would advise you to avoid in titles: puns, cuteness, jokes. They cloy easily and can create negative reactions. Also be wary of poetic titles— I mean pretentious—or titles that have esoteric or unfamiliar words in them. Avoid foreign words totally. An audience has to be able to remember the title.

If you cannot come up with what you think is the perfect title, go with one that is at least straightforward: *Hair, Scenes from a Marriage, Mr. Mom.* Each of these defines the essence of the piece. This is a good rule to follow: What is my story about? What is the essence? Defining this for yourself will almost always lead you logically and easily to a suitable title. If it does not, even simply, use your main character or characters' names: *Annie Hall, Kramer vs. Kramer, George Washington.* (I would not, however, have used *Sakharov.* It is foreign, obviously, and, to most of the audience, meaningless. I would have tried instead to capture the tragic circumstances of his life in the title.)

Place names in titles can help. *Beverly Hills,* for example. There was a time in the forties and fifties when New York in the title was thought to be valuable. Then, in the late sixties, that turned to poison. The country wanted nothing to do with the Big Apple, though I think that is changing again. I found in the early seventies that Las Vegas or Hawaii in the title added audience interest. That's death these days. I would again avoid foreign place names, since given the shabby education—the chauvinistic education—of Americans in the past twenty years, nobody, it seems, knows or cares where anyplace is if it is outside the United States.

Neil Simon's stated approach to titles is to try to come up with a phrase that is already in the language—*Come Blow Your Horn, Only When I Laugh*—on the theory that everytime someone utters the expression he is promoting your wares. On a practical level, this finally is what it is all about: helping your script succeed. Helping it find an audience. In television especially, if a title can add a few share points—one, even—it is worth taking the time to find that title.

I feel equally strongly about characters' names in a script. When these names ring right to me they help crystallize what I feel and think about the characters. I spend a lot of time on naming the people before I begin to write. Ordinarily, for my main characters, I use simple given names: John, Bill, Ed, Harold, Tom, David, and so on for the men. For the women, Sarah, Katherine, Elizabeth. For younger women, I will go to the "trendy" names of Wendy, Tammi, Lisa, Tiffany, and Cher if these underscore what I want the character to say. The rarest I have used are Eunice and Anabelle, which in the latter instance was a "given" from the novel by another person that I adapted. Anabelle felt right to me so I kept it. The leading male character in the novel was called Rowland. I changed that quickly to Alex. Straightforward names provide easy audience access to likeable characters. Wimpy or very offbeat names may set up unconcious barriers. Exception: Felix Unger is an inspired choice for the prissy character in Neil Simon's *The Odd Couple.* And, which may have come first, gave Simon that wonderful "F.U." joke.

I like exotic or funny names only for lesser characters and, again, only if the names reinforce a character's personality or circumstance, which is the proper yardstick to use. The name should aid in defining the character. I had a hell of a good time naming Samantha's entourage in *Once Upon a Beverly Hills.* I enjoy especially her hairdresser, Amadeus Portman, her makeup woman, Candida Mojeleski, and her psychic, Astrid McBride. These names may seem to you at first to be ridiculous, but the world in which they live is ridiculous and people in it make ridiculous adaptations to it. Those names in that town are not unbelievable. I know people who are self-inflicted with names like that, an observation that I think adds insight about the milieu. Another example of names signaling a subtext statement can be found in the way the second and third generation immigrant groups who poured out of the cities and into the suburbs sometimes named their children: Sean Ginsburg, Daphne Lipschitz, Skip Petrocelli, and Heidi Zakarios. These names were not meant as cruel jokes by sadistic parents but were messages to express the parents' dreams and goals and values. A hold on the past and an urgent need to move away from it.

Earlier, I spoke of a 2-hour television movie being divided into seven acts to accommodate the commercials. Given the 96 minutes of playing time, this does not mean that each act has to be 13.7 minutes in length or 96 divided by 7. On the contrary, avoid it.

As an additional tactic for success, my first act nearly always runs 20 minutes. Yes, that does mean that I have to have shorter acts later on to come out on time. But, your first act in television is your most important act. You must hook the audience there or kiss it goodbye. Nowadays especially—and this will intensify—a vast number of viewers sit there with their little hand-held clickers—those electronic guillotines—and can barely restrain themselves from chopping off a program every thirty seconds. I know other how-to books stress the importance of the ending as well as the start of the picture. No doubt, your ending should be satisfying to the audience, but I say it again: in television I will trade you five great act sevens for one great act one. Act one has got to grab the audience and hold it.

One clear way for a first act to engage the audience is length. If your first act is 17 to 20 minutes long, the audience almost has to stay to the half-hour at least, because even if viewers find your show eventually wobbly, they will, if the first act has been engaging, be too committed to get much out of the competition. Make act two, if you can get away with it, long also, Or, make it shorter, so act three can be long. One of these configurations will fulfill our next tactic: "bridging" the break, or "the half-hour." If your act lengths can vary from the standard 28:30 half-hour so that you are in program content while the other networks and stations are in commercials, or in program content while the oncoming competition which your audience may be tempted to sample, is about to begin, you have the best chance for holding the audience when it is most likely to leave you.

As you may have guessed, my last act is seldom longer than five minutes, even shorter if I can manage it.

As a telling example, study Johnny Carson's formating. He is a master in a particularly sticky mine-field of commercials—in late night, it is six commercials every half-hour and a four-plus-minute break at midnight. Notice his long opening, his bridging of the midnight break, and his short—

sometimes only a minute or even five seconds—last act. Carson does not care if you stay up for David Letterman by giving you a big finish. He is worried about Carson and 11:30 (Eastern and Pacific). A term for all of this is "front-loading."

The reality of acts and intervening commercials seems, at first, a major obstacle for a television drama writer. How do you establish your rythyms, your flows, your beats and cresendos with all of these interruptions? On closer examination and application, you will find that the commercial breaks that force you to the seven acts merely constitute a form. A form different from those for theatrical movies, plays, novels, or, if you will, sonnets, but like the forms for these, a framework that in its challenge is part of the excitement of writing. I have used the tennis court example, but nearly all sports are intensified by boundaries and rules. The same insistence applies, though not always so vividly, in other fields. For instance, you cannot plead successfully in court without adhering to the rules of law, nor launch a space satellite if you break the laws of physical nature.

The goal then is to accept the seven-act form and make it work for you. Use the breaks to your advantage.

When I was doing "Tonight" and "The Merv Griffin Show," I made it a point to use the commercial breaks to affect the flow of the programs. Within a couple of minutes either way, I could call for a break or hold one back. If a guest or segment was playing very well, I would let it play, postponing the break as long as I could, or until a significant "high" was reached, then quickly signal going to the break. If a guest or segment was stillborn or dying, I would call for the break much sooner—fast—so that we could bring on a next guest or element and get the program going again. Merv was especially adept at this. He and I had a series of visual signals worked out—I always sat line-of-sight to him—to control the pulse and energy of the program. Since these kinds of programs are unscripted and unrehearsed, this technique, though you can get pretty good at it, remains fluid and uncertain.

In a structured drama, your opportunity to control pacing can be—or should be—more concrete. You can plan ahead of time how you will end each act. You can construct what are called, traditionally, "cliff-hangers." It is not easy—none of this is—but it is necessary and deeply satisfying when you can do it.

There are other advantages to the seven-act form, but first let's consider the cliff-hanger aspect of act endings. The phrase came into use after the protagonist in a silent film was left, literally, hanging from a cliff, but I prefer to keep in front of me a Pearl White incident (Pearl White was the star of a silent movie serial called *The Perils of Pauline*). She is being tied to the railroad tracks with the train fast approaching when—TO BE CONTINUED. Perfect. What an act ending. If this will not bring an audience back (the following week in movie-movie serials) or hold them over the commercial break in television movies, what will? This does not mean that all act endings have to be so blatant and melodramatic, but it does serve as an example that you should keep clearly in mind as you devise your own act endings. It has application in love stories, comedies, family or psychological and social dramas, as well as its more obvious use in adventure, crime, war, western, horror, and disaster stories. What is my "Pearl on the tracks"? It is the question to ask yourself each time you conclude any act but the last one.

Look at the act endings of *Drop-Out Father*. Each one is designed to hold the audience over the break. Not so obviously as poor, put-upon Pearl knotted to the rails, but they are subtle equivalents.

End of Act 1

Series of petty, personal disasters ending with Ed's wallet being stolen by a pickpocket.

End of Act 2

We know Ed has decided to change the absurd life we have seen he is living when, as a powerful symbol, he shoots the television set and smiles. (How is that for biting the hand that feeds me?)

End of Act 3

The family is in high anxiety and realizes the changes to come as Ed burns everybody's credit cards.

End of Act 4

Ed has begun his new life, alienated from all family members except daughter Elizabeth, who is also wavering. Will he have resolve to pursue the new life? Will he and his wife get back together—and how? Will he also lose Elizabeth?

End of Act 5

It is getting on in the script, so Katherine and Ed are back together—maybe. From her "redecorate" line, we know there is still a period of adjustment ahead, an adjustment that may or may not work. There is still doubt as to whether they will make it.

End of Act 6

Act 6 is very short, you will note. Katherine and Ed are back together definitely now and headed toward a good new life together. The marriage, as the act ends, is reconsummated. Not a cliff-hanger exactly, but a very nice "high" for an act this late. (You do start to have to tidy up matters.) And, for an end-end to this act—in a comedy, for certain—I have used another technique with the last line: "It'd put us in a higher tax bracket," which is what is called a "snapper"—a surprise laugh line or event that provides a lift to get out on.

End of Act 7

> Again, the act is short. All loose ends are tied off. Everyone is happy. (This *is* television, remember.) Katherine has a speech that states the theme of the script: "To thine own self be true," rather than trying to live your life according to someone else's real or imagined expectations. I could have ended the story there. Everyone is functioning and the future looks bright. Katherine's speech even brings a tear to many viewers. But this *is* a comedy, so there has to be surprise—a lift—a snapper—a laugh to get out on.
>
> That is the entire purpose of Grandpa and his new Chinese girlfriend. Grandpa's line, "I guess I'm going through my middle-age crisis," is pure technique, designed to get a laugh and to give symmetry to the piece, since this is where Ed started. But I do like the resonance of the line also. It has a positive quality in it regarding aging. You may think Grandpa is a "dirty old man," but if he can believe he is having his mid-life crisis at eighty, there is hope for all of us.

All in all, I think I had strong, suitable "Pearl-on-the-tracks" for the first four act endings. Five is not bad and even six will hold you, since, if the film has worked to this point, you now like this couple very much and are happy they are making love again. You will certainly want to stay for the last act to share their joy; you can now trust that this is what they and you will have, and it may solace you for the arson, mayhem and murder about to arrive on your late local news. Especially when you learn your home team has lost.

How do you begin writing and shaping a television movie script? If it is an original, anything decent that I have written begins with a personal feeling, commonly some angst or other. Then I begin to think about this feeling. *Once Upon a Beverly Hills,* for instance. I have been in show business—television—all my adult life. I am grateful for the rich and varied opportunities and experiences it has given to me and to my family. For a good part of my career I lived in New York. For the past six years I have lived in Los Angeles. That was the beginning—for me.

But what about you? What do you have to contend with? Characters, of course. Plot and action. Incident and detail. Structure—the story line—going from point A to B to C and all the way to Z. Theme and milieu. Exposition. Dialogue.

Let's take them one at a time. For me, theme and milieu usually come first. What is bothering me? What do I want to write about and what do I want to say about it? All right. In this case, show business–Los Angeles is bothering me. I want to talk about it, but since no one is going to give me two hours of television time to do a personal monologue, I have to have somebody talk for me—a character. Characters. I have my milieu. My theme is that there has to be more to life than a network pickup and a Porsche. I have already arrived at characters. One of the main characters, I know, will by my alter ego, will speak my personal say, experience my emotions. The supporting characters will act on my main character, forcing his actions and attitudes, reactions and judgments.

Who is this main character? He cannot be a stick figure spouting my undigested ideas. He has to have height, weight, age, coloring, a look. More importantly, a personal history. Traits. I begin with a man who like myself is from another town but now has to be in Beverly Hills whether he wants to be or not. A man like myself who has trouble adjusting to it. It cannot be me. I am too experienced, too much a part of the problem over the years to establish a clearly defined, credible crisis of identity. My man should be a purer man, a more innocent man, a man totally removed from and unexposed to show business. What part of me is innocent? The Indiana part—of my youth? The small-town part? Before I knew about show business? Yes. Good. I can write that. I know the language and the attitudes. I know such men. And, a small town is a more definite contrast to Beverly Hills than New York or another large city. So, my man will be from a small town in Indiana. I make up a town. Darwin, Indiana. Population, 10,000.

What does my man do? It ought to be something visible and familiar to an audience. A druggist, maybe? Everybody comes in contact with a druggist. Everybody in a small town would know him and he would know everybody. I want my man to represent the old values. I want him to be hard-working, honest, giving, and educated. Economically comfortable, but not rich and not powerful. Respected at home, but a nobody in Beverly Hills. A druggist seems ideal.

Little by little, an entire character grows in my mind. I write it down. I give him a name. An innocent, Midwest WASP name. Harold Thayer. That works for me very well. I know a very decent, honorable, moral Harold, and Byron's "Childe Harold" comes to mind. I also free-associate a last name. I hit on Thayer. From Sylvanus Thayer, "Father of The Military Academy" at West Point. This says to me discipline, duty, self-sacrifice—a touch rigid and stuffy. Harold Thayer it is. The name alone begins to free me to know my man. I see him now, physically and psychologically. I build a life for him and write down his biography.

I know nothing of my story yet except for this emerging man and the simple fact that he is about to have to leave his happy life in a small town in Indiana to go live in Beverly Hills. A tortoise on the fast track.

I know also he will have a teen-age son, because I want the boy to go to a school similar to Beverly Hills High School and go through the events and people that John Shanks experienced. I cannot use John. Well, some parts of him. His sunny nature and good heart—and good looks. His observant wit. But, otherwise, since he was raised in Manhattan, John is too sophisticated to stand in for my Indiana teen-ager. This boy has to be in culture shock. I use some parts of myself from when I was a teen-ager in Indiana. I incorporate other Indiana kids I know. I call him, because it is close to John, Jamie. Jamie Thayer.

My man, of course, must have a wife. One wife for life. I begin to get a picture of her. Solid, home-town girl, high-school sweetheart, domestic, devoted to family. Because she is a woman and a woman with a husband and children, she is more flexible than a man. More romantic. This will allow her to be a conflicted bridge between her husband's resistance to the new life and the new life itself, which she (like my own wife, Ann) begins to enjoy. What's her name? Simple, straight forward. Helen, Maude, Pat, Jane—Eunice? Yes, Eunice. The name of one of my grandmothers. Eunice Thayer. Harold and Eunice Thayer.

Soon I have detailed biographies on Harold, Eunice, and Jamie Thayer. But why do they have to go to Beverly Hills?

I realize that this couple would be likely to have more than one child. Who is the other child? Nothing clear comes. Maybe, though, I could use the second child as a device, an instrument for getting the family to California. I want to talk about show business—California, right? So, what in the lives of these people would put them in that world? What could they possibly have that would make that world interested in them? I do not want Jamie the son to be in show business. I want him as an observer as well as a bemused participant. I've got it! A daughter. They have a daughter. A beautiful daughter. Hollywood is very interested in beautiful daughters. That's it. I'll give Jamie an older sister—seventeen, eighteen—who is beautiful and becomes a star. This would worry the hell out of the decent father. He would not want to hold his children back, but he would certainly be fierce in his desire to protect them, especially a daughter. The family has to join her in California to look after her. Perfect. What is the daughter's name? Should be a star name. I'd like it to be a trendy name. But why would Eunice name her daughter in a trendy fashion? What would influence her? Television, of course. She would pick a name from someone she liked on television. TV, TV, TV—Whitebread. WASP. Elizabeth Montgomery! Her character's name. On "Bewitched"! That show would have been on around the time of the daughter's birth. Samantha. Samantha Thayer. *All right.* That's how I go about it.

It does not always come easily, but you will be amazed how logically the writing begins to come when you have your core characters clearly in mind.

It needs no great leap of imagination, for instance, to figure out that a beautiful girl like Samantha from a small town would enter and win beauty pageants. This leads naturally to Hollywood "finding" her.

Next, I work on the structure—the "through line"—the story line. How do I open, where do I want to end, and what happens in between?

One gray-beard expression of this three-part story form skeleton is, "Boy meets girl, boy loses, girl, boy gets girl." Another is, "Get a guy up a tree, throw rocks at him, get him out of the tree." More formally, these are called the three acts. Every screenplay and television play has them. There is first and always the problem or the conflict. The three acts then are:

establish the problem, confront the problem, resolve the problem.

In *Once Upon a Beverly Hills* the problem is: A small-town, Midwest family has to move to Beverly Hills. The confrontation is a collision of their old ways against this new life. I confront them with all the hype, shallowness, venality, glitz, and obscene materialism of that town. The resolution is that the family members find some contentment and victory in coming to terms with their new world, without surrendering themselves or their traditional values.

Particularly in a comedy, I do not want to grab the audience by the lapels and lecture them. I want to entertain as I make my points. I want the audience to laugh. I begin by jotting down a number of specific incidents or experiences that I have had personally. Probably even painful at the time. But that's all right. Pain makes the best comedy. I jot down other people's experiences that I have heard about. I jot down milder experiences I have had, which on their own would not amount to much but can if I inflate them. Exaggerate them for comedy.

I make another list, a categorical list of California phenomena: mansions, hairdressers, agents and entourages, Mexican household help. The high school. Trashy TV shows. California cops, mega-producers. Spoiled, neurotic kids of wealth. The beach. The cars. Always the cars. I begin to make connections of these with my characters.

I put Samantha into a television show that is a combination "Dukes of Hazzard" and "Li'l Abner" in which she is a Daisy Mae. I call it, so you will know right away that it is a hayseed program and she is the star, "The Chick from Chickasaw County." This easily provides a rationale for my entourage characters. Samantha would logically have one.

I work on establishing the problem. No one, not even an innocent small-town druggist is foolish enough to pack up and abandon his life for a first season of a show. Everybody in the country is an expert on television and knows how fast programs can be canceled. So, to make the move credible, the show has to be a big smash, going into its second season, which means I have to figure out how the family handled Samantha being in California during the first year of the show. Ah. The mother, Eunice, went with her while Harold and Jamie stayed at home. That's good. That means Eunice has had a taste of "the good life" and her daughter's new fame. This will inevitably create tension between Harold and Eunice.

The "what ifs" begin to multiply. The answers come logically. What if they live in a mansion? A mansion requires help. What if, for the first time in their lives, they have domestic help? What if these modest people are suddenly in the frenzied media spotlight? What if this Midwest druggist is faced with health foods, health clubs, trendy fashions, fancy cars, lots of money, hot tubs, homosexuals, complex home security systems, and hard drugs? Hard drugs. The first joke pops into my head. I see Harold at a Beverly HIlls party saying, "I'm a druggist." And a fast-tracker answering, "Far out, I'm a user."

In my first draft, I had the family already in Beverly Hills. I opened very

"hot" with scenes intercutting two helicopters. In one are two police officers who are watching a couple making love on the hillside next to the
HOLLYWOOD sign, when a radio call comes in for them to go to a house
in Beverly Hills where Dobermans have a man thought to be a robber
trapped in a tree. In the other helicopter is Rhonda Guzman, a Hollywood
gossip queen and television interviewer. She is getting shots of Rodeo High
for use in her special on Samantha and her family. Both helicopters then
arrive simultaneously at the mansion where the Thayers are living. It is the
morning after the family's arrival in California and Harold, as at home in
Indiana, has gone out to get the morning paper. No one told him about
the silent burglar alarm under the stairway carpet, which he has set off,
which has summoned the police. While getting the paper, Harold has the
front door close and lock behind him. He is in pajamas. That is when the
guard dogs attack and he runs up a tree. Farfetched? I dont't think so. I
know Harold is a creature of habit. Nothing could be more in his character
than his going out for the morning paper. It is his new environment—with
dogs and alarms and celebrity interviewers and cops who have ideas for
TV shows—that creates havoc—funny havoc in his life. It is a wild scene,
but credible and logical. It could happen.

Since CBS wanted a quieter start and to see the family first in its life
back home in Indiana, this first-draft first-act opening became the second-
act opening in the final script. I opened in Indiana, as you have read in the
first ten pages of the script. That new first act has as its comedy high point
a scene that is a gala at the local high school to celebrate "Samantha Thayer
Day." I used some of the kinds of entertainers that I know perform in these
small-town events. While I knew they could be funny, I knew I would
never have screen time to present them all or at length. I hit on the device
of having Samantha's agent, impatient to get out of "Hicksville" and back
to Beverly Hills, pacing backstage at the gala and demanding of Samantha's press agent the schedule for the gala. As the press agent reads off each
cornball act, we intercut a brief excerpt from each act out front, on-stage.
This is very "filmic." Here is the scene:

19   EXT. DARWIN HIGH SCHOOL GYM-DAY

      Facade of the high school gym, a big banner across the front
      which reads: ''SAMANTHA THAYER GALA.'' We HEAR ''RUFFLES
      AND FLOURISHES'' being played, as we--

                                                      DISSOLVE TO:

20   INT. DARWIN HIGH SCHOOL GYM-DAY

      The gym is packed, about 1,000 people. At one end is the high
      school band, which is playing ''Ruffles and Flourishes.''
      In the center of the basketball floor, four 10-year-olds,

two CUB SCOUTS, two BROWNIE SCOUTS face each other, as from the ceiling, coming down on wires, there is a furled American flag. The flag stops belt-high in the space between the fading ten-year-olds. Two scouts hold the bottom of the flag casing, while two scouts remove the ties which hold the flag furled. The flag begins to unfurl as it rises and the band goes into ''The Star-Spangled Banner.''
EVERYONE is standing.

At the other end of the gym is a stage. On it, Samantha, on a throne, flanked by Harold, Eunice, Jamie on one side, and Mayor Breedlove and other dignitaries on the other. ESTABLISH this scene, then--

                                                            CUT TO:

21   INT. DARWIN HIGH SCHOOL GYM-THE STAGE, BACKSTAGE-EVENING

We can SEE the throne and stage figures in the background. Foreground are Samantha's entourage and various acts (self-evident when we get to them) waiting to go on. We OPEN on Max Taber, pacing and looking at his watch. He summons Paige Turner, who carries a clipboard with papers on it.

                          MAX
              Paige--bring me the program.

                         PAIGE
                   (from her clipboard)
              Next is the American Legion Drill
              Team.

22   INT. HIGH SCHOOL GYM FLOOR-EVENING

We SEE the DRILL TEAM in action. This is the first of a SERIES OF INTERCUTS, out-of-time, with appropriate APPLAUSE and SOUND EFFECTS.

23   INT. BACKSTAGE-EVENING

                         PAIGE
                 --Then a spoon player.

24   INT. GYM FLOOR-EVENING

We see the spoon player in action.

25   INT. BACKSTAGE-EVENING

                         PAIGE
              Flaming baton twirlers.

26   INT. GYM FLOOR-EVENING

We SEE the flaming (working with fire) baton TWIRLERS in action.

27   INT. BACKSTAGE—EVENING

                    MAX
          It's a five hour show.

27   CONTINUED: (2)

BUMPKIN, carrying a calf, enters.

                    MAX
               (continuing)
          Who's he?

                    PAIGE
          Herschel Buckner. He's a calf-
          lifting champion.

                    MAX
          There's an act we can cut.

                    PAIGE
          We can't, Max. He got out of a
          hospital bed to come here.

                    MAX
          For what?

                    PAIGE
          Double hernia. He follows the
          basketball team. Then, the town
          historian with a slide show of Samantha's life.

28   FULL SCREEN PROJECTION OF PHOTOS OF SAMANTHA, AS APPRO-
      PRIATE. FIRST PHOTO IS OF AN INFANT.

                    TOWN HISTORIAN (V.O.)
          It all began when Samantha Thayer
          won her first contest--slide, please.
          ''The Miss Indiana You Must Have Been
          A Beautiful Baby Pageant.'' Sponsored
          by the Hoosier Milk Producers' cooperative.
          Then time flew and before we knew it,
          she was ''Miss America Pre-Pubescent.''
          It's upside down.
               (the slide)
          Then came, ''Miss Corn Bread and Bean
          Festival,'' ''Miss Cattle Breeders'
          Association,'' and ''Miss Wheat From
          The Chaff.'' All this, while she
          maintained a C-plus average--and

there's never been a whisper of scandal
unlike so many of our young twirps.
A cheerleader--a baton twirler--and
a scholarship student at Ivy Proctor's
Ballet & Hula Academy. This God-fearing
girl was on her way to pre-veterinary
college, when fate stepped in and said,
''Whoa there, young lady--just a darned
minute.'' That's when she won ''The Miss
Cosmos'' contest--as the most beautiful
girl in the whole world--light-skinned
or dark. Da-da! Hollywood beckoned--
and the rest is history.

29   INT. BACKSTAGE-EVENING

PAIGE
Then Mayor Breedlove makes his
speech.

MAX
We won't get out of her till
Tuesday. When's Samantha on?

PAIGE
Right after Breedlove.

MAX
By that time, she'll be playing
character parts.

30   INT. HIGH SCHOOL GYM-EVENING

We SEE Breedlove at the podium.

BREEDLOVE
And in conclusion--the world will
little note nor long remember what
we say here, but because of this
prettly little girl from Darwin,
wholesome television will not
perish from the earth. Samantha's of the people,
by the people, and
for the people--so help us all.
Here's our own--Samantha Thayer.

The crowd goes wild, everybody stands. Breedlove helps
Samantha from the throne, and brings her to the microphone,
then goes back to his chair. Band plays ''Back Home Again In
Indiana.'' When all settles--

SAMANTHA
I'd like to open with a prayer.

```
                    BREEDLOVE
             (to dignitary next to him)
          She can't do that here--this is
          school property.
```

This written scene, of course, came considerably later in the writing. After I had the theme and milieu and the biographies of the main characters, I began to work on the structure—the story line. Here are my early notes.

Start with the house maybe. Must establish Jamie as a nice kid. Meet the entire family. Harold is resisting going to California. How demonstrate? Don't get out of bed? Local town gala to honor Samantha? Good, quick way to show their life there contrasted to what it will be in Beverly Hills. Show that Harold and Eunice have a very loving marriage. How? Would they sell their house? Probably not yet. Too big a break. Rent it then. Harold is in bed. Maybe he wants to take their bed to California. Bed powerful symbol of love and marriage.

Helicopter to introduce California—maybe something at the HOLLYWOOD sign. Quick establish. See the Thayers in their new Beverly Hills mansion, but also must establish Rodeo High. Maybe meet the first of the Hollywood types—Samantha's entourage, agent, make-up, hair, etc., in Indiana. That's good. They'd be blown away by a small town back there. Good line: one of the entourage emerges from motel in Indiana, looks around, and says, "It's really eerie—I haven't seen a single Mercedes." Okay, now in BH, intro more Hollywood types. Mansion needs domestic help, people to run it. Let's have a hustling, good-hearted butler. Maybe has his whole family working at the house. Fernando. Street-wise, lovably larcenous, new wave immigrant chaser of the American Dream. Probably illegal immigrant. Get Harold up a tree in culture shock.

Jamie in his first day at school. Time frame then at the start is late August in Indiana scene, early September now. He is fifteen, too young to drive a car. Big problem for a kid in Beverly Hills. How get around? Bike from home. Establish bike in Indiana—maybe he has a paper route back there. Fernando is butler-chauffer. They have a limo. Fernando wants to take Jamie to school in a limo. Jamie is in shock from this, of course, and refuses. Fernando says, you can't walk—nobody walks in BH. He goes on his bike. Good chance to meet his principal new high school friends. On his bike, he runs into (literally when his bike is demolished by a collision) two kids in a Ferrari. These will be sixteen-year old Anastasia (good BH name) Mandeville. She is rich witch daughter of Aaron Mandeville, the high-powered producer who owns, among other shows, Samantha's program. Jamie will fall instantly in love with her. For several acts, she will ignore him—but finally they will get together. Other kid is my Asa.* Make him

---

*I already had fairly solid bios of Anastasia and Asa. Asa Mandeville, 15, is Anastasia's half-brother: adorable, witty, neurotic existentialist. Intellectual.

also physically puny and hypochondriachal. He and Jamie become best friends. Both outsiders by Rodeo High School standards. We see the school for the first time. Work in the parking lot scene John described: New expensive cars in the students' lot. Beat up, used cars in the teachers' lot. Good opportunity here to also show California vanity plates. Asa: "It's the only literary tradition we have." Jamie has to go to the principal's office to register. Asa leads him there. On the way, they meet some of the exotic kids—druggies, punks, the suntan team.

I need a high school student villain—a punk rocker maybe. Scuz Spittle. Call his band "Toxic Waste." They are *bad*—and the costuming should be fun—but Jamie has to triumph over Scuz after some scary confrontations. Make Scuz Anastasia's boy friend. She has very low self-esteem under brittle exterior. (Most of these kids do.) I don't want Jamie to beat Scuz by resorting to violence. How then? Wit. He outwits him. Then, maybe, if I get stuck, Fernando can help Jamie when it has to get physical. God, violence always seems to have to be the solution. Maybe Fernando has a big family. Lots of brothers and sisters whom he calls on in a crisis. The brothers can beat the band. Scuz has Anastasia hooked on some kind of drugs. Big problem in the school, but don't get hung up there too seriously or darkly.

Anastasia though has to have some crisis to help her see finally that Jamie is a clear choice over Scuz. Okay. School dance. Scuz's band is playing. He gives Anastasia drugs. Then, she drives. Car accident with her driving. I've already set her up as a lousy driver, even without drugs. Does she get hurt? No. Asa. Asa gets hurt, riding with her. That would bring her to her senses more than if she hurt herself. And, Asa will be funnier in traction—his look, his comments. (Don't kill him.) Maybe he is bandaged head to foot, but "it cleared up my allergies." That sort of thing.

What about Harold's adjustment? He has to adjust to life in BH. Some conflict between him and daughter Samantha. Use Mandeville the producer? Does he seduce Samantha? Too heavy for TV comedy. Ah. He signs her for a movie-movie in which she will have to appear nude. Adam & Eve, maybe. That would outrage Harold. Get him anxious about losing his family and values. He will be appalled at Samantha's growing vanity and callousness. He will confront Mandeville. His innocence will triumph over Mandeville's cynicism. This will make him look good again to Samantha— and to himself. It can be the denouement scene of "old" values against selfish values.

Harold must also be disapproving at first of Fernando. Of his scheming, his if-not-breaking-the-law, his bending it into pretzels. It's Harold's by-the-book rules against Fernando's street rules. How do they get to respect each other and become friends? The Mandeville scene would win Fernando's respect—Harold standing up to a big shot. Then, Fernando can find Harold a Los Angeles drug store to buy—in a "normal" neighborhood. He can urge Harold to teach him the business.

End on the police helicopter spying on Jamie and Anastasia kissing beneath the Hollywood sign. Good symmetry."

This rough story line was enough to make me believe I could start scripting scenes. I did make a refinement of the outline first, adding more detail of actual scenes, arranging them sequentialy, breaking them into acts, and devising act endings. At that point, a lot of writers put their sequential scenes and acts on index cards or on a chart pinned to the wall. It may work for you, but I find that approach too tyrannical for my taste. The outline stares at you constantly, dominating your choices. I prefer to have my scene and act outline on a number of pages on my desk along with the script pages. That way, when a new idea hits me, I can shuffle the outline pages until they are out of view and for that moment lost, which gives me freedom to pursue spontaneously the new idea or scene. Still, the outline is there to dig out and see afresh when I need it as the measure of the new material.

With the first rough notes I had on *Beverly Hills* and the refined outline, I knew where I was going. I knew the structure would carry me through. When I began to write, of course, there were lots of zigs and zags. New scenes came in. Some favorite scenes and lines fell out. Especially those that did not advance the story or were not in character. This is very important. Do not get infatuated with every word or even every scene or minor character. These may be good. These may be very good. These may be the best you have ever written. But if they do not serve the overall needs of the script, if, in fact, they are distorting or diverting the story, you have to be ruthless in getting rid of them.

The script of *Once Upon a Beverly Hills* essentially followed the outline I had prepared, and it worked. I think you do not have to follow an outline slavishly, if it is dead-ending on you or if you see that it is forced in moving from A to Z. But never, never start writing the script until you have an outline. If you are going wrong off the outline, rework the outline. The problem is probably there. Or even farther back. You don't know your characters well enough. If you write a script without a through line from the start, you will be wandering off into a writer's wilderness. Playing without boundaries or a net. You do not have to know every detail when you begin the script, but you have to know where you want the characters to end up.

To guide myself in making an outline, indeed, in making up a story, the most important thing for me is to know what each character *wants.* Every human relationship or meeting is some kind of negotiation, intellectual or emotional, of individual wants. People are trying always to get what they want—what they need or think they need—whether they are conscious of the want or not. It may be subconscious: I want people to like me. It may be very conscious: I want him to hire me. It may be passive or aggressive. It is usually multilayered.

Knowing what each character wants provides you with what is called a "subtext." These interacting powers of the characters' individual psyches will add deeper meanings to all your writings. They will affect everything your characters do and say—or do not do or say. Or cannot do or say at the moment but may, will, or must later. That gives your story torsion.

Keep in mind, as I am sure you know from your own life, that characters have conflicting wants, simultaneously. Harold Thayer, for instance, wants his life as he has known it in Indiana. But he wants to protect his daughter and to be with his wife, which means he has to go to California. The collisions of these two basic wants shape how he feels and behaves. They color and inform his entire existence. They put him in conflict within himself and with others.

So, as you write, ask yourself and keep asking yourself, what does my character want? How does it harmonize or conflict with his other wants or the wants of other characters? Ask yourself about each line, each action, each scene: Is this consistent with those wants? Does it advance the story, which is nothing but the working out of these wants?

Your prior understanding of who the characters are—their histories and personality traits—will motor how they go about getting what they want. How can I know how Harold Thayer will proceed or react in any given situation, if I do not know in great detail who he is?

Be aware, of course, that television is not terribly interested in subtext or subtlety. Most things are stated and acted out bluntly, hit on the head, to provide quick and easy audience understanding. Plot Pontius Pilots all. The hook, the twist, the gimmick get the coins. Still, even potboiler characters will be enriched if you know what they want. Even "The A Team" wants something.

Theme, milieu, characters, story-line structure. That brings us to scripting and to exposition, dialogue and incident and detail.

Exposition. This is the craft aspect of exposing to your audience what it needs to know about the characters and the action. Traditionally, exposition has been used as a term to define what the audience must know that has happened in the past—the back story. I will use the term more generally, as a label for revealing not only the past but the present circumstances. Even experienced writers have difficulty with exposition, and beginners trip all over themselves, most commonly by telling too much too soon and too nakedly.

The classic cliché example of bad exposition is having a maid or butler talking on the phone with someone, saying, "Yes, Mr. and Mrs. Thayer—that's Harold and Eunice—will be arriving today from Indiana, where they ran a drugstore, to start their new life in California, where they have to live now because their beautiful seventeen-year-old daughter, Samantha, is a big television star. Her brother, Jamie, who is fifteen, starts school tomorrow at that very posh Rodeo High. Yes, I think you're right. All of them will have a hard time adjusting to their new lives. Certainly, Mr. Mandeville, I will tell them you called. You are the Mr. Mandeville who produces

Samantha's show, "The Chick from Chickasaw County," and all those other television shows and movies, aren't you? The one who has two children—Anastasia and Asa?"

That, of course, is not bad. It is horrible. Exactly how not to do it.

You expose the necessary information about a character or situation through the character's own words or deeds; through another character's view or knowledge about the first character; through symbols; through a range of possibilities where it would happen naturally in life that information is compressed and imparted. For an example of the latter, say someone is briefing a character about another character or situation. Pure James Bond movie. After opening by hitting you between the eyes with a scorching hot-action scene to get your attention—it is usually the end of one case—the Bond pictures slow down to let M explain what Bond (and we) have to know about the case that will constitute the substance of the movie. This briefing technique was also used successfully in "Mission Impossible." In the first minute of every episode, our heroes were filled in on who the villains were and what evil they were doing. Our heroes knew (as we did) some of the obstacles that would be facing them. Another natural example of compressed information would be a character answering a policeman's questions or a doctor's. Another still is using a television or radio broadcast. Making a public speech.

In some cases—*The Winds of War*, for example—large chunks of exposition can be handled by a voiceover narrator. This is particularly useful—and forgivable—when there are slabs of history to impart.

A character within the drama can also serve as a voiceover narrator. Think of detectives Sam Spade and Mike Hammer giving you the exposition straight.

Still, always be wary of these "crutches" and of giving exposition in big gulps. It is clumsy craft, and there is the danger that no one can or will work to remember it.

Go back to those first ten pages of *Once Upon a Beverly Hills*. Study how I have "exposed" information the audience must have in order to know the characters, their pasts, their present circumstances, and where they and the story are aiming.

In shot 1, we find out through symbol—the moving van—that a move is going to happen. I don't say it, but I prepare you for it. We learn from the sign that we are in Darwin, Indiana, and that it is a small town—I have put the population 10,000 on the sign. We know somebody important lives there when we read on the sign "Home of Samantha Thayer." The HIGH CORN ALL AROUND tells us our time frame. It is late summer.

In shot 2, we know from the television trucks and police cars that something or someone at this scene is of public importance.

Study each succeeding shot. More and more information is rolled out. I don't give you everything in one gulp. Keep in mind that you must begin to introduce and reveal characters and story direction simultaneously with the barebones exposition. Through page 5, remember, I am also allowing for the main title credits to be supered over the action and dialogue, so the information cannot be too dense or you will miss it as you are also reading the credits.

Notice the use of the front page of the newspaper in shot 6. This is a further example of compressed information, a technique that too frequently is used arbitrarily. But, in this case, I believe it is natural and justified, because the newspaper plant is part of the life of one of our major characters. Jamie has a newspaper route. It is organic for him to be there and to see the front page, while we learn from it, which keeps it from appearing to be learning.

Look at Eunice's speech in shot 9. Its function is pure exposition. I need the audience to know Harold's occupation and that he and Eunice have rented their house. To advance the story and tighten the conflict all I needed Eunice to say is, "You can't back out now." But, to get in the other information, I have set it up so she can buttress her argument for not backing out. The true purpose is to tell the audience for the first time something it has to know, but the cover for that is that she seems to be reminding Harold, which is natural, why he cannot back out: "The house is rented. You've sold the drugstore. You can't—" People talk that way. She knows he knows the house is rented and that they have sold their business, but she tells him because it seems he has forgotten these circumstances and the consequences if he acts otherwise. It is a reinforcement of her contention of what his first duty is and why. The next time you meet a stranger on a plane, a train, a bus, or in a bar—wherever—listen to his talk. Listen for exposition. We all reveal ourselves, but pay attention to *how*.

Stay with shot 9 a moment longer. Eunice's continued speech, "You can't—" is a naturalistic flourish. I don't need the line for any specific information, but I like having Harold interrupt her, because we break off what we are saying all the time, and we interrupt each other, or ourselves, all the time. This touch makes the dialogue more vital, more realistic, and, therefore, more believable. If you do use this technique, you should know in your own mind what the character was going to say if he or she had finished. In this case, Eunice was going to say "You can't stay here. Where would you live? What would you do? What would *we* do? What would people think?"

I like the content of Harold's interruption. It has nothing to do with Eunice's speech. He has introduced entirely different subject matter. I like this because it again is the way we talk. Frequently, we do not respond directly because we are distracted by our own thoughts or by outside stimulation; or we are avoiding. We do not listen. I like the interruption for another technical reason. It helps "hide" Eunice's exposition. The audience has found out in her speech what I think it needs to know, but I have then quickly distracted the audience from dwelling on the exposition as "educational" rather than its being organic to the scene. There is more bang-on exposition in Eunice's speech in shot 11. What she is really saying to the audience is, "You have to know my daughter and I have been living in California for a year while my husband and son were living in Indiana if you are to care about us as people and understand our story." But I have hidden that, I hope, and gotten beyond it quickly by moving to the new idea that she and Harold love each other, which is further exposition. Then, so that that does not become a pudding, I use a snapper to get out of the scene: "I am not gonna drive a foreign car." That line works on its own, on the face of it and gets a nice kind of laugh. The audience feels Harold's vulnerability while recognizing foreign cars as a symbol of southern California high life. It is an empathetic laugh. But the line is also valuable to express Harold's deeper want or subtext. What he is really saying with the line is, "I'm warning you, Eunice. I am not going to change who I am. I want to be who I am." An audience will recognize that the line is an omen of some kind of conflict and crisis to come. It will stay interested in Harold and Eunice to find out what that is, even though I leave them at that point to go to other characters.

"I am not gonna drive a foreign car" is a line that serves to demonstrate what is called "preparation." Which means that you prepare an audience for what is coming later. All of us recognize in a commonsense way that real life seldom prepares us for the random, chaotic, irrational, cruel—and often joyous and pleasant—incidents that strike suddenly in our individual lives. But to apply this unclothed truth in drama, and I include comedy, is a risk of the highest order, unless that is your theme. Otherwise, it almost always spells the failure of a script.

A novice writer recently brought me a script that committed this sin of no-preparation twice. In the first instance, the script opened with high interest and good film technique. It showed an infant's christening in church with voiceover sound intercuts of a man and woman talking about their lives and relationship. It grabbed. I had the right to assume that the man and woman talking were the parents of the baby and that I was being directed, willingly, because it was well done, to consider the wisdom or rashness, the bravery or thoughtlessness of bringing a child into the world.

Nothing of the sort. On page 9, our voiceover, unmarried couple—two of four main characters—dismissed the christening event very casually—the man was the baby's uncle at least—which had no relevence to them or to where the movie began to go from then on. The parents and baby were never seen again. I felt very cheated—had. The writer had hooked me on the christening. I committed my interest to the people on-screen and to the event, only to be told, "Forget that." That is not what the picture is about at all." It was a scripting shell game and I stopped trusting the writer and the script at that point.

The second violation was worse. The story was ambling along beyond the opening in a very languorous style, which was not inappropriate to the characters presented, telling me about 1980s Yuppies and their inability to love and make commitments. It sought to be a comedy of manners about this generation. Then, suddenly—one of the main characters, one of the men, is coming home alone one night and is robbed, shot, and nearly killed by an anonymous assailant whom we never see again. This comes very near the end of the script. Sure, I know it happens in life, as the writer said, defending his choice when I asked him about it, but it cannot happen in a script. Nothing in the story up to that point had carried me toward it. Nothing had prepared me for such a violent and arbitrary twist. There had been no hint whatsoever that perhaps part of what the author wanted to say is that we live in an absurd and dangerous society. Okay, not a bad theme, but not the one he had led me to. Following where he was taking me, I was involved with middle and upper-middle-class angst in relationships, exploring his two men and two women in their early thirties who were trying to work out their sexual identities and their need for and fear of love and obligation. Bang. The shooting, without setup or warning, was too wrenching. And it led nowhere. It was not even used as a trauma that changed where our main characters were going. The fellow shot was in and out of the hospital with almost no effect or further reference. Again, the writer had broken trust with the reader. With the audience.

I asked him why the shooting was there. Why had he put it in? That was jarring enough, but further compounded by his dropping any consideration of its consequences. He said he felt he needed "something dramatic" close to the end. Of course. All the books tell you that—you need a big moment next to closing. But what the books assume, even when they do not declare it specifically, is that the big moment must be in keeping with the logic of the script up to that point. An audience will follow you into the wildest, most ridiculous terrain if you maintain an inner script logic from start to finish. What you cannot do is establish one logic, then jerk the audience over to another.

Do I mean to say you can never surprise the audience? Absolutely not. That is an important part of what you must do. But the surprises must be consistent with what has led up to them and with what is to follow. The double sting at the end of *The Sting* is pure story magic. It is enormously surprising and has been hidden well. But it is not illogical with what has come before. That is what makes it so satisfying. So inevitable.

The opening of *Beverly Hills Cop* is equally effective. We see Eddie Murphy in a scam in which he seems to be a crook. Police arrive. All hell breaks loose. A powerfully inventive chase ensues. The cops "catch" Murphy. Bingo. He turns out to *be* a cop. A shell game? No. A surprise? Yes—and wonderful. And logical according to what is to come. We know now that Murphy is unorthodox in his methods. A rebel. But a good rebel. A hero who will flout all kinds of authority, but for the right reasons and, in the end, will strengthen legitimate authority and institution. We know all of this from the start, so we can trust the writer and the picture. Sit back and enjoy.

Dialogue. The spoken word. Two or more characters talking. That seems simple enough. You have heard it all of your life. In movies, on television, as part of your life-life. You know that in television and movies the dialogue is there to provide the chief means of exposition and story advancement. The characters talk to each other to tell the audience what the action and plot are. In many primitive shows, the dialogue does little else, or does its little else poorly.

In too many shows, everyone speaks alike. They use the same vocabulary, the same cadence, the same grammar and syntax. All voices are reduced to the single voice of the writer and are enslaved to the story. This is feeble craft, of course, though a lot of writers make a tidy living spewing out these monolithic mouthings for shows that demand nothing more complex than that you give the characters different names and genders.

But you and I know from life-life as opposed to primal screen life that no two people talk alike, and we know that no one person speaks the same in all situations. You talk one way in the morning, another late at night. You talk one way when you are trying to make a good impression, another when you are relaxed, another when you are under various levels of emotional stress or exhilaration. You talk differently to a parent, a boss, an employee, a brother or sister, a friend, a good friend, or a lover or stranger.

Whatever the mood is or the circumstance or whoever the speaker is, a person's talk is individual. It is as particular as a person's handwriting, signature, or fingerprint. True, we do drift without thought into the common pool of linguistic clichés; peer groups (teens, for example) and professions (physics, computers, medicine, education, sociology—television) beget their own argots, often intentionally arcane; and archaeological shards of language from Shakespeare, the Bible and other lesser poets and scribes, whether we recognize the sources or not, litter the commons of our uttered soundscape. But dialogue, when it is written right, which means hearing it right, which means understanding it right, captures the human individual reality. Speech reveals character, personality traits, history of family and place, education, occupation, emotional and mental states, chronological age, and, occasionally, even physical health. Speech identifies. It identifies each of us uniquely.

Successful dialogue is script speech that combines what the audience needs to know about plot, exposition, and story with this plausible, individualized characterization.

Don't be surprised and don't give up if your first efforts at dialogue read or, more importantly, "talk" stiffly or artifically. Chances are you will also commit that other beginner's sin: talking too much. Overexplaining. Oververbalizing.

Some writers say for themselves and advise for others that you should plow ahead and "get it down," even if the dialogue, as you go, is stilted. They claim, at the least, that this will have carried the story, plot, and action forward. I myself have committed this kind of automatic or mechanical dialogue writing, but I hate doing it that way. I prefer to move ahead a line at a time. I prefer to build a solid base for everything that follows. I find that anything that "gets down" wants to survive and therefore is harder to get rid of when it is wrong, and allows falsity to build on falsity. A script, if you will, is an organism, and if you let it grow with damage in the genes, there will be damage in the living whole. Remember the adage "One mistake has many children."

I do understand, however, that when you are beginning, you will have all the separate aspects of craft to piece together, and that in attempting to weave and master these—plot, incident, action, story structure—your dialogue may suffer. A technique that demands a careful building of a line at a time may inhibit or even defeat your ability to conquer the other technical requirements. There is the danger that you may even give up. First of all, don't do that. Secondly, you will have to find your own route, the approach that works best for you. This is a human construct, not mathematics. I suppose the process is akin to walking. The first goals are to remain erect and go forward. It is only when you have incorporated these that you can concern yourself with a personal gait and style, with skipping, running, leaping, jumping, and dancing. So, if you must, forge ahead to see if you can complete a scene, an act, a script. Then go back and try to repair the spoken damage. But, as quickly as you can become adept at scripting, confident that you can tell a complete story, I persist in urging you to try to get each line right as you go. It will also take you to new invention. This is doubly important in comedy that strives to get its laughs out of serious reality, since laugh lines or actions require logical setups in order first to punch or hurt before earning the honest laugh of recognition.

As an exercise in getting dialogue right, take four real characters in your life. People you think you know pretty well. A parent, for instance, a sibling, a best friend, or a teacher. Think about how they speak. Listen to them. Listen for subtext. What are they really saying? Listen for pet expressions and rhythms. Grammar. Do they use the right verb forms? "He don't see it my way," for example, instead of the proper "He doesn't see it my way." The incorrect personal pronouns? "Him and me went to the store" instead of "He and I went to the store." Speech hesitations or fills, such as "uh," "Like," "well," and "you know." What about vocabulary? What about accent? What about dropped endings of words? Does one swear a lot or never or under stress only? Does one make inadvertent spoonerisms?* That is, transpose the initial sounds of two or more words, such as

---

*A noun that came into usage because of an English clergyman and educator at New College, Oxford, William Spooner (1844–1930), who was notorious for this kind of error and who might have said about writing a screenplay, not "find your personal way" but "wind your personal fray." Which turns out to be rather sensible advice.

I have "giles to mow" instead of "miles to go." Or malaprops?* Such as "now you're adding incense to injury."

Generally, people of different generations use different words and phrases to express similar ideas. Geographic locations produce differences. Education will affect the choice of words, the grammar, the syntax. People for whom English is a second language will probably have an accent or, if the accent is gone, will continue to have a speech rhythm born of their first language. They will place words in sentences in different order. They may eliminate altogether certain parts of speech. The English add questions at the ends of declarative sentences. There is Brooklynese, jockese, Harvardese, surferese. There is black English. The variations are endless.

When you have selected your four people, pick a single idea to be expressed. For example, "I'm hungry." How would your father or mother express that notion? Your brother or sister? A friend? Your dad might say, "I could eat a horse." Mom, maybe, if she's on a diet, or feeling guilty about not being on a diet, "I know I shouldn't, but I've got to eat a little something." Bro or Sis? "Hey, man, I need some groceries" or "Pig-out time." Your English teacher might say, "I'm famished."

Try the notion "I'm tired." You will get "I'm whipped." "I'm bushed," "Burned." "Collapsing." "On the rims, baby." "*Très fatiguée, mon cher.* "Blood—I be beat." "Man—I'm so beat Jack Kerouac seem like a game show host." "Exhausted." "Shut down." "Shut off." "Off-duty." "We're talkin' cast party for *Night of the Living Dead.*" You get the idea.

When you have captured and written down the different ways the same idea is expressed by the four people in your life whom you have chosen, consider the contexts in which they have said it. Might they have said it differently in another setting? With other people? Subject to differing emotions? At another time of the day, week, year, life?

As you train yourself to listen to how people speak, you will realize quickly that hardly anyone speaks in complete or extended sentences. Unless we are William F. Buckley, Abba Eban, suitably educated, or in a formal setting, we tend to speak in sentence fragments that are crowded with run-ons, interjections, detours, hesitations, fills, and mangled tenses, cases, numbers, and grammar. (Buckley has a penchant for parentheticals.)

Frequently, as I have pointed out, we do not respond directly when answering another person. Even when we are listening, we may edit our responses or, simply, we may not understand. We talk at each other or by each other rather than to each other.

As an example, look at shot 6 of *Drop-Out Father*. Read it. Ed has no perception of one's need to change one's name for religious or romantic

---

*A noun came into usage after a character named Mrs. Malaprops so misused words in *The Rivals*, a 1775 stage comedy by the Irish-born English writer R. B. Sheridan; she might have said about screenwriting, instead of "It's a way to earn a buck," "It's a way to buck an urn." H'mmm.

reasons. He works from the only idea he has in his background: A daughter changes her name when she gets married. So, even though he is listening carefully in the scene, he is responding at cross-purposes to what he is being told. Also, Muhatma-Arthur focuses on his girl as Indira, while Ed thinks of the same person as Peggy. This fuels the confusion as to what grandmother's name is or was, which confusion leads to a laugh. More of Ed's character is revealed in his correcting himself. We could properly guess that Peggy's true given name is Margaret but that the family has always used the affectionate derivation "Peggy" by which to refer to her. When Ed corrects himself from "Peggy" to "Margaret," we can bet the grandmother was never called other than Margaret, a fact Ed is conditioned to respect.

There is a further example of misunderstanding in shot 41 in the scene between Katherine and her psychiatrist, Dr. Simon. Dr. Simon is asking Katherine how she feels about sex and about not having sex now that Ed has locked himself in their bedroom, which has forced her to sleep in the guestroom. At first, she thinks Dr. Simon is inquiring about the bedroom. As you see, she says, "Well—the blue in there is totally wrong. And the drapes. Oh. You mean Ed."

While we have Dr. Simon here, let me share a secret. I named him Doc Simon and planted it early on in the script only so I could make the joke later, when Katherine introduces him to Cannon Rush, of Rush mistaking him for Neil Simon, who is known to insiders as Doc Simon. Contrived? Not going forward a line at a time? Certainly. But Simon is not strained as a psychiatrist's name, and the mistake of identity is not at all out of character for Rush. Indeed, it helps to define it. He is exactly the kind of man who would work at knowing this kind of information whether he knows the people personally or not, to project that he does and that he is "with it." Further, he is the kind to be very impressed with celebrities and to gush in their presence. (The scene in question is in shot 53.)

I am sure you can find better examples elsewhere of how people speak as separate individuals, but since I don't want you to put this book aside to search through others—I may never get you back—turn to shot 21 in *Drop-Out Father*. It is the scene in the screening room at the advertising agency. The characters in the scene have just finished viewing the new GUN deodorant commercial.

The art director, Tony, is cynical about the entire process but realist enough to know he must go through it and earn approval of his work in order to get the money to maintain his way of life. He is confident of his talent, which gives him more ease in the meeting than the others. He can afford to be flippant.

Draper Wright, the account executive who has no demonstrable, marketable talent such as Tony's, is Type-A and outer-directed, especially nimble at adapting himself in the face of power. See how sychophantic he is to the boss, Cannon Rush; as capable of quick personal aboutfaces in order to please as he is quick, in front of the boss, to point out the shortcomings of others. (As Oscar Wilde said, "It is not enough that I succeed, but that my friends must fail.") Because he wants to appear as more his own man than he is, Wright has developed a habit of positing all he says in sports metaphors. This makes him, at least in his mind, tough and masculine. He is, in truth, a trembling pillar of pudding.

Cannon Rush has been to the Norman Vincent Reagan school of optimism. He talks in slogans. Slogii. Superlatives. Ad mottoes. Mixed metaphors. Who cares or knows if what he says makes any sense? He learned a long time ago that the music, the hum, of what he says is much more important than the words and content. He is a skimmer, a headline reader, an opportunist, a fast mover, an est graduate. He is the kind who goes to Europe not to experience anything really but to be able to say he has been.

Ben is an educated black Yuppie on a lower management level. He is doubly, triply anxious to dispell in whitey's mine any sharecropper dust that may be clinging to his psyche or persona. He bends his tongue out of shape over a tortuous King's English spiced with Latin to distance himself from "down home" or even Harlem. He certainly can and does speak differently with a brother.

Gloria is also a junior executive trying to prove how smart she is. Just as Ben knows Rush looks to him to be the house black, "ergo," the spokesperson for all blacks, Gloria knows Rush looks to her to be the house feminist speaking for all women everywhere, which, because she is very recently out of college, she believes she is supremely qualified to do. The argle-bargle of her classrooms further taints her speech. Alone or with close friends, she swears like a dock hand.

These two characters, Ben and Gloria, appear in only this one scene, but even with such minor characters, I work hard to make them clearly individual.

There are some other things you can do to get your dialogue right. I believe these additional tools will help you with the other elements of craft as well.

First, learn to play act. Become each character. Pick someone you know. Try to act and talk as this person does, to the extent that you know the person. Try to imagine the parts you don't know and fill these in. I suppose you could go around doing this in restaurants or on street corners. I was thinking more specifically that you can do it in private, so you won't get arrested. As you write. Truly, deeply try to put yourself in each character, male or female. Feel, think, act from inside that person out. Then "write" the person. Actors obviously use this technique. It is worth borrowing to sharpen your craft, as well as humanness.

Next, read aloud what you have written. Even if you're a lousy actor or reader, you will hear enough to know if you have it right. You will discover awkward constructions and artificiality. You will find which lines are hard to say. If you know actors or simply a few intelligent friends who like to read aloud, organize a gathering and let them read what you have written before you send your material out into the world. While these group readings can be enormously instructive, they may also send you diving into your bed to hide under the covers for a week. But you will survive, come out, start again, and be a better writer for it.

Another helpful device in dialogue: using it to move you from scene to scene. Carefully constructed, dialogue that ends an outgoing scene can tie into dialogue in an incoming scene without appearing to be artificial. This permits you not only to sustain momentum and understanding from scene to scene but to intensify them. You need not start each new scene from zero. A couple of examples: Look first at the transition from shot 8 to shot 9 in *Once Upon a Beverly Hills.* Jamie's "out" line, "Come on, guys—she's my sister," tells us immediately to whom Eunice is referring in her "in" line, "She's only seventeen." It provides a means to say what you have to say about a subject without the picture becoming stagnant. You can reveal story and character faster and more richly by getting at the material and people through a variety of shorter scenes.

Now look at *Drop-Out Father,* at Peggy's last line in shot 56. "You think they'll get a divorce?" This gives me a bit of a Pearl-on-the-tracks billboard for the incoming confrontation scene between Katherine and Ed, which opens with Katherine saying, "Don't touch me." Now the audience is hooked on paying renewed attention with heightened anxiety, thinking maybe they will divorce.

What do you do in constructing dialogue when you are beyond your personal understanding or depth? Say, you need to write a Russian person speaking English or a Zulu or Zen Buddhist or a kid from Bedford-Stuy-vesant in Brooklyn, and these are outside your experience or earshot? A) Expand your life. B) Start today tuning in on everybody who comes in touch with your life, either in person or through radio and television news and information programs. Or, for that matter, *American Bandstand* and *Soul Train.* Sensitize your ears and your intellect, so that you can store inside yourself as many "voices" as possible against the day when you will need one of these. C) Under an immediate need, fill in by trying to meet someone who has the authentic sound just before or, if you have to, right after you write. Beyond "street" experience in this regard, nearly all big cities and universities have associations, organizations, or individuals who are representative of the various voices you might need. D) Under an immediate need, get to the library. Find books, periodicals, newspapers, foreign-language English grammars that speak in the particular voice you need. You will get a sense of vocabulary, speech pattern, and cadence. This latter, of course, is the least satisfying, but not unhelpful in a pinch.

Withal, I caution you not to reproduce language in script that is too phonetically exact and idiomatic. See much of Eugene O'Neill to realize how irksome this is to read. If you write the spirit, not the law, good actors and directors will know what you want and will be able to give it to you.

In the meantime, your script will not be inpenetrable to producers and others whom you want to read it.

I spoke earlier of the common mistake of "saying too much." You have to work to keep scenes and dialogue as tight as possible. First, film is, obviously, a visual medium. "Show it" if you can. If you can't, relax. Film is also a powerful sound medium. I think, in fact, especially in television, where the audience is not always paying close visual attention, if you have to choose, sound dominates. If you doubt me, watch the picture on television with the sound turned down. Now, black out the picture and turn up the sound. What do you think? Right? Even paying attention, you comprehend more with only sound than with only picture. The power of spoken words is difficult to sustain with an audience if there are too many words. Or words where action will say it better.

As I have told you, I am more into words than I am into car crashes, so dialogue is vital to me. Therefore, I have to work intensely to get the words right and to keep the scenes aurally taut, since I have fewer action bits to rely on. William Goldman, in his fine and funny book, *Adventures in the Screen Trade,* gives some excellent advice in this regard. It is posited in one of those lasting expressions that is as tangible and useful as a landmark is for a mariner. He said, "Start each scene as late as possible." For me, he means to get rid of all the naturalistic clutter in a scene and to reduce, without sacrificing a sense of reality and complexity of character and action, the scene and the words to their essences. Others have said it differently—that good writing can be defined by "what is left out."

With this in mind, look at shot 65 in *Drop-Out Father.* It is Katherine in a session with Dr. Simon. I don't attempt the whole fifty minutes of a therapy hour, but I hope I give a sense of its entirety and of Katherine's state of turbulence. I don't diffuse focus with a lot of extraneous "hello," "how are you," "have a chair." I come in late, for the last minute of the session only. There is absolutely no warmup or foreplay before "the moment." The scene's essence for me is that Katherine is going through the disintegration of her established world in a way that Ed has already experienced, which we have seen. I need *this* scene—Katherine needs this scene—in order to bring her around logically to sharing Ed's new view of life and to point her toward how they may be able to live from now on—together.

Of course, when we first met Katherine, we saw a woman who, despite some psychological heave and yaw, could have gone on with her life in her accustomed accommodations to it, but the changes in Ed have produced frightening convulsions in her. I don't spend pages on that. I express it in her first short speech: "I don't know what I'm saying. I'm not making any sense at all. I've lost control, I've lost my husband—"

We know immediately and without overexplaining that Katherine is losing the life she has been used to and that the entire session in Dr. Simon's office has been a reflection of that.

Within seconds of entering the scene, we know that Katherine has depended all along on certain institutional frameworks to define and sustain herself; that the most important of these, her traditional suburban marriage, has already fallen apart, and that another, psychotherapy, which has been a significant prop, is about to go as well: "I've lost Dr. Simon— he's asleep. He's actually sleeping. Wake up!" At the end of the scene, he is dismissive and insensitive (though accurate in his understanding of Katherine) as she is pleading for her life! That is what the scene is about: the death of her old order. This has to happen to her personally in order to get her back with Ed. I think I stick to that point without distraction or unnecessary buildup or wind-down. I entered the scene "as late as possible," or at least as late as I knew how to, and got out of it just as quickly. (This collapse of her world is further reinforced by the shocking revelation of her women friends in shot 73 and the chilling attitude of her lawyer in shot 69.)

Making a scene funny poses an added challenge. I have given you the serious definition of shot 65, but having accomplished that level, I then had to make it funny also. How? For one, by playing off some of the elements of therapy with which an American audience is familiar, as in Dr. Simon's first line coming out of sleep: "It's your mother—*my* mother." Everybody knows it is our parents who mess us up, right? The same order of understanding is there about "crazy" and "disturbed" and "the hour is up." This is fairly easy "recognition" humor—our shared recognition of customs, phenomena, public personalities or events. It is connecting unexpected frames of reference. Let me give you an example through a joke that just came to mind. You know Dracula, right? You know AT&T's phone slogan, right? Now see Dracula in a phone commercial saying, "Reach out and bite someone." You recognize the backstory of Dracula and the phone slogan. Putting these together becomes a recognizable surprise—and a laugh. If you did laugh. If you didn't, how about this one? Richard Nixon in the same phone commercial: "Reach out and wiretap someone." Or, Nero, with Rome burning in the background, "Reach out and torch someone."

Self-putdown works. As in Katherine's blaming herself for her troubles. "Am I that boring?" (That Dr. Simon would fall asleep at the most critical moment of her life.) "No wonder Ed left me."

I always find self-putdown more engaging in comedy than the putting down of others. When it works, I not only laugh, I am touched by the character as well. I have always favored Laurel over Hardy, Keaton over Chaplin, Newhart over Rickles, Benny over Burns. Mastroianni over Cary Grant. Woody Allen over Bob Hope and Richard Pryor over Eddie Murphy. I am a fan of all the people I have just named, but I am a sucker for comedy that combines funny with vulnerability and defenselessness.

But this kind of comedy is not very fashionable right now. The central comedy motif of "right now" (and it has, more or less, always worked) is to set up a publicly powerless young Everyman who nevertheless seems to have superhuman powers and who wins over the representatives of established might. Not only wins, but, along the way, makes authority look idiotic and ridiculous. It is a nice, consoling fantasy for the powerless audience and the current kids are loving it, which means Hollywood is grinding it out by the ton. If Hollywood does not overkill, this trend is worth watching. The fantasy contains a strong message of rebellion.

Baby-Boomers, having consolidated their own rebellion of the late sixties and early seventies, have for a while now been turning to personal concerns and toys for grownups in their Yuppied pop culture choices, as expressed for the former in *Kramer vs. Kramer, Flashdance, Tootsie, Terms of Endearment,* and *The Big Chill* and, for the latter, in the hi-tech hardware movies of George Lucas's *Empire* trilogy. But the new kids are signaling a rebellion that cries out, Beat the system, the boss, the book, the boardroom—the powerful. Among its many virtues, mostly Eddie Murphy, I think *Beverly Hills Cop* owes some of its enormous success to its strong appeal to this rebel need. (I have left out three other blockbusters that appeared over the same time period: *Close Encounters of the Third Kind, E.T.,* and *Ghostbusters.* I view these as religious pictures—the first two are reworkings of the Christ myth, the latter deals with devil spirits—the past, old folks, old ideas?—which are first confronted at the New York Public Library—a major symbol of the past, old folks, and old ideas. So, rather than rebutting my theory, I believe these movies affirm the rebellion-to-be that I am speaking of. Their successes—they are all very well done, which, of course, contributes—say there is widespread dissatisfaction with our established gods and religions and the mess we have made of things, which is a necessary precondition of restlessness and which will eventually lead to change.)

All else being equal then, if this trend continues, as I believe it will, since the sense of powerlessness in the young is so pervasive, the Democrats will win in 1988. *If* they cast themselves as the lone rebel against the system. One saw the first blush of this in Gary Hart, but he turned out to be the wrong man in the wrong year, and Reagan himself had coopted the role of the Lone Ranger. By 1988, Reagan will look the epitome of establishment and boss—and goodbye. Bush, Baker, Dole, and the other Republicans will not fill his boots. Keep in mind that the Beatniks, James Dean, and Sal Mineo in the Eisenhower fifties presaged first Kennedy, then the temblors that followed.

What has this got to do with television and television writing? You can bet that programmers in their zeal to follow (not lead) societal currents *(Beverly Hills Cop),* whether they understand the underlying phenomenon or not, are right now trying to fashion such "rebel" shows and movies. You, of course, want to be part of this action, though I do think it is too soon to push along this line in television. Remember, the Baby-Boomers constitute the bulk of the television audience, and now that they are parents and heads of households, they are watching "Bill Cosby" and "Kate

& Allie" and the consumer-porn soaps, "Dynasty," "Dallas," et al. The "rebel" shows—the rebel comedies—should, moreover, be just right for television in the late eighties and early nineties, as today's teen-agers become more attractive consumers to the advertisers, and the Yuppies get the wind knocked out of them. (Already, the Silicon Valley is showing itself not to be The Garden of Eden.)

Getting back to comedy, another technique is used in shot 65—counterpoint: Katherine's extreme mental pain playing against Dr. Simon's detachment. Simon's detachment in contrast to Katherine's eddying ego is sharpened by a small but conscious and, I think, effective device. Out of seven sides (speeches) in the scene, Simon, in six of them, calls Katherine by her first name. Ordinarily, when characters in a script call each other by name this much, it is a sure sign of amateur writing, the writer not trusting the audience (nor himself) to know or to remember the characters without this constant (and annoying) reminder.

But in the case at hand, Simon wants to assert his authority and promotes that by talking to Katherine as though she is a child. That is his view of their relationship. His condescending repetition of her name works to solidify this perception of Simon's—and our sympathy for Katherine's turmoil. There are other people who, to gain your confidence, establish a kind of shotgun friendship and disarm you, overwork this first-name business as well, which would justify its excessive usage in a script in order to depict them accurately: Salesmen—of the used-car stripe—stewardesses, and politicians being interviewed on television: "Well, gosh, Sam, Ted, Barbara, Peter, Tom, Dan—nobody can say—Sam, Ted, Barbara, Peter, Tom, Dan—we meant to lose—Sam, Ted, Barbara, Peter, Tom, Dan—248 Marines in Lebanon—Sam, Ted, Barbara, Peter, Tom, Dan—David, Bryan."

Speaking the unspeakable but the clearly thinkable usually gets a laugh. Who would ever expect a psychotherapist to say Dr. Simon's last line in shot 65? "Every week it's something, Katherine." "Being inside" Dr. Simon, I was certainly thinking it in this situation. I was feeling the overload of angst this man hears from his patients everyday. I knew that as a psychotherapist I was professionally trained to keep a distance, but I was also feeling that I could not get too excited over each individual calamity in any case, if I wanted to survive. I knew I had been listening to this nice woman for a long time and had become lulled over these sessions to the music of her typical small, middle-class tics and twitches, so that today, because I have taken an antihistamine for a cold and fallen asleep, I miss her suicide reference and the entire import of her problems after she has wakened me. Shrinks are human too. I want simply to get her out of the office, so I say what I am feeling, which comes out a shock—and a laugh.

Look, if a lifeguard saves a drowning woman, it isn't funny. If, however, just before he gives her mouth-to-mouth, as she is lying there blue and unbreathing on the beach, he says to her, "There's something you should know—I have trouble with commitment," it begins to be.

What all of these examples have in common is surprise. That is the common denominator of comedy. You have to turn a thing we know or expect on its head. But, it has to be a turn of degree—180, to be sure—and not of kind. It should only surprise the audience (and the other characters, perhaps), never the character saying or doing it. Otherwise, the audience won't believe it. In the opening number of the remake of *To Be or Not to Be*, you laugh at Mel Brooks and Anne Bancroft as Polish performers in Poland in 1939, doing Fred Astaire and Ginger Rogers and singing an American pop song in Polish, because it is such a silly and delicious surprise. But you believe it, because their characters believe it. They are seriously doing what song-and-dance people all over the world were doing in 1939, since Astaire and Rogers and American music were so hot.

The last surprise in shot 65 was on me. The line that I least expected to got the biggest laugh, in three different screenings. It is Dr. Simon's line that follows Katherine saying, "Dr. Simon, my life is spilling out and you were sound asleep."

Then he says, "not sound, Katherine, fitful."

Comedy. Go figure. Hey, how 'bout this one? Hitler is on the horn in a beer hall in Munich: "Reach out and putsch someone."

William Goldman's advice applies, of course, to action as well as words. The abiding concept for pictures and words is compress. Compress. Compress. Do I need this scene at all? If I do, what do I need it to say and to show? How can I use it to get to the next scene or act or the ending? Have I made the scene short, crisp—essential?

I think these questions have always been worth asking in any literary form. I admire poets—good ones—for working most fiercely among writers to achieve this principle of reduction. A word, a line, a stanza can stand for volumes, giving away nothing in insight or complexity.

To ask yourself these questions nowadays is more essential than ever. The spirit of the times, the fashion is contained in "the bottom line." Net-net. And velocity is virtue. That explains in part why I was able to design a revved-up "Good Morning America" that would overtake an ambling "Today" show, though now the breakfast tables may be turning. The number of segments was increased, and none ran longer than five and a half minutes. Most segments varied from one to two to two and a half to three. The audience wanted that kind of coverage and that kind of pacing, especially in the morning. At the same time, the audience never felt rushed, I think, because at the center was the comforting, deliberate ease of David Hartman. Peace of mind is an equally strong yearning in our hyper-times. Whether it is because people catch on faster or are less willing to pay attention for any length of time, that they demand to get things fast, I am not sure. Something of both, I believe. This is especially true with entertainment drama form. The audience is very hip, having seen so much television and movies. They know the way. The twists, the climbs, descents, and straightaways. They know the fauna too. You have got to keep the viewers moving or you'll lose them.

I recognize all of this as a hard fact of American life, but in many ways it is a reality that saddens me. There are so many human and earthly riches that need more time in order for us to comprehend and savor them. Or to savor them and to be awed by the mysteries. These get lost or truncated in our speeding culture. We are a more ignorant, less feeling society because of it. We know too much about tax shelters and too little about shelters of the spirit.

Still, I am a creature of my place and time. If I have a scene that runs even four or five pages, I get nervous. Can I hold you? I get nervous looking at any page that has a block of more than six or seven lines in a single speech. Will you tune out? You can imagine my anxiety, then, about one scene in *Drop-Out Father.* Look up shot 55. It is two full pages of Ed McCall ruminating. I was not alone in my doubt. Everyone who *saw,* even without reading, those pages would make a rote response: "You're gonna have to cut Ed's speech in 55." I myself was so conditioned that I never disagreed, but each time I sought to edit the speech, something inside me resisted. As large as it loomed on paper, there was no fat in it for me. Eliding it was putting saw to bone. Long or not, I argued to myself, this speech has to be an exception. It works. I need it. It is what the whole damn movie is about. It'll hold. I know it. I think.

I needn't have worried. Dick Van Dyke, a superb dramatic as well as comedy actor, gave me everything I wanted from the speech and more than I had any right to expect. He was gentle, intelligent, moving, and unmawkish. As willing to expose himself as the character was compelled to get back to first truths, no matter what the risks or consequences. Van Dyke's emotional honesty in this long monologue set up the burning of the credit cards that comes at the end of the scene (and the act), so that it got not only the expected (and easy) laugh but a stabbing depth of serious feeling as well. I saw many viewers at screenings sitting moist-eyed—even crying—and laughing at the same time. I thank Van Dyke for giving me both, which is what I was feeling when I wrote it.

In no way are you to take economy of line literally. Goldman does not mean for you to do that either. Not every speech or scene must be reduced to three-frame cuts and muteness. Drama is not MTV. While it worked for him, if everything were leveled to "yup" and "nope" and Gary Cooper, our film and television literature would be a desert of feeling and understanding. Rather think Paddy Chayefsky. I think no screenwriter in our time has combined such disciplined selection of observation with such precise power of language and moral legitimacy. His work, particularly in *Marty, Hospital,* and *Network,* defines Mark Twain's dictum that "the difference between the right word and the almost right word is the difference between lightning and the lightning bug." You know this applies not merely to words but to every aspect of writing television drama.

Let's move on to two other aspects: incident and detail.

Who can forget "our song" from *Casablanca*? Paul Henreid lighting two cigarettes at the same time and handing one to Bette Davis? The two contrasting lobster scenes in *Annie Hall*? Dustin Hoffman's *Tootsie* in bed with Jessica Lange? *That's* love, kiddies. This detail in "showing" it is the real thing.

Or on a darker journey, consider *Death of a Salesman*. It opens on stage with Willy Loman coming home for what will be the last time, carrying his suitcase and his sample case. Arthur Miller could have had Willy leave his cases in the car, which that night might have been truer to the character's life, since Willy is so tired, but Miller wanted us to see that tiredness instantly and as though it were our own. When Willy comes on stage by himself, bearing the nearly unbearable weight of those cases, we know the terms of the play immediately. We are to be in the company of a man whose exhaustion is spiritual as well as physical. He is beaten in his soul. His fatigue is permanent and terminal. Those cases say it.

While we are here, let's back up a moment to the business of naming characters. Consider the name Miller has given his central figure: Willy Loman. The boyish, powerless, dismissable "Willy." (I have always thought President Carter was harmed by the diminutive "Jimmy." These matters are impossible to measure precisely, and I am not saying that this was Carter's only problem with the people, but I believe he would have been perceived as being more effective had the populace thought of him as the stronger "James" or even "Jim." Kennedy, for instance, enjoyed two nominative blessings in being called "Jack"—a strong name and a warm name in its being a friendly nickname for John—and JFK, a monogram echo of the residual good-will then pertaining to FDR. I do not want to make too much of the power of names, but I do not want you to ignore them either as usable tools of communicating thematic ideas and character qualities.)

Consider Willy's last name, Loman. It provides an easy journey to metaphor—Low Man, as in Everyman. Also, Loman lacks grab, bite, potency to stay in people's minds. It neither inspires nor intimidates. It is gray, amorphous. Probably the amputated trunk of a longer unspellable immigrant name. The words together, Willy Loman, constitute a small, powerless, forgettable name, which clearly helps define what Miller wants us to know and to feel about this man. The irony is that because Miller's illuminating talent made him a transcendental figure, Willy Loman is a name that is fixed forever in the pantheon of world literature.

Incident and detail. These can be defined separately, but I find them so tightly wedded that I always think and speak of them as one. However, for now, I will try to treat them separately. Incident is defined in Webster's as "an occurrence of an action or situation that is a separate unit of experience." It names "Happening" as the synonym. Every scene in a script must *be* an incident that complements the whole of the script and contributes to our three acts, either to reveal, confront, or resolve the "problem" of the script.

In *Drop-Out Father*, the problem is Ed McCall's middle-age disillusionment with the way he is living his life. Given this problem, I have to create incidents to attend it. I believe each scene in the script has at least one workable incident, but for purposes of analysis, let's examine shot 28. Ed is having lunch with his business colleague, Draper Wright. I have been setting up the script's problem in various smaller ways that have been building into larger and larger ways since page 1. By shot 28 I need a denouement of the setup, the revelation of the problem. I need an act one ending. (Although the scene, in television form, is in act two, it is, in the classic three act form of drama, the end of act one.) Until now, Ed has been reacting to the revelation of the problem. Something must happen in this scene, an incident that pushes him to act on the problem. Something that moves him into act two or confrontation of the problem. The incident I selected is death. Draper Wright's death. This incident certainly works to move the script into act two, but in choosing it, I also get a perverse pleasure out of its being not just *a* death, but Draper Wright's death. What delicious, malicious glee in getting even, through him, with all the health-food/physical-fitness aficionados, as nettlesome to me as religious fanatics, who act so superior when they find out I smoke, drink occasionally, love rich sauces and pralines-in-cream ice cream and believe, from having coughed for fifteen minutes after waking, that I have had a strenuous daily workout.

Death tops the list of a range of dramatic incidents that do ignite changes in people's actions. A problem may have been smoldering in a person for whom it will burst into flames given a significant incident of combustibility such as a death, an illness, a birthday, an anniversary, a reunion, a divorce or separation, a job loss, an exotic vacation or a holiday. Depression, suicide, falling in love, hyperkinetic activity, renewed courage, happiness—the full universe of human acts, states, and emotions can be kindled by such incidents and will burn according to the particular fuels of character and circumstance.

These can be set off as well by what seem to be very small incidents. My personal favorite example of this kind is contained in a *New Yorker* cartoon. A couple is coming out of a Chinese restaurant and they are obviously arguing. The woman says, "It wasn't the egg roll, Harry—it's been the whole last year."

While my choice of incident, Draper Wright's death, may have been malicious, it was not capricious. Nor must such choices ever be. Wright's death is logical—in character. He was an A-Type in extremis—a nervous wreck—rigidly in harness and vulnerable to this kind of sudden and massive trauma. It figures that he would have a coronary blowout. The death of any other character in the script would not have served the purposes of my script's problem and would have, on the contrary, worked against it. Having chosen a death as the incident that would force Ed to confront the problem, it had to be Draper Wright's death. I had no choice, although one can always force a bad alternative.

Wright's being two years younger than Ed reinforces the choice. This sharpens Ed's sense that life is finite and that his own might be running out soon—wasted. Further, despite their differences in style, Ed knows that he and Wright have more values in common than not and sees in Wright's exaggerated behavioral adaptations to these values how absurd his own system of dealing with them has become. Wright's death brings Ed to a crystalline view of Wright's wayward life and of just how far he too has been traveling in the wrong directions. He is now compelled to see if he can, if you will, find his way home. How logically then the next scene came. I have Ed at his house, at least, if not yet his true home.

Setting Wright up as a health-food/physical-fitness freak was simply garnishing the main dish—his death. It was one of those credible 180-degree turns I have described. I did not break the logic. This trendy health-nut salvation fits this anxious, insecure, outer-directed man. I knew at his death the audience would be shocked and surprised and, because I had not broken trust, would laugh.

Sometime after I wrote *Drop-Out Father*, while it was no laughing matter, there was a parallel in the death at a fairly young age of the fitness-jogging guru, Dr. James Fixx. This was front-page news the country over, because it shook for millions what had become an article of faith: Running will keep you alive. What a jolt, then, what a confrontation with personal mortality, what *An Appointment in Samara*, to be faced with the death of a chief priest of this certitude, and to have to know again, as with all absolute truths, it ain't absolutely so. (The running laity felt great relief, of course, when it was learned later that Dr. Fixx had had hereditary heart impairment and that because of this he might have died even sooner had he not been a runner. Whether this latter proposition is true or not, it was widely declared to be true and became the laminated myth of consolation.)

The choice of Draper Wright's death in shot 28 is incident. All else in the scene, in support of the incident, is detail—the minute, specific working out of the particulars.

Webster's first definition of the word detail is "extended treatment of or attention to particular items." It gives "particular" as the synonym. In his own Sisyphean efforts to improve my efforts, my book editor, Ed Barber (you see, it is not just in art that people have allegorical names), admonished me constantly, "God is in the details." This is a pronouncement full of Old Testament resonance and one I have tried earnestly to internalize. It goes right in there with Goldman's "Start each scene as late as possible" and Twain's "lightning and the lightning bug."

Examine the details in scene 28 of *Drop-Out Father*. See if you think I have made good choices. Specific choices. Choices that speak to the script's problem and of the script's characters.

First off, I have placed Ed and Wright in the executive dining room high above the city. This is not an arbitrary choice of setting. I believe the setting says something specific about the script's problem and the characters in relationship to it. In this room, they are hermetically sealed from "life," and the room's décor, starkly modern and impersonal, bespeaks further the alienation of these two men.

Ed has never cared much for Draper Wright and now, in the throes of discovering his urgent need for a new order in his own life, is shorn of his usual controls to hide this feeling. He is uncharacteristically impatient, smokes more than he normally does, and is on his third glass of wine, which he almost never has at lunch.

I give the detail of the kinds of topics that are usually discussed during the foreplay phase of one of these lunches, before the players get down to the true topic of business, and, to show Ed's impatience, I put this material into his speech.

Wright, for his part, is a man who has worked his entire adult life in a field in which the star players are creative types—writers and art directors—which he is not. Because of this, he is always intimidated by the very talented copywriter Ed. Wright's sense of intimidation, of course, gets converted into jealousy, then into resentment, and, finally, into anger. This is, in fact, pretty much Wright's emotional pattern, not just with Ed but with life in general. Since he lives a total falsity, far removed from his nature, he is in a chronic state of anxiety and frustration. Over the years, to avoid this truth and to live with himself, he has tried any number of consumeristic salvations, the most recent of which is his desperate insistence on good physical health habits. To show this, I give him the yogurt and mineral water for lunch and the action of zealously performing isometric exercises. As Ed gets annoyed at these and then challenges Wright's entire way of living (because inside he is challenging his own way of living), Wright's fear of the truth about himself begins to mount. I show this by intensifying the exercises and increasing the number of spoken sports references. I even have him defend his creativeness—"I self-express." I work him into a state of stress so great that he is willing to have a showdown with Ed, an act of honesty so foreign and novel to him that, coupled with his deeper rage, it stops his heart and kills him.

Knowing my man Ed McCall, and having chosen the larger character details of Wright's health kick and jockese way of expressing himself, the finer details of dialogue in this scene came very naturally. It is not a one-liner but a serious critical judgment when Wright chastizes Ed by saying, "The other day you even made fun of Vince Lombardi." It is not a joke but a symptom of the reality of their terms of communication when, at the close of the scene, Ed exclaims over Wright's dead body, "You're only forty-five! You jog—and eat yogurt. Draper—you can't die—it's only the third quarter!"

I think the detail choices in shot 28 work pretty well. I know for certain that they are the best I could come up with. Otherwise, and finally, of course, you and the audience have to judge.

Let me say something about adaptations. Since originals, which offer the least certitude and security to buyers, are increasingly difficult to sell, as I have said, you will be writing a lot of television screen adaptations of materials from other sources. The materials will come from novels, short stories, plays, commercials, songs, books of biography, history, journalism, and science—and true stories. The true stories may have surfaced in newspapers, magazines, "60 Minutes," "20/20."

Each of these sources presents an array of problems and opportunities. If the source is a novel, the novel may range from the barely disguised screenplay-type to one such as *The Old Man and the Sea,* in which most of what counts is in the interior consciousness of the old man. A play may be rich in language and ideas but devoid of action. A history piece may present a splendid story but lack detail and character psychology and motivation. True stories may present fascinating character and incident, even detail, but, as with life always, be messy in structure and through line, having no clear beginning, middle, and end. Obviously, some of these materials will be easier to adapt than others, and all seem to present some easing of the writer's tasks in that they provide a theme, a story or concept, characters' names and biographies, milieu, and plot points. Frequently, however, these "givens" can make the tasks more difficult, since they inhibit the freer choices available in pure invention.

Either way, when you are writing an adaptation script, you must adhere to all the elements I have been writing about. You must identify the story's problem, set forth its revelation, confrontation, and resolution. You must provide exposition, plot points, action, character, incident and detail and dialogue. You must approach the material not as it is but as it is usable according to these movie form strictures. You are not writing a novel, a short story, a play, a history, or a true life. You are writing a screenplay, which is only *based* on one of these. You must treat this base material as though it were merely some of the steps I have spoken of in the evolution of an original work—parts of the process that you would have had to go through in any case, except now these have been done or lived for you by someone else. Certainly, some of these source materials will have loomed larger in the public mind than others—millions of people know *Gone with the Wind* or *Thornbirds* as a book, for instance—and because of this you will be under obligation to be true to the needs of this prior form. Or, you may be bound by factual or legal considerations. Weighing these necessities as you must, resist as much as you can a wooden conformity to them. You must not allow yourself to become enslaved to the dictates of the material in its previous form. I am not saying throw out Scarlett and Rhett or the facts of *The Killing Fields,* or the spirits of these stories, but I am saying judge them and select from them as characters and details for a screenplay rather than for a novel or a real life. Represent them with the same or applicable truths—the qualities that must have made these source materials desirable for adaptation in the first place—but apply the techniques of the screen, which are different from those of the earlier forms.

In its simplest example, these other forms can succeed by telling; a television movie can only tell by showing. Everything must be seen or externalized. That which in other forms may be vital from within the minds of people must be converted into people's actions or spoken thoughts in film, or must be sacrificed. Also, a movie handling of the material must be accomplished in a finite time frame. In most cases this demands cutting and compression, but it sometimes means adding, as in the case of Ernest Hemingway's very lean account of *The Killers*.

You must be savage in modifying some characters, dropping others, or, with others still, making composite figures. You will have to invent new scenes and characters. You will have to throw out or adapt narrative and dialogue descriptions of visuals and actions, when these visuals and actions can be seen rather than described. A life in life or in a book may be extraordinarily complex and abound with attendant personalities, incidents, and details. You can use no more than a few of these in a film. You must try to select the key characters, moments, incidents, and details, those that will make the best movie (and hope that these stand in for the truths of the greater reality).

For instance, you do not have to know everything Remarque tells you about his soldiers' sensitivities and the obscene carnage in which they are participating in *All Quiet on the Western Front*, if you can come up with what the film of it showed: a soldier's disembodied hand reaching out of the trench to grasp a flower lying on the lip of the field in no man's land—then the sound of a shot, the hand twitches and falls still—the flower lost. You know in seconds of the beauty that is possible in life and the horror that can kill it.

Be wary of taking book dialogue whole into your script. There is read speech, which is often quite different from spoken speech. While the dialogue in a book may seem and be right to the eye, it can be terrible to the ear. The test, again, is to read this book dialogue out loud.

I have done only one screen adaptation thus far. A novel, *Paper Castle*, the one I mentioned earlier that became *He's Fired, She's Hired*. (I have been through the reverse process. *Love Is Not Enough* was a screenplay that I used to build the novel.) "Castle" was 387 manuscript pages—not a giant book—that had to become 110 script pages. More importantly, the book had to become a television movie. Every choice I made was dictated by the hook or concept that had first grabbed CBS's interest: a married couple who want to maintain an upper-middle-class life-style even after the middle-aged husband gets fired from his high-paying job and do so by devising a scam to get the wife a good job in the husband's field. As it did not in the novel, a form that permits more distractions, detours, flashbacks, reminiscences, and other inner thoughts than film, everything I selected had to complement that basic idea and cleanly drive it forward.

For instance, there is in the book an entire substory of the couple's black maid, who makes her own stylish clothing. She goes onto a game show, wins, and with the prize money founds her own designer label. I liked this black maid and the fact that she was so atypical, but there was no way I could stop and tell that story. I kept her in the script but showed her talent quickly (I made her a jazz pianist) and her independence in ways that could be integrated with and help propel the script's main problem. I did not even deal with how she and the heroine-wife, who had become very close personal friends, had met, or how their relationship had evolved, which took up several pages in the book. I did retain their close friendship by devising scenes that showed this as it pertained to the script's problem, the husband being fired and the wife being hired. For example, the maid and the husband have a scene in which it is important that they get to know each other to serve the "confrontation" needs of the script. The maid until now has disapproved of the husband, seeing him only as a self-concerned, workaholic, absentee family member; the husband, now forced to stay at home, knows nothing about the maid, and she has been right about him. As they warm to each other, the husband apologizes to the maid for knowing so little about her. The maid says, "You're wife knows it all. We talk—a lot. We're best friends." The husband says, sheepishly, "Then I guess you know about me." The maid says, "She sees a lot of good in ya." In three lines, we know of her personal friendship with the wife, her opinion of the husband, and her independence as expressed in her blunt speech.

A couple of other things about this maid character. Small things maybe, but very important to me. Black maids are such a widespread indictable reality in American society and have been seen so often on the screen that you are always in danger of making one hackneyed in a script. I know they exist in life, and I know the suppressed anger and frustration that manufacture the fat, but I just could not serve up another Aunt Jemimah-type maid with a "nigger" name. In the book, she was "big-boned" and named "Mayflowers." Judy Rand, the author, had space and time in the novel to give the character depth and scope, thus keeping her from being a cliché, but I would not be able to do that in the script and was afraid I would end up with only another fat lady with a fatuous name. It is not that I wanted to censor reality. I wanted to present the real sense of the richer character Ms. Rand had written. I didn't want the audience to be obstructed from getting to know this more complex character by its own conditioned reflexes to fat black media maids. Sometimes you have to alter a life truth, when it has been over used, into a movie truth. The movie truth may be a life rarity or even a falsity, but it will seem like a life reality because it is fresh and the audience can experience it openly without precondition.

As the writer, I insisted in the film directions that the maid specifically not be fat, and I changed her name to Serena. I thought Serena stayed in the tradition of how many black women are named without at the same time being ridiculous or demeaning. The name also spoke to me of the wise and stablizing influence the character has on the family in its crisis.

Sharing my feelings, Ann Shanks, the producer of the movie, was vig-ilant in protecting the casting of this part (as she is in casting all parts, large and small). We were blessed when the very talented, very powerful Nov-ella Nelson was available to take the role. In her capable hands, the black maid was anything *but* "another mammy maid."

There are two more challenges in *Paper Castle* I want to tell you about. First, before either, the exposition, or back story.

There are two lead characters, the husband and the wife. The husband has announced to the advertising trade press (he has been the creative director of an agency) that he has resigned from his job, though really he has been fired. (Most organizations will abet significant employees in this face-saving lie.) He has *said* that he wants to write a book. He has gotten three months' severance pay, so the family will not starve immediately. The husband does sent out résumés and make phone calls, but he knows that at his age (forty-eight) and salary level (100 thousand) nobody is going to rush to hire him. He begins to convince himself that maybe he can make some money by writing a book—a thriller—but that he and his family will have to sell their house and change their super-charged consumer life in order to survive. He wants to move to Vermont. "Vermont-Vermont?" the wife says, "And run a motel or something?" Oh no. She is set up as having been a very poor girl who now cherishes deeply her home and upper-middle-class existence. She will *not* give it up. What to do? *I'll* get a job," the wife says. At first the husband scoffs at her ability to work or earn, but then he hits on the idea that she could work—could do what he does—or did. She is younger (thirty-eight); she is a woman, and women always get paid less. Someone might hire her if they can fake an employment résumé, a body of work, and an unmarried biography for her. She will "front" the copywriter's job and he will do the work for her from home, which means that even if she only makes half what he did, at least they can cover the mortgage, while he tries to write a book.

They have to approach someone in advertising who has respect for the husband but whom the husband has not seen for a while, which means that that someone may have bought the story he gave to the press as to why he left the agency. That someone is someone he can approach to get his wife—now not his wife but his advertising "protégé"—a job. The scam works. The comedy comes in how the husband and wife each respond to their new situations, and in some close calls of their scam being uncovered, and then, finally, in getting caught and getting out of getting caught. The happy ending.

The details of this backstory and the scam are critical information for the audience to have and to understand, so that it can enjoy the confron-tational details and the details of the resolution to come. All of this took—I've forgotten for sure—but at least fifty to sixty pages to set forth in the novel. I would have to compress it to ten at most. Furthermore, unlike a book, I could not have the couple sitting around discussing it. What a boring picture that would be. I had to have things happening—visual action. To solve the problem, I hit on the idea of using a "flash-forward," the term for incidents that take place in future time. The husband begins to describe his plan for the scam and for what he and his wife will do. This is in the present. I continue this present time narration in the voiceover soundtrack, as the picture dissolves from the couple in the present to the wife in a montage of scenes in future time, "acting out" what is being verbally narrated. This technique permitted me to compress information and time, which advanced the story quickly. It also permitted me to make the visuals much more varied, energetic, and entertaining, without sacrificing what the audience had to know.

Here it is, beginning at shot 28 in the final script. It came in at eight script pages.

26   CONTINUED:

                          ANABELLE
              Emily says I should get a job.

                          SERENA
              Doing what?

                          ANABELLE
                        (shrugs)
              Retailing, maybe.

                          SERENA
              No.

                          ANABELLE
              No?

                          SERENA
              You're a buyer, not a seller.
              Oh, he left you a note. Wants
              you to have lunch with him out
              there.

                                                        CUT TO:

27   EXT. GARAGE STUDIO—DAY

CAMERA, SLOW ZOOM IN, as Serena talks.

                          SERENA (V.O.)
                        (cont'd)
              Amazing what he's done to the
              place in two months. Weather—
              stripped the windows, painted
              the walls, stained the floors,
              put in track lighting--filing
              cabinets, desk, chairs, a couch--
              still looks like a slum.

28   INT. GRIER HOUSE, ALEX'S STUDIO ABOVE GARAGE – NOONISH

Alex is seated before a word processor on his desk. He is
just finishing the page we SEE on the video screen, which is
titled ALEX GRIER'S SUICIDE BUDGET.* (Actual info for this
is at the end of the script.) He hits the print—out button
after we and he have read the screen. As the machine begins
to print out, he gets up and goes to a Mr. Coffee. Pot is empty.
He and we SEE a manila folder lying next to the pot, marked:
UNTITLED THRILLER by ALEXANDER GRIER; DO NOT TOUCH. . He picks
it up by one corner and when it opens, nothing falls out.
There is nothing in it. He walks the folder back to the desk
and shoves it into the center drawer.

                                              (CONTINUED)

28   CONTINUED:

Anabelle pushes open the door with her foot and enters. She
is carrying a large lunch tray. She refers to the print-out
action.

                    ANABELLE
          What's that? Does your James
          Bond solve it all with a computer?

Alex, when the print-out machine now clicks off, rips off
the paper and hands it to Anabelle, who has set down the tray.

                    ANABELLE
                  (reading)
          What is this? Suicide budget?

                    ALEX
          It's a print-out of our income
          and out-go for this year--with
          a salary. And next year--which
          is only ten months away--without
          a salary. Alive, I'll be deeper
          in debt than Brazil, maybe all
          of South America. Ah, but dead--
          you and the children would have
          my profit-sharing, social security
          and four hundred thousand dollars
          in life insurance. Twice that if
          I can make it look accidental.
          Hence, the title: ''Suicide Budget.''
          What's for lunch?

                    ANABELLE
          These figures can't be right.

                    ALEX
          I'm deeply moved by your reaction.
          Listen, Belle, we're going to have
          to sell the house.

                    ANABELLE
          Then we'd better make it a suicide
          pact. I'm not moving.

                    ALEX
                  (holding it up)
          I'd like you to read this prospectus
          from Vermont.

                    ANABELLE
                  (not taking it)
          Vermont-Vermont?

                                      (CONTINUED)

168

28   CONTINUED:

> ALEX
> (still with the brochure)
> It's called Vermont Business
> Opportunities.

> ANABELLE
> Oh, no. I'm not going to
> Vermont. What and run a motel
> or something? I'm not going
> anywhere. Our home is here.

> ALEX
> Read those figures, then tell
> me you've got a better idea.
> What difference does it make
> anyway, where we live? As
> long as we're all together?

> ANABELLE
> It makes all the difference.

> ALEX
> What happened to ''Till Death Do
> Us Part''?

> ANABELLE.
> That's death, not Vermont. This
> is my home. Our home. The only
> one I ever wanted or want. It's
> my world, my being. There's not
> a room, a niche, a space that
> isn't furnished--cluttered with memories. Our
> children were
> raised here--conceived here.
> And when I die, I want to die
> here.

> ALEX
> (nods, quietly)
> Of starvation.

> ANABELLE
> What about your book? It's only
> been two months.

> ALEX
> You want to see my book?

He gets the folder from the drawer and hands it to Anabelle.

> (CONTINUED)

28   CONTINUED:

ANABELLE
It's empty.

ALEX
Writing a stick-'em-up thriller
turns out not to be the same as
writing for ''Stick-'Em-Up'' Deodorant.

ANABELLE
Okay. You had to find that out.
You can't say you didn't try, when
you go back to work.

ALEX
I've sent out over a hundred
resumes. Thirty-some calls--
mostly unreturned.

ANABELLE
Then I'll find a way to pay the
mortgage--somehow. I'll get a job--

ALEX
Doing what?

ANABELLE
I don't know. Right this minute.
Other women do it. I worked once.

ALEX
You were at the agency for a year.
Twenty years ago. You never learned
to read your own shorthand. You
always put the carbon in backwards.
Now, you have to know computers and--

ANABELLE
Well then, maybe I'll do what you
do--did. How hard can that be? I
certainly know how to sign my name
for lunch. You can teach me the
rest. How to throw darts, three-
dimensional tic-tac-toe. I can
probably find the club car on my
own.

ALEX
Holy light bulb. That's it! That's
it exactly. They wouldn't have to
pay you what they pay me. Least,
we'd cover the mortgage, till I--
then maybe I could write a book, if
I weren't so paralyzed about the money.

(CONTINUED)

28   CONTINUED:

> ANABELLE
> Dr. Kaufman told me there'd be
> symptoms.

> ALEX
> It's fantastic, Belle.

> ANABELLE
> What are you talking about?

> ALEX
> Advertising. You. It's a
> classic. My big idea, finally--
> and you're it. My monument. My
> immortality.

> ANABELLE
> I'm going back to the house, Alex.

> ALEX
> Belle, Belle--sit down and listen.
> Here's what we're going to do.

29   EXT. RIVERTOWN TRAIN STATION – MORNING

Anabelle, among commuters, waits for the train. She carries
a 3/4'' video cassette and a large black portfolio. The train
arrives and she gets on.

> ALEX (V.O.)
> We're gonna make you me and get
> you a job. I'll give you my demo
> cassette of commercials, my print
> portfolio. We'll have to edit
> them--only go back the last ten
> years, since you're ten years
> younger. . . younger. . .That's right--
> we'll have to fake you a background.

30   INT. COMPUTER SCREEN READOUT OF ANABELLE'S ''RESUME''*(*See
back of script for copy.)

> ALEX (V.O.)
> We'll give you a really beautifully forged resume.
> You're such a
> knockout though, you'll probably
> get hired on looks alone. But
> you're gonna need a flashier
> make-up.

> ANABELLE (V.O.)
> Alex, you know, of course, I'm not
> a writer. I'd be scared to death.

(CONTINUED)

171

31   EXT. GRAND CENTRAL STATION – MORNING

Anabelle comes out of the station, amid crowd, and fights
for a cab. Gets it.

>   ALEX (V.O.)
>   I'll teach you. No, better yet--
>   I'll do it. Right from here.
>   Once you're hired, you can bring
>   the work home--or call me from
>   the lobby and I'll write the junk
>   on the phone.

>   ANABELLE (V.O.)
>   We'd never get away with it. Who's
>   going to hire me?

32   EXT. MADISON AVENUE, MODERN BUILDING IN THE FIFTIES – MORN-
       ING

Start on Madison Avenue street sign, PAN OFF to SEE Anabelle
getting out of a cab in front of a modern building.

>   ALEX (V.O.)
>   Yeah, who, who? Let's see, it's
>   got to be a guy who doesn't know
>   I was fired--somebody who bought
>   the story I gave to Advertising Age--
>   about resigning to write and seek new challenges.
>   Somebody who loves
>   me, but hasn't seen me for--that's
>   it--it's not a guy--it's a woman.

33   INT. MADISON AVENUE MODERN BUILDING FOYER – MORNING

Anabelle, at the building directory, finds ''FREDDIE FOX,
3507.''

>   ALEX (V.O.)
>   A woman named Freddie Fox. She's
>   perfect.

>   ANABELLE (V.O.)
>   How perfect? How much did she
>   love you?

34   INT. ELEVATOR, MADISON AVENUE MODERN BUILDING – MORNING

Anabelle looks up at company names, above door, and sees 35-
-MOYNIHAN, MERTZ & NUSSBAUM ADVERTISING.

>   ALEX (V.O.)
>   It was all business. She's
>   Executive Creative Director at
>   Moynihan, Mertz and Nussbaum.
>   She tried to hire me once.

                                              (CONTINUED)

34   CONTINUED:

> ANABELLE (V.O.)
> Why don't you call her for
> yourself?

35   INT. CORRIDOR, 35TH FLOOR, MADISON AVE. MOD. BLDG. – MORN-
> ING

Elevator door opens, Anabelle comes off.

> ALEX (V.O.)
> I'm over-qualified. Only job
> she could give me is her own.
> But you can come in at a much
> lower salary--we'll have to lie
> about your age.

> ANABELLE (V.O.)
> (taking out a compact mirror)
> I'm only thirty-eight.

36   INT. CORRIDOR, 35TH FLOOR – GLASS DOORS – MORNING

Anabelle walks towards glass doors, inscribed with agency
name.

> ALEX (V.O.)
> With your looks I think--let's
> say--thirty-three--and that'll
> be your asking salary. Maybe
> thirty-five.

> ANABELLE (V.O.)
> I liked thirty-three.

> ALEX (V.O.)
> I meant your salary.

37   INT. 35TH FLOOR RECEPTION AREA – MORNING

Anabelle goes through glass doors, talks to RECEPTIONIST
#1. Pantomime that she's got the wrong spot. Anabelle comes
out the glass doors and starts for the other end of the corridor.

> ANABELLE (V.O.)
> I like thirty-five. What about
> the children's ages?

> ALEX (V.O.)
> Make Emily eight and Lexy six.
> Tim'll have to go altogether.

(CONTINUED)

37   CONTINUED:

> ANABELLE (V.O.)
> Alex!

> ALEX (V.O.)
> I'll tell Freddie you were a
> brilliant and talented protege
> of mine. You took time off to
> ''re-evaluate your personal life.''
> Women in business do that all the
> time. You got a divorce probably.
> Yes, definitely. Besides, Freddie's
> a feminist. She wants to see other
> women get ahead. Let's see,
> graduated Ovington College in 19--

> ANABELLE (V.O.)
> I didn't graduate--

> ALEX (V.O.)
> Nobody ever checks. Especially
> there. Who'd lie about that college?

38   INT. 35TH FLOOR CORRIDOR - MORNING

Anabelle goes through the glass doors at opposite end of the
corridor, towards RECEPTIONIST #2.

> ALEX (V.O.)
> Now, the hardest part's the job
> interview. Very tricky. We'll
> go for a mid-February appointment
> with Freddie--that'll give us six
> or seven weeks. We'll work every
> day. Starting now. Okay? Alex
> Grier's crash course in creative
> advertising--or Machiavelli 101.

39   INT. RECEPTION AREA - MORNING

> ANABELLE (V.O.)
> It'll never work. Can you go with
> me?

> ALEX
> No, but by the time we're finished,
> I'll be in your head the whole way.
> I'll be there--in spirit.

Anabelle looks into a large mirror on the wall. Alex is suddenly there, waving.

(CONTINUED)

39   CONTINUED:

                    ALEX
          See? What'd I tell you?

                  ANABELLE
                (whispering)
          What about my name? It's the
          same as yours, you know.

                    ALEX
              (not whispering)
          That's easy. Use your maiden
          name. Anabelle Loomis.

Alex makes an ''O'' with his thumb and first finger, and
vanishes.

Anabelle takes a deep breath, then faces Receptionist #2,
who is reading a romantic novel and does not look up.

                  ANABELLE
          Excuse me. I'm Anabelle Loomis--
          to see Freddie Fox. I have an
          appointment.

                                        FADE OUT.

                    END OF ACT ONE

You have been introduced in what you have just read in shot 39 to the start of the solution of the second challenge I wanted to tell you about. As you see, I made Alex, who was not really there, "visible" to Anabelle—and to the audience. I used this device in several following scenes because I wanted to keep Alex on screen: A) Alex was a star part. I could not have him disappear for long stretches while I told Anabelle's story. B) the device gave me a lot more comedy possibilities. C) the device was justified psychologically. Anabelle was at first very frightened about what they were doing and she was very unsure of herself in the new situation. I put Alex "in her mind," from time to time, which is when she and we see him "pop in" on screen, as her way of reassuring herself. When Anabelle is certain at one point in the story that she has gotten very good at the job, which she does get to be, I get rid of the device. It is a nice moment of her emergence as a person in her own right when in that scene Alex is standing with her in the conference room, "in her mind," telling her how to do things, and she asserts herself by saying, "Alex, please, I want to do this on my own. Thanks for everything, but—" and she snaps her fingers. Alex disappears—"pops out"—and never again returns in this guise.

This device was not in the novel, since, in that form, a major character can stay off-stage a long time without getting lost in the reader's mind. And, of course, there is no major star under contract being kept waiting in the wings in a novel. The device is my own invention for the script, so I alone, not Ms. Rand, must be held responsible for whether it works or not.

The best way to learn about adapting material is to try it. Take a fictional story—preferably one in the public domain—or a real-life story and try seeing it as a film. Try showing it. Take a scene in *Madame Bovary*, for example, or *'Twas the Night before Christmas*. Dickens and Kipling are user-friendly for adaptation since both wrote so filmically. Or, for a real story, if you remember Jeremy Levin, the CNN reporter who was kidnapped by Shiite Moslems in Lebanon and who later "escaped," try writing your version of these events and characters. These particular suggestions may miss the mark for you, but other examples are abundant. As a beginning exercise, be sure to take one that you feel close to and passionate about.

A further suggestion. When you see the announcement of a television movie or miniseries that you know is an adaptation of a novel, say, get the novel, read it, make your own adaptation outline, then watch it on television and see what the adapter did and how that compares with your approach.

One afterthought about comedy. If you have written something that you, the buyers, director, actors, everybody thought was funny on first exposure, don't waver and give up on it later when somebody wants to cut it because it is "not funny." "How could we think *this* was funny?" Since comedy is surprise, of course it is not funny after two or more script revisions, countless reads, several scene rehearsals, and any number of takes. How could it be? But, if the first judgments were correct and everyone can keep the faith, it will be funny to the audience seeing and hearing it for the first time.

Another afterthought about writing. The old inspiration/perspiration ratio. It *is* mostly perspiration, they're right. Every human achievement is "the drudging doing." You have got to go to wherever it is you go to write, sit down and try for it on a disciplined, regulated schedule, whether that careless, fickle, endlessly betraying bitch of a muse comes with you or not. You will learn you do not need a favorite room, either. A favorite pencil, pen, or super-whamo machine.

It is a stupendous high when that muse baby is with you in the rush of an idea, but most of the work and, honestly, most of the good work comes when you are sitting on the hard bench in the stern auditorium of your own emotions, intelligence, and doggedness, building your own doggy shelter, even if you seem to be doing nothing but hitting your thumb with the hammer each time you try. The other side of this is that by ignoring your need for an inspirational fix and sticking it through, even when your bottom hurts and your brain is a Twinkie, you can tease the muse out of hiding. No muse wants to think you can do it on grit, and alone.

That's it. I think I have pretty much run out of things to tell you about how to write a movie for television. Don't be disappointed. No how-to book ever taught anyone absolutely how or what to write. Read the books. I have. In each you may find something you can use—a key, a chord, a concrete "there, there" that helps you in a specific way you would not have thought of or acted on otherwise. It is better still to read scripts than read about them. Best of all is to live a life that gives you something to say. So write. If write is what you want. Write and write and write until it is stupid to continue, which usually means that no one will pay you for it, or until you die.

The best I or any book can do is put you on the road to Oz, but you have got to make the journey on your own, remembering always that the true destination is yourself.

Drop-Out Father

By the time this book will have been published, which should be a kind of period point *30* on the piece, it will have been seven years since, lying in bed one 3:00 A.M. I had the idea for *Drop-Out Father* in January 1979. "The Pure Idea." At the time, we were working through our company, Comco, under an umbrella deal with MCA-Universal, having been brought there by Al Rush, one of the premier gentlemen and gray matters in our business.

The idea in the form of a verbal presentation was first pitched to Len Hill, then vice-president of movies for television at ABC, on February 16, 1979. In those days, we always pitched first to ABC out of a quaint personal loyalty born of my having so recently worked there. Hill rejected the idea immediately, before we had finished talking about it and without even taking the written presentation that you read in chapter 2. "Too soft," he broke in. He rejected four other ideas Ann and I pitched in the same meeting with equal brusqueness and infallible television certiorari. I thought I handled it very maturely. I refused the urge to tip his desk over and never went back to see him during the rest of his tenure at ABC, the technical term for which is called cutting off your buyers to spite your scripts. (Hill left ABC to become an independent producer, of "The Dukes of Hazzard," for one.)

We went to see Deanne Barkley next, then the vice-president of movies for television at NBC. That was on February 20, 1979. Deanne was a friend of many years in New York and a woman who, before she became an executive, had had experience producing and writing television programs—a rarity. She had been a key force, working with Barry Diller, in the success of ABC's Tuesday and Wednesday *Movie of the Week* before moving up and over to NBC. (Currently, she is a vice-president at

Commworld, a major independent production company.) Deanne is intelligent, witty, and, I do believe she will not mind my saying so, a kind of Madwoman of Encino in the way of Jean Giraudoux's *The Madwoman of Chaillot*. She is or was a serial marrier, who once said, cheerfully, "I wish I could pick spouses as well as I pick scripts." Ann and I held the party for one of these earlier weddings at our apartment in New York. We like her.

This meeting at NBC was our reunion, the first time we had seen her since moving to California. Also in the meeting was Deanne's associate, Jane Deknatel, a tall, striking woman out of England, cum *Vogue*, who later moved into Deanne's job, then into David Susskind's company, then into HBO, then into "Indy Prod." Is it any wonder that our contact books are looseleaf? *Drop-Out Father* was third on our list of five ideas—the same list we had pitched to Hill. The first two ideas were heard in full and rejected courteously. As we began to talk *Drop-Out*, Deanne came forward in her chair, tugged at her shawl, and said, "That's it. I like that. Let me see." We showed her the written presentation. "Yes, good, we can develop this. I'll talk to Paul" (Paul Klein, then head of programming at NBC). We did not pitch ideas four and five.

Ann and I had a report that Deanne recommended the idea to Klein on February 26. We were called in for a meeting on March 13 and told we had a script deal. We were to work with Deknatel as the supervising executive on the project. Less than a month had gone by since our first meeting. Two months since I had had the idea. Pretty good. Things were moving.

On March 22, accompanied by Robert Harris, who dealt with NBC for Universal, we had our first "creative" meeting with Deknatel. We discussed the original written presentation and I agreed to a number of changes and refinements that NBC wanted in the outline. "Marvelous," Jane said. "You can start writing—just as soon as the deal is set." Ann and I didn't know it this happy day, but we were about to become a kind of *Bobbsey Twins*-Theseus entering the television version of Minos' Labyrinth at Knossos, to face the Minotaur.

First, the Fred Silverman rule at NBC had gathered its full tempest force, and heads began to roll. Paul Klein for one very considerable one. Then, there were changes in business affairs, the department at each network that negotiates the deals after programming says it wants a project. March became April became May, on the thirty-first of which, in a status report meeting with Al Rush to discuss our various projects, we asked him to push personally on the NBC deal. He said he would. May became June became July and you could hear the rattle of the tumbrils and the swooshthwack of the NBC guillotine echoing out of Burbank, but there were Citizens Barkley and Deknatel still alive, still in their jobs. On July 12 Jane and Irwin Moss, the new vice-president of business affairs, called to say NBC was going ahead. They were prepared to negotiate on *Drop-Out Father*.

(Our deal with MCA-Universal was to end September 1. Since none of the other larger projects—series—that both parties had anticipated were panning out, Rush graciously said we could keep *Drop-Out Father* as our own project without Universal's involvement.)

Our attorney, John Schulman, a rumpled, rapid-talking giant, of tender heart and steely mind—presently general counsel for Warner Bros.—began talking to NBC. By August 7 NBC had submitted the first draft of a contract. By August 13 John had countered with changes and comments. It snowed paper from then back and forth between Burbank and Beverly Hills until, on September 25, John was able to send our signed agreement to NBC. Despite the delays, I read this September 25 date as a good omen. I had gotten out of the army on September 25. September 25 was the date of our wedding. I joined ABC on September 25. We had signed for our California house on yet another September 25. But then, armies, weddings, jobs, and homes are as nothing compared to a movie deal. NBC did not sign the agreement. Talks reopened and another paper flurry ensued until both parties finally agreed to and signed a new contract in December 1979. The script delivery date of the earlier contract, January 11, 1980, was changed now to May 15, 1980.

Oh, yes. I had not written a word yet.

When the news came that I could begin to write, I was in New York, commuting to Los Angeles on weekends, where I was producing (and co-writing) two one-hour specials called *Omnibus*, pilots for a possible new series to be sprung from a distinguished 1950s cultural series of the same name that had been hosted by Alistair Cooke and produced by Robert Saudek. Our host was Hal Holbrook. To get him, I flew one morning from New York to Los Angeles to have lunch with him to tell him about the show, then flew back in the afternoon to New York, thinking long thoughts on the plane about Lewis and Clark, the Donner party, the Mormon migration, and other poignant and painful western treks, and I was out of sorts because I had seen the in-flight movie. These *Omnibus* hours were for ABC and Marble Arch Productions, Inc., then headed by Martin Starger.

Some of *Drop-Out Father* was written in California, some on commuter 747s and DC 10s and L1011s and mostly in a small, sunless room at the back of the Dorset Hotel in New York, to the accompaniment of TNT explosions that rocked the entire building. Next door, they were blasting out hardrock for the foundation of the Museum Tower, which later rose on the site.

I delivered the *Omnibus* hours (Ann was preparing three half-hour television shows and finishing a book) in April and the first-draft script of *Drop-Out Father* on May 14, 1980.

On July 10 I received a letter from Irv Wilson, a sympathetic figure who always seems to me like an escapee from Woody Allen's *Manhattan*, and a friend who had become vice-president, motion pictures for television, at NBC. (Deanne Barkley and Jane Deknatel were gone.) Here is the letter.

NBC
Entertainment

A Division of
National Broadcasting Company, Inc.

3000 West Alameda Avenue
Burbank, CA 91523 213-840-3854

Irv Wilson
Vice President
Motion Pictures for Television

July 8, 1980

Bob Shanks
Comco Productions, Inc.
2237 N. New Hampshire
L.A., Ca. 90027

Dear Bob:

After careful evaluation, we have
decided to pass on DROP-OUT FATHER.
We feel the concept does not meet
our 1980/81 needs.

I truly appreciate the fine job
you did, and am sincerely sorry
that this couldn't work.

All the best,

Irv Wilson

Irv Wilson

IW/vs

cc: D. Considine, D. Gilbert,
    B. Title, H. Cloud, K. Danaher,
    J. Agoglia, S. Maier

I called Steve Mills, a former ABC colleague who was now vice-president, motion pictures for television for CBS. Mills is a soft-spoken fellow Midwesterner with whom I have always had a quiet but honest rapport, a solid citizen, equally dependable in a social situation, business, and, I suspect, in a life boat, were that required.

We set a lunch date for July 29. I gave him the script of *Drop-Out Father* for what is called in the business "a free read." Usually, when a property has been developed by one network, which then rejects it, that network is entitled by contract to get the full amount of its script investment paid back if the writer (or owner) can turn around and sell the script to another network. This is called "turnaround," as in, "I have a script in turnaround." Our attorney had done something better. He got NBC to agree to let us "buy-back" the script for $15,000, a fraction of what NBC had paid for it. We were allowed to keep the additional money and gain unencumbered ownership of the property.

I spoke to Mills a few weeks later. He had read the script and liked it, although he saw some problems with it in detail, and overall thought it was "soft." What this television shorthand, "soft," means is that there is no high concept in the property—no tangible hard action such as war, car crashes, explosions, jeopardy, murder—that kind of thing. No sex. No promotable angle. I could not disagree. *Drop-Out was* soft by this definition, though from my own considerable network programming experience I believed its human values and humor would attract and hold an audience. We left it that CBS would only get involved if a star of their liking would agree to play Ed McCall. Mills gave me the names of three male stars who would be acceptable to CBS. We sent the script immediately to the agents of all three. One of these I thought was dead wrong for the part, another I liked very much, and the third would have been passable. The first responded that he was "dead wrong for the part"; the one I liked, though he was in his fifties, thought the part was too old for him. (He had a male sex symbol/action-bachelor image and did not want ever to be perceived by the audience as a man with wife and children and mortgage.) The third wanted to own the movie outright.

I reported all of this to Mills. By now it was October of 1980. I also told him how I thought I could make changes in the script to solve some of the problems he had with it. He said he would have others at CBS read it to see how they felt. In early December I got a call that Ann and I should join Mills for lunch on the tenth at LaSerre, a popular and pricey saltlick for show business creatures, a short BMW safari down Ventura Boulevard from Mills's office on Radford Street in Studio City.

Others at CBS had read the script and liked it. Among these was Nancy Bein, a young associate/executive whom Steve brought to the lunch. (She is now director, motion pictures for television at CBS.) It was the first time we had met. Nancy Bein is a tall, slender, fine-haired blond with translucent skin and a faint-sounding voice of calm. Her look is delicate in the way of a Tennessee Williams heroine ("Julie Haydon," Ann says, referring to the actress who played Laura in *The Glass Menagerie* when it opened on Broadway), but the look is misleading because there is nothing fragile about her professionally. She is focused, perceptive, and, in her always quiet way, punctilious about the projects she supervises. Ann and I and Nancy hit it off right away when she announced that she liked *Drop-Out Father* and thought it was very funny. It was the beginning of a lasting (and less narrowly defined) friendship with her and her husband John Chamberlin.

Steve said at the lunch that CBS would make a deal to rewrite *Drop-Out*, according to their thoughts about it. Nancy would be our day-to-day contact.

Schulman started all over with CBS business affairs. By January 24, 1981, a "deal memo"—a one-pager, in case you have not been paying attention, that sets forth the major provisions of the parties' mutual understanding, was in place. (The contract got completed and signed in May of 1981.) Ann and I met with Nancy in her office on February 23 to go over her notes in detail on the NBC draft of the script. I turned in the revised script on March 25. On April 7 I met again with Nancy in her office to go over her notes on the revision. I completed the polish and turned in the revised-revise on April 10. CBS had by contract until June 22 to exercise its option to make *Drop-Out Father.*

April 10 became May 10, then 20, then perilously close to June and still no word came from CBS about a "pickup." "Pickup", remember, means that the buyer (in this case CBS) agrees to pick up a script—go forward to make a movie from it. Then, on a Friday, after five in the afternoon, May 29, Steve Mills called and said the network was giving us a pickup on *Drop-Out.*

"I thought about waiting till Monday," he said, "since you might be gone. But I took a chance. Thought if I got you, it might be a nice thing to have for the weekend."

And so it was. *So it was!* Ann and I broke out the Dom Perignon. Prematurely, as it happened. For who knows which and how many reasons, a start date for pre-production and shooting never got set. May became June became July became August became September became October became November became almost give up. We had with CBS's approval sent the script by then to Dick Van Dyke, whom Ann and I wanted. We knew he would be good. Dick liked it and had agreed to do it—only if it could be done in January. CBS had also approved our first choice for Katherine, Mariette Hartley, whom we had met and gotten to like during another show on which we had worked. We had sent Mariette the script. She had read it, liked it, and agreed to do it—*if* Van Dyke did it. (Also, money and all that stuff had to be right, of course, for her and for Van Dyke.) Mariette's representative, Arlene Dayton, said it was not a "deal breaker," but could I rewrite act one to put in Katherine? In the present draft she did not appear until act three. With CBS's approval of how I could do that, which

I thought was a very good idea for the script and for the potential rating if we could get Mariette, the answer to Arlene was yes.

Finally, we got a call from CBS and went to see Nancy Bein on December 2. Could we, she asked, be ready to shoot the first week of January? "Yes, absolutely," Ann said. She would let us know. We went back on December 4. The same question from Steve Mills, who said his production people were doubtful. We said that we were not. We could do it. I will give the production details in the next chapter, but, for now, that day we got a go. The picture was shot in January (with Ann carrying most of the production daily details), cut in February, recut in February and early March, scored and mixed, and delivered in April 1982. Now, we had to wait some more.

We were notified in the first week in September that the picture would air as a special and open the CBS season on Monday, September 27, 1982.

And so it did. Ann watched it at home in California. I watched it in a hotel room in Detroit, where she and I were doing another show. We spoke on the phone afterward and agreed it "seemed okay." The next morning we got the overnight ratings. Shares were in the mid to high 40s in New York and Chicago and in the mid to high 30s in Los Angeles. Not bad. Then the nationals came in. *Drop-Out Father* got a 23.8 rating and a 37 percent share of the viewing audience. According to the Nielsen total audience figure for that year, 117,454,050 people were watching television that night and 43,458,800 of these were watching *Drop-Out Father*. It was the highest rated two-hour movie on all three networks—made-for or theatrical—for the entire 1982–83 season. As of this writing, CBS has not had a higher-rated two-hour made-for-television movie since.

Forty-three million viewers. It had taken well over three years or 44 months or 193 weeks or 1,351 days to get the picture to them since "The Pure Idea."

As an epilogue to the story, *Drop-Out Father* got one Emmy nomination, won a prize in the International Film & Television Festival of New York, and in March 1984 was nominated for a Writers Guild of America Award (the Guild's year is a year behind). Ann and I got gussied up, went to the WGA Awards Banquet at the Beverly-Wilshire Hotel Ballroom on April 5, and heard, with what we hoped were chipper countenances, a presenter intone that another script had won. That final dubious pleasure had taken another 18-plus months or 79 weeks or 553 days to occur.

Why am I telling you all this!? Why am I making you bathe in all this blood over the dam? Because you have to, you must, understand in a corpulscular way what you will be up against. What can happen to you. Or not happen. We were lucky. *Drop-Out* got written, it got made, it got on, it got good numbers, it won some accolades and prizes, we made some money and had a good time with it. Equal effort is likely to have to be made without the prospect of any of these things happening. You have got to know that.

You have got to have other resources and other projects in order to survive—economically and in your psyche. During this time span from idea until *Drop-Out* aired, Ann and I, together or separately, also produced a network pilot, directed a network movie, did three network specials, did nine *American Life Style* programs for syndication, a ninety-minute program and a thirty-minute program for ABC Arts, for whom we were also consultants, a ninety-minute program for CBS Cable, an hour pilot for Warner-Amex, ten one-hour specials for The Playboy Channel. We published two books, bought stage rights to others, "took" over a thousand meetings, had over a hundred projects rejected, and went to New York dozens of times, Europe seven times, and Africa once. Otherwise, if we had been waiting for—depending upon—*Drop-Out Father*, we probably would have gone bankrupt and insane. I do not want that to happen to you. Or, he said blithely, for you to get discouraged, depressed, and defeated. You will get discouraged and depressed, but maybe you won't get defeated, if, coming in, you know the truth of how it is likely to be.

Now. Read *Drop-Out Father*, don't be afraid to laugh out loud a couple of times and I will meet you at the end—in the chapter on producing.

CBS TELEVISION NETWORK
PRESS INFORMATION
TELEVISION CITY
LOS ANGELES, CALIF. 90036

September 13, 1982

Following are cast and production credits for "Drop-Out Father," new motion picture-for-television to be broadcast as a special movie presentation, Monday, Sept. 27 on the CBS Television Network:

ON AIR: 9:00-11:00 PM, PT

ORIGINATION: Hollywood and locations in New York (film)

FORMAT: Contemporary comedy

STARRING: Dick Van Dyke (Ed McCall)
                                 Mariette Hartley (Katherine McCall)

SPECIAL APPEARANCES BY
(IN ALPHABETICAL ORDER):   George Coe (Kannon Rush)
                                 William Daniels (Draper Wright)
                                 Monte Markham (Tony Malgrado)
                                 Arthur Rosenberg (Marty Zimmerman)
                                 George Wyner (Dr. Lefkowitz)

ALSO STARRING: Claudia Lonow (Peggy McCall)
                                 Charles Bloom (David McCall)
                                 Michael Cummings (Bud McCall)
                                 Jacques Aubuchon (Dr. Simon)

INTRODUCING: Martha Byrne as Elizabeth McCall

PRODUCED BY: CBS Entertainment

PRODUCERS: Ann Shanks
                                 Bob Shanks

WRITTEN BY: Bob Shanks

DIRECTED BY: Don Taylor

DIRECTOR OF PHOTOGRAPHY: Gerald Perry Finnerman, A.S.C.

EDITOR: Tom Stevens

SOUND MIXER: Andrew Gilmore

SOUND EDITOR: Sam Horta

ART DIRECTOR: Albert Heschong

MUSIC: Peter Matz

(More)

ADD "DROP-OUT FATHER". . .Matz

CO-STARRING:

Ray Singer (Doug)
Jeff Altman (Harry)
Rhea Perlman (Tawny Shapiro)
Terry Hard (Muhatma)
Jeffrey Richman (Hairdresser)
Bruce Gray (Austin Morrow)
Ned Wilson (Charleton Hart)
Frank Ronzio (Angelo)
Bill Erwin (Grandpa)

FEATURING (ALPHABETICALLY):

Siv Aberg (Housekeeper)
Jose Aleman (Mean Kid)
Dallas Alinder (Commuter #4)
Sandy Barry (Muffy)
Shelly Batt (Gloria Levin)
David Boyle (TV Announcer)
Ed Call (Capt. O'Malley)
Bobby Duncan (Willie)
Israil Juarbe (Jose)
William Lithgow (Dr. Furness)
Marianne McAndrew (Diane)
Richard Penn (Commuter #3)
Ben Powers (Ben Brown)
Celia Wellman (Beth Anne)
Terry Wills (Commuter #1)

EXECUTIVE IN CHARGE OF
 PRODUCTION:

Bernard Oseransky

DIRECTOR OF PHOTOGRAPHY, N.Y.:

Ronald M. Lautore

SOUND MIXER, N.Y.:

Peter Ilardi

PRESS REPRESENTATIVES:

Allan Cahan (Hollywood)
Bob Higgins (New York)

<u>DROP-OUT FATHER</u>

#1310-3211-0805

Written by
Bob Shanks

CBS ENTERTAINMENT
4024 Radford Avenue
Studio City, California 91604
© CBS Entertainment, 1982
All Rights Reserved

<u>FINAL DRAFT</u>
December 21, 1982

<u>DROP-OUT FATHER</u>

<u>ACT ONE</u>

FADE IN:

1   EXT. UPPER MIDDLE–CLASS HOME IN CONNECTICUT SUBURBS – DAWN   1

SLOW ZOOM in from full of the house to upstairs bedroom window
as we hear voice–over Announcer on radio.

(MAIN TITLES WILL BE SPACED APPROPRIATELY THROUGH PAGE 3)

> RADIO ANNOUNCER (V.O.)
> The consumer price index rose 1.1
> percent last month, according to
> Commerce Department figures to be
> released later today. That's the
> news –– and now back to Wally
> Winkler and 'Good Morning, Punk.'

2   INT. SEMI–DARK BEDROOM – THE McCALL HOME   2

ED McCALL is 47, good–looking, but sallow and anxious. He is
lying in bed, sleeping fitfully in his upward mobility. Next
to him is his wife, KATHERINE, 45. She is attractive. She bolts
up in bed, in sleep and says:

> KATHERINE
> (in her sleep)
> Donahue cares!

Katherine falls back in bed, open–mouthed and snoring. Her
outburst has stirred Ed McCall. He groans, reaches out to the
end table for a cigarette in the pack lying next to the clock-
radio from which we continue to hear the broadcast.

> RADIO ANNOUNCER #2 (V.O.)
> LISTEN, FREAKS, You think the news was bad,
> wait'll you hear the punked–out
> weather report. Rain this morning
> from Cape May to Block Island ––
> with a fifty percent chance of snow
> by evening.

Ed McCall finds his cigarette and lights it.

> RADIO ANNOUNCER #2 (V.O.)
> (continuing)
> So, we need a little flash and
> trash, right? Get it on, baby,
> it's 6:45 A.M., Eastern Vicious
> Time.

(CONTINUED)

2   CONTINUED: 2

Ed McCall sits bolt upright.

                    RADIO ANNOUNCER #2 (V.O.)
                         (continuing)
                    Here's Deborah Dee-licious
                    Harry with --

Ed snaps off the radio, jumps out of bed and moves OUT OF THE
FRAME, as:

                    KATHERINE
                         (in her sleep)
                    No, Phil. Phil, it isn't right.

3   INT. BATHROOM – McCALL HOUSE   3

Ed looks into the mirror above the sink.

                    ED
                    Old. That's an old-looking person.
                    How can you be old? You haven't
                    even grown up.
                         (studying his hair)
                    Gray. Definitely gray -- what's
                    left of it.

He starts to rub his hands through his hair, but a pain in his
shoulder grabs him.

                    ED
                         (continuing)
                    Uh. Tennis shoulder. Tennis?
                    Bursitis -- age, decay. The
                    decline and fall of Ed McCall.

He starts to shave as we. . .

                                                           CUT TO:

4   INT. McCALL KITCHEN   4

ELIZABETH McCALL, age 12, bright, pretty, charming, sitting
at the breakfast table, eating and reading ''Scientific American.'' A small, counter television set is turned on. We hear
the following SOUND from the television set. Elizabeth ignores
it.

                    ANNOUNCER (V.O.)
                    Tonight, a night of special specials
                    -- starting at 8 Eastern -- 'Crash
                    Baxter's Nashville St. Patrick's
                    Day.'

                                                      (CONTINUED)

3A   EXT. McCALL HOUSE – DAY   3A

Ed exits house, looks for newspaper and finds it in a birdbath.

3B   INT. McCALL KITCHEN – DAY

Elizabeth at the breakfast table.

Big unrelated laughtrack LAUGHTER and APPLAUSE.

> ANNOUNCER (V.O.)
> A laugh-filled country riot. Then
> at 9 -- the Junk Sports Jamboree
> tests the brawniest, bustiest Playboy
> Bunnies competing against baseball's
> highest paid free agents.

SOUND: GIGGLES and GRUNTS.

> ANNOUNCER (V.O.)
> (continuing)
> Stay tuned at 10 o'clock -- It's
> Randi Stamp in the spectacular
> 'Sex On Ice.'

Big ice show MUSIC.

This following television set dialogue continues under:

> ANNOUNCER (V.O.)
> (continuing)
> That's tonight -- a night of
> special specials -- and it all
> begins at 8 o'clock Eastern,
> 7 Central.

During the above close-off of the on-air promo, Ed McCall
enters. He is showered and shaved and dressed -- J. Press. Tweed
jacket, tie, grey slacks, button-down shirt. He is carrying a
water-soaked New York Times.

> ED
> The kid threw the paper in the
> birdbath again. You can't read Reston
> in a wet Times.

Ed sticks the paper in the clothes dryer which he turns on. He
starts to make a cup of coffee. Again, we hear, in the clear,
SOUND from the television set.

(CONTINUED)

4   CONTINUED: (2)   4

> HOST (V.O.)
> (on television)
> Welcome back to 'Wake Up, America.'
> Our next guest is Dr. Martin Furness,
> a Columbia University professor
> who's written this really
> fascinating -- though I gotta
> say for some of us -- disturbing
> new book. It's called 'Meeting
> the Male Menopause.' Good morning,
> Doctor.

Ed McCall winces.

The following television set dialogue is now UNDER Ed and Elizabeth.

ED
Damn, you seen the lid for the coffee pot?

ELIZABETH
You ought to drink tea.

ED
I don't like tea

ELIZABETH
Coffee causes cancer, I read.

ED
Doesn't everything?

PROFESSOR (V.O.)
Good morning, Mr. Hart.

HOST (V.O.)
You can call me
Charleton. We're
just folks here.

PROFESSOR (V.O.)
Oh yeah. I'm a little
nervous. It's my
first time on TV.

HOST (V.O.)
Of course. Now, Dr.
Furness. . .

PROFESSOR (V.O.)
Call me Marty.

HOST (V.O.)
Yes. What _is_ the
male menopause,
exactly?

Ed puts bread in the toaster. Now he looks and listens to the television set. The following television set lines are FULL UP.

> PROFESSOR (V.O.)
> (on television)
> It hits most men in their forties,
> Mr. Hart -- uh -- Charleton.
> Occasional or severe impotency.
> Unexplained aches and pains.
> (MORE)

(CONTINUED)

4   CONTINUED: (3)   4

                              PROFESSOR (V.O.) (CONT'D)
                    Depression. A terrifying sense
                    that more life is behind than
                    ahead.

The following television set lines are UNDER Ed and Elizabeth,
until Ed turns the set off.

ED	HOST (V.O.)
(to Elizabeth)	That's pretty
You watching this?	frightening,
	Professor. And all
ELIZABETH	men go through this
Not really.	phase?
ED	PROFESSOR (V.O.)
Why's it on?	Nearly everybody,
ELIZABETH	Charleton. Especially
(shrugs, accepting facts)	men.
I don't know. It's always on.	

        Ed turns the set off, goes to a cabinet, pulls out an empty jar
        of instant coffee.

                              ED
                    We're out of instant? Damn.

Ed lights a cigarette, checks the dryer, Times is still wet. Ed
gets whole milk from fridge and sugared cereal from pantry.

                              ELIZABETH
                    Grandpa called last night. He
                    says Aunt Maggie wants to stick
                    him in a home.

                              ED
                    My sister wouldn't do that.

                              ELIZABETH
                    Then Aunt Maggie called. Our
                    share of the home is a thousand
                    a month.

                              ED
                    See? My sister would do that.
                    A thousand?

                                                    (CONTINUED)

4   CONTINUED: (4)   4

                            ELIZABETH
            It's very nice, she said. It has
            arts and crafts and ping-pong and --

                               ED
            He's 80 -- not 8.

                            ELIZABETH
            Aunt Maggie says Grandpa's foolin'
            around with his housekeeper.

                               ED
            No wonder the place is such a mess.

                            ELIZABETH
            He's threatening to marry her, Aunt
            Maggie said. That's impossible,
            isn't it?

Ed is putting orange juice concentrate in the blender.

                               ED
            Why?

                            ELIZABETH
            You know. He is 80. People half
            his age can't -- 'do it' -- can
            they?

Ed has turned on the blender, and, distracted by Elizabeth's
question, has forgotten to put on the lid. Juice goes all over.

                               ED
            Men can till they die!

                            ELIZABETH
            Okay, okay. What do I know?

                               ED
            Too much and not enough.

Ed has cleaned up the juice, puts the juice container in the
fridge and checks the toaster.

                               ED
                         (continuing)
            The toast didn't toast.

                            ELIZABETH
            You cut yourself shaving.

                                                        (CONTINUED)

4   CONTINUED: (5)   4

> ED
> I was going for the wrists --
> and missed.

Ed sees what Elizabeth is reading. Over her shoulder, he kisses her on top of her head.

> ED
> (continuing)
> Well, one literate child out of
> four. That's not bad these days.

> ELIZABETH.
> Being the youngest, I escaped the
> permissive influences of the Viet
> Nam period. My problem's over-
> achieving. You missed my Science
> Fair last night. I won first
> prize.

> ED
> Oh, God, Elizabeth. I'm sorry.
> Honestly. I had to work.

> ELIZABETH
> What time'd you get home?

> ED
> Three. After, I guess. The
> train's don't --

Ed, standing up, is by now eating a bowl of cereal.

> ELIZABETH
> You missed your dream state.
> You're gonna be irritable today.
> You shouldn't eat those sugar-
> coated cereals. Very bad for you.
> Negative nutritional value. And
> whole milk's full of saturated
> fats. How can you smoke and eat
> at the same time?

> ED
> Elizabeth. Give me a break,
> huh? It's early for --

VERY LOUD ROCK MUSIC explodes. Ed McCall jumps in his seat and looks up at the ceiling.

> ED
> (continuing)
> Good God, what's that?

(CONTINUED)

4   CONTINUED: (6)   4

ELIZABETH
Your son David is up.

ED
Now all of Connecticut is up.

ELIZABETH
Can you give me my allowance?

ED
Get it from Mom, okay? I'm a
little --

ELIZABETH
She always takes an extra sleeping
pill when you work late. She won't
be alive till about noon.

ED
(yelling)
David -- turn it down!

The last is said as Ed McCall gets up and exits the room.

ELIZABETH
I told you you'd be irritable.

5   DAVID'S ROOM   5

Ed McCall is pounding on the door. The MUSIC is deafening.

ED (O.S.)
David? Turn it down, hunh?

There is no response. Ed finally BANGS violently on the door.
It opens. DAVID McCALL, 17, handsome and long-haired, stands
there with a guitar around his neck. David continues to play
the guitar as he stares at his father as though his father had
lost his mind.

DAVID
You okay, Dad?

ED
Some people over in Rhode Island
called about the music, okay?
Turn it down.

(CONTINUED)

5   CONTINUED: 5

DAVID
It is down.

Ed looks through the door at David's unkempt room.

ED
The same people do your room
as ransack our embassies?

DAVID
Dad. I need $50.

ED
What?

DAVID
$50.

ED
I can't hear you.

DAVID
I need a new muffler.

ED
We just bought a new carburetor.

DAVID
That's not a muffler. What can
I say?

ED
Say you've found a job.

DAVID
There aren't any. I look.
Times are hard.

ED
When I was your age, I --

DAVID
I know, but -- I can't go to the
Korean War, Dad. It's over.
You like the new ''Endangered
Animals'' album?

ED
(nods, despairingly)
Better than root canal surgery.

6   INT. McCALL KITCHEN   6

Elizabeth is still at the table eating as Ed McCall reenters.

(CONTINUED)

6   CONTINUED: 6

                          ELIZABETH
            My allowance?

                          ED
                    (nods, goes to his pocket)
            Five, right?

                          ELIZABETN
            Ten.

                          ED
            Ten?

                          ELIZABETH
            As it is I barely make it -- with
            inflation.

Katherine wanders into the kitchen like a zombie. She is an
attractive woman, but right now is totally out of it from the
effects of the sleeping pills she has taken. She has curlers in
her hair and is wearing an old tartan bathrobe (Ed's) and ath-
letic socks. She goes to the fridge, takes out the orange juice,
goes to get a glass, pours juice half in and half out of the
glass. Ed and Elizabeth watch. Katherine goes catatonic. Ed
takes the juice container from her hand and looks right in her
face.

                          ED
            Katherine -- Katherine?

                          ELIZABETH
            I think she fell asleep.

                          ED
            Katherine -- listen to me. Wake up.
            Do you hear me?

                          KATHERINE
            Tom Snyder had a woman on came
            back from the dead.

                          ED
            I'm glad she made it.
                    (to Elizabeth)
            My God, you could take her appendix
            out. How can she do that standing
            up?

                          ELIZABETH
                    (shrugs)
            Horses do. My allowance? Please.

                                            (CONTINUED)

6   CONTINUED: (2)   6

Ed forks up the $10.00 as PEGGY walks in. Peggy is 19, a sopho-
more at Vassar. She is in a flannel nightgown. She is very
pretty, but very depressed and does not speak. She pretends to
see no one. She goes to the fridge and takes out a yogurt.

                    ELIZABETH
                (continuing)
        Oh, yeah--I forgot to tell you.
        Peggy's home.

                    ED
        That's why I saw her car in the
        garage last night.
                (Peggy ignores them)
        Is she all right?

                    ELIZABETH
        Of, sure -- if you mean
        Legionnaire's Disease or anything.
        Vassar just isn't relevant. She
        can't find herself there.

                    ED
        I know she wasn't born to be an
        anthropoligist, but --

                    ELIZABETH
        Daddy? You have a cigarette in
        each hand.

He does. He laughs nervously and stubs one out as a tall YOUNG
MAN, not unattractive, with horn-rimmed glasses, enters the
kitchen. The Young Man is wearing a turban and Eastern garb with
sandals. He goes to the fridge and removes an egg. All watch,
except Katherine who is still sleeping. The young man prays
over the egg, then devours it whole -- shell and all.

                    ELIZABETH
                (continuing)
        That's Muhatma. He used to be
        Arthur Emschweiler from Lancaster,
        Pennsylvania. He's from Vassar,
        too. Or was. Muhatma, this is
        my dad.

Muhatma greets with prayer hands under the nose.

                    MUHATMA (YOUNG MAN)
        Peace and earthly patience, Good
        Father.
                (MORE)

                                              (CONTINUED)

6   CONTINUED: (3)   6

>   MUHATMA (CONT'D)
>   (whips out pamphlet from gown)
>   Here, have a pamphlet.

Muhatma continues to chop and eat nuts throughout the rest of
the dialogue.

>   ED
>   Yeah, how are -- ?

>   ELIZABETH
>   He's Yang to Peggy's Yin.

>   ED
>   Huh?

>   MUHATMA
>   Indira makes me whole.

Ed looks around as though he has missed someone.

>   ED
>   Who's Indira?

>   ELIZABETH
>   Peggy. She changed her name.

>   ED
>   That was my grandmother's name!

>   MUHATMA
>   Indira?

>   ED
>   Peggy! Margaret!
>   (thinks)
>   You don't mean you changed your
>   last name? You two aren't --
>   God forbid -- married?

>   MUHATMA
>   We are eternal opposites joined.
>   The Universal male and female
>   in oneness through all time and space. We are --

>   ED
>   That sounds married.

David enters, guitar around his neck.

>   (CONTINUED)

6   CONTINUED: (4)   6

                          DAVID
            They're just livin' together.
            They want to shack up here till
            they re-incarnate, change kharmas,
            underwear or something.

                          PEGGY
            David!

                          DAVID
                 (to Ed)
            How 'bout it, Dad? I need the
            car to look for work.

                          ELIZABETH
            Girls, he means.

                          ED
            How he manages it in a Trans-Am
            with bucket seats is--

                          DAVID
            Manage what?

                          ED
            Do I have to spell it out?

                          DAVID
            You mean s-e-c-k-s?

                          ED
            You are kidding me?

                          DAVID
            You know I can't spell. You bug
            me enough.

    He smiles broadly.

                          ELIZABETH   .
            Cars are out anyway. He goes to
            their rooms. Or they come to his.

                          ED
            Here? In the house?

                          ELIZABETH
            Theirs, mostly.

                          ED
            With their parents there?

                                          (CONTINUED)

6   CONTINUED: (5)   6

                    ELIZABETH
          Sure. Well, not in the room.

                    DAVID
          Never on school nights. Or
          before exams. Can I have $50?

                    ED
          Okay. Have Mom give you--

                    DAVID
          Mom's broke.

David gives Katherine a cheek kiss.

                    DAVID
               (continuing)
          Mornin', Mom.

Katherine groans, still out of it.

                    KATHERINE
          Mornin', Phil,

                    ED
          She can't be broke. She just
          cashed a check Monday for a
          hundred.

                    DAVID
          Yeah, that's what she said last
          night.

The PHONE RINGS. Ed comes out of his shock to answer it,
Katherine starts to topple.

                    ED
               (to David)
          Hold her.
               (into phone)
          Hello? Yes, operator, I'll accept
          the charges. Hi, Bud. Of course,
          it's me. I live here. What's up?
          No, she isn't. Well, she is up, but--She took a pill. Well,
          ask me. You can ask. I'm your
          father.
               (in shock again)
          How much? For what?
                    (MORE)

                              (CONTINUED)

6   CONTINUED: (6)   6

                     ED (CONT'D)
           (long pause)
For--a--kiln. A kiln? Bud,
can we talk about this later?
There's some kid here in an
orange muumuu named--

                PEGGY
He's not a kid, Daddy.

                  ED
Muhatma--Peggy's friend--

                PEGGY
Call me Indira.

                  ED
And your mother--That's not
true, Bud. I _do_ take you
seriously. Bud--Bud, you
made ashtrays at camp. You're
in college to be a doctor!

Ed looks at the phone as he holds it away from him.

                  ED
           (continuing)
He hung up on me.

                PEGGY
He's sensitive. We all are.
Can't you understand that--
bad Karma?

Peggy storms out in tears. Muhatma bows out after her.

              ELIZABETH
I forgot to tell you. Bud also
called last night.

               DAVID
He's found himself.

              ELIZABETH
In ceramics.

                  ED
           (goes to Katherine,
             still out)
Katherine, we've got to talk!
                (MORE)

                          (CONTINUED)

6   CONTINUED: (7)   6

                  ED (CONT'D)
There's a bald—headed Yang in
Peggy's bedroom. She's quit
college. Katherine?! Bud wants
to make pottery!

                  KATHERINE
He can make potty, Ed. He's 21.

                  ED
Katherine, listen to me. Wake up!

                  ELIZABETH
Daddy, it's 7:30.

                  ED
My God, my train. I'm gonna miss
it. Will she be alright?

                  ELIZABETH
Oh, sure. I always walk her back
to bed.

                  ED
You tell Peggy not to leave this
house till I get home and sort
this out.

                  ELIZABETH
Okay, Daddy——have a nice——

                  ED
Don't say that, Elizabeth.

                  ELIZABETH
I understand.

Ed nods, comes to Elizabeth and kisses her on the head.

                  ELIZABETH
            (continuing)
Daddy? The back of your tie's
longer than the front.

Ed sighs, slumps.

                  DAVID
Dad? What about the fifty?

                  ED
            (furiously, into
            his pockets)
Here, take it.
                  (MORE)

                          (CONTINUED)

6 CONTINUED: (8) 6

      ED (CONT'D)
     (hurling money
     at David)
  Take it all. Everything!

Ed exits. Elizabeth looks after him.

      ELIZABETH
  That's not a happy man.

      KATHERINE
  Is it time for Richard Simmons yet?

7 INT. McCALL GARAGE 7

Ed McCall uses a jump cable from a new Continental in the garage
to start up the beat-up station wagon he drives away in. In the
driveway, as he backs up, we see a souped-up Trans-Am and a white
Volkswagen convertible.

8 EXT. ANOTHER SUBURBAN HOUSE-DAY 8

A man named DOUG gets into Ed's station wagon.

      ED
  Morning, Doug--sorry I'm a
  little late. You won't believe
  what--

      DOUG
  Mary Alice left me, Ed--for
  her shrink.

Station wagon exits as we . . .

         CUT TO:

9 EXT. ANOTHER SUBURBAN HOUSE-DAY 9

A man named HARRY gets into Ed's station wagon.

      ED
  Hiya, Harry.

      DOUG
  Mary Alice left me, Harry--for
  her shrink.

      HARRY
  Don't shout. Nobody shout. I
  got a hang-over on a hang-over.

Station wagon COUGHS and bucks, but pulls away as we . . .

         CUT TO:

10   EXT. YET ANOTHER SUBURBAN HOUSE–DAY   10

A man named WARREN jumps into the station wagon.

                          ED
          Warren.

                        WARREN
          God, Ed, where you been? You're
          late. We're gonna miss the train.
          I can't miss the train. I got a
          national sales meeting at nine
          straight up and my kid spilled
          Hawaiian punch all over my
          presentation!

                        DOUG
          Mary Alice left me, Warren––
          for her shrink.

                        HARRY
          Why do I drink like that? Why?

                        WARREN
          Anybody got a valium? We ran out.

Station wagon pulls away as we . . .

                                              CUT TO:

11   EXT. TRAIN STATION, STAMFORD, CONNECTICUT–DAY   11

The train is in the station as Ed, Doug, Harry and Warren and
OTHERS run to board it, through the rain.

12   INT. TRAIN CAR–DAY   12

The car is crowded. The CAMERA SEES Ed McCall and others as they
move through it looking for seats. In order coming down the
aisle, they are Harry, Warren, Doug and Ed.

                        HARRY
                (half over his shoulder
                 to the others)
          My kid was first––first––in
          his class at Yale. Now he's making
          wallets in the Village.

Harry finds a seat, jumps in quickly. Now it is Warren, Doug and
Ed coming along the aisle.

                                          (CONTINUED)

12   CONTINUED: 12

> WARREN
> (half over his shoulder
> to the others)
> This new girl I been seeing can't
> understand why my wife and I have
> compatible birth signs.

Warren finds a seat, jumps in quickly. Now it is just Doug and
Ed.

> DOUG
> (to himself)
> How could she do that?

Dough finds a seat and slumps into it, nods to guy next to him
whom he obviously knows.

> COMMUTER #1
> (to Doug)
> Can you believe it? My secretary
> forgot my wife's birthday.

> DOUG
> Mine left me for her shrink.

> COMMUTER #1
> Your secretary?

> DOUG
> My wife.

> COMMUTER #1
> Wow. I was worried for a minute.

The car is full. Only Ed does not get a seat. He sees, back to
his friends, and is frustrated.

The train jerks, but does not move forward. Ed is thrown to a
stop next to COMMUTER #4, who looks at him eye-to-eye.

> ED
> Sorry.

> COMMUTER #4
> Here. Take my Times.

> ED
> Oh thanks. They were out at the--

> COMMUTER #4
> I'm not gonna read the Times any
> more. Any paper.
> (MORE)

(CONTINUED)

20.

12   CONTINUED: 12

> COMMUTER #4 (CONT'D)
> What's the point?
> Crime. Corruption. Radiation.
> The Russians. Bella Abzug. It's
> too much. I can't take it any
> more. Do you hear me? Hear me?
> I can't take it!

Ed knows he has met a man going mad; he smiles and eases away as
we . . .

CUT TO:

13   INT. PLATFORM OF TRAIN BETWEEN CARS   13

There is a CONDUCTOR standing there as Ed enters.

> ED
> Shouldn't we be moving by now?

> CONDUCTOR
> We're not going anywhere.
> There's been a breakdown--
> all along the line.

Ed McCall closes his eyes and nods in acceptance. A MAN brushes
by him--

> MAN
> Oh, excuse me.

Man rushes off the train

> ED
> That's okay--stop--hey--
> you stole my wallet!

FADE OUT.

END OF ACT ONE

ACT TWO

FADE IN:

14 INT. A STYLISH BATHROOM   14

A MAN'S SILHOUETTE is seen through a blurring glass shower door. The water is on full.

15 INT. STYLISH BEDROOM   15

A BEAUTIFUL YOUNG WOMAN lies in a satin nightgown on satin sheets. She looks troubled.

16 INT. STYLISH BATHROOM   16

Same as SHOT #14.

17 INT. STYLISH BEDROOM   17

The Beautiful Young Woman turns sensuously in the bed and reaches to open the drawer of an end table. She takes out a pistol, modeled on a .44 Magnum.

18 INT. STYLISH BATHROOM   18

Same as SHOT #14.

19 INT. STYLISH BEDROOM   19

In WIDE SHOT now, as we see the bathroom door (open) in the background as, in the foreground, the Beautiful Young Woman gets up out of the bed, with the pistol in her hand. Slinking, she walks towards the bathroom door.

20 INT. STYLISH BATHROOM   20

The Man is out of the shower. We see that he is young and almost as beautiful as the woman. He has a towel around his waist. With a second towel, he is drying off.

                          HANDSOME MAN
                          (calling out)
              Honey? Have you seen my deodorant?

The Beautiful Woman appears in the doorway. We see her through the mirror. The Handsome Man sees her, too.

                          HANDSOME MAN
                          (continuing)
                  Hi, honey, where's my--

                                               (CONTINUED)

20   CONTINUED: 20

> BEAUTIFUL WOMAN
> Try this, 'honey.'

She has raised the pistol and aimed at him. The Handsome Man
sees it and turns. He laughs, but is in shock and fear.

> HANDSOME MAN
> Hey--what's the joke?

> BEAUTIFUL WOMAN
> No joke, 'honey.' Put 'em up.
> Up, I said.

The Handsome Man does put them up.

> HANDSOME MAN
> Hey--come on.

> BEAUTIFUL WOMAN
> It's the only way.

> HANDSOME MAN
> Is that thing loaded?

She nods.

> BEAUTIFUL WOMAN
> I'm sorry. I've tried everything.
> Everything else there is to try.

> HANDSOME MAN
> Honey. You gotta believe me.
> Yes, I am a physically active man,
> but I meant no offense--ever.

> BEAUTIFUL WOMAN
> I love you too much.

She brandishes the gun.

> HANDSOME MAN
> Don't!

She does. She ''fires'' the gun, which emits a spray of deodorant. She fires it into both of his armpits. He acts wounded,
very sensuously. He closes his eyes and grimaces in pained
ecstasy.

> HANDSOME MAN
> (continuing)
> I love you!

(CONTINUED)

23.

CONTINUED: (2)

The **FRAME FREEZES** on the couple. ''Supered'' over the picture
is the word ''GUN.''

ANNOUNCER (V.O.)
Gun--kills wetness and odor.
Gun--for 24-hour personal
protection, every day of your
life--scented or unscented.
Gun--for the eighties--the
ultimate deodorant.

As the editor's marks on the end of the film appear, we--

CUT TO:

21   INT. SCREEN ROOM—VERY STYLISH   21

We see the editor's marks run out and the screen go white, as
the lights come up in the room. Seated there are CANNON RUSH,
55, silver-haired, imposing blue-pin-striped president of
Cannon Rush, Allison & Perkins, a major advertising agency;
TONY MOSCONI, 45, wearing an exotic shirt open to show his chest
hair (gray) and a gold chain. He is wearing large tinted glasses
which darken in the sunlight. He is eating sunflower seeds.
His hair is permed. He is the art director of the agency. There
is also DRAPER WRIGHT, 45, the group vice-president account
executive, who is three-piece all the way, with his vest holding together his nerve ends, which he further controls with
Gelusel; and BEN BROWN, 30, a black version of Draper Wright;
and GLORIA LEVINE, 25, an Ivy-League know-it-all who is mur-
derously earnest and ambitious.

For a moment no one speaks.

TONY
Well?

Still silence. All eyes go to Cannon Rush, as Ben fights his tie
knot, Gloria nods, play-acting deep thought, and Draper clears
his throat and takes a Gelusel. Only Tony doesn't look. Cannon
has his hands raised together just under his nose, as though in
prayer, and continues to stare at the screen.

TONY
(continuing)
Look, we didn't figure to win an
Oscar, but--

A rear door opens and Ed McCall comes barreling in, out of
breath.

(CONTINUED)

24.

21   CONTINUED: 21

                              DRAPER
                    Well, there you are. Good afternoon.

                              ED
                    What's the verdict?

                              DRAPER
                    The screening was for nine, Ed.
                    Nine sharp. Does Bradshaw come
                    in late for the Super Bowl?

                              ED
                    Draper--go pad your expense
                    account. Come on, Cannon. Nobody's
                    gonna talk 'til you do. We all
                    know that. Tony and I think it's
                    pretty good.

                              CANNON
                         (out of his spell)
                    Good? You said good? No, Ed,
                    not good.

                              DRAPER
                    That's exactly what--

Cannon freezes Draper with a look.

                              CANNON
                    It's a breakthrough. A classic.
                    Socially relevant. Frightening.
                    Powerful. Devastating.

                              ED
                    Yeah, but did you like it?

                              CANNON
                    You're a genius, Ed. A brilliant
                    concept. You too, Tony. The art
                    direction is beautifully perfect.
                    Geniuses. Genii. Both of you.
                    What do you think, Ben?

                              BEN
                    I agree, Mr. Rush, per se. I was
                    concerned about the gun motif and
                    the sensitivity to stereotype in
                    the black community, but these are
                    upward mobile success images, so
                    simply substitute the personae, per
                    se, and, ergo, with black actors,
                    it will have equivalent impact in
                    'Soul Train.' No trouble per se.

                                             (CONTINUED)

21   CONTINUED: (2)   21

> CANNON
> I don't know what you said, Ben.
> But--I like it. Uh, Gloria?

> GLORIA
> Intense anthro-socio-psychological
> impact. The concept of the woman
> shooting the man--and making the
> man the sex object in the shower
> is very now--very acceptable.

> CANNON
> Draper?

> DRAPER
> A homerun with the bases loaded.

> CANNON
> We'll have to test it, of course.

> DRAPER
> Oh, gosh, absolutely. You don't
> get to the Series without spring
> training.

> TONY
> Anybody see any problems with the
> Gay community?

All shake their heads no, except Ed who tries to keep from
breaking up. Cannon rises. Draper, Ben and Gloria jump to their
feet.

> CANNON
> Ed, Tony--I wish they gave the
> Nobel Prize for commercials.
> (shakes their hands)
> Multo grazie. Ciao. Draper--
> I want to see you a minute.

Cannon, Draper, Ben, Gloria move to the back of the screening
room. Gloria is last in line. Tony turns to look at her back-
side.

> TONY
> How can you hate that broad--
> from behind.

> ED
> Is multo grazie Swedish?

> TONY
> Per se, mother.

(CONTINUED)

21   CONTINUED: (3)   21

                              ED
              You believe him? He's whiter than
              John Davidson.

                             TONY
              You should've seen Draper. He took
              three Rolaids during a 30-second
              screening.

                              ED
              At least he didn't say 'We got
              this one for the Gipper.'

We see Draper, as the others exit, come back to Tony and Ed.

                            DRAPER
              We got problems, gentlemen.

                              ED
              What happened to the Nobel Prize?

                            DRAPER
              Break your lunch dates if you have
              them.

                             TONY
              No way--I've got a stew from
              Lufthansa--on a short turnaround.

                            DRAPER
              It's your jobs, gentlemen--with
              a lot of rookies coming up. We
              need the big play.

                              ED
              He says he loves it.

                            DRAPER
              Not Gun. The new toothpaste--
              Starteeth. He hates it.

                              ED
              So much for Stockholm.

                            DRAPER
              The executive dining room at one?
              And come to play.

22   INT. OFFICE HALLWAY-IN FRONT OF ELEVATORS   22

Ed and Tony wait for an elevator. A bronze plaque on the wall
spells out CANNON RUSH, ALLISON & PERKINS.

                                                 (CONTINUED)

22 CONTINUED: 22

> TONY
> Ever notice the intials of Cannon,
> Rush, Allison and Perkins?

> ED
> C.R.A.P. I never noticed. I don't
> believe grown men do what we do
> for a living.

> TONY
> Trash for cash.

Elevator door opens. A bent, bizarre-looking OLD MAN MESSEN-
GER gets off, carrying a large package. Ed and Tony get on.

> TONY
> (continuing)
> You rather end up 70 and a messenger
> boy?

> ED
> Maybe he's happy. There's gotta
> be more to life than money. And
> deodorants shot from guns.

23 INT. ELEVATOR   23

Ed is smoking.

> TONY
> You're right. There's alimony and
> child support and analysts and--
> you hung over?

Ed shakes his head no.

> TONY
> (continuing)
> Why's your hand trembling?

> ED
> It is?

> TONY
> About nine on the Richter scale.
> And what'd you do to your chin?
> I've seen shaving cuts, but--

> ED
> It's not easy to kill yourself with
> a Norelco. That's my second suicide
> reference today.

(CONTINUED)

23   CONTINUED: 23

> TONY
> People who talk about it usually
> do it, they say.

> ED
> They do? I don't know what's wrong
> with me, Tony. That's why I'm
> going for a physical this morning.
> You know the truth? I think I'm
> cracking up. I can't handle
> anything the way I used to. My
> heart's pounding. My hands tremble.
> I can't sleep. Concentrate.
> Nothing seems important. I don't
> care anymore. My work, my family
> --my life--have no meaning. I
> can't feel anything. I have no
> feelings!

> TONY
> Then why are you shouting?

> ED
> I am?

Elevator door opens, Ed starts to get off. Tony stops him.

> TONY
> Not our floor, pal.

> ED
> It looks like our floor.

> TONY
> They all do.

A pretty, but prudish young killer WOMAN gets on. She is probably a vegetarian. She looks at Ed's cigarette, as shocked as
though he were exposing himself. The elevator door closes.

> WOMAN PRUDE
> It is a crime punishable by law
> to smoke in elevators.

Tony corners the woman.

> TONY
> But not to have sex. I think I'm in love with you.

(CONTINUED)

23   CONTINUED: (2)   23

> WOMAN PRUDE
> (going into her purse)
> I'm trained for Mace.

Elevator door opens. Ed and Tony get off.

24   INT. LONG, STYLISH CORRIDOR   24

with lots of glass and desks and workers. Ed and Tony walk along.

> ED
> Are you crazy? We could've been tear-gassed.

> TONY
> That's what you really need. Not
> police woman there, but a pliable
> 22-year-old with long--

> ED
> Oh, thanks. I've got a daughter
> almost that age.

> TONY
> (turned on)
> Yeah? You ought to bring her
> around.

> ED
> You're sick. Besides, she's got
> a yin.

> TONY
> A what?

> ED
> A boyfriend--in a nightgown and
> sandals.

> TONY
> Kink-y. You could use my place.

> ED
> For what?

> TONY
> Girls. It's unbelievable how
> available . . . and I've got this
> fantastic new waterbed.

(CONTINUED)

24   CONTINUED: 24

                              ED
          I get seasick.

                              TONY
          Me, too. I take Dramamine.
                    (to a beautiful young
                    thing at a desk they
                    pass)
          Betsy, Betsy--be patient. Your
          turn's coming.

BETSY ignores Tony.

                              TONY
                    (continuing; to Ed)
          It'd tide you over the middle-age
          crisis you're going through.

                              ED
          I'm not having a middle-age crisis.
          Something's really wrong.

                              TONY
          Middle-age isn't?
                    (to another beautiful
                    young thing at a
                    Xerox machine)
          Laura, Laura--make a copy of
          yourself and send it to my place.
                    (to Ed)
          Let me tell you where you're at--
                    (distracted by
                    another beauty)
          --look at that chest on accounts
          receivable. Umm.
                    (to Ed)
          You're thinking--why am I killing
          myself over work that's meaningless?
          Why do I make so much money and
          never have any? What have I
          accomplished with my life? Why've
          my kids turned out to be jerks?
          Is that really the woman I married?
          Why is sex boring? Why do I turn
          now first to the obituary page?
          Is this it--is this all there is?

                              ED
                    (stunned because it
                    is what he's feeling)
          Did I get smashed and tell you all
          that?

                                        (CONTINUED)

24   CONTINUED: (2)   24

                            TONY
              You didn't have to. I've been
              through it. My middle—age crisis
              started at 28.

                            ED
              How long did it last?

                            TONY
              I don't know yet. I'm still in it.
                      (to another beautiful
                      young thing)
              Yolande, Yolande——if it feels
              good, it is good.

Ed obviously disapproves of Tony's behavior. Tony sees. They
have reached Ed's corner office.

                            TONY
                      (continuing)
              Look, Ed. When man has an unlimited
              expense account, a corner office,
              and stock options, and still isn't
              happy, he's gotta do something.

                            ED
              You're right. Something's got to
              change. But what?

                            TONY
              Buy a sports car.

                            ED
              How can you afford a Ferrari?

                            TONY
              I default on my alimony.

Another beauty walks by. Tony follows her.

                            TONY
                      (continuing)
              Tiffany, Tiffany, wait. About last
              Thursday——and the sour cream.
              I can explain.

CLOSEUP of Ed——desperate.

25   INT. ED McCALL'S CORNER OFFICE—VERY ELEGANT   25

Ed enters his office. His secretary, TAWNEY SHAPIRO, is seated
at his desk, watching ''The Phil Donahue Show.''

                                            (CONTINUED)

25   CONTINUED: 25

Tawney is no beauty. She gets up as Ed enters, but without guilt
at being found in his chair.

                          TAWNEY
                     (indicating TV)
               'The Phil Donahue Show.' The
               president of our National Secretaries
               Union is on, discussing sexual
               abuse in the office. Your mail
               is ready.

She stands at his desk. He goes by desk, turns off TV, goes to
the windows to look down on Manhattan.

                          TAWNEY
                     (continuing)
               Your physical's at ten, remember.
               You didn't eat anything, I hope.
               You weren't supposed to. Draper
               Wright and Starteeth is one o'clock
               now--upstairs. Mr. Wright called.
               I tried to move your accountant
               to tomorrow, but he said it's got
               to be today absolutely. You've
               had two postponements already and
               now they're threatening to audit
               you three years back. He's 11:45.
               I told the doctor to rush your
               check-up. I moved your story
               conference on Space Age Bras to
               four. Your wife called. Somebody
               left a newspaper in the dryer and
               your shirts came out printed, and
               a muskrat crawled into your septic
               tank and died. The whole house is
               backed up. The plumber says $900.
               Should she go ahead? Your father
               called. He's getting married and
               wants your blessing. Not to worry,
               they signed a prenuptial agreement.
               Your sister called. She needs your
               signature to have your father
               committed. Then Charlie Schwartz
               from graphics. They think they've misspelled
               Bacayazi on half a
               million billboards. Ernie Dunlop.
               He needs copy approval on the new
               lip gloss, Joystick, and Gary Knox
               from the bank. You're overdrawn
               was the message. Mr. McCall? Good
               morning? Where do you want to
               start.

                                                    (CONTINUED)

25   CONTINUED: (2)   25

                                    ED
               We really do look like ants.

                                  TAWNEY
               What?

                                    ED
                        (turning to her)
               Tawney, could you get me a cup of
               coffee, please?

                                  TAWNEY
               Mr. McCall, tsk, tsk, tsk. I'm
               sorry, but remember the agreement.
               That was a major issue in the
               strike settlement. No personal
               checkbooks, or errands--and no
               coffee.

                                    ED
                        (on the brink)
               Oh, Tawney, for God's sake, come
               on--

                                  TAWNEY
               Haven't you even read the summary
               of the agreement?

Ed walks towards her menacingly, backing her towards the door
through which she exits by the end of his speech.

                                    ED
               Yes, yes, I read it. It's fascinating.
               I didn't see a word about shorthand
               skills or speedwriting even or
               sending out letters with typos and
               misspellings--and punctuation
               because 'it feels right'--or do
               we still think, Ms. Shapiro, the
               semi-colon is the large intestine.
               And there was nothing about phone
               calls to your mother and out of-
               work brother and girlfriends, and
               leaving at four when I'm out of
               town; or reading cheap novels at
               your desk, which is a mess by the
               way; or watching soap operas in my
               office when I'm out to lunch; or
               doodling your boyfriend's name
               permanently into my leather desk
               set--
                                  (MORE)

                                                      (CONTINUED)

25   CONTINUED: (3)   25

                              ED (CONT'D)
                    And--as for sexual abuse in the
                    office, Ms. Shapiro, Mr. McCall
                    thinks you are safer than--
                    Lillian Carter.

Tawney exits in shock, pulling the door closed behind her. Ed
collapses against the door, his face in his hands. He tries to
get a hold of himself. He finally walks to his desk and picks up
the first letter on the pile. He reads aloud.

                              ED
                         (continuing)
                    'Dear Mature Manager: Isn't it
                    about time you thought cemetery
                    plots?'
                         (crumples the letter
                         slumps in the chair)
                    My God, I am having a breakdown.
                         (touches out a number
                         on the phone)
                    This is Ed McCall. McCall, as in
                    magazine! Tell Dr. Lefkowitz I'm
                    coming over--now.

26   INT. DR. IRVING LEFKOWITZ'S OFFICE   26

DR. LEFKOWITZ is ''holding'' on the phone as Ed enters, putting on his suit jacket. Ed has just finished his physical.
Lefkowitz motions him to a chair. Ed sits.

                           LEFKOWITZ
                    I'll just be a minute, Ed. How'd
                    the physical go?

                              ED
                    Your new proctologist lacks charisma.

                           LEFKOWITZ
                         (into the phone)
                    Charlie? How you doin'? Yeah,
                    Irving Lefkowitz. Im gonna pass
                    on that avocado ranch. No, I know.
                    It's just I got a chance to get
                    into this condo conversion in
                    Florida, and, in my bracket, the
                    shelter's better. Hunh? No, no
                    problem. The tenants're thrown
                    out already.

                              ED
                    As Hippocrates said, 'I shall do
                    no harm.'

                                                        (CONTINUED)

26   CONTINUED: 26

> LEFKOWITZ
> Sure I'm still interested in the
> orchid deal. Not personally.
> For my pension plan. Yeah, let
> me know. Okay. Ciao.
>   (picking up Ed's chart)
> So, let's see. Good Lord, Ed.
> What've you done to yourself?
> This blood pressure looks like
> an NBA score.

There is an INTERCOM BUZZ.

> LEFKOWITZ
>   (continuing)
> Hold that thought.

Lefkowitz picks up.

> LEFKOWITZ
>   (continuing)
> Yeah?
>   (punches line)
> Joe. How should I be? I think
> we ought to sell Control Data and
> National Semi-Conductor. Yeah.
> What d'you know about Skin-Vid--
> over the counter? I hear they got
> great pornos for the home video
> market. Yeah, check it out, hunh?
> Ciao.
>   (hangs up; to Ed)
> Where were we?

> ED
> Irving, look, I know it's an
> imposition, and maybe I ought to
> catch you on the golf course, but--

> LEFKOWITZ
> Oh, right, a wreck, you're a wreck,
> Ed. Worse than a year ago. You
> exercising?

> ED
> Tennis, a little. Except with the
> bursitis, I--I can't lift my arm.

> LEFKOWITZ
> You know that Henny Youngman joke?
> Guy goes to the doctor and says,
> 'Doctor, it hurts when I go like
> this,' and the doctor says, 'Don't
> go like this.'

> ED
> Irving, I came here 'cause you're
> a doctor and I feel lousy--just
> flat-out lousy. I think something's
> wrong.

(CONTINUED)

                      LEFKOWTIZ
Really? What?

                           ED
I don't know. You're the doctor--
according to the wall.

                      LEFKOWITZ
You seem okay to me, Ed.

                           ED
You just said I was a wreck.

                      LEFKOWITZ
Could be, I said. Could be. Heart attack,
stroke, cancer. You're a prime
candidate for all three.

                           ED
Will I get a volume discount?

                      LEFKOWITZ
               (checking chart)
This your real age?

                           ED
Yes. Why?

                      LEFKOWITZ
Most guys lie these days. I been
thinking of getting an eye job
myself. What do you think? Ed,
listen, our age, you gotta expect
some aches and pains.

                           ED
My dad's 80. He's getting married.
To a woman 45.

                      LEFKOWITZ
               (laughs)
You hear the one about the old guy
who got married to a young thing?
Somebody asked him wasn't that a
big risk? and he says, 'Yes, but
if she goes, she goes.'

Ed puts his head in his hands.

                      LEFKOWITZ
               (continuing; writing
               out prescription)
Here--get these tranquilizers.

                                  (CONTINUED)

26   CONTINUED: (3)   26

                              ED
          I don't want <u>pills</u>!!

                         LEFKOWITZ
          You don't?

The INTERCOM BUZZES.

                         LEFKOWITZ
                        (continuing)
          Hold that thought.
                        (punches line)
          Yeah? Bernie--long time, no see. 'An
          actress a day keeps the--?
          Yeah, yeah. What're you selling?
          Sure, I'll make a million. He's
          got what? Bernie, how many could
          there be? Sure, it sounds good,
          but how do we know they're really
          locks of Elvis Presley's hair?
          Oh. He was his barber. Yeah?
          Yeah?--

Ed McCall gets up, goes to the wall, takes down the diploma there
and breaks it over his knee.

27   INT. ACCOUNTANT'S OFFICE   27

Ed McCall is there with MARTY ZIMMERMAN. Zimmerman is over-
wrought and overweight. He has a cold. He is going through papers
in front of him. There is a desk plate that says, ''Martin Zimmerman, C.P.A.''

                             MARTY
          Doctors--shrinks mostly--the
          schools, the mortgage, the new roof
          we couldn't anticipate. The cars,
          of course, and the car repairs.
          Heating oil. And gas. We're about
          4000 over our annual budget.

                              ED
          Already?

                             MARTY
          We'll have to sell some stock.

                              ED
          What about the commodities you
          bought? Can't we--

                             MARTY
          I'm still right about commodities.
                             (MORE)

                                               (CONTINUED)

27   CONTINUED: 27

> MARTY (CONT'D)
> It wasn't all commodities. Just
> the pork belly futures. Oy. Pork
> bellies, I shoulda known. Anyway,
> look at the bright side. We've
> got very good tax losses this year.

> ED
> I own pork bellies?

> MARTY
> Now about the audit. It's a tough
> one, Ed. The IRS guy is new, young
> --an idealist--especially on
> travel and entertainment. He wants
> to go back three full years. Did
> you bring the diaries?

Ed hands them over.

> ED
> They really are phonied up.

> MARTY
> I didn't hear that, Ed.

> ED
> Strange system, we all cheat on
> our taxes.

Marty covers his ears.

> MARTY
> Ed, I don't like this kind of talk.
> Legitimate deductions, that's what
> we do.

> ED
> Come on, Marty, be honest--with
> me, at least.

> MARTY
> I don't like talking about honesty.

> ED
> That's the whole point. If
> everybody just paid a straight
> percentage tax, the government'd
> get the same money and we could
> all be good citizens again.

> MARTY
> Are you crazy?

> (MORE)

(CONTINUED)

27   CONTINUED: (2)   27

                        MARTY (CONT'D)
            I'd be out of business.
            Accountants <u>and</u> lawyers.

Ed gets an idea.

                        ED
            How much am I over budget?

                        MARTY
            Four thousand--and change.

                        ED
            How much for the audit?

                        MARTY?
            For me? My fee, you mean? 4000--
            about.

                        ED
            Marty--you're fired.

28   INT. EXECUTIVE DINING ROOM—DAY   28

The room is very stark, modern, rich. Windows look out on soaring Manhattan. Draper Wright and Ed have just finished lunch,
Ed obviously is on his third glass of wine.

                        DRAPER
            Now that's a lunch--yogurt and
            mineral water. You better start
            watching the old waist--

                        ED
            Draper. Look, we've talked sports,
            our kids, my tennis, your boat,
            the economy, your wife's hysterectomy
            --and Tony's definitely not going
            to show. Now, you're really not
            interested in my girth. Let's
            talk <u>Starteeth</u>.

Draper gets up, goes to a wall and presses with his hands against
it. He walks his feet away from the wall at an acute angle. He
is doing an isometric exercise. He looks like a suspect being
frisked.

                        ED
                    (continuing)
            Is the wall falling?

                                        (CONTINUED)

28   CONTINUED: 28

> DRAPER
> Just a little isometrics to keep
> in shape. And alert. Every play
> could be the game winner.

> ED
> You look like a guest on 'C.H.I.P.S.'

> DRAPER
> Keeps the old stomach flat.

> ED
> Talk to me, Draper.

Draper turns to Ed very seriously, but during the scene he continues to do exercises.

> DRAPER
> We got our Starteeth knocked out,
> old buddy. A total K.O.

> ED
> Salute! It's a dumb product and
> nobody needs it. I'm sorry I
> dreamed up the name.

> DRAPER
> Ed, we're not giving up. My gosh,
> that's not the attitude that's
> gonna get us across the goal-line.

> ED
> Come on, Draper. I'm not a client
> --and this is not 'The Wide World
> of Sports.'

> DRAPER
> Some of us still take this
> profession seriously, Ed. Every
> day is bottom of the ninth, two
> outs, bases loaded and me at the
> plate. Maybe I shouldn't say
> this, guy, but--

> ED
> You're gonna bunt.

> DRAPER
> I have to say it, Ed.

> ED
> Cannon told you to, right?

(CONTINUED)

28   CONTINUED: (2)   28

                    DRAPER
          We've both noticed it. It's--
          your attitude.

                     ED
          My attitude? What about my work?

                    DRAPER
          The work is good, nobody--

                     ED
          Good? It's the best in town.
          What do you mean, attitude?
               (referring to another
               Draper exercise)
          Will you please stop that?

                    DRAPER
          We'd like you to care. You used
          to care. You used to be a great
          team man--a play-maker, a leader
          --M.V.P.

                     ED
          I'm sorry I missed bedcheck. What
          else did Cannon have to say? Or
          should I call him coach?

                    DRAPER
          You want it straight?

                     ED
          That'd be a first.

                    DRAPER
          It's half-time and you're down by
          ten big ones.

                     ED
          Oh. Draper, will you can it with
          the jockese?

                    DRAPER
          You don't like me, do you, Ed?

                     ED
          Oh, I don't dislike you. I just--
          we're different, that's all.

                    DRAPER
          We're creative too, you know.
          You think dealing with clients
          is any easier than writing copy?

                                        (CONTINUED)

                            ED
                 No, I know. But look at you,
                 Draper. From what I can see, your
                 creativity is lunch and cocktail
                 parties. See how you're handling
                 it? Yogurt and mineral water.
                 That's not a fully-expressed
                 artistic life.

                          DRAPER
                 Just 'cause I don't drink at lunch
                 --or stuff myself. I have fun--
                 I dream. I self-express.

                            ED
                      (sympathetic to them
                       both)
                 Oh, Draper, be honest--for one
                 naked nano-second, face it. You
                 hate it--all of it. You're a
                 nervous wreck. If you ever open
                 that vest, your nerve ends'll jump
                 out and electrocute you. Don't
                 you see? You're killing yourself
                 --not to mention my enthusiasm
                 for organized sports.

                          DRAPER
                 Look who's talking? Smoking,
                 drinking. Just because I take
                 care of myself. Care about what
                 I do. Because I exercise and jog
                 and get plenty of sleep and eat a
                 balanced diet. And try to keep a
                 healthy mental attitude. What do
                 you do? The other day you even
                 made fun of Vince Lombardi.

                            ED
                 Okay, okay. Let's skip it.

                          DRAPER
                 Oh, no. Now that we're into this,
                 I'm going to finish. You can tell
                 me later to drop dead, but now I'm
                 going to--finish.

Draper suddenly seizes his chest. His mouth goes open. He is
having a massive heart attack. His head drops on the table. He
is dead.

                            ED
                 Draper? Is that another exercise?
                          (MORE)

                                              (CONTINUED)

28   CONTINUED: (4)   28

> ED (CONT'D)
> Stop it, will you? Draper? Are
> you--dead?

Ed goes to him, shakes him.

> ED
> (continuing)
> You can't be! You're only 45!
> You jog--and eat yogurt. Draper
> --you can't die--it's only the
> third quarter.

29   EXT. THE McCALL HOME—IN THE DRIVEWAY—NIGHT   29

Ed enters in the station wagon. He ''buzzes'' the garage door.
It opens. It is filled with Peggy's furniture. He gets out.
ENGINE continues to RUN for a minute, COUGHS, DIES with a WHIM-
PER.

                                        CUT TO:

30   INT. THE McCALL HOUSEHOLD—LIVING ROOM/FAMILY ROOM—NIGHT   30

Ed enters. He is beaten, catatonic, the walking wounded. All
the lights in the house are on. He goes through the living room.
No one is there. He goes to the family room. There is no one
there either, but a TELEVISION set is ON. Turns it OFF. (As he
leaves each room, he, by habit, turns out the lights.)

31   INT. KITCHEN—NIGHT   31

Ed enters. TV is ON. He turns it OFF. He goes to fridge. There
is a note Scotch-taped on the front. He removes it and reads:

INSERT SHOT—THE NOTE

> ED (V.O.)
> (internal voice)
> 'Ed--At my group session 'til
> ten. Dinner in oven. Love, etc.,
> Katherine. P.S. Furniture in
> garage is Peggy's. Will explain
> later.'

Ed goes to oven. He opens it and pulls out a TV dinner. He exam-
ines it, takes it to the wastebasket and dumps it. He turns out
light and exits as we--

                                        CUT TO:

43A. (TO BE INSERTED IN POST. O.C. DIALOGUE FOR PAGE 43, SCENE 31--
THE TELEVISION VOICES)

LIVING ROOM:

ANNOUNCER (V.O.)
On Big City News tonight, Kent Clark
has a heart-warming story about Shep,
the Collie dog who needs a heart
transplant and the generous folk
who raised the money to get him one.
Also--an old man starves to death in
New Jersey apartment. Film at eleven.

KITCHEN:

ANNOUNCER (V.O.)
Tonight on the late late movie--
''Terror At The Convent.''
Be sure to watch as a psychopathic
killer hijacks a busload of nuns
returning from a St. Patrick's Day
parade and holds them hostage at
the convent. Dina Bostwick stars
as Mother Superior in this timely
holiday horror story.

32   INT. UPSTAIRS HALL—NIGHT   32

Ed comes up steps, like Willie Loman.

33   INT. HALL—IN FRONT OF ELIZABETH' ROOM—NIGHT   33

Ed ENTERS FRAME, knocks at the door. There is no answer, but he
tries the door and it opens. Smoke FILLS the FRAME. You can see
nothing of the room——only smoke.

> ED
> Elizabeth! Are you all right?

> ELIZABETH (O.S.)
> Oh, hi, Daddy. Can we talk later?
> I'm right in the middle of a
> science experiment.

Ed nods, closes the door and leaves quietly.

CUT TO:

34   INT. HALL—DOOR TO DAVID'S ROOM—NIGHT   34

Ed ENTERS FRAME and knocks at the door. There is quiet and no
answer. He knocks again. Still no answer. He tries the door. It
is, surprisingly, unlocked. Ed opens the door and sees David
and a TEEN-AGE CONFECTION OF A BLONDE sitting up in bed, beneath
the covers, kissing. Both David and Blonde have stereo earphones on. Ed bolts from the room and slams the door, slumping
outside against it. He takes a deep breath and moves on, as we—
—

CUT TO:

35   INT. HALL—OUTSIDE PEGGY'S DOOR—NIGHT   35

Ed ENTERS FRAME and knocks at Peggy's door.

> PEGGY (O.S.)
> Hara Krishna. Enter in peace.

Ed opens the door. Peggy (Indira) and Muhatma, dressed in
Eastern garb, are sitting in lotus positions on the floor in a
room that is now bare except for grass mats and faded Indian
pillows. They are smoking from a large water pipe.

> MUHATMA
> Welcome, giver of Indira's life.
> What's mine is yours. Want a
> pamphlet?

(CONTINUED)

35   CONTINUED: 35

Again, Ed bolts the room, slams the door behind him and slumps
against it. He then moves on, beaten, as we—

CUT TO:

35A   INT. McCALL MASTER BEDROOM—NIGHT   35A

The lights in the room and the TELEVISION set are ON. Ed enters
and slumps on the edge of the bed. For a moment, he listens to
the television (words to follow). Then he gets up, walks heavily to the closet, drags out a shotgun and box of shells and
returns to the edge of the bed. Methodically, he loads the
shotgun as he continues to watch the television. When the gun
is loaded, he at first rests his chin on the upright barrels of
the gun. Then, almost casually, he BLASTS away at the television set. He is pleased for the first time today, for many
todays. He drops the gun, gets up and walks to the bedroom door.
He locks it, then comes back to the bed and turns down the covers. He gets in bed, fully—clothed. He pulls the covers over
his head.

Words and VISUALS for the TELEVISION set during the above
action:

                         ANNOUNCER
              Tomorrow on 'Wake Up America,' be
              sure to watch as Charleton Hart
              visits Delphi Penitentiary and
              talks to a woman who, in a simple,
              heart-warming prison ceremony,
              will marry the man who's serving
              3 to 15 for raping her.

              Then—on everybody's favorite
              game show—your happy-go-lucky
              host, Dickie Luft, will try to
              give away $5000 in cash and two
              free weeks in Hawaii to the parents
              and kids of divorce who tell it all
              on 'Family Secrets.'

              Then, in the afternoon, on America's
              number one continuing drama, Luke
              learns Lydia thinks she's pregnant
              by another man, while Laura's on
              her idealistic way to Poland. At
              2:30 Eastern time—on 'Love In
              The Wind.'

              That's tomorrow—
                              (MORE)

                                              (CONTINUED)

35A   CONTINUED: 35A

ANNOUNCER
'Wake-Up America,' 'Family Secrets'
and the award-winning 'Love In The
Wind.'Stay-at-home, play-at-home television
entertainment for the entire family.
And its free.

NEW ANNOUNCER
Most people who suffer from
irregularity also know the
agonizing pain of throbbing
headache. Now-----for the millions
all over America who endure this
double agony, there's relief in a
single tablet. The new Omni-----
an amazing scientific breakthrough.
Be rid of the double trouble--
fast and gentle, like these
satisfied users.

ANOTHER VOICE
It really works.

2ND OTHER VOICE
Thank you, <u>Omni</u>.

NEW ANNOUNCER
That's <u>Omni</u>, O-M-N-I. America's
first combination headache remedy
and laxative. <u>Omni</u>-----Available
in Live Alone and Family Size.

FADE OUT.

<u>END OF ACT TWO</u>

ACT THREE

FADE IN:

36   EXT. FRONT OF HARRY'S SUBURBAN HOUSE—DAY   36

A Volvo pulls up in front. Doug is driving. Harry, obviously hung—over, gets in.

               DOUG
      Hi, Harry. I had a cable from
      Mary Alice——from Vienna. She
      and her shrink visited Freud's
      original office.

               HARRY
      Doug——s'hh. Think of me as a
      hospital zone.

37   EXT. FRONT OF WARREN'S SUBURBAN HOUSE—DAY   37

Volvo with Doug and Harry pulls up. Frantic Warren gets in.

               DOUG
      I heard from Mary Alice, Warren——

              WARREN
      I got the most important meeting
      of my life at nine sharp——and
      look at this presentation. My kid
      glued the pages together. Where's
      Ed?

               DOUG
      Still sick, his wife said, but
      their cleaning lady told our
      cleaning lady he's locked himself
      in his room. In bed. For the
      last three days.

               HARRY
      My head feels like Leonard Spinks talks.
          (Options: 1. Howard Cosell
          2. Alexander Haig.)

38   AFTER EACH OF THESE SCENES, WE SEE ED IN HIS BEDROOM PROGRES-   38
    SIVELY A MESS. WE SEE THE BEARD GROWING.

Here he is starting to read ''War & Peace.''

               ED
      I always wanted to read this.

                          (CONTINUED)

38A INT. McCALL KITCHEN–DAY   38A

KATHERINE is standing, pacing, tries and fails to open a bottle of wine with its opener.

> KATHERINE
> (talking on the wall
> phone)
> Mom, it's been four days.
> (listens)
> Mom, I've tried talking to him.
> It's not easy--through the door.
> I told him Dr. Simon said if
> things were bothering him, he
> ought to talk about it. Get it
> out in the open.
> (listens)
> Well, he threw something at the
> door--and it shattered. I think
> it was that lava lamp you gave us.
> Now he's got the stereo up full
> blast. 'The 1812 Overture'--
> time after time after time.
> (listens)
> Starve him out? Mom, that's what
> you told me about sex. What is
> he eating? He must be starving.
> He must look like Howard Hughes did
> at the end.
> (listens)
> No, Mom--it's okay. Really.
> We don't actually need a lava lamp.

39   INT. ED McCALL'S OFFICE–DAY   39

Tawney Shapiro has just picked up the phone.

> TAWNEY
> Ed McCall's office. Oh, good
> morning, Mr. Rush. No, he isn't.
> I know it's been five days. You
> don't have to shout. Well, what
> am I supposed to do?

Rush obviously says something rude on the other end of the phone.
Tawney is in shock.

> TAWNEY
> (continuing)
> Mr. Rush!
> (hangs up)
> Wait'll the Grievance Committee
> hears about this!

40   INT. ED'S BEDROOM–DAY   40

Ed is further along in ''War & Peace'', ''1812 OVERTURE'' is
BLASTING now. He is eating a hot fudge sundae.

                                                        (CONTINUED)

41   INT. A PSYCHIATRIST'S OFFICE–DR. HAROLD SIMON–DAY   41

Katherine is sitting on the leather (if possible) Eames chair.
DR. SIMON has a beard and, as Katherine talks, he is cleaning
his pipe in a lascivious manner.

>   KATHERINE
>   But, Dr. Simon, it's been six
>   days now and he's still in bed.
>   He still has the same clothes on.
>   He refuses to unlock the door. I
>   could kill him.

>   DR. SIMON
>   Anger is good. Have you thought
>   of trying sex?

>   KATHERINE
>   Doctor––we have four children
>   remember? Course, as you know,
>   it hasn't been as often lately.
>   And now––with the door locked.
>   I've had to sleep in the guest
>   room.

>   DR. SIMON
>   How do you feel about it?

>   KATHERINE
>   Well––the blue in there is
>   totally wrong. And the drapes.
>   Oh. You mean Ed.

42   ED   42

in his bedroom––farther along in book. ''1812 OVERTURE'' GOING
STRONG. Ed is eating Kentucky Fried. Häagen Dazs ice cream in
container nearby.

43   INT. KITCHEN–DAY   43

Elizabeth is on the phone. David, with stereo headset on, a
guitar around his neck, is getting cold pizza out of the fridge.

>   ELIZABETH
>   I did listen at the door last
>   night and heard him say, 'I'm
>   not okay, you're not okay.'
>   I know it's been seven days,
>   Aunt Maggie, but that doesn't mean
>   insanity runs in the family. My
>   Daddy is not crazy––Grandpa either.

                                              (CONTINUED)

44 ED   44

in his bedroom. Farther along in his book. He is eating a Big
Mac. Containers all over the place. ''1812 OVERTURE'' PLAYS
ON.

45 INT. GRANDPA'S BEDROOM—DAY   45

Grandpa is on the bed. Start CLOSEUP on him. On the phone.

> GRANDPA
> I'm fine, Katherine, how are you?
> (covers the phone,
> speaks to someone
> O.S.)
> It's my daughter—in—law.
> (into phone again)
> Yes, we're married all right——
> and very happy. Well, thank you.
> How's that? Ed's been in bed
> eight days and you can't get him
> out?

Reveal HOUSEKEEPER in bed next to Grandpa.

> HOUSEKEEPER (OLGA)
> (Swedish)
> Like father, like son.

46 ED   46

in his bedroom. ''1812'' is BLARING. He is deeper into ''War
and Peace''. He is eating a Mrs. Smith's Cherry Pie with his
hand and drinking milk from a container.

47 INT. BEAUTY SALON—DAY   47

Katherine is getting a comb—out from a MALE HAIRDRESSER

> HAIRDRESSER
> Nine days? Men. Has he done
> anything like this before?

> KATHERINE
> Never. He's the most responsible
> person I know. He votes in off—
> year elections. He won't even
> let you change your age on your
> driver's license.

> HAIRDRESSER
> I read once about a man in Cleveland.
> He stayed in bed for thirty years.

(CONTINUED)

51.

47 CONTINUED: 47

                         KATHERINE
           Thirty years?

                         HAIRDRESSER
           Course, that was Cleveland,
                    (finishes)
           Don't you love it?

48 ED   48

    in his bedroom. ''1812'' CONTINUES. He is ¾ way through ''War
    and Peace''. He is eating Twinkies.

49 EXT. DINING PATIO AT COUNTRY CLUB TENNIS COURTS   49

    Katherine with THREE HOUSEWIVES.

                         MUFFY
           Ten days?

                         DIANE
           Put everything in your name--
           then have him committed.

                         BETH ANN
           I'm sure there's another woman.

                         KATHERINE
           No. Ed's always been faithful.
           I told you--he chose me at that
           wife-swapping party?

50 ED   50

    in his bedroom. ''1812'' ONE MORE TIME. ''War and Peace'' com-
    ing to an end. He is eating French Fries.

51 EXT. SIDE OF McCALL HOUSE—UNDER MASTER BEDROOM WINDOW—DAY   51

    Start MEDIUM CLOSEUP on a bucket being lowered on a rope from
    the window. CAMERA TILTS DOWN and WIDENS as it FOLLOWS the bucket
    until we see Elizabeth standing on the ground waiting. David
    rushes up with a MacDonald's package.

                         ELIZABETH
           Where've you been? It's only five
           blocks.

                         DAVID
           The cops stopped me. I told Dad
           I needed a new muffler.

                                              (CONTINUED)

51   CONTINUED: 51

> ELIZABETH
> He gave you the money for one.

> DAVID
> I had to buy guitar strings. And
> the Stones album.

Peggy (Indira) and Muhatma arrive.

> PEGGY
> What are you two doing?

David hands food bag to Elizabeth.

> DAVID
> I gotta split. Say hello to Ravi
> Shankar for me.

> PEGGY
> Elizabeth--what are you doing?

> ELIZABETH
> Doing. Doing. What am I doing?
> I'm an 'A' student, I'll think
> of something. Shouldn't you two
> be meditating or facing east or
> whatever it is--Darn, David
> forgot the Twinkies.

> PEGGY
> Are you feeding him? Daddy? Does
> Mom know?

> ELIZABETH
> He's gotta eat.

> MUHATMA
> He should eat brown rice and seaweed.

> ELIZABETH
> All he wants is junk food--tons
> of it.

> PEGGY
> He'll never come out if you feed him.

> ELIZABETH
> You want him to starve?

> PEGGY
> If he doesn't, we will.

(CONTINUED)

53.

51   CONTINUED: (2)   51

ELIZABETH
Afraid you and Muhatma the Mooch
might have to go to work?

MUHATMA
Earning money is against my
religion.

PEGGY
(trying to grab food
bag and bucket)
I'm not gonna let you ruin our--

ELIZABETH
Pull, Daddy, pull!

The bucket, filled, moves up fast and out of reach.

PEGGY
Muhatma--do something! Arthur!

MUHATMA
It is useless to intervene in our
own affairs.

ELIZABETH
He must be great to make out with.

Peggy grabs Elizabeth and twists her arm behind her back and
pushes her toward inside the house.

52   INT. McCALL KITCHEN (OR LIVING ROOM)-DAY   52

OPEN right ON a weird-looking vase being placed by Bud, who has
made the vase. CAMERA STARTS PULLING BACK to reveal Bud and
Katherine.

KATHERINE
Oh, Bud, I'm so glad you're home.
And your pottery is wonderful.
Very mature. You've come a long
way since Camp Wacamac. But I
knew then you had talent.

BUD
You really think so, Mom?

KATHERINE
I do. Just remember, a thousand
years from now, when they dig up
Stanford, it'll be your pots that
tell the story.

(CONTINUED)

52 CONTINUED: 52

>   Bud
> You don't mind I'm not going to
> be a doctor?

Peggy rushes in, dragging Elizabeth by the arm. Muhatma follows.

>   PEGGY
> Mother! Elizabeth's been sneaking
> him food.

>   ELIZABETH
>   (wrenching free,
>   rubbing wrist)
> I thought you people were supposed to
> be non-violent.

>   PEGGY
> Daddy's made us the laughing stock
> of the neighborhood and she's
> helping--

>   ELIZABETH
> I don't care about the neighborhood.
> I care about him. He's my daddy
> and I love him. Even if he is
> crazy. At least, he's home for
> a change.

>   PEGGY
> He's humiliated us. I've never
> been so humiliated.

>   ELIZABETH
> Oh, no? What about the night of
> the Prom? When you had a cold
> sore on your lip.

DOORBELL RINGS.

53 INT. McCALL FRONT DOOR AND ENTRANCEWAY-DAY   53

DOORBELL RINGS AGAIN. David, with guitar, and headset around his neck, comes in and opens the door. FIREMAN CAPTAIN O'MALLEY stands there, with an axe.

>   O'MALLEY
> This the McCall residence?

>   DAVID
> You could say that. I call it
> Disneyland North.

>   (CONTINUED)

53   CONTINUED: 53

                    O'MALLEY
          I'm from the Fire Department.
          We had a call--

Katherine enters.

                    KATHERINE
          It's for me, David.

                    DAVID
          That figures.

                    KATHERINE
          Hello, I'm Mrs. McCall.

                    O'MALLEY
             (checking his
             clipboard)
          Right. I'm Captain O'Malley. You
          wanted a door broken down?

                    KATHERINE
          That's right. My husband's. He's
          been locked in for eleven days.

                    O'Malley
          Oh. Well, we've been on strike.

                    KATHERINE
          No, that's all right. I just
          called this morning. Don't you
          have anything smaller than an axe?

Cannon Rush barges in. Tony Mosconi is with him.

                    CANNON
          Katherine? I'm Cannon Rush.

                    KATHERINE
          Of course, you are. Hello. What
          a nice surprise, Mr. Rush. Uh,
          this is Captain--?

                    O'MALLEY
          O'Malley, M'am.

                    KATHERINE
          Cannon Rush and--

                    TONY
          I'm Tony. Hey, no wonder Ed keeps
          you hiden in Connecticut. You're
          gorgeous.

                                (CONTINUED)

KATHERINE
Well, thank you. I have coffee,
if any--oh, these are my children.

Peggy, Elizabeth, Muhatma and David have gathered.

TONY
(eyeing Peggy)
Himalayas.

CANNON
I want to see him, Katherine--
now. I know what he's up to.

KATHERINE
Well, your timing is perfect, Mr.
Rush. Captain--uh? Forgive me,
I'm terrible at names.

O'MALLEY
O'Malley, M'am.

KATHERINE
O'Malley--was just about to
break down the door.

Dr. Simon enters.

DR. SIMON
Sorry I'm late, Katherine. You
said left on Paradise Lane. It's
right.

KATHERINE
I'm sorry. Mr. Rush--everybody--this is
Doc Simon.

CANNON
Oh, how do you do? I love your
plays. Especially 'The Odd Couple.'
Very funny, very funny.

KATHERINE
This way, everybody.

All start moving upstairs.

TONY
You ever get to the city,
Katherine? May I call you
Katherine? For a matinee, maybe?

(CONTINUED)

54   INT. THE McCALL MASTER BEDROOM—DAY   54

The room is a mess. Ed McCall has a beard. He is in bed. In the
same clothes. He is finishing ''War and Peace,'' aloud, from
the last page. We continue to read the title of the book clearly.
''1812'' STILL PLAYING.

> ED
> '. . . and to recognize a dependence
> not perceived by our senses.'

He closes the book triumphantly.

> ED
> (continuing)
> That's it.

He sits up and throws the covers back, goes to the STEREO and
turns it OFF.

> ED
> (continuing)
> Now. Time to get on with my life.
> I wonder what day it is?

He shrugs. He picks up a small piece of paper from the bed. This
is in one hand. Then, he picks up another in the other hand. It
is a <u>long</u> piece of paper.

> ED
> (continuing)
> The current pros in my life.
>
>> (re short paper)
>> And the cons.
>> (the long paper
>> unfurls)
> But no more. I'm changing all of
> it. There's going to be a new
> Ed McCall. First, I'll have a
> meeting with Katherine and the
> kids.
>> (smiles)
> First, I'll unlock the door.

Ed goes to the door, unlocks it and opens it, just as O'Malley,
the Fireman, is about to bring his axe down through it. O'Malley, propelled by the force of his own motion, comes plummet-
ing into the room, burying the axe in the carpet, and crashing
his head into the far bedroom wall. O'Malley slumps to the floor,
knocked out. Katherine, Cannon Rush, Tony, Dr. Simon, Peggy,
Bud, Elizabeth, David and Muhatma enter the bedroom.

> ED
> (continuing; a
> big smile)
> Well——what a nice surprise.

(CONTINUED)

54   CONTINUED: 54

> KATHERINE
> Look at this room. I'll have to
> clean it before the cleaning
> woman sees it.

> ED
> (re-born, rushes to
> embrace Katherine)
> Oh, God, Katherine, am I glad to
> see you. I've got so much to
> tell you.

> KATHERINE
> (reacting to his
> odor, held in his
> embrace)
> You've gained weight--and
> you've got a beard.

> TONY
> You could use a little <u>gun</u>
> deodorant, old buddy.

> CANNON
> All right, McCall. Stop goofing
> around. Acting crazy. I know
> what your game is. I ought to
> fire your--

> ED
> All right, I accept.

> CANNON
> You've had another offer, haven't
> you? Another agency. Winfield,
> right? I'll never let you out
> of your contract

> ED
> You honestly think that's what this
> is all about? Cannon--I've been
> battling for my soul in this room.
> For my life. I want out.

> KATHERINE
> But, darling, you're the one who
> locked yourself in.

> ED
> More than you know, Katherine,
> but we're gonna be free now.

                                        (CONTINUED)

54   CONTINUED: (2)   54

                              CANNON
                   That's what you think! Blackmailer!

                              TONY
                          (whispering to Peggy)
                   Here's my card, Indira. You'd be
                   great in commercials--and I have
                   this new curry powder account.
                   We'll have lunch.

                              KATHERINE
                   What happened to the television?

                               ED
                   I shot it.

                              KATHERINE
                   You shot?--It was the lava lamp. I knew it.

                              CANNON
                   All right, Ed. I haven't got all
                   day. You win. A new contract.
                   Big raise, extra vacation and--

                               ED
                   Cannon--everybody--I'm not
                   going back.

                              O'MALLEY
                          (from the floor,
                           half conscious)
                   Unnnnnn.

                               ED
                   Who's that?

                              KATHERINE
                   Oh. A nice fireman named, uh--
                   I'm sorry. What's your name
                   again?

                              O'MALLEY
                   Ohhhhhhhh.

                              KATHERINE
                   That's right. O'Malley.

55   INT. McCALL KITCHEN-EVENING   55

      Katherine, Bud, Peggy, Elizabeth and David are seated around.
      Ed is standing.

                                            (CONTINUED)

55   CONTINUED: 55

                              ED
          No. Despite the last several days,
          I'm not crazy. I'm saner than I've
          been for--well, a long, long
          time. That's why I wanted this
          family meeting. I want you all to
          know--I'm going to change my life.
          You might say, I'm dropping out.
          I'm tired of giving and not getting
          much back. Gimme. Gimme. Gimme.
          It means your lives'll change too.
          Your lives.

Ed studies their faces, warmly. He walks around the table behind
each child as he talks about him or her.

                              ED
                        (continuing)
          Bud. Edward Andrew McCall, Jr.
          Remember, Katherine? We were in the
          Village, married less than a year,
          seeing 'The Fantastiks', and
          suddenly--there was a blizzard
          and no cabs and I stopped this
          couple from New Jersey. They
          thought I was trying to steal their
          car till I explained. They took us
          to the hospital and you were born,
          Bud, four hours later. Seven pounds,
          nine ounces. The couple from New
          Jersey sent you a birthday card
          every year for years and years.

                              BUD
          They still do.

                              ED
          I'd lost track. Then you, Peg--
          Indira. Five pounds, five ounces.
          So tiny and fragile and pale; they
          kept you in an incubator for two
          weeks. Then we kept you in our
          room, with the temperature so high
          we could hardly breathe. But then
          the color came into you like a
          springtime. You were the gentlest,
          sweetest piece of life that ever
          stirred. Bud was in the living
          room by then--on a sofa bed--
          and we knew it was time to leave
          the Village.
                           (MORE)

                                        (CONTINUED)

55   CONTINUED: (2)   55

                              ED (CONT'D)
          A promotion, Connecticut, a car--
          two cars. And then you, David, nine
          pounds of you. Your mother said
          you'd be a boy. Jumping for life
          in her stomach so hard you'd wake
          her in the middle of the night.
          You were rock and roll before you
          were born. Then later came
          Elizabeth. And no, you were not
          an accident. But, I wasn't there
          when you were born--for the first
          time. But I was very successful.
          A vice-president, wanted by ten
          other agencies, working 12, 14, 18
          hours a day. All of it for all of
          you, I thought. I'm sorry, Elizabeth.
          You're the only one I didn't teach to
          ride a bicycle. Did I ever take you
          to the circus?

Elizabeth shakes her head no.

                              ED
                         (continuing)
          I always thought there'd be time the
          next day, tomorrow. I thought it
          would last forever. Now--I hardly
          know you at all. Any of you. Somehow,
          it all slipped away--on commuter
          trains and planes and dinners left in
          the oven--when I ate home at all.
          The weekends I wasted watching games
          on television. Or slept. I lost
          you--all of you. You, too,
          Katherine. The shining October girl
          I first saw leaving the campus book
          store with an arm full of Emily Dickinson
          and Simone de Beauvoir and the
          morning sun in your hair. I loved
          your mother before I met her. But
          even more when I did. A radiant,
          intelligent girl who graduated
          with honors and talked for hours
          about poets and books and doing
          something with her life. Now--
          here we all are--in the biggest
          house on the block--
          I'm changing it.
          All of it.

                         KATHERINE
          What--kind of change, Edward?

                                                    (CONTINUED)

55   CONTINUED: (3)   55

Ed goes to a wall cabinet and takes down a can of charcoal
starter.

> ED
>
> It's a long list, darling.

He pulls out an actual list.

> ED
> (continuing)
> Do you have your credit cards with
> you?

Everyone acknowledges that they do.

> ED
> (continuing)
> May I have them, please?

> KATHERINE
> I don't understand what--?

> ED
> You'll see. I won't keep them long.

Everyone passes his credit cards to Ed, who pulls out his own.
He takes the bowl from the center of the table and empties the
wax fruit. Ed pours the fuel into the bowl and then puts the
credit cards in.

> KATHERINE
> Ed--what are you doing?

Ed lights a match and ignites the contents of the bowl.

> KATHERINE
> (continiuing)
> Edward!

> EVERYONE
> Dad! Daddy!

> ED
> That's number one.

He looks at his list as we . . .

FADE OUT.

END OF ACT THREE

ACT FOUR

FADE IN:

56   INT. McCALL KITCHEN—LATER THE SAME NIGHT   56

OPENS ON the refrigerator door slamming shut as the CAMERA PULLS BACK to reveal David, guitar around his neck, Sony Walkman earphones on, juggling American cheese, bologna, mustard, bread and a Coke from the fridge to an opposite counter. As he crosses, we see Peggy speaking on the wall phone. Though we cannot hear the music, David can and he snaps his fingers to it through this scene.

> PEGGY
> (on the phone)
> I said he's selling our cars,
> Muhatma. Our cars, don't you
> understand? You'll have to walk
> around Poughkeepsie. Besides,
> I'm not talking to you——ever
> again.

Elizabeth enters carrying ''Psychology Today.'' She goes to counter and takes an apple from basket. She sits at the kitchen table.

> PEGGY
> (continuing)
> How could you go to New York and
> leave me here? I hope you get
> dog do in your sandals.

Peggy slams the phone down.

> ELIZABETH
> Muhatma's in New York?

> PEGGY
> I told you, genius. We were both
> going till Daddy destroyed my life.
> Fifty-dollar-a-plate dinner at
> the Waldorf and I have to miss it.
> Everybody'll be there. Jane
> Fonda's the speaker.

> ELIZABETH
> I hadn't read she was against
> hunger.

> PEGGY
> Elizabeth——Jane Fonda is against
> everything worthwhile!
> (MORE)

(CONTINUED)

56   CONTINUED: 56

> PEGGY (CONT'D)
> (thinks this over as
> Elizabeth looks
> puzzled)
> That--didn't come out quite
> right.
> (grabbing David)
> David--stop snapping your fingers!

David removes one earpiece and looks at Peggy as though she were insane.

Bud enters, furious and frustrated.

> BUD
> He's hopeless. There's no talking
> to him--What're we gonna do?
> All our lives Dad promised he'd
> pay for our college educations.
> He can't go back on it now.

> ELIZABETH
> Bud--you <u>were</u> supposed to go to
> classes. You hadn't been since
> December.

> BUD
> He had no right to call the school.

> DAVID
> Least you and Peggy got a chance
> to be college drop-outs.

> PEGGY
> Will you please call me Indira?
> And how can you stuff yourself--
> now?

> DAVID
> I've only got a year left.
> Eighteen and we're out on our own,
> Dad said. I'll probably starve.
> What am I gonna do?

> ELIZABETH
> Do what you're always saying you
> want to do. Form a band. That's
> really all he's saying to all of
> us. If Peggy wants to be Indira,
> fine. And Bud wants to make
> pottery, that's okay, too.
> (MORE)

(CONTINUED)

56   CONTINUED: (2)   56

ELIZABETH (CONT'D)
We can be what we want to be, but
we have to work at it and earn it.
Do it on your own.

DAVID
Easy for you. You're 12. You got
six years of food, clothing and
shelter to go.

ELIZABETH
Well, I grant you, being an overachiever has its advantages. With
my grades, I'll be able to get a scholarship.

PEGGY
If you don't get raped and killed
living in the city.

DAVID
Mom's not going to the city. You
heard her. Me either.

ELIZABETH
I don't know--the city might be
great. Think of all the resources.
The suburbs are pretty provincial
and boring.

DAVID
All my friends are here.

ELIZABETH
That's a good example of what I
mean.

BUD
Can you get unemployment if
you've never had a job?

PEGGY
You think they'll get a divorce?

57   INT. McCALL'S BATHROOM AND BEDROOM—SAME NIGHT   57

Katherine comes slamming into the bathroom and bangs the door
closed behind her. She is in a nightgown and Ed's old bathrobe,
but very appealing. She is distraught and angry.

(CONTINUED)

57   CONTINUED: 57

She opens the medicine chest and knocks over some vials of pills
(there are lots of them) before finding the one she wants. She
shakes out two pills and swallows them with water. Ed enters
and tries to put his arms around her from behind.

                         KATHERINE
          Don't touch me.

                         ED
          Katherine. Can't we at least
          discuss it? You're the one who's
          always saying--

He tries again to touch her.

                         KATHERINE
          Don't touch me. I mean it. What's
          to discuss?

                         ED
          Our lives.

                         KATHERINE
          Our lives? You certainly took
          care of those.
          You read
          off your list of points like some
          maniac Martin Luther.
          You made all the decisions. You
          don't need my opinion.

                         ED
          I do.

                         KATHERINE
          No, you don't! What you want is
          my approval.

                         ED
          That, too.

                         KATHERINE
          Well, forget it! I like my life
          just the way it is--was. My
          home. I'm happy--
                    (she begins to sob)
          --very happy! Damn you!

                                        (CONTINUED)

57   CONTINUED: (2)   57

She pushes past him into the bedroom. Ed follows. She goes to
the busted television.

                            KATHERINE
                          (continuing)
                 Damn. I can't even watch Carson
                 --since you shot the television.
                 Uhhhhh.

She goes to the bed, gets in and covers her head. Ed sits down
on the edge of the bed.

                            ED
                 Katherine, I don't think either
                 of us has been very happy for a
                 long time. I think we've settled.
                 Accommodated. Here, too--in
                 bed. It's not a life to fall
                 asleep with a pill--silent and
                 untouching--watching the
                 'Tonight' Show.

Katherine sticks her head out.

                            KATHERINE
                 Don't blame me for that.

                            ED
                 I don't. I know.

                            KATHERINE
                          (sitting up)
                 I've--accepted--the way things
                 are. It's more than most people
                 have. What'd you expect out of
                 life? To be 20 forever?

Ed gets up, goes for a cigarette.

                            ED
                 Course not.

                            KATHERINE
                 I thought you'd stopped smoking.
                 Wasn't that number eight on your list
                 of things to change?

                            ED
                 I'm just playing with it.
                 Katherine, I don't hate my age or
                 50 or 60 or 80. I hope I will be.
                            (MORE)

                                              (CONTINUED)

57   CONTINUED: (3)   57

                       ED (CONT'D)
But with whatever life I have left,
I want to enjoy it. Enjoy it,
live it--feel it.

                       KATHERINE
I know what this is about. Why
don't you just be honest and say
it? There's someone else. You
want a divorce. No, you--

                       ED
Is that what you think?

                       KATHERINE
I've read Passages. I watch
'Donahue.' I know more than you
think I do.

                       ED
Oh, God, Katherine. Not at all.
There's no one. There never has
been. I love you--or I did.
I want to explain.

                       KATHERINE
What do you mean--did?

                       ED
I mean--I do. But admit it.
We have drifted away from each
other. Our interests. God,
there's more to life than waxy
build-up and Tupperware parties.

                       KATHERINE
I have never been to a Tupperware
party in my life.

                       ED
Lunch every day with the girls
then, at the tennis club, or
exercise groups or group therapy,
plus Doctor Simon, you know what
I mean.

                       KATHERINE
I most certainly do not.

                       ED
When's the last time you read a
book that didn't have a pirate and
a blond with heaving bosoms on the
cover?
                       (MORE)

                                (CONTINUED)

57   CONTINUED: (4)   57

> ED (CONT'D)
> (finds one on her
> end table)
> See? <u>Lust In New Orleans</u>. Or
> discussed politics or poetry or
> painting? You spend hours
> watching television made for
> bubbleheads.

> KATHERINE
> Bubbleheads? You think I'm a
> bubblehead?

> ED
> You haven't grown. You've gone
> backwards. So have I. And I
> will go crazy if we don't change
> it.

> KATHERINE
> We cannot, I will not, live in
> the city.

Ed follows in.

> ED
> Why not?

> KATHERINE
> You don't have a job for one thing.

> ED
> I'm going to work. I told you.
> But no more workaholic. No more
> work as escape. Or just to buy
> things. I'll always work. Maybe
> I'll only earn half as much or a
> third or a quarter, but we'll be
> together and live. For each other.
> Maybe you could work, even. You
> used to be so ambitious in the old
> days. Full of ideas and plans--

> KATHERINE
> But what about the children?

> ED
> They may really become somebody
> --valuable. Self-reliant and
> proud of themselves. I know now
> they're shocked and angry, but--

(CONTINUED)

57   CONTINUED: (5)   57

                              KATHERINE
                    We promised them college.

                                ED
                    I never promised a four-year grant
                    for dropping out--or 'finding
                    yourself.'

                              KATHERINE
                    What if they don't find themselves?

                                ED
                    They will. You'd be surprised how
                    fast, when they have to pay their
                    own way.

                              KATHERINE
                    It doesn't seem fair. All their
                    friends are--

                                ED
                    Lost, dropped-out, on drugs, or
                    bubbleheads.

                              KATHERINE
                    We brought them into this way of
                    life.

                                ED
                    Katherine--they can go to college
                    --if _they_ want to. Not limp
                    through to half-please and half-
                    defy us. If they're serious,
                    they'll work for it, and we'll
                    help, whatever it is they want to
                    do. Really do.

                              KATHERINE
                    You're sure--there's no one else?

                                ED
                    Positive.

                              KATHERINE
                    No, I just can't do it, Ed. I'm so
                    scared.

                                ED
                    Me, too. Isn't it wonderful?

58   INT. McCALL KITCHEN-DAY   58

     Elizabeth sits alone at the table, eating her skimmed milk and
     bran.

                                              (CONTINUED)

58   CONTINUED: 58

She is reading <u>Atlantic Monthly</u>. Ed enters, wearing a turtle
neck and sports jacket. He has shaved his beard. They look at
each other.

                              ED
                    Well, today's the day.

Elizabeth nods, but does not speak nor even keep eye contact.

                              ED
                         (continuing)
                    You know Mom's not coming.

Elizabeth nods again, head down.

                              ED
                         (continuing)
                    I thought she was--till I got
                    this lawyer's letter-charging
                    desertion.

                          ELIZABETH
                    I think the ladies at the club
                    talked her into it. They've got
                    a lot invested in divorce.

                              ED
                    Have you--made your decision?
                    Mom agreed you could make your
                    own choice.

                          ELIZABETH
                    Some choice. I'm packed.

                              ED
                         (truly pleased)
                    That's great, Elizabeth. We'd
                    better go, then.

                          ELIZABETH
                    I want to go--but--I have to
                    ask you a question first.

                              ED
                    Sure. What?

                          ELIZABETH
                    The other night--at the family
                    meeting?

                              ED
                    Yes? What?

                                              (CONTINUED)

58   CONTINUED: (2)   58

> ELIZABETH
> Well, you mentioned everybody's--
>   (gets up and starts
>   out)
> --Oh, it's not important. A
> fourth child's not exactly a
> novelty.

Ed stops her, looking her in the face.

> ED
> I can tell by your lower lip it's
> extremely important. What is it,
> Elizabeth?

> ELIZABETH
> Do you--do you know how much I
> weighed at birth?

> ED
> Sure. Eight pounds even. Why?

Elated, Elizabeth jumps on her father, hugging him and kissing him.

> ELIZABETH
> Oh, Daddy, Daddy, I love you.
> They'll come around, you'll see.
> We'll have a great life in the
> city--a tremendous adventure!

59   INT./EXT. MONTAGE OF NEW YORK CITY--DAY & NIGHT   59

Ed and Elizabeth in New York at:

A)   LINCOLN CENTER
B)   GUGGENHEIM MUSEUM
C)   MUSEUM OF MODERN ART
D)   MUSEUM OF NATURAL HISTORY
E)   HOT DOGS IN PARK
F)   THE METROPOLITAN MUSEUM

60   EXT. FRONT OF FOUNTAIN SIDE OF PLAZA HOTEL--EARLY EVENING   60

Ed and Elizabeth get in hansom cab. Rest of scene is in hansom cab.

(CONTINUED)

60   CONTINUED: 60

ELIZABETH
Daddy, I love theatre and museums,
and staying at the Plaza, but
we're gonna go broke.

ED
It's only been a week.

ELIZABETH
We've got to find a place to live
though--really live.

ED
Okay, okay. We'll start tomorrow.
Let's pick up a paper later.

ELIZABETH
Imagine getting the morning paper
the night before. I love cities.

ED
I love you.

ELIZABETH
I've got to find a school, too.

ED
We will. We will. But tonight
--there's one more thing we've
got to do.

61   EXT. BRICK WALL—CITY—CLOSEUP—CIRCUS POSTER—NIGHT   61

RINGMASTER (V.O.)
Ladies and gentlemen--children
of all ages--welcome: To The
Greatest Show On Earth!

PULL BACK to reveal Ed and Elizabeth. They grin at each other
and run off, hand in hand.

62   EXT. FACADE OF OLD BUILDING IN SOHO—DAY   62

SLOW ZOOM into top-floor windows.

ED (V.O.)
Well, here it is. A loft in SoHo,
where all the artists live. Good
school nearby.

DISSOLVE TO:

ELIZABETH
You'll never get Mother here.

ED
I couldn't get Mother Teresa here.
What do you think, Elizabeth?

63   INT. SOHO LOFT—DAY   63

                              ELIZABETH
              I don't know. I feel like I'm in
              a documentary.

                              ED
              The price is right.

                              ELIZABETH
              They paying us?

                              ED
              Hey——what happened to the
              tremendous adventure?

                              ELIZABETH
              Is it my fault I was raised upper-
              middle?

                              ED
              Okay, I grant you——right now
              it's horrible, but with a little
              paint and some thrift shops, I'll
              bet we can turn this place into
              something——really terrible.

Elizabeth smiles, despite herself.

                              ED
                        (continuing)
              Come on, Elizabeth. What do you
              think?

                              ELIZABETH
              That middle age is even more
              frightening than adolescence.
                        (running to him
                        for hug)
              Oh, Daddy, I miss Mommy.

                              ED
                        (holding her to him)
              So do I, baby. So do I.

                                              FADE OUT.

                         <u>END OF ACT FOUR</u>

ACT FIVE

FADE IN:

A64   INT. McCALL KITCHEN—DAY   A64

Katherine is in Ed's old bathrobe. She is drinking coffee, half-
listening to the television set and is on the telephone.

From on the TELEVISION set we hear the following. CAMERA is on
Katherine, listening on the phone with an occasional ''Uh,
hunh.''

                    ANNOUNCER (V.O.)
          Tonight's movie-of-the-week—
          an international premier. Robert
          English stars as Cliff Janson, the
          heroic American amputee who fights
          his way to Olympic glory and the
          Gold in 'One-legged Hope.'

                    ACTRESS (V.O.)
          Cliff—you're crazy—you can't
          compete—you've only got one leg.

                    ACTOR (V.O.)
          But I've only got one dream, Eve.
          I'm going for the Gold.

                    ANNOUNCER (V.O.)
          'One-legged Hope,' a heart-warming
          story of insane courage, based on
          a partially true story. Parental
          discretion advised. 'One-legged
          Hope'—nine o'clock Eastern,
          eight o'clock Central. We now
          return to 'Love In The Wind.'

SOAP OPERA MUSIC.

                    KATHERINE
          That's all very nice, Elizabeth.
          Now tell me the truth. Has anyone
          molested you?
                    (listens)
          And you haven't been mugged?
                    (listens)
          Of course, I'm not disappointed.
          I'm just worried about you,
          Elizabeth; that's all.
                    (listens)
          Are you eating?
                              (MORE)

                                        (CONTINUED)

A64   CONTINUED: A64

KATHERINE (CONT'd)
(listens)
Twenty-one?! We can't afford
Twenty-one! Elizabeth, you should
know--I filed papers to get you
back. You bet I'm angry. But Dr.
Simon says anger is healthy. Oh,
my God, that reminds me--I'm
late for my appointment. I'll
call you later, okay? Remember
what I said: Take a taxi to
school--and don't go anywhere without that
police whistle I sent you.

64   INT. SAME SOHO LOFT-DAY   64

but the place has been transformed. It is painted white, the
windows are sparkling and the floors are varnished. Two trees
and several plants are in place. There are rugs, a not-bad couch
and floor pillows. A dining area, sleeping areas, lamps and so
on. Elizabeth is just hanging up the phone, which Ed sees as he
enters, carrying a large bundle.

ELIZABETH
What's that?

ED
(begins to unwrap it)
You'll see.

It's unwrapped.

ELIZABETH
Daddy, what is that?

ED
A genuine Tibetan Yak skin. I
bought it from a man at the
Chinese restaurant--on the
corner.

ELIZABETH
I hate killing animals.

ED
This one died of old age or suicide. I
thought it'd go great on this wall
--it's really bare.

ELIZABETH
A Yak skin. Your drums arrived.

(CONTINUED)

64   CONTINUED: 64

                                ED
                   They did?

Elizabeth points to the drums, set up. There is a palm tree
painted on the base drum. Ed goes to them, tries them out. He is
terrible.

                                ED
                          (continuing)
                   All my life, I've always wanted to
                   play drums--and learn to speak
                   French. I signed up--at the New
                   School. And bought some
                   conversational records.

Ed looks around.

                                ED
                          (continuing)
                   Oh--you hung the painting there.
                   It's good there. This place
                   really looks great. Not bad for
                   five weeks, honey.

                             ELIZABETH
                   It's okay--if you like nouveau
                   down-trodden.
                          (she smiles and goes
                           to him for a hug)
                   I love it--sort of.

                                ED
                   Was that Mom? On the phone?

                             ELIZABETH
                   Yes.

                                ED
                   How is she?

                             ELIZABETH
                   Miserable--like you.

                                ED
                   Did she ask about me?

                             ELIZABETH
                   No, but she filed the custody
                   papers to get me back.

65   INT. KATHERINE'S SHRINK'S OFFICE-DAY   65

She is lying on the couch talking.

                                            (CONTINUED)

65   CONTINUED: 65

Dr. Simon is asleep, which she does not see at first.

                              KATHERINE
              I don't know what I'm saying. I'm
              not making any sense at all. I've
              lost control, I've lost my husband--
                        (she turns and sees
                        Dr. Simon sleeping)
              --I've lost, Dr. Simon--he's
              asleep. He's actually sleeping.
              Wake up!

                              DR. SIMON
                        (jolted; semi-
                        conscious)
              It's your mother--my mother. Oh.

                              KATHERINE
              Dr. Simon, my life is spilling out
              and you were sound asleep.

                              DR. SIMON
              Not sound, Katherine, fitful.

                              KATHERINE
              I'm going crazy! Am I that boring?
              No wonder Ed left me.

                              DR. SIMON
              We never say 'crazy,' Katherine.
              Just--understandably disturbed.

                              KATHERINE
              Understandably disturbed? I
              could kill myself!

                              DR. SIMON
              Now, now, Katherine, we'll work
              it out. You'll see--next week.

                              KATHERINE
              Next week?

                              DR. SIMON
              The hour is up, Katherine.

He turns small clock to her.

                              KATHERINE
              But--

                                                    (CONTINUED)

65   CONTINUED: (2)   65

                         DR. SIMON
             Katherine--you know your problem
             with respecting other people's
             time.

                         KATHERINE
             But I'm in desperate trouble. My
             husband's in trouble. My
             daughter's--

Dr. Simon is steering her towards the door.

                         DR. SIMON
             Every week, it's something,
             Katherine.

66   EXT. SOHO STREET-OUT FRONT OF THEIR LOFT BUILDING -DAY   66

Ed and Elizabeth come out of the buildings. There are lots of
art galleries and interesting shops and restaurants--and
people.

                         ED
             I'm famished. What do you feel
             like today? Japanese, Thai, Czech,
             French, Italian?

                         ELIZABETH
             Daddy, this week alone I've had
             calamari, scungili, teriyaki,
             sushi, curry, moussaka, coq au vin
             and smoked eel, uck. Couldn't we
             just have some Campbell's soup and
             a tuna sandwich?

                         ED
             Elizabeth. You don't sound happy.

                         ELIZABETH
             Oh, I'm ecstatic, aren't you?
             Daddy--I want you to go out with
             Tony tonight.

                         ED
             Oh, no, I don't think so. I'm
             gonna call and cancel.

                         ELIZABETH
             You can't.

                         ED
             Why?

                                          (CONTINUED)

66 CONTINUED: 66

> ELIZABETH
> I can't stand you hanging around
> the loft morning, noon and night
> beating those stupid drums—and
> your French is lousy.

Elizabeth runs ahead. Ed runs after her.

67 INT. BEAUTY SALON—DAY   67

Katherine is getting combed out from the HAIRDRESSER.

> HAIRDRESSER
> He was actually asleep?

> KATHERINE
> I couldn't believe it.

> HAIRDRESSER
> I won't tell you what my shrink
> did, but it sure cured me in a
> hurry. So, how are the kids?

> KATHERINE
> Oh, great. Bud's had the flu for
> seven weeks—ever since, you
> know. David got sent home from
> school for saying something rude
> to the guidance counselor—and
> now I see he's sleeping with his
> Snoopy dog again—the one he had
> when he was five.

> HAIRDRESSER
> I never stopped. How's my little
> Peggy?

> KATHERINE
> Fine. She and Muhatma're selling
> flowers—from our garden—at
> the toll booths on the New England Thruway.

> HAIRDRESSER
> (finished)
> There. Don't you love it?

> KATHERINE
> (nodding; looking
> in mirror)
> But what's it for? Who's it for?

> HAIRDRESSER
> Men are such beasts.

(CONTINUED)

68   INT. BAR RESTAURANT—NIGHT   68

Ed and Tony are at a table with two beautiful Lufthansa STEW—
ARDESSES. All are laughing as we FIND them. The Stews get up.
Ed has shaved off his beard.

                    STEWARDESS #1
          Enshuldigen, bitte.

                    TONY
          Where you going', baby?

                    STEWARDESS #1
          Wie sagen sie——the ladies' room?

                    TONY
          Oh, sure.

He and Ed half—rise.

                    TONY
              (continuing)
          Hurry back.
              (when they are gone;
              to Ed)
          Are you crazy? You got a fraulein
          strudel practically on a platter
          and you spend the whole night
          talkin' about your wife and kids.
          Nobody wants to hear about your
          wife and kids. I don't want to
          hear about your wife and kids.
          Gretchen and Brunhilda don't want
          to hear about your——

                    ED
          I can't help it. I miss them.
          Katherine especially.

                    TONY
          I hate goin' out with beginners.
          What happened to the new Ed McCall?

                    ED
          He feels very old and lonely
          suddenly.

                    TONY
          I could tell you weren't Field
          Marshall Von Swinger.

                    ED
          Would you be? Katherine's lawyer's
          killing me, three of my kids won't
          talk to me.
                    (MORE)

                                        (CONTINUED)

68 CONTINUED: 68

> ED (CONT'D)
> I have no idea what to do for work.
> The whole--upheaval--seems--
> stupid now. I don't know what to
> do.

> TONY
> Do me a favor. Do yourself a
> favor. Just fly along with the
> Red Baron, okay? We'll go back
> to my place. Play a little Wagner
> --take a Dramamine--

> ED
> Girls are not what this is all about,
> Tony.

> TONY
> They aren't?

Ed gets up to leave.

> TONY
> (continuing)
> Where are you going?

> ED
> Auf Wiedersehn, Tony.

> TONY
> Hey come back. You can't decide
> these things now--till you've
> tried it to the 'Valkerie'!

69 INT. LAWYER'S OFFICE–DAY 69

Katherine is seated across from AUSTIN MORROW, a lawyer.

> AUSTIN
> The custody hearing on Elizabeth's
> set for the 18th. I've enjoined
> him from selling the house and
> your car. He'll have to meet the
> payments. Plus your allowance and
> support for Peggy and David.
> Actually, with his own expenses
> and my fees, it's more than before.
> Now he'll have to go back to work
> if Cannon'll take him back--and
> ask for a raise. Perhaps take a
> second job as well.

(CONTINUED)

69   CONTINUED: 69

> KATHERINE
> Austin--you sound so gleeful.
> Ed McCall is your friend.
>
> AUSTIN
> Of course--why do you think I've
> been so lenient? But we have to
> put it to him, as they say.
>
> KATHERINE
> I don't want to 'put it to him.'
> Or hurt him. I love him.
>
> AUSTIN
> In a big job in a big house in
> Stamford, Connecticut, fine. But
> in a loft, Katherine, in Greenwich
> Village? Out of work? With no
> cars, no colleges--no tennis
> club?
>
> KATHERINE
> We were happy in the Village--
> before.
>
> AUSTIN
> Don't get sentimental, Katherine.
> It jeopardizes every good divorce
> settlement.
>
> KATHERINE
> Divorce?
>
> AUSTIN
> Of course. You don't think for a
> minute, given my reputation, I'm
> interested in half-measures, do you?

70   EXT. ''ARTISTIC'' RESTAURANT FACADE-DAY   70

Ed and Elizabeth have just finished eating lunch.

> ED
> How was it?
>
> ELIZABETH
> Compared to what? I've never eaten
> Icelandic food before.

(CONTINUED)

70   CONTINUED: 70

> ED
>
> Me either. That's the fun. You
> didn't touch your reindeer.

> ELIZABETH
>
> It made me nauseous. I kept
> thinking about Rudolph.

> ED
>
> There's a new sculptress--at the
> Radical Women's Gallery. Very
> interesting, I read. Everything's
> done in pantyhose. Want to go?
> Desire tous--m'accompanique, mai
> a--a?

Bad French sentences.

> ELIZABETH
>
> Daddy, I mean it. Stop changing
> the subject, and stop torturing
> the French. What are you going
> to do about working? Mom's gonna
> get custody for sure if you don't
> have a job.

> ED
>
> I've been thinking about it. Je
> pense.

> ELIZABETH
>
> Owning a flower cart in the park
> or writing reviews of dirty books
> for a pornographic newspaper is
> not thinking about it.

> ED
>
> Sacre bleu! The whole idea was to
> explore things. Courage, ma petite
> --Something'll turn up.

They pass a store that says: ANGELO'S PHOTO STUDIO: WEDDINGS,
GRADUATIONS, BABY PICTURES. The windows are full of examples.
There is also a sign which reads, ''Bizness 4 Sale. Owner
retiring.''

> ED
>   (continuing)
> See? I could be a photographer.

> ELIZABETH
>
> All right. Do it.

(CONTINUED)

70   CONTINUED: (2)   70

> ED
> He'll be there tomorrow. Let's
> go to the park.

> ELIZABETH
> No. Right now. Go ask.

> ED
> Seriously?

> ELIZABETH
> You had a dark room at the house.
> You used to take pictures.

> ED
> That's right, I did. I did a
> portrait of you once.

> ELIZABETH
> Forget that. Nude on a blanket
> and ten months old.

> ED
> Okay, let's see what the story is.

71   OMITTED   71

72   INT. PHOTOGRAPHIC STORE-DAY   72

Ed and Elizabeth and ANGELO, a 70-year-old man, crinkly and
kind. Ed is signing a paper.

> ED
> I don't believe this. But there
> it is. And my check. A thousand
> now--the rest on Monday.

> ANGELO
> Bene. Grazie. Now I canna go
> home--to Sicily--and die in
> my family, in peace.

> ED
> Are you--

> ANGELO
> Not a right away. Now I strong like
> a bull. Someday. Domani.
>   (looks around)
> I'll a missa this--a good life.
> Always a people when they happy.
> Weddings, graduations, babies.
>   (MORE)

(CONTINUED)

72   CONTINUED: 72

> ANGELO (CONT'D)
> I helpa them hold the happiness,
> forever. They have--for when
> it's not so good.

> ED
> I hadn't thought about that. It's
> really honorable work.

> ANGELO
> Tell me, you gonna change the name,
> hunh, outside?

> ED
> Well, I don't think so. Part of
> what I'm buying is goodwill,
> remember.

> ANGELO
> Bene, bene. Brava, Senor McCalli.
> Buena Fortuna.
>   (shakes Ed's hand)
> You sure you don't want the pony,
> huh?

73   EXT. COUNTRY CLUB PATIO—DAY   73

at a table near the tennis courts. Katherine is there with THREE
HOUSEWIVES. They are having lunch.

> BETH ANN
> I still think there must be
> another woman somewhere.

> DIANE
> I'm not surprised you do, Beth Ann.
> Your Walter had them everywhere.

> BETH ANN
> Not anymore.

> DIANE
> Imagine. Dropping dead in a Ramada
> Inn in Bridgeport. And so young--
> relatively.

> BETH ANN
>   (studying an enormous
>   diamond on her finger)
> But so well insured, darling.

(CONTINUED)

73   CONTINUED   73

KATHERINE is finishing a hot fudge sundae.

                        MUFFY
            Katherine--that's your third hot
            fudge sundae this week--for lunch.

                        DIANE
            Our dear Katherine is wavering.
            Definitely, dangerously wavering.
            Psychosomatic eating--and--did you
            know? She actually drove into the
            city last Sunday to see Ed.

                        MUFFY
            Katherine!

                        BETH ANN
            You didn't.

                        KATHERINE
            We didn't connect. Same time--
            he and Elizabeth were driving out
            to see me.

                        DIANE
            Not only that. She stopped the
            separation proceeding.

                        BETH ANN
            Katherine!

                        MUFFY
            You can't. You're not going to go
            live in that slum.

                        KATHERINE
            Why not? Didn't look so bad to me.

                        BETH ANN
            But you can't give in now.

                        DIANE
            We can't let you. I'd never forgive
            myself. We've got to stay united and
            help you be strong.

                        KATHERINE
            To do what?

                        DIANE
            Diet--and divorce.

                        KATHERINE
            I don't want a divorce. I want Ed.

                        BETH ANN
            In that jungle? Growing old without
            furs and diamonds?

                                        (CONTINUED)

73   CONTINUED: 73

> DIANE
> You'll see, Katherine. It's either
> divorce or lose all this.

> KATHERINE
> All this what?

> DIANE
> Everything we all have.

> KATHERINE
> And what is that? Come on--I'd really
> like to know. I've been thinking about
> that a lot lately. What do we have?

> DIANE
> You know. Stamford. Cars.
> Shopping.

> KATHERINE
> Things, ladies. That's what we have.
> Things. Doctors. Hairdressers. This
> club. God, I'm beginning to sound like
> Ed.

> DIANE
> Whoever thought Ed'd go crazy like
> the rest of them. I always--liked Ed.

> BETH ANN
> I remember--New Year's Eve.

> DIANE
> Just a friendly little kiss.

> BETH ANN
> It looked like you were trying to
> take his tonsils out.

> BETH ANN
>   (to Katherine, who is puzzled)
> Oh--I thought you knew.

> DIANE
> Who's ready for another martini?

> BETH ANN
> That's your third already.

> DIANE
> Four's my lucky number. Katherine,
> a little drinky-winky?

Katherine shakes her head no.

                                              (CONTINUED)

73   CONTINUED: (2)   73

Housewives trade looks.

                          BETH ANN
                Katherine——is Ed working yet?

Katherine shakes her head no.

                          BETH ANN
                     (continuing)
                What'll you do for money?

                          KATHERINE
                He will, I'm sure. Just——not
                in the rat race anymore.

                          DIANE
                I hope my rat doesn't get any
                ideas.

                          KATHERINE
                I thought I might look for a job.

                          DIANE
                That's what we've been thinking
                about. We're all your friends,
                Katherine——you know that.

                     MUFFY AND BETH ANN
                That's right. We're your friends.

                          DIANE
                With Ed gone now all these weeks
                ——and——you must get——you know
                ——lonely.

                          BETH ANN
                And the money problem's no joke,
                Katherine. We all know that.
                Struggling to make ends meet.

Muffy and Diane laugh.

                          BETH ANN
                     (continuing)
                No pun intended. Even with
                husbands doing well.

                          KATHERINE
                Right. So?

                          MUFFY
                Well——we thought——you're still
                too attractive to just——sit on
                the shelf and——

                                              (CONTINUED)

73   CONTINUED: (3)   73

> **BETH ANN**
> Katherine, we have a little
> business proposition. We--we're
> all in it. Only two days a week
> really. But the money's terrific--

> **DIANE**
> And the work's not bad either.

> **MUFFY**
> We take turns at each other's
> houses. You know. It's a lot of
> fun really. The attention anyway.

> **BETH ANN**
> Better bed than dead.

> **MUFFY**
> Or bored.

> **KATHERINE**
> Doing what? Avon parties?

> **DIANE**
> Not exactly. Uh--we--uh--
> entertain.

> **BETH ANN**
> Men. Lots of them.

> **KATHERINE**
> Some kind of home franchise selling,
> you mean?

They all stare at her. She finally gets it.

> **KATHERINE**
> (continuing)
> Oh--my God, you mean--?

They nod.

> **KATHERINE**
> (continuing)
> And you want me to--do that?

                                          (CONTINUED)

74   INTERCUT MONTAGE OF ED AND KATHERINE   74

ED   KATHERINE

A) FRONT OF HOUSE, hammering FOR SALE sign into lawn with small rubber mallet.

B) IN STUDIO. Photographing a squalling baby.

C) DR. SIMON'S OFFICE. Katherine pulls mallet out of bag and breaks Simon's clock.

D) STUDIO. Photographing a bride and groom.

E) LAWYER'S OFFICE. Katherine tearing up brief and snowing it on desk.

F) IN STUDIO. Photographing twin graduates.

G) TENNIS CLUB PATIO. Katherine takes pitcher of ice tea from Waiter, dumps it on Housewives.

H) STUDIO. Photographing ''Miss Chinatown.''

I) FRONT OF McCALL HOUSE. Katherine watches younger couple--the wife pregnant--the husband pulling out of the lawn the FOR SALE sign. Katherine hands the husband the house keys as the newspaper boy throws the newspaper and it lands in the bird-bath.

J) STUDIO. Photographing OLD COUPLE, 50th Anniversary.

K) IN JAM-PACKED STATION WAGON. Katherine and David come up on thruway on-ramp and see Peggy and Muhatma hitch-hiking. Muhatma holds up handmade sign that reads ''Peace--and Portland, Oregon.'' All wave and smile or laugh their way. As wagon LEAVES FRAME, we see sign saying ''New York City,'' 35 miles.''

(CONTINUED)

75   INT. LOFT—NIGHT   75

There are large, impressive photo blowups around the loft now.
Not just weddings, etc. Ed and Elizabeth are at the table, with
the remains of a dinner. Ed holds a glass of wine. In front of
him is a Twinkie with a candle in it.

                         ELIZABETH
            Did you make a wish?

                            ED
            You crazy? Of course. I'm a
            veteran at this, you know.

                         ELIZABETH
            Then--blow.
                 (he does)
            I really should have bought a cake,
            but--

                            ED
            You were broke after the Ansel
            Adams book. It's a wonderful gift,
            Elizabeth. You'll be broke for
            months.

                         ELIZABETH
            Years. But you're worth it.

                            ED
            You're gonna be late. Marche,
            marche.

                         ELIZABETH
            I feel so mean, leaving you on
            your birthday. I'm gonna call and
            cancel.

                            ED
            No, you won't. I'm fine. I want
            you to go. I can't standing having
            you around the loft morning, noon
            and night. Remember?

                         ELIZABETH
                 (nods)
            You mean it?

                            ED
            No, but you can't cancel your first
            date.

                                        (CONTINUED)

> ELIZABETH
> It's not a date, Daddy--really.
> Eight of us are going to the
> Planetarium.

> ED
> John asked you personally, didn't
> he?

> ELIZABETH
> Yes, but Im using my own bus pass.

> ED
> It's a date. Thirteen. So fast.
> Come here.

Elizabeth does. Ed embraces her and kisses her.

> ED
> (continuing)
> You're going to be a wonderful
> woman, Elizabeth. Just like your
> mother. Lucky you--you even
> look like her.

> ELIZABETH
> I wish--never mind.

> ED
> So did I--on the Twinkie.

> ELIZABETH
> You shouldn't tell. It won't come
> true.

> ED
> A superstitious scientist?

> ELIZABETH
> You sure you'll be okay?

> ED
> Absolument. Now go.

> ELIZABETH
> What if he tries to kiss me?

> ED
> It depends on how you feel.

> ELIZABETH
> He's okay, but he's got braces.
> I'm afraid of cutting my lip.

(CONTINUED)

> ED
>
> Then I'd wait awhile.

Elizabeth nods, goes to mirror for a final check.

> ELIZABETH
>
> Oh, gross—I'm getting a pimple
> on my nose.

> ED
>
> Scram! Allons!

She does. Ed wanders over to where she has been. He looks into the mirror.

> ED
> (continuing)
>
> Allo--old friend--mon vieux.
> Quelle damage.

Ed shrugs, goes to stereo. Puts on FRENCH CONVERSATIONAL RECORD, then goes to drums and plays. He answers the machine twice—Bonjour. ''Bonjour.'' Comment allez-vous? ''Comment allez-vous?''

THE DOORBELL rings. He goes to answer it.

> ED
> (continuing)
>
> Elizabeth, now what? I--

He opens the door and there is Katherine. She is holding A SUIT-CASE. FRENCH RECORD should slowly fade out during scene so that we forget it.

> ED
> (continuing)
>
> Katherine!

> KATHERINE
>
> Happy Birthday, Ed.

> ED
>
> Oh, yeah--thank you.

> KATHERINE
>
> I--didn't get you anything.

> ED
>
> That's oh--it's the thought that counts.

> KATHERINE
>
> I thought about something.

> ED
>
> You did? Well, that's--

(CONTINUED)

93A.

75   CONTINUED: (3)   75

                         KATHERINE
          A Smith & Wesson or Colt .45--your
          favorite wine with strychnine.

                            ED
          Oh. Still mad, hunh?

                         KATHERINE
          Furious. Enraged. Berserk.
          Nothing serious, of course.

                            ED
          Then?

                         KATHERINE
          Why am I here?
                              (MORE)

                                        (CONTINUED)

75. CONTINUED: (4)   75.

Ed nods.

> KATHERINE (CONT'D)
> I don't know why I'm here. I don't
> know why you're here--except it's closer to Bellevue maybe.

> ED
> You want to come in?

> KATHERINE
> No.

> ED
> Oh.

> KATHERINE
> Yes. To stay. I think.

> ED
> Katherine! You mean it?

> KATHERINE
> No.

> ED
> (looking at suitcase)
> Oh. But--isn't that a suitcase?

> KATHERINE
> Yes. Maybe. It certainly looks
> like one, doesn't it? But it's
> not a big one. The big ones're
> downstairs--in the car--with David--
> with the motor running--in case I
> change my mind.

> ED
> That's fantastic.

> KATHERINE
> This is only an overnight bag, Ed.

> ED
> Okay. Then we could--try--overnight.
> (He reaches for the bag)

> KATHERINE
> (Clutches bag. They are both
> holding it.)
> No, wait. If--I--do--try--move in--
> decide to--are you going to stay?
> You're not going to join a sect,
> are you? Or run off to sea or the
> Peace Corps?

                                        (CONTINUED)

75   CONTINUED: (5)   75

                              ED
          No. This is it. Maybe Toledo
          for the summer, but--

                          KATHERINE
                    (seizing at her suitcase)
          Don't kid, Ed. You're dealing with
          a woman who still thinks you need a
          brain scan.
                    (pause)
          Well--aren't you going to ask me in?

                              ED
          But I--did.

                          KATHERINE
          Ask me again.

                              ED
                    (gently takes the suitcase
                    and escorts Katherine in)
          Katherine--please come in.

                          KATHERINE
                    (stepping in, but then she
                    stops)
          No, wait. I forgot to ask. Do you
          even want me back?

                              ED
          Oh, yes--Katherine, of course.

                          KATHERINE
          I still don't think this is going
          to work. Just tell me--did your
          stomach hurt as much as mine?

                              ED
          Miserable--morning, noon and night.

They embrace.

                              ED
                    (continuing)
          Oh, Katherine, I've missed you so much.
                    (they break embrace)
          Come in, come in.

Katherine goes by him into the loft and studies the place.

                              ED
                    (continuing)
          Well, what do you think?

                          KATHERINE
          It's wonderful. Really. Course,
          we'll have to re-decorate.

                                              (CONTINUED)

94B.

75   CONTINUED: (6)   75

> ED
> (smiles, shakes his head)
> Welcome home, Katherine. Welcome
> home.

FADE OUT.

END OF ACT FIVE

ACT SIX

FADE IN:

76   INT. CORRIDOR OF A NEW YORK SCHOOL—DAY   76

David and Elizabeth walk along. David turns to her after a
passing kid has said ''Sit on it, Gringo'' in Spanish to him.
David is carrying his guitar in a case.

                    DAVID
          What did he say?

                    ELIZABETH
          You'll learn. I can swear in
          Yiddish, Spanish, Black English,
          Chinese, Serbo-Croatian--

A cute, macho, Puerto Rican kid, JOSE, approaches.

                    JOSE
               (to Elizabeth)
          Que pasa, baby?

                    ELIZABETH
          Hi, Jose--come sta?

                    JOSE
               (a sexy little
               body movement)
          Chi chi boom. Gringo--bingo!

David is furious, starts to react.

                    ELIZABETH
          David, relax. Just keep walking.
          Do a Clint Eastwood here, you
          wouldn't last five seconds.

                    DAVID
          He can't talk to my sister like
          that.

                    ELIZABETH
          Like what?

                    DAVID
          Like you were some kind of--

                    ELIZABETH
          Friend. I'm his friend. We're in
          science class together. Believe
          me, he has a lot of respect. Now,
          be cool--you're not in Connecticut
          anymore.

                                        (CONTINUED)

76   CONTINUED: 76

> DAVID
> I'm not even in America.

> ELIZABETH
> David, you've got to stop
> resisting. You've been here
> two months and--

> DAVID
> Great. I should be up for parole
> soon.

> ELIZABETH
> I wish you'd lighten up.

> DAVID
> Darken up, don't you mean?

Elizabeth is stopped by this racist remark. She looks at David
in shock.

> DAVID
> (continuing)
> Well, it's true, isn't it? I
> never saw so many blacks--and
> foreigners.

> ELIZABETH
> So?

> DAVID
> So--aw, nothing. Come on.

> ELIZABETH
> Schlameil.

> DAVID
> What does that mean?

77   EXT. FRONT STEPS OF SCHOOL-DAY   77

Elizabeth and David come out of school door and head down steps.

> ELIZABETH
> What do you want for dinner? I'm
> gonna cook--and you'll help.
> Mom's got work tonight.

                                                        (CONTINUED)

> DAVID
> Again? She's never home, with
> that dumb job.

> ELIZABETH
> The Human Resources Center is not
> dumb.

> DAVID
> I liked it better when she was in
> therapy instead of giving it.

> ELIZABETH
> I think it's great. She's really
> helping people.

> DAVID
> If you're an ex-addict or on
> probation.

They have passed three black guys on the steps, who are looking
at David and his guitar, rather menacingly on first impression. One of the three, WILLIE, speaks.

> WILLIE
> Hey, man--hey.

> DAVID
> Yeah?

> WILLIE
> Can you like really crank that
> thing?

> DAVID
> Hunh?

> WILLIE
> You know, play. That is a guitar
> you got in there, right?

> DAVID
> Sure.

> WILLIE
> Well, look, man, we got a band, you
> know, and somebody dropped a dime
> on our lead guitarist. He had
> himself a little sideline business,
> you know, and the cops like busted
> him. Dig? Anyway, we got a gig
> Saturday night. A hot one--for
> bread--and no guitar. I like
> seen you around school and, you
> know, want a try?

(CONTINUED)

77   CONTINUED: (2)   77

                          DAVID
              Well, gee. I don't know. I--

                        ELIZABETH
              I can dig it. He'll be there.

Willie soul slaps hands with Elizabeth.

                          WILLIE
              All right, little sister.

78   INT. MUSIC CLUB—NIGHT   78

It is dark.

                      EMCEE (BLACK V.O.)
              Brothers and sisters--The Black
              Hats and Paleface.

Lights come up. The BAND PLAYS. The Band consists of three black
teenagers--drums, keyboard, base--in big bad Clint Eastwood
black cowboy hats--and David on guitar. Establish David is a
hit with the group.

                                              CUT TO:

78A   ELIZABETH   78A

watching Band, radiant.

                                              DISSOLVE TO:

79   INT. THE LOFT—DAY   79

We see as CAMERA PANS the loft that the furniture is now half
thrift shop and half Early American from the Connecticut house.
Katherine's influence is everywhere. The CAMERA PICKS UP Ed
leaving kitchen area carrying a tray which bears two compotes
of fresh fruit, glasses and a bottle of champagne. The CAMERA
FOLLOWS him into the bedroom area. Katherine is in bed, sitting up, reading the Sunday New York Times. She is wearing an
''I Love New York'' tee-shirt (the kind where for love is a
heart). Also, glasses. Ed is in jeans, no shirt nor socks. Ed
pours the champagne.

                        KATHERINE
              Champagne? For breakfast?

                          ED
              To Katherine--den mother of the
              huddled masses.

                                              (CONTINUED)

                         KATHERINE
                    (reading
                    the <u>Times</u>)
              To a ''promising, photographic talent--
              witty, powerful, humane.''

                         ED
                    (clinks his glass to hers)
              Thank you.

                         KATHERINE
              I didn't say it. The New York Times
              did.
                    (reading from paper)
              ''The current group exhibition at
              The Victor Jonas Gallery includes
              five photographs by Ed McCall which
              mark the debut of a promising photographic
              talent--witty, powerful, humane.

                         ED
              Whadda they know?
                    (clinks glasses again,
                    they drink)
              We got to get up soon. Go buy a Christmas tree.

                         KATHERINE
                    (still reading paper)
              We will, we will.

                         ED
              Do you really have to go to City
              Hall this afternoon--on Sunday?

                         KATHERINE
              Yes, and you ought to be marching
              with me. You know how important those
              funds are to the center--they're
              cutting off everybody.

                         ED
              You ought to run for president.

                         KATHERINE
              Maybe I will.

                         ED
              You're marvelous. I can't believe
              how good you are with those kids.

                         KATHERINE
              You can't be all those years in
              therapy and not learning something.
              But I'm quitting. I'm going back
              to school. I don't want to just
              assist. I want to be a full-fledged
              therapist.

                                             (CONTINUED)

79   CONTINUED: (2)   79

>   ED
>   You'd be a damned good one.
>
>   KATHERINE
>   McCall? This hasn't been easy,
>   you know. These last seven months.
>
>   ED
>   I know.
>
>   KATHERINE
>   I didn't think I could ever forgive
>   you for the way you disrupted our lives.
>   But--now--thank you. I feel so alive
>   again. And useful.

Ed starts to kiss Katherine. She pulls back.

>   KATHERINE
>   You never did tell me what happened
>   at that New Year's Eve party with Diane?
>
>   ED
>   Are you kidding. Nothing--to
>   speak of.
>
>   KATHERINE
>   I'll bet, she said, wiping that stupid
>   grin off her husband's face.
>   (flirting)
>   I could still take the girls up
>   on their offer, you know.
>
>   ED
>   You know what? You'd of made
>   a fortune.
>
>   KATHERINE
>   (shakes her head)
>   It would have put us in a different
>   tax bracket.

They laugh, embrace and kiss.

>   FADE OUT.

END OF ACT SIX

<u>ACT SEVEN</u>

FADE IN:

80   INT. LOFT—NIGHT   80

CAMERA BEGINS TIGHT on hand struggling with angel on top of a
Christmas tree. PULL BACK to reveal Ed balancing precariously
on a small kitchen ladder as he stretches to put the angel on
straight.

>ELIZABETH
>Left, Daddy, left. It's still
>crooked.

>ED
>Okay, now?

>KATHERINE
>Perfect. Leave it. Come down
>from there before you break your
>neck.

>ED
>(coming down)
>Whew. Not bad. Could use some
>more ornaments.

>KATHERINE
>It's beautiful.

>ELIZABETH
>Our best one ever.

>KATHERINE
>Now sit down and drink your eggnog.
>Are you lighting that cigarette?

Ed was about to.

>ED
>Hunh? Oh. No. I--

>KATHERINE
>What's the matter with you? You
>been jumpy all day.

>ED
>I don't know. David ought to be
>here.

>ELIZABETH
>He's got a gig.

(CONTINUED)

80 CONTINUED: 80

                          KATHERINE
            A concert.

                             ED
            On Christmas Eve? What is that?
            Hark, the Herald Angel rocks?

                          KATHERINE
            You're the one who taught us about
            change.

DOORBELL RINGS.

                          ELIZABETH
            I'll get it.

She goes.

                             ED
            It's not right, though.

                          KATHERINE
            What?

                             ED
            Nothing. You know, I was just
            thinking--

                          KATHERINE
            They're fine, Ed.

                             ED
            Sure. They talk to you, at least.

                          KATHERINE
            They'll talk to you. Give them
            time.

                             ED
            Maybe I was too hard. Maybe I
            ought to--

                                                    CUT TO:

81 INT. LOFT DOORWAY—NIGHT   81

   Elizabeth opens the door and Bud is standing there. Before she
   can exclaim, Bud puts his hand over her mouth. They enter towards
   living area.

82   INT. LOFT—LIVING AREA—NIGHT   82

> ED
> (without turning
> around)
> Who is it, Elizabeth?

We see Bud and Elizabeth behind their parents on the couch.

> Bud
> Merry Christmas, Dad.

> ED
> (turning; surprised,
> but grateful)
> Bud.
> (gets up, rushes
> to him)
> Bud.
> (embraces him)
> Son.

83   INT. LOFT—KITCHEN—DAY   83

Elizabeth and Katherine are preparing dinner.

> ELIZABETH
> I still think we should've done
> the turkey cacciatore.

> KATHERINE
> Not on Christmas Day. Think of
> poor David.

> ELIZABETH
> You'd think he'd outgrow macaroni
> and cheese by this time.

> KATHERINE
> How are the yams?

84   INT. LOFT—LIVING AREA—DAY   84

Ed, Bud and David. Ed is pouring champagne.

> BUD
> Oh, thanks. So, anyway, I'm
> enlarging the Cambridge store
> and I should have one in Newton open
> by the first of March—-and with
> the order from Filene's—-that's
> the big department store in Boston—-

(CONTINUED)

CONTINUED:

> ED
> Right.

> BUD
> --I'm gonna have to hire ten or
> twelve more people and buy another
> kiln.

Ed looks at an advertising flyer in front of him.

> ED
> McCall Ceramics, Inc. Fantastic,
> Bud. Really, I just feel terrible
> you didn't come to me.

> BUD
> No. This time I had to prove it
> to myself. And do it myself.

Katherine enters with Elizabeth and pours herself more champagne.

> KATHERINE
> Not entirely. Remember who co-
> signed with you at the bank? The
> working woman, folks, with her own
> credit rating.

> ED
> How could you two keep that
> a secret for seven months?

> BUD
> I made her swear. In case I
> bombed.

> ED
> No way. Your ashtrays were always
> the best in camp.

DOORBELL RINGS. Elizabeth starts to go to the door.

> KATHERINE
> Wait, Elizabeth, Let your father
> get it.
> (Ed looks puzzled)
> Well--go on--answer it.

> ED
> You didn't invite your huddled
> masses, did you?

> KATHERINE
> Just get it.

(CONTINUED)

CONTINUED: (3)

Ed is at the door. He opens it cautiously. There stand Peggy,
very pregnant, and a transformed Muhatma. They are both in
regular clothes.

>   PEGGY
> Merry Christmas, Daddy.

>   ED
> Indira, I--

>   PEGGY
> It's all right, Daddy. I'm Peggy
> again. You remember Arthur--
> Muhatma? He's gone back to school.

>   ED
> Muhatma, of course--I didn't
> recognize you without your pigtail.

Katherine rushes over.

>   KATHERINE
> Hello, darling. Arthur.

She and Peggy embrace.

>   PEGGY
> Mom.

Ed sees that Peggy is pregnant.

>   ED
> Are you?

>   PEGGY
> Any minute actually.

>   ED
> You are--married?

>   PEGGY
> Daddeee--of course. And if it's a boy,
> we're going to name him
> Edward.

>   ED
> Well--in that case, come in.

INT. LOFT – DINING AREA – EARLY EVENING   85

    Ed, Bud, Arthur and Peggy are at the table, ad–libs. Katherine
enters right away with the turkey on a platter. Elizabeth brings
Ed the carving tools. Katherine sets the turkey in front of Ed.

>   ED
> Now––who wants dark––light?
> And one of the drumsticks––
> cause I'm having the other one.

    Everyone calls out his preference, as Ed carves. Katherine goes
to her place at the table, ''dings'' on a glass with her knife.
She raises a glass after all are silent.

>   KATHERINE
> We all know on this day about The
> Three Wise Men who came bearing gifts
> of gold and frankincense and myrrh.
> Here's to my husband––your father––
> To Ed. The fourth wise man––who
> brought us the gift of ourselves.

>   ALL
>   (raising their glasses)
> To Daddy. To Daddy.

>   ED
>   (really moved)
> To our family.

>   DAVID
> What is myrrh?

DOORBELL RINGS.

>   ED
> Katherine?

>   KATHERINE
> Not me.

>   ELIZABETH
> I'll get it.

    Elizabeth goes to the door. Door opens. GRANDPA and a GORGEOUS
CHINESE GIRL, traditionally–dressed, enter. Other family
members come to him.

>   GRANDPA
> Merry Christmas, everybody. Say
> hello to Song Lee––Santa's little
> helper.

    The others, especially Katherine, welcome Song Lee. Ed pulls
his father aside.

(CONTINUED)

CONTINUED: (2)   85

> ED
> Dad--what happened to Hilda, the
> housekeeper?

> GRANDPA
> I kept growing--and she didn't.

> ED
> You old dog, you.

> GRANDPA
> (smiles sheepishly, shrugs)
> I guess you could say I'm going
> through my middle age crisis.

Ed laughs, as we

INT. LOFT – OVERVIEW – EARLY EVENING, CONTINUOUS   86

ELEVATED CAMERA SHOT. We see everyone go to the table and begin
the business of eating. They ad—lib, laugh and so on as

CREDITS ROLL.

> FADE OUT.

THE END

5

How to Produce One

For most of my adult life I have been a television producer, but even so, I cannot provide a satisfactory explanation of the producer's role. Even the most remote civilian seems to focus clearly on writing and directing, but producing remains elusive. Of course, I know a few unfocused producers as well, but I am a game expositor, so I will try again here to make comprehensible to peers as well as the pure in heart the role of the producer; in this instance, as it pertains to movies for television.

First, there is no distinct producer-personality profile. Producers come in all kinds of psychological and physiological types and sizes—and all genders. They range from tall and tan and young and lovely to short and fat and old and ugly. From Snow White to Machiavelli-with-warmth. It is likewise a coat of many colors when it comes to family and geographic background, quantity and quality of formal education, and early-career routes and training.

A few producers were raised rich or have married rich; many more were poor, some painfully; and most were middle class. They are black, Oriental, Latin, but predominantly white, predominantly male. They are Jewish, WASP, Roman Catholic, and Other. A few have Ph.D.s or LL.B.s, several dropped out of high school, and most have some college or one degree, from schools that range from Harvard to something like the San Fernando Valley Institute of Fine Arts—and Plumbing.

Some producers began in the mail room or as messengers, in little theater or local television. Some started as network ushers or gofers or secretaries. Or relatives. There are ex-actors and performers. Agents. Ex-hairdressers. Ex-cops and military officers. Bored housewifes. Some producers are actors still, or writers or directors. Or bored housewives. Or relatives. Many, and these increasingly dominate, are lawyers and accountants, M.B.A.s and ex-agents.

Producers are drawn to the role because they love the business—the art, even—and have creative talent. They are drawn to the role because they don't give a damn about the content but see an easy buck, and lack creative talent but love to be proximate to it. Some are workaholics, some are glamorholics. Some are totally engulfed. Some are totally in golf.

All of this is to say you too can be a producer.

I have little patience or respect for the dilettantes, the avariccios, the inpenetrable amateurs and the fakers who crowd the ranks of television producers, and I hate to see you come into the field if you are going to add to this overpopulation; but if you come in, learn it well, and do it right, welcome. The role can be honorable, creative, and rewarding, in your pocket and in your heart and in your mind. It is an involved, caring, imaginative person trained for the task who deserves the name of producer and whom I will use to define the role.

There are categories of producers. There are executive producers, supervising producers, hyphenate-producers and on-line producers.

Executive producer typically means the owner of the picture or the owner's chief managerial representative. In our umbrella deal with Charles Fries, for instance, our movies would credit Charles Fries as executive producer. David Wolper and Dick Clark in their companies would get credit on their movies as executive producer. While the title can represent more or less active involvement and creative involvement, as it does in the three names mentioned, it more often represents equity and management and less than day-to-day responsibility for the project.

Supervising producer on a movie for television ususaly indicates a high-level associate producer or production manager, one of sufficient clout and experience to warrant the more elevated title. He is there to manage the nuts and bolts of production and to ride herd on the budget. He can be of enormous help to a producer or he can be a management spy. Andy Gottlieb was the especially praiseworthy supervising producer on *Drop-Out Father*.

Hyphenate-producers are director-producers or writer-producers, people who began as directors or writers but who wanted to add the producer role in order to protect their work. Sometimes it works in reverse. I began as a producer and became a writer and occasional director. Performing these two or more roles gives the person more clout and creative participation than if he were performing one.

The on-line producer is charged with day-to-day responsibility for getting the movie made. He is or should be okay on budget and logistics but usually is a stronger creative player. He may own some equity or net profits in the project or may simply be a hired hand brought in by a network, studio, or executive producer to supervise the project. You rarely see the credit "on-line producer." "On-line" simply means he is *there*, on-the-line, the ultimate responsible party.

It is this latter producer with whom we are most concerned here.

No one makes a movie alone. The French auteur theory that declares that there is an "author" of a film is bunk. In theatrical films, the director who is the auteur-designee does seem to lead, to be preeminent in the establishment and execution of a taste and vision about a project (or gets the credit away); and some who come immediately to mind—Bergman, Fellini, Buñuel, Welles, and Woody Allen—can stake a serious auteur claim. But stars, writers, producers, art directors, directors of photography, composers and musicians, technicians and crews—and studios—contribute, more or less, to the authorship of a film, an assertion to which all but auteur manqués would agree.

In television, these same team players contribute in parallel ways, but here the guiding force is not the director but the producer. Producer is the core role in television from start to finish, and it is the producer who is or should be, the keeper of the dream.

What does a producer do? The functions and the performance of the functions vary depending on the personality and experience of the person in the role, and on the kind of television show it is, but, for movies for television, here is what a producer does or should do: Exert the controlling vision. Find or invent the property. Sell it to the network as an idea. Hire a writer to make a script according to the producer's view of the material. Work with the writer (and the network) on script direction, revisions, and broadcast standards considerations. After the script is finished and approved, hire a production specialist to make a script breakdown and preliminary budget. Comb that budget for snares. Adjust the script for savings if necessary. Make or be involved in the making of a final budget. At every step, exercise controls and make decisions to stay within the final budget. Meet the payroll, pay taxes, and honor the appropriate union contracts. Secure insurance. In coordination with a network, hire the key behind-the-camera personnel—i.e., a production manager, the director, the director of photography (on the director's recommendation but with the producer's approval), the art director, a casting specialist, a location manager, the editor, and the composer. (Additional personnel is hired by the director or the production manager, with the producer's approval.) Work with the director (and the network) on casting, about which the producer should be very fussy. (Elia Kazan told me once that a good fifty percent of his effectiveness as a director came because of whom he had cast.) Work with the location manager and director on selecting locations, with the manager securing permissions to shoot. Join in planning the production schedule. Supervise the shoot—*in loco parentis*—as a parent on the set everyday, protecting and pampering the cast and director and crew as well as disciplining any of their peccable acts during working hours. Host the wrap party. Oversee and/or dictate the final cut of the movie. (The network has final-final say.) Fight for a favorable air date, devise and coordinate (with the network) the advertising and promotion, arrange for industry and review screenings, set up subsequent distribution deals, and submit the picture for awards.

Also, write a lot of thank-you letters, because a lot of good people deserve them.

Because in earlier chapters I have related in some detail the fabrics of finding a property and selling it, and, from the writer's view, the making of a script, I will not go over these steps here but will try to provide you with an analysis of the subsequent steps.

It is the producer's role on script to work with the writer ahead of time to define the characters and to establish the story structure. When the script is completed, the producer serves as the first audience, then as an editor, as with book and magazine editors, to cut, alter, and revise the first-draft script as necessary in accordance with the producer's vision. The producer serves as liaison between the writer and the network, getting the writer to understand and to make the changes required by a network; defending the writer's (and the producer's) version of the script to the network. This formulation applies to subsequent drafts and the polish. The producer should not submit the script to the network until the changes he wants are incorporated.

In our case, when I am the writer as well as the co-producer, Ann and I suffer the marital equivalent of the Chinese curse of "May you live in interesting times." Our script meetings are not confined to the civilities of business days or hours with appointments in offices or over lunch or on the phone. Our conferences are just as likely to take place as we are driving on a freeway, doing the dishes in the kitchen, doing whatever in our bedroom or bathroom, on a weekend or at 3:00 A.M. When there are particularly sticky creative disagreements, the entire history of our marriage may be invoked. Ann, who remembers with stunning clarity every detail of my every transgression during every year of our relationship, while I can summon only a vague atmosphere of continuing injustice, carries a decided edge in these sessions. Certainly, I have heard of writers and producers hurling curses and heavier objects at each other, but I would suppose that I am the only writer in television who has been threatened with being locked out of his own house by a producer. Still, we have never called in the Writers Guild or the divorce lawyers on each other. Somehow, we survive and come out enjoying the process. I must confess, if you promise to keep it quiet, that as I have gone from wanting her not to change a word, to listening and responding carefully to what she has to recommend, it has gotten better—and so have my scripts.

Conjugal or not, the writer in television must finally bend to the producer, which again is the chief reason so many writers work to become writer-producers.

Though the network has the final contractual say, these working relationships among writers, producers, and networks are running excitations of off-the-contract human negotiation and persuasion.

On *Drop-Out Father*, Ann and I were fortunate to work with CBS's Nancy Bein. More than a few network executives arrogantly misuse their positions to back into the roles of producer and writer on the cheap. I remember one green junior executive at ABC summoning veteran writers and producers to his office to lecture them as though they were schoolboys. Bein, on the other hand, knew her role both in the uses of its power and in its restraints. She acted with intelligence and grace. Her script notes were specific, insightful, and mostly agreeable. When we disagreed, she would hear us out and keep it our way if we were able to make a case. Frequently, her flagging of a weak spot, without trying to write it for me, would lead me to a new and better solution. She performed as an effective "blocking back" with her own and other areas of the network.

We had similar positive experiences with Ellie Sidel, CBS's movie executive in New York, and with Bob Silberling, a CBS television movie vice-president in California, who is excellent on script and in production crisis and even better in life and human relations.

Beginning with Steve Mills, who is their boss, you get the sense with these CBS people that you are allies, not adversaries. Partners in the process, not slightly clever peons being dictated to by corporate patroons. I mention these executives not simply to flatter and follow the dictum of a friend who once said, "Never kick a star when he's up," but to emphasize that their approach is as commendable as it is not universal.

This state of emotional, intellectual, and aesthetic negotiation and persuasion obtains for the producer in his ongoing dealings with the director and all other creative participants on a picture. A competent-confident producer, moreover, will not hire good people in order to obstruct them from performing their jobs. Certainly, no producer who does will be able to do so to the same good people more than once. Good production people are in constant demand and are very independent. They will not long suffer producers who are stupid and indecisive; who are constantly interfering; or who are bullying and nickle-and-diming a production team. Ann and I try to hire these best people, communicate our vision to them precisely, treat them as we like to be treated ourselves, and support them in every way we can. One producer whom I admire has said it more succinctly, "Get the best and get out of their way."

Sadly, that is not always possible. With the best credentials and intentions, serious and legitimate creative differences do arise. In such instances, the producer in television, because he is ultimately responsible, must prevail, even if this means replacing a writer, a director, or any other creative person on the picture, except major stars. It is almost impossible to replace a star. There have been instances, but this means shelving the footage and starting again, or abandoning the picture entirely.

Generally, stars behave professionally, though nearly all of them do have their personality tics and warts. I don't blame them. It is their faces, their personas that are visibly at risk in every picture. The women have the added burdens of hair and makeup. What is often described as "ego" is more often fear—high anxiety about their looks and their performances—

the "nakedness" that actors have to experience. They are permanently in jeopardy of making fools of themselves in public. Ann and I empathize with this vulnerability. We honor the talent. We *like* actors. We do everything we can to make actors feel comfortable and confident and free to give. Still, you will occasionally run into a snag. Or worse, into an unredemptive son of a bitch or a no-talent. If one of these latter is a star you, as the producer, will have to endure, strengthened by the notion of the limited time you will have to put up with it; and affecting what you can, keeping in mind the overriding goal of getting the best picture possible "in the can" finished.

When a producer makes a deal for a television movie with a network, he may get a small supervisory or development fee (1 to 10 thousand dollars) to compensate his work during the scripting stage. If the script is picked up, the producer (with the development fee folded in) gets 30 to 100 thousand dollars per two hours as the fee for his work, depending on his experience and talent. If it is an in-house (network-owned) picture, the producer may get some share of net profits, if he had the idea for the picture. If the network had the idea, the in-house producer may simply be hired as an employee at a fixed fee.

If it is an outside production or package in which the network licenses the film for x runs over a period but does not own it, the producer will get his work fee as part of the production budget, plus a share that can range from total ownership to some equity, royalties, and a percentage of net profits, if the film is his idea and has been placed through a studio, major independent, or distribution company.

All producing entities, whether a network, studio, major independent, or smaller cottage-industry producer, have to be signatory to union contracts. Among these are SAG—The Screen Actors Guild; SEG—The Screen Extras Guild; DGA—The Directors Guild of America; WGA—The Writers Guild of America; AFM—The American Federation of Musicians; and the craft locals representing art directors, camera people, sound people, props people, gaffers (lighting and electricians), grips (stage hands), wardrobe, hair, makeup, costume designers, set decorators, stunts, editors, publicists, carpenters, painters, and production secretaries. These are most often the locals of IATSE—called "Yatsey" or "The IA"—which is the acronym for the International Association of Theatrical and Stage Employees and Technicians.

The SAG contract establishes for actors minimum wages—called scale—with minimum rehearsal days and hours for a day and for a week. Wages and hours are determined by the length of a program and its use—in local, regional, and network broadcast, cable, pay cable, home cassette, and foreign markets. There is a minimum scale for principal performers, and various others for those speaking fewer than five lines—called "under five"—and for specialty acts, voiceover, looping voices, dancers, singers, groups, and choruses. There are provisons that ask for guaranteed days of employment, meal and rest periods, credit, wardrobe, hair and makeup demands, retakes, understudies, stand-ins and dance-ins, stunts, vacation, holiday and overtime compensation, remotes, auditions, travel requirements (first class when available), dressing rooms, and sundry working conditions. The contract binds employers to full payments to pension and welfare plans and health and insurance plans. The SEG contract establishes similar rights for extras.

DGA represents directors, associate and assistant directors, unit production managers, production managers, and production assistants on television films. (DGA has jurisdiction throughout television, tape or film or live, and in radio.) For all of its members, the DGA contract governs scale wages, working conditions, credit, and the director's rights to the cut of a picture. A number of specifics are similar to SAG's contract, including per diem rates (food and daily spending money), first-class transportation, lodging on location, and health, pension, and welfare plans totally funded by the employer. There are established reuse fees for all subsequent distribution forms and markets, domestic and foreign.

WGA represents *all* writers in television (and radio), including writers of movies and mini-series. The WGA contract covers much of the same terrain as SAG and DGA contracts do for their members. Again, there is a health and pension and welfare plan paid for by producers. Working terms and credit are defined, as well as scale payments and residual payments for all subsequent runs, uses, and markets.

AFM is a national union with separate locals in individual communities. It covers musicians in all mediums from nightclubs to televison. Its contract parallels the others in its provisions. IATSE and NABET the same, without residual payments.

Keep in mind that with what I have just set forth you know next to zero about the unions. I am simply pointing you toward knowing what you do not know but will have to get familiar with as you become a producer. You yourself as a producer-for-hire may want to joint the Producers Guild of America, which looks after producers' rights, with management.

I will not give you more detail here and now, because when you are there and then, the details will be different. When you are ready to produce, all of the unions will provide you with specific, up-to-the-moment contracts and information governing the area of your concern.

Your eventually knowing all of this to a point is valuable and necessary, but I do find that even experienced producers, us included, do not know the minutiae of every applicable union contract. Since these are so complicated, prolix, and proliferous, producers rely on experts—lawyer, accountant, executive in charge of productions, associate producer, production manager, unit manager, and first and second assistant director—to establish knowledge and to maintain order at the various steps along the way. You will find that many creative producers have producer partners or chief lieutenants who are union and financial specialists.

Producers must by law pay social security and carry workmen's compensation and personal and property liability insurance. Networks will require that you carry these in larger amounts than government requires. Networks further demand a completion bond—a form of insurance that guarantees that either the picture gets completed and delivered as agreed or that there is money available to reimburse the financial outlay in the event of trouble.

There are additional critical coverages for a producer to have: E & O, negative and cast insurance.

E & O—errors and omissions—insurance safeguards the producer from people who might claim that a picture was their idea; or aver that the picture has defamed or libeled them or has invaded their privacy; and other chest-pain possibilities. For instance, a number of criminals have claimed recently that their transgressions were the direct faults of movies they had seen on television. In our litigious society, it is not a long jump one day for the victim of such a crime or, heaven help us, the criminal himself, to sue a producer for inducement of the felony.

Negative insurance shields the producer against his film footage being lost, stolen, damaged, or defective in manufacturing. This protection should begin from the day the film is purchased through to completion of a satisfactory answer or composite print that is kept separately from the original negative.

Cast insurance protects the producer from death, injury, illness, or other failure to perform by members of the cast. This insurance is especially necessary when you have stars or names in a picture. Imagine if you had been an uninsured producer when Natalie Wood was killed in the midst of a production.

Producers also insure for life, health, and accident for *all* personnel on a picture. The insurance companies usually demand physical examinations of all principal cast and production people. Weather insurance is available but extremely expensive, so most producers go without it and hope for the best. There are other policies, for hazardous acts and locales, for example, but here, once more, an insurance expert should be involved to tailor coverage for your particular circumstances. All of this insurance coverage is a pass-through expense that must be included in your picture budget. About the only insurance not available is coverage for a bad picture.

Television movie budgets vary but, as of this writing, range from a network paying 1 million to a 1.3 million per hour. Figure an average of 2.3 million dollars for a contemporary two-hour film. Beyond this, when the script is completed and approved, you will want an expert to work up a production budget. Even if you don't, others will demand it—the network, the studio, the major independent—whoever is the ultimate financial entity. These organizations have full-time staff experts to make movie budgets. In addition to this support service, as applicable, Ann and I spend a few hundred dollars out of our own pockets to hire a free-lance movie financial specialist to give us a detailed budget breakout. This provides a secure standard for comparison—and ground for civil questioning in the case of unexplained disparities.

The assigned production manager on a picture will be responsible for the day-to-day maintenance of the budget. There are also outside companies for hire who specialize in keeping financial records, adhering to union contracts, meeting payrolls, and paying the bills and taxes. There is a union accountant assigned to each production.

Here following are the budget form Ann and I use; the preliminary below-the-line one-page budget for *Drop-Out Father* (which apparently was prepared before the pickup by CBS and was used in making the decision to go forward); and a copy of one day's production control status report (which is updated and published every day of production) for *He's Fired, She's Hired*, nee *Paper Castle*. All forms differ in some degree from network to network and from studio and production company to studio and production company, but all provide for the same basic information.

THE PRIMAL SCREEN

TITLE _____   PICTURE NO. _____

DATE PREPARED _____

ACCOUNT NUMBER	DESCRIPTION	DAYS, WKS, OR QUANTITY	RATE	TOTALS
1	STORY –			
	A. STORY PURCHASE			
	B. TITLE PURCHASE			
	TOTAL STORY			
2	CONTINUITY AND TREATMENT			
	A. WRITERS			
	B. STENOGRAPHER			
	C. MIMEOGRAPH EXPENSE			
	D. RESEARCH EXPENSE			
	TOTAL CONTINUITY AND TREATMENT			
3	PRODUCER			
	A. PRODUCER			
	B. ASST. PRODUCER			
	C. SECRETARIES			
	TOTAL PRODUCER			
4	DIRECTOR			
	A. DIRECTOR			
	B. SECRETARIES			
	C. PENSION CONTRIBUTIONS			
	TOTAL DIRECTORS			

TITLE _____ PICTURE NO. _____

DATE PREPARED _____

ACCOUNT NUMBER	DESCRIPTION	DAYS, WKS, OR QUANTITY	RATE		TOTALS	
5	CAST					
	BUYOUTS		125%			
	PENSION H&W CONTRIBUTIONS					
	TOTAL CAST					
6	BITS					
	BUYOUTS		125%			
	PENSION CONTRIBUTIONS					
	OVERTIME ON BITS					
	FITTING CHARGES					
	TOTAL BITS					

TITLE _____ PICTURE NO. _____

DATE PREPARED _____

ACCOUNT NUMBER	DESCRIPTION	DAYS, WKS. OR QUANTITY	RATE	TOTALS
7	EXTRAS			
	OVERTIME FOR EXTRAS			
	FITTING FOR EXTRAS			
	SERVICE FEES FOR EXTRAS			
	ADJUSTMENTS FOR EXTRAS -			
	STAND INS			
	SCHOOL TEACHER'S			
	STUNT PEOPLE			
	STUNT ADJUSTMENTS			
	BUYOUTS 75%			
	PENSION H&W CONTRIBUTIONS			
	TOTAL EXTRAS			

TITLE _____   PICTURE NO. _____

DATE PREPARED _____

ACCOUNT NUMBER	DESCRIPTION	DAYS, WKS. OR QUANTITY	RATE	TOTALS
8	**PRODUCTION STAFF SALARIES**			
	A. PRODUCTION MANAGER			
	B. UNIT MANAGER			
	C. 1st ASST. DIRECTOR			
	SEVERANCE			
	D. 2nd ASST. DIRECTOR			
	SEVERANCE			
	E. EXTRA ASST. DIRECTORS			
	F. SECRETARIES			
	G. DIALOGUE CLERK			
	H. SCRIPT CLERK			
	U. DANCE DIRECTOR			
	J. CASTING DIRECTOR & STAFF			
	K. TECHNICAL ADVISOR			
	L. FIRST AID			
	M. LOCATION AUDITOR			
	TOTAL PRODUCTION STAFF			
9	**PRODUCTION OPERATING STAFF**			
	A. CAMERAMEN			
	1. 1st CAMERAMAN			
	2. CAMERA OPERATORS			
	3. FOCUS ASST. CAMERAMEN			
	4. ASST. CAMERAMEN			
	5. CAMERA MECHANICS			
	6. COLOR DIRECTOR			
	7. STILL MAN			
	8. STILL GAFFER			
	9. PROCESS CAMERAMAN			
	10. ASST. PROCESS CAMERAMAN			
	11. EXTRA CAMERA OPERATORS			
	12. EXTRA CAMERA ASSISTANTS			
	13. O.T. CAMERA CREW 43-48 HOURS			
	TOTAL ACCT. 9-A			

TITLE _____   PICTURE NO. _____

DATE PREPARED _____

ACCOUNT NUMBER	DESCRIPTION	DAYS, WKS. OR QUANTITY	RATE		TOTALS	
9	**PRODUCTION OPERATING STAFF (Contd.)**					
	B. SOUND DEPT.					
	1. MIXER					
	2. RECORDER					
	3. BOOM MAN					
	4. CABLEMAN					
	5. CABLE BOOM MAN					
	6. P.A. SYSTEM OPERATOR					
	7. DREAM OPERATOR					
	8. SOUND MAINTENANCE					
	TOTAL ACCT. 9-B					
	C. WARDROBE DEPT.					
	1. WARDROBE DESIGNER					
	2. WARDROBE BUYER					
	3. 1ST WARDROBE GIRL					
	4. 2ND WARDROBE GIRL					
	5. 1ST WARDROBE MAN					
	6. 2ND WARDROBE MAN					
	7. TAILOR					
	8. SEAMSTRESS					
	9. EXTRA HELP					
	TOTAL ACCT. 9-C					
	D. MAKE-UP AND HAIRDRESSING					
	1. HEAD MAKE-UP MAN					
	2. 2ND MAKE-UP MAN					
	3. HEAD HAIRDRESSER					
	4. 2ND HAIRDRESSER					
	5. BODY MAKE-UP GIRL					
	6. EXTRA HELP					
	TOTAL ACCT. 9-D					

TITLE _____   PICTURE NO. _____

DATE PREPARED _____

ACCOUNT NUMBER	DESCRIPTION	DAYS, WKS, OR QUANTITY	RATE		TOTALS	
	PRODUCTION OPERATING STAFF (Contd.)					
	E. GRIP DEPT.					
	1. 1ST GRIP					
	2. BEST BOY					
	3. SET OPERATION GRIPS					
	4. EXTRA LABOR					
	5. CAMERA BOOM OPERATORS					
	6. CRAB DOLLY GRIP					
	TOTAL ACCT. 9-E					
	F. PROPERTY					
	1. HEAD POOPERTY MAN					
	2. 2ND PROPERTY MAN					
	3. 3RD PROPERTY MAN					
	4. OUTSIDE HELP					
	5. EXTRA HELP					
	TOTAL ACCT. 9-F					
	G. SET DRESSING DEPT.					
	1. HEAD SET DRESSER					
	2. ASST. SET DRESSER					
	3. SWING GANG					
	4. DRAPERY MAN					
	5. ASST. DRAPERY MAN					
	6. NURSERY MAN					
	7. EXTRA LABOR					
	TOTAL ACCT. 9-G					
	H. ELECTRICAL DEPT.					
	1. GAFFER					
	2. BEST BOY					
	3. ELECTRICAL OPERATING LABOR					
	4. GENERATOR OPERATOR					
	5. ELECTRICAL MAINTENANCE MAN					
	6. RIGGING & STRIKING CREW					
	7. WIND MACHINE OPERATOR					
	TOTAL ACCT. 9-H					

TITLE _____

PICTURE NO. _____

DATE PREPARED _____

ACCOUNT NUMBER	DESCRIPTION	DAYS, WKS, OR QUANTITY	RATE		TOTALS	
9	PRODUCTION OPERATING STAFF (Contd.)					
	I. LABOR DEPT.					
	1. STANDBY LABORER					
	2. ASST. LABORERS					
	TOTAL ACCT. 9-I					
	J. SPECIAL EFFECTS					
	1. HEAD SPECIAL EFFECTS MAN					
	2. ASST. SPECIAL EFFECTS MAN					
	3. PLUMBER					
	TOTAL ACCT. 9-J					
	K. SET STANDBY OPERATORS					
	1. CARPENTER					
	TOTAL ACCT. 9-K					
	L. SET STANDBY PAINTERS					
	1. PAINTER					
	TOTAL ACCT. 9-L					
	M. SET WATCHMAN					
	1. WATCHMEN					
	TOTAL ACCT. 9-M					
	N. WRANGLERS					
	1. S.P.C.A. MAN					
	2. HEAD WRANGLER					
	3. WRANGLERS					
	O. MISCELLANEOUS					
	GRAND TOTAL SET OPERATING SALARIES					

TITLE _____ PICTURE NO. _____

DATE PREPARED _____

ACCOUNT NUMBER	DESCRIPTION	TIME		RATE				TOTAL	
10	**SET CONSTRUCTION**								
	A. Art Director								
	B. Asst. Art Director								
	C. Sketch Artist								
	D. Draftsman								
	E. Set Supervisor								
	F. Material & Supplies								
	G. Construction Supervisor								
	H. Miscellaneous								
		LABOR		MATERIAL					
	1								
	2								
	3								
	4								
	5								
	6								
	7								
	8								
	9								
	10								
	11								
	12								
	13								
	14								
	15								
	16								
	17								
	18								
	19								
	20								
	21								
	22								
	23								
	24								
	25								
	26								
	27								
	28								
	29								
	30								
	31								
	32								
	33								
	34								
	35								
	36								
	37								
	38								
	39								
	Rigging Labor Grip								
	Striking								
	Backings								
	Greens								
	TOTAL SETS								

TITLE _____   PICTURE NO. _____

DATE PREPARED _____

ACCOUNT NUMBER	DESCRIPTION	DAYS, WKS, OR QUANTITY	RATE		TOTALS	
11	SET OPERATION EXPENSES					
	A. Camera Equipment Rentals					
	B. Camera Equipment Purchases					
	C. Camera Car Rentals					
	D. Camera Crane Rentals					
	E. Wardrobe Purchased					
	F. Wardrobe Rentals					
	G. Wardrobe Maintenance					
	H. Grip Equipment Rented					
	I. Prop Equipment Rented					
	J. Props Purchased					
	JJ. Prop Man's Petty Cash Exp.					
	K. Props Rented					
	L. Props - Loss & Damaged					
	M. Set Dressing Rentals					
	N. Set Dressing Purchased					
	O. Draperies Purchased & Rented					
	P. Nursery - Purchased & Rented					
	Q. Process Equipment Rentals					
	R. Make-up Purchases					
	S. Hairdressing Purchases & Rentals					
	T. Electrical Eauipment Rentals					
	U. Electrical Equipment Purchased					
	V. Electrical Power					
	W. Rentals on Picture Cars - Trucks - Planes - Wagons - Livestock, etc.					
	X. Miscellaneous Rentals & Purchases					
	Y. Generator Rental - Gas & Oil -					
	Z. Special Effect Purchases & Rentals					
	Total Set Operation Expense					

TITLE _____   PICTURE NO. _____

DATE PREPARED _____

ACCOUNT NUMBER	DESCRIPTION	DAYS, WKS, OR QUANTITY	RATE	TOTALS
12	**CUTTING FILM LABORATORY**			
	A. EDITOR			
	B. ASST. CUTTER			
	C. SOUND CUTTER			
	D. MUSIC CUTTER			
	E. NEGATIVE CUTTER			
	TOTAL LABOR			
	F. NEGATIVE ACTION RAW STOCK			
	G. NEGATIVE SOUND RAW STOCK			
	GG. TAPE RENTAL			
	H. DEVELOP ACTION			
	HH. DEVELOP SOUND			
	I. PRINT ACTION			
	II. PRINT SOUND			
	J. MAGNASTRIPE - PRODUCTION			
	JJ. MAGNASTRIPE - SCORE & DUBBING			
	K. COLOR SCENE PILOT STRIPS			
	KK. 16MM COLOR PRINTS (FROM CCO)			
	KKK. INTER-NEGATIVE			
	L. SEPARATION MASTERS			
	LL. INTER-POSITIVE			
	M. ANSWER PRINT			
	MM. COMPOSITE PRINT			
	N. FINE GRAIN PRINT			
	NN. PANCHROMATIC (FG)			
	NNN. 16MM PRINTS			
	O. FADES-DISSOLVES-DUPES & FINE GRAIN			
	OO. REPRINTS			
	P. TITLES, MAIN & END			
	Q. CUTTING ROOM RENTAL			
	R. CODING			

TITLE _____   PICTURE NO. _____

DATE PREPARED _____

ACCOUNT NUMBER	DESCRIPTION	DAYS, WKS. OR QUANTITY	RATE	TOTALS
12	CUTTING FILM LABORATORY (Contd.)			
	R. PROJECTION			
	S. MOVIOLA RENTALS			
	T. REELS & LEADER			
	U. CUTTING ROOM SUPPLIES			
	V. STOCK SHOTS			
	W. PROCESS PLATES			
	X. SALES TAX			
	XX. CODING			
	LABORATORY SUB-TOTAL			
	TOTAL CUTTING FILM LABORATORY			

TITLE _____   PICTURE NO. _____

DATE PREPARED _____

ACCOUNT NUMBER	DESCRIPTION	DAYS, WKS. OR QUANTITY	RATE	TOTALS
13	**MUSIC**			
	A. Music Supervisor			
	B. Director			
	C. Composer			
	D. Musicians			
	E. Singers			
	F. Arrangers			
	G. Copyists			
	H. Royalties			
	I. Purchases			
	J. Miscellaneous			
	K. Instrument Rental & Cartage			
	L. Librarian			
	Total Music			
14	**SOUND**			
	A. Royalties			
	B. Dubbing Room Rental			
	C. Pre-Score Equipment Rentals			
	D. Scoring Equipment Rentals			
	E. Labor for Dubbing & Etc.			
	F. Sound Equipment Rentals			
	G. Miscellaneous			
	H. Transfer Time			
	Total Sound			
15	**TRANSPORTATION STUDIO**			
	A. Labor			
	B. Car Rentals			
	C. Truck Rentals			
	D. Bus Rentals			
	E. Car Allowance			
	F. Miscellaneous			
	G. Gas & Oil, - Generator - Mileage			
	H. Wranglers Cars			
	I. Livestock Transportation			
	Total Transportation			

TITLE _____   PICTURE NO. _____

DATE PREPARED _____

ACCOUNT NUMBER	DESCRIPTION	DAYS, WKS, OR QUANTITY	RATE	TOTALS
16	**LOCATION**			
	A. TRAVELING			
	B. HOTEL			
	C. MEALS			
	D. LOCATION SITES RENTAL			
	E. SPECIAL EQUIPMENT			
	F. CAR RENTALS			
	G. BUS RENTALS			
	H. TRUCK RENTALS			
	I. SUNDRY EMPLOYEES			
	J. LOCATION OFFICE RENTAL			
	K. GRATUITIES			
	L. MISCELLANEOUS			
	M. SCOUTING & PRE-PRODUCTION			
	N. POLICE SERVICES & PERMITS			
	O. CONTACT MAN			
	TOTAL LOCATION			
17	**STUDIO RENTALS**			
	A. STAGE SPACE			
	B. STREET RENTALS			
	C. TEST			
	D. VACATION ALLOWANCE (STUDIO)			
	E. SURCHARGE ON RENTALS & STUDIO CHARGES			
	F. MISCELLANEOUS EXPENSES			
	G. DRESSING ROOMS - PORTABLE			
	H. OFFICE RENTALS			
	TOTAL STUDIO RENTALS			
18	**TESTS & RETAKES**			
	A. TESTS PRIOR TO PRODUCTION			
	B. TESTS DURING PRODUCTION			
	C. RETAKES AFTER PRINCIPAL PHOTOGRAPHY			
	D. PRE-PRODUCTION EXPENSE OR SHOOTING			
	TOTAL TESTS & RETAKES			

TITLE _____   PICTURE NO. _____

DATE PREPARED _____

ACCOUNT NUMBER	DESCRIPTION	DAYS, WKS, OR QUANTITY	RATE		TOTALS	
19	PUBLICITY					
	A. ADVERTISING					
	B. UNIT PUBLICITY MAN					
	C. ENTERTAINMENT					
	D. TRADE AND NEWSPAPER SUBSCRIPTIONS					
	E. PUBLICITY STILLS SALARIES					
	F. PUBLICITY STILLS SUPPLIES EQUIPMENT					
	G. PUBLICITY STILLS LAB. CHARGES					
	H. STILL GALLERY RENTAL & EXPENSE					
	I. Trailer					
	J. PRESS PREVIEW EXPENSE					
	K. SUPPLIES, POSTAGE AND EXPRESS					
	L. MISCELLANEOUS					
	TOTAL PUBLICITY					
20	MISCELLANEOUS					
	A. VACATION ALLOWANCE					
	B. RETROACTIVE WAGE CONTINGENCY					
	C. SUNDRY UNCLASSIFIED EXPENSE					
	D. COSTS IN SUSPENSE					
	E. SET COFFEE					
	F. WATER & ICE					
	TOTAL MISCELLANEOUS					
21	INSURANCE, TAXES, LICENSE AND FEES					
	A. CAST INSURANCE					
	B. NEGATIVE INSURANCE					
	C. LIFE INSURANCE					
	D. MISCELLANEOUS INSURANCE					
	E. COMPENSATION & PUBLIC LIABILITY INS.		%			
	F. SOCIAL SECURITY TAX		%			
	G. PERSONAL PROPERTY TAX					
	H. MISCL. TAXES AND LICENSES					
	I. CODE CERTIFICATE - MPPA					
	J. CITY TAX AND LICENSE					
	K. UNEMPLOYMENT TAX		%			
	L. PENSION PLAN CONTRIBUTION ACTORS DIRECTORS WRITERS		%			
	M. HEALTH & WELFARE CONTRIBUTION					
	N. PENSION PLAN – CRAFTS		%			
	TOTAL A/C 21					

TITLE _____

DATE PREPARED _____

ACCOUNT NUMBER	DESCRIPTION	DAYS, WKS. OR QUANTITY	RATE		TOTALS
22	GENERAL OVERHEAD				
	A. FLAT CHARGE				
	B. CORPORATE OVERHEAD EXPENSE				
	C. CASTING OFFICE SALARIES				
	D. ENTERTAINMENT - EXECUTIVES				
	E. TRAVEL EXPENSE - EXECUTIVES				
	F. OFFICE RENTAL AND EXPENSE				
	G. AUDITOR				
	H. TIMEKEEPER				
	I. SECRETARIES				
	J. PUBLIC RELATIONS HEAD				
	K. PUBLIC RELATIONS SECRETARY				
	L. LEGAL FEES				
	M. OFFICE SUPPLIES				
	N. POSTAGE - TELEPHONE & TELEGRAPH				
	O. CUSTOMS BROKERAGE				
	P. CONTINGENCY				
	Q. GENERAL OFFICE O.H.				
	R. FILM SHIPPING				
	TOTAL GENERAL OVERHEAD				
	GRAND TOTAL				

PRODUCTION BUDGET

DEAR-CUT FATHER — NEW YORK/LA. COMBINED BUDGET.
WORKING TITLE

EST. NO. WORKING BUDGET #2   CBS STUDIO CENTER   PROD. NO. _____

EST. DATED 7/10/81   Film Budget   PRODUCER _____

STARTING DATE _____   DIRECTOR _____

FINISHING DATE _____   Local   Dist.   SCRIPT DATED 4/9/81

FILM/SCOPE _____ Studio Loc.   Loc.   PGT. FOOTAGE _____

| DAYS BUDGETED | 1ST UNIT | 3 | 14 | 2 | IDLE | HOLIDAYS | TRAVEL | TOTAL 19 |
| 2ND UNIT | | | | | | | | |

DESCRIPTION	PAGE NO.			TOTAL BUDGET
01 SCREENPLAY	1			
02 PRODUCER'S UNIT	2			
03 CAST EXTRAS ONLY	3	56955		
05 DIRECTION	4			
MUSIC				
ROYALS, FEES, RIGHTS, OTHER				
TOTAL ABOVE THE LINE				
49 TELECINE	5	3000		
56 INSURANCE	6	—		
58 SECOND UNIT	6	—		
59 TESTS	6	—		
66 SET DESIGN	7	27700		
67 SET DRESSING	8	65371		
71 AMORTIZATIONS	9	—		
73 MUSIC	10	—		
74 SET CONSTRUCTION	11	169472	MC CALL HOME - PRACTICAL LOCN	
75 SET OPERATIONS	12	53407		
76 PROPERTY	13	40221		
77 WARDROBE	14	58805		
78 MAKEUP AND HAIRDRESSING	15	26842		
79 ELECTRICAL	16	66861		
80 CAMERA	17	94155		
81 PRODUCTION SOUND	18	30655		
82 STUDIO TRANSPORTATION	19	34465		
83 PICTURE VEHICLES-SPECIAL EQUIP.	20	11600		
84 LOCATION TRANSPORTATION	21	148245		
85 LOCATION EXPENSE	22	128679		
86 SPECIAL EFFECTS	23	17316		
87 MINIATURES	24	—		
88 POST PRODUCTION SOUND	24	25629		
89 TRICK AND MATTE SHOTS	25	—		
90 STOCK SHOTS AND PROCESS SHOTS	25	2000		
91 FILM	25	40286		
92 LABORATORY	26	50128		
93 OPTICALS, INSERTS AND TITLES	26	14000		
94 EDITORIAL	27	72983		
95 PRODUCTION STAFF	28	68855		
96 PUBLICITY	29			
97 ADMINISTRATIVE EXPENSE	29	17424		
98 FEES AND STAGE RENTALS	29	42075		
99 EXTRA TALENT	30	—		
TOTAL BELOW THE LINE		1316,174		
TOTAL BUDGET				

REMARKS:

BUDGET PREPARED WITHOUT ASSISTANCE FROM A PRODUCER,
DIRECTOR, CAMERAMAN OR CHOSEN SITE LOCATIONS.
CREW RATES BASED ON NEW PGA CONTRACT & 3rd YEAR
BEGINNING AUG 1st 1981 FOR IA AGREEMENT. INCLUDES
PROJECTED ESTIMATE FOR 1981-82 STUDIO CENTER RATE (?)

SHOOTING SCHEDULE = 2 DAYS DIST LOCATION-NEW YORK
14 DAYS LOCAL LOCATIONS -LA.
3 DAYS CBS STUDIO CENTER
19 DAYS TOTAL

PRODUCER _____   PRODUCTION MANAGER _____

UNIT PRODUCTION MANAGER _____   PRODUCTION ACCOUNTANT _____

PRODUCTION CONTROL STATUS REPORT

TITLE: "PAPER CASTLES" 0310-2932-0164

DATE: _THURS 9/21_

BELOW-THE-LINE BUDGET: $ 1,294,051 US
TOTAL OVER/UNDER EST. TO DATE: $ _– 793_ US
CURRENT B-T-L EST. TO COMPLETE: $ _1,293,258_ US

COMPANY IS ONE DAY BEHIND SCHEDULE

ABOVE-THE-LINE:

		THIS DATE	TO DATE

EXTRAS: _WED. 9/20_ Budget: $_____ (____ people)
14TH DAY WED. 9/20 Actual: $ _____ (____ people)

THIS DATE $_____   TO DATE $_____

TOTAL EXTRAS: $ _+ 1919_

BELOW-THE-LINE:

	DATE/DAY	FROM	TO	WORK HRS	PAY HRS		PAGES
BUDGET:	_9/20 14TH_	_7:00 AM_	_7:30 PM_	_11.5_	_13.5_		
ACTUAL:	_9/20 14TH_	_8:00 AM_	_8:30 PM_	_11.5_	_13.5_		_2 7/8_

BUDGETED TOTAL PAY HRS: 243.00 HRS

ADJUSTED TOTAL PAY HRS: _289.75_ HRS

SCHEDULED PGS TO DATE: _____

ACTUAL PAGES TO DATE: _68_

TOTAL MINUTES TO DATE: _81:13_

B-T-L ESTIMATE FROM PREVIOUS REPORT: $ _1,292,692_ US

	OVER/UNDER THIS DATE	OVER/UNDER TO DATE

WED. 9/20 -- 14TH DAY: _$ 11,505 U.S._
$11,505 US = one 13.5 hr shooting day

OVER/UNDER THIS DATE $ _0_   OVER/UNDER TO DATE $ _+33,073 U.S._

See back page for detail on B-T-L information   _+ 566 U.S._   _– 33,866 U.S._

UPDATED B-T-L ESTIMATE AS OF THIS DATE: $ _+ 566 U.S._ $ _– 793 U.S._

(OVER)

14ᵀᴴ DAY __WED ⁶/₃₀__ "PAPER CASTLES"

		+/- THIS DATE	+/- TO DATE
SET CONSTRUCTION	(labor)		− 2500
	(rentals)		
	(purchases)		
PROPS	(labor)		− 1500
	(rentals)		− 2000
	(purchases)		
SET DRESSING	(labor)		− 4200
	(rentals)		
	(purchases)		
WARDROBE	(labor)		− 2200
	(rentals)		− 4000
	(purchases)		− 2800
MAKEUP/HAIR	(labor)		− 1500
	(rentals)		
	(purchases)		
GRIP	(labor)		− 3000
	(rentals)		
	(purchases)		− 2000
ELECTRIC	(labor)		− 4000
	(rentals)		
	(purchases)		
CAMERA	(labor)		− 1000
	(rentals)		
TRANSPORTATION	(MILEAGE MONEY TO LOCATION)		+ 3600
	(labor)		− 4500
	(rentals)		− 2500
LOCATION	(MEAL MONEY)		+ 5000
	(labor)		− 1600
	(~~catered meals~~) HOTELS & PER DIEM		+ 9000
	(site rentals)		+ 960
	(OFFICE EQUIPMENT, SURVEY EXPENSE, MISC)		− 7473
FILM FOOTAGE	(Budget: __5500__ ' per day)	+ 566	+ 1067
	(Actual: __7440__ ' this day) +1940' @ .3650 ≝		
OTHER:	1. 2ᴺᴰ UNIT (COMM'L)		− 11,200
	2. ASS⁴ ART DIRECTOR & SET DESIGNER		+ 10,000
	3. PICTURE CARS & DRIVERS		− 2000
	4. PRODUCTION STAFF		− 1200
	5. SAVINGS IN PREP		− 3520
	6. EQUIPMENT RENTAL ON DOWN DAY		+ 1200

TOTAL THIS PAGE: $ + 566 $ − 33,866

NOTES: COMPANY IS ONE DAY BEHIND SCHEDULE

By the time we went into production on *Drop-Out Father*, the below-the-line budget had been pared by $46,682 to $1,269,492. On *Paper Castle (He's Fired, She's Hired)*, despite being one day over our shooting schedule, we finished under budget.

"Below the line" traditionally means fixed costs. "Above the line" means variable costs. In television, above the line means the creative elements of cast, script, producer, director, music, royalties, fees, and rights. Under below the line in television, not to say that some of the elements are not creative, come the craft items and equipment, administration, and nuts and bolts.

As you can see, particularly from the daily production control status report, there are extremely tight financial controls in television movies. The daily report is a helpful dictator, letting you know exactly where you stand and, if you are over, forcing you to make changes in the script and production requirements in order to bring the picture back on budget.

In *He's Fired, She's Hired*, for instance, Ann Shanks, who was producing the pricture, got the director to cut two small scenes completely, eliminate a couple of others by folding their content into other larger scenes and by rescheduling a scene that I had written as an interior, and that would have taken considerable time to light, as an exterior scene, which, playing in sunlight, went faster.

I mentioned earlier something called broadcast standards. At CBS it is called program practices. At ABC it is called broadcast standards and practices. NBC splits the responsibilities into two sections, broadcast standards; and compliance and practices. In industry shorthand, these are the censors.

Because of their responsibilities to government regulation—the FCC—a self-regulating industry code—the NAB or National Association of Broadcasters Code—their affiliated stations, and a heterogeneous viewing audience, networks are fastidious in their concerns about subject matter, taste, language, and attitudes in scripts and shootings. These standards departments are autonomous and have veto power even over their own programming departments.

While every producer can recount stories of foolishness, obtuseness, abstruseness, and plain arbitrary stubbornness on the part of the representatives of these departments, I think they perform sensitively and realistically. In a democracy with its massive and disparate television audience and its many young watchers, some system of restraint and discretion is obligatory. If the networks did not exercise control, the government—especially in the current fundamentalist atmosphere—might, which is the curse of television in most of the rest of the world.

What does this leave us with? Electronic mental tapioca? Sometimes. But I think that is more often the fault of ratings-chasing creators and programmers rather than departments of standards. Also, I can think of no serious social, moral, or political theme or subject, no matter how controversial, that has not or could not be dealt with in a television movie. The responsibility resides with the producers and the programmers to expand television's sights, to reveal previously hidden societal truths and allow for unpopular views. If they can do so skillfully, without gratuitous violence and cretinous language, the "censors" will not stop them.

If you wish for "snuff" pictures, *The Texas Chainsaw Murders* and other greater and lesser putrefactions on your network channel, you and I part company. Yes, under our Constitution, everything on film or in print, as odious as it may be to others, should be available to individuals on a paid or private basis, but it does not belong on broadcast television. Of course, "We should be eternally vigilant against attempts to check the expression of opinions that we loathe," as Justice Oliver Holmes said, but never in the history of the American Constitution has the right to freedom of speech been supposed or judged to be absolute. Holmes also put this side of the proposition aptly as part of a 1919 Supreme Court decision, "Free speech would not protect a man in falsely shouting fire in a theatre."

Producers (and writers) can and must work to broaden the reach and substance of television by fighting sincerely to extend the boundaries of the permissible rather than cynically to up a rating. Some of us have done it, and television has come far from the bad old bluenose, racist, sexist, mindlessly patriotic, myopically middle-class days of twin beds and married-only love making. Stepinfetchit, brainless blonds, John Wayne clones pulling out hand grenade pins with their teeth are rare now, as are presidents made of marble and cheery suburban homes with cheery husbands, wives, and children where only cakes get battered and the truth abused.

If you believe you have material in your script that is important morally and intellectually, fight for it. Even if you deem some of it harmless and inoffensive except to a few self-anointed saints on Earth, fight for it. Television, especially television comedy, has to offend someone or risk becoming the communications equivalent of a capon. Be in the vanguard, as Holmes also said, "of the felt necessities of the times." But if you know you are defending material the real purpose of which is to titillate, exploit, slander, or demean, do not cry censorship when it has to come out.

Much of the business of broadcast standards departments has to do with matters other than content and taste. For instance, the departments guard against the misuse of commercial names—"plugs"—and absolutely forbid, as the law does, any mention of a product or service in exchange for money, gifts, or favors, except in those cases where a waiver is granted and a clear disclaimer is present in the film. The departments guard against invasion of citizen privacy and against legal risk and try to assure factuality.

These departments register and file all written idea submissions, read all scripts, attend all rough cut and final screenings. They can insist on changes at every step. Every network contract stipulates that all other provisions are dependent on a broadcast standards department's acceptance of the film.

Here following are the broadcast standards notes for *Drop-Out Father*. The handwritten notations are Ann's and came out of a meeting with members of the department to negotiate the original comments.

CBS/BROADCAST GROUP

CBS Inc., Television City
7800 Beverly Boulevard
Los Angeles. California 90036
(213) 852-2345

Dear Andy:

Re: "Drop-Out Father"
     Final Draft Dated 12/21/81; Received 12/24/81

Following are our Program Practices requests:

Page 1   Please be sure Wally Winkler is fictitious or cleared
                for use. Same for "Good Morning Punk".

Page 2   Please be sure "Crash Baxter's Nashville St. Patrick's
                Day" is fictitious.

Page 4   Dr. Martin Furness should be a fictitious name for the
                Columbia University Professor. Same for the book title
                "Male Menopause".

Page 6   Instead of "do it" could Elizabeth say "do anything"?

Page 7   Please qualify Elizabeth's remarks about "sugar coated
                cereals" by indicating: "...some people say..." or
                similar. Please clear the Pink Floyd music.   *Rolling Stones*

Page 8   Though it's not apparent in the script, we assume David
                will be attired in more than his guitar. Should he be
         OK   wearing a t-shirt, please be sure it is free of commercial
                identification. And, the guitar should not be identifiable
                as a particular brand.

Page 11   *OK* Please be sure Arthur Emschweiler (from Lancaster, Pennsyl-
                Ref vania) is fictitious or cleared for use.

Page 12   I believe the correct expression is yin and yang.
and later

Page 13   As previously requested, please delete Ed and David's graphic
                remarks about sex in a Trans-Am. Something oblique might
                be acceptable. In any event, please delete the commercial
                name and use a generic reference.

Page 17   In the garage, please avoid featuring the identification
                of the vehicles parked there.

CBS Broadcast Group: CBS Television Network. CBS Entertainment. CBS Sports. CBS News. CBS Television Stations. CBS Radio

Page 18   Instead of "Hawaiian Punch", please use a generic
                     reference.

Page 21   As previously indicated, please avoid showing that
and later   portion of the nude man's silhouette between waist and
                     knees. Also, please be sure the beautiful young woman's
                     attire provides adequate coverage in all respects. When
                     she fires the "Gun" deodorant, please avoid a close-up
                     of his armpits being sprayed. The product name should
                     be fictitious.

Page 25   Please delete Tony's use of "mother" which has an unac-
                     ceptable connotation in this particular context.

Page 26   Instead of "Rolaids", please have Tony use a generic
                     reference.

                     Also, delete the "Lufthansa" references here and later.

                     "Starteeth" should be a fictitious product name (here and
                     later).

Page 27   Please delete the "C.R.A.P." joke inasmuch as the   WKRP
                     expression is not in general use on the Network.

Page 30   Instead of "Dramamine", please use a generic reference.

Page 31   Please delete Tony's "sour cream" reference   The sexual
                     connotation seems in questionable taste.

Page 32   We assume "Space Age Bras" is fictitious. Please ensure
                     that "Bacayazi" is fictitious. Please name the lip gloss
                     something other than "Joystick".

Page 34   Instead of "proctologist", please use another speciality.

Page 39   Instead of "hysterectomy", please name a different
                     surgical procedure.

Page 42   Draper's heart attack should be carefully staged to avoid
                     an exaggerated or horrifying effect. When he's shown
                     dead, please avoid open, staring eyes.

Page 44   When we peer into David's room, please have both teens
                     fully clothed and on top of the covers.

                     Please delete water pipe and similar paraphernalia.

Page 45   Instead of "raping" please have Announcer say "assaulting".

Page 50   The housekeeper must be up to her armpits in sheet (if she
                     is in bed).

Page 51   Please avoid identifying Twinkies.
and later

Page 52   Please delete "Twinkie" reference and use generic.

Page 53   We trust that "Camp Wacamac" is fictitious.

Page 56   To be acceptable for broadcast, Tony's "matinee" ref-
                  erence must clearly be a reference to theatre rather
                  than a "nooner".

Page 63   Please do not identify "Psychology Today".

Page 65   Bathroom footage should be free of commercial identifi-
and later   cation.

Page 69   Please be sure "Lust in New Orleans" is fictitious.

Page 71   Please avoid identifying "Atlantic Monthly".

Page 72   Montage footage (New York City) should be free of com-
                  mercial identification.

Page 73   Please clear use of the circus poster and avoid featuring
                  "Ringling Brothers, Barnum and Bailey" name.

Page 75   For reasons of taste, please delete the "amputee/one-
                  legged" elements of the Announcer's copy.

Page 79   Footage of the Soho street should be free of commercial
and later   identification.

                  Instead of "Campbell's Soup" please use a generic
                  reference.

Page 81   Please delete all Lufthansa identification and references
                  to "Red Baron".

                  Please ensure that all spoken German is acceptable for
                  broadcast.

Page 82   "...tried it to the 'Valkierie'..." sounds suggestive.
                  Please rework the line to tone it down.

Page 84   "Radical Women's Gallery" should be fictitious. Same
                  for "Angelo's Photo Studio".

Page 86   Please delete the unflattering reference to Ramada Inn.

Page 88   If we are to keep the "Struggling to make ends meet"
                  line, we will want to lose the "No pun intended" line
                  to avoid the prostitution connection.

Page 89   As previously requested, please rework the dialogue to
                  delete the housewives' prostitution scheme.

Page 90   Instead of "Miss Chinatown" please use a fictitious
                  title.

"Drop-Out Father"   Page 4

Page 93   If an actual French conversational record is used, please
                 clear it for broadcast, and be sure the material is
                 acceptable for air.

Page 94   Please clear use of the "I Love New York" t-shirt logo.

Commercial identification is to be avoided as in:

Page 2   kitchen and props (appliances, food containers,
                     magazine, etc.)
Page 3   newspaper
Pages 4 & 5   instant coffee, milk container, cigarette pack, electric
                     appliances, cereal carton
Page 18   train station
Page 43   TV dinner
Page 48   wine bottle
Page 49   ice cream and fried chicken packages
Page 51   Twinkies and McDonalds

Casual profanity and the casual usage of "God" seem at an acceptable level.
We would appreciate your not exceeding scripted indications.

As for routine production cautions, please clear with this department or
avoid use of commercial identifications that appear on exteriors and
props. There should not be legible telephone numbers except for 555 pre-
fix followed by 2000 or a number higher. Personal and commercial names
should be fictitious or cleared for broadcast. Program Practices must
approve in advance any agreements involving on-air exposure or credits in
exchange for money or production assistance.

Sincerely,

Carol Isaacs
Senior Editor
Program Practices

December 29, 1981

Mr. Andy Gottlieb
CBS Studio Center
4024 Radford Ave.
Studio City, CA 91604

cc: Nancy Bein, Paul Bogrow, Stan Hough, Steve Mills, Bill Self,
     Elsie Walton

CI:sp

As you can see, the requests are reasonable to begin with; and, in many instances, in which we made reasonable arguments, the script items stood. For example, in the page 13 note, I took out "Trans-Am" but was able to keep the "s-e-c-k-s" sequence. CBS accepted it as an honest revelation of broad teen-age behavior in the eighties—and of our faulted educations (How many good spellers do you know these days?) Ed McCall's attitude, moreover, was disapproving of his son's behavior, one more item in his view of contemporary life as a hodgepodge of wayward values.

I use the names of commercial products frequently in my scripts—never for personal gain, but because they are so present in our lives. People talk, think, and act because of product identifications and images. Products are metaphors. I agreed to alter these usages where a generic name would work as well: for instance, "fruit juice" for "Hawaiian Punch"; but CBS yielded when the specific name was logical or underscored a point. For instance, "Rolaids" stayed in since no one goes around saying "antacid tablets." The same for "Dramamine." I still don't know the generic name for that substance. "Pink Floyd" had to go since we could not clear the band's music. I came up with "Endangered Animals," for which John Shanks and his band "Line One" provided the music.

As you see from Ann's notated "yes" and "OK," most of what we believed we needed, we were able to keep. By the by, "hysterectomy" stayed in and so did "proctologist" and "C.R.A.P." "Twinkies" fell out.

Much of all of this is influenced by the overall meaning and tone of a script. The standards people at CBS knew that *Drop-Out Father* had serious intentions and a valuable theme. They worked with us to preserve its textures and its purposes.

As broadcast standards is reviewing the script, it is also sent to an outside company called deForest Research. DeForest makes a meticulous examination of the script, tracking all character names, places, and references, to real people, events, products, and institutions to flag potential conflicts and problems. They check for factual accuracy, translate foreign usages, and trace copyright and trademark owners as appropriate. They clear usable phone numbers. None of this research is binding on the producer or the network. It is an advisory service, but its advice is respected and applied. Here is one page of the deForest Research examination of *Drop-Out Father*, a report that ran to seventeen pages in total:

> de Forest Research
> December 23, 1981
> <u>For: CBS ENTERTAINMENT</u>

<u>RESEARCH ON: ''DROP-OUT FATHER'' By Bob Shanks</u>

<u>OPENING NOTE – LOCALE</u>: The indicated locale of this teleplay is Stamford, Connecticut. However, due to possible conflict mentioned below (see Cast List re ''Ed McCall''), in conversation with Mr. Shanks, he has asked us to change the locale to GREENWICH, Connecticut. Therefore, in addition

to all standard sources, all names have been checked in that actual community.

<u>CAST</u>
<u>COMMENT</u>   Radio Announcer, p.1

Radio Announcer #2, p. 1   Identified in dialog as Wally Winkler. We find one prominent person with this name: a physician in Switzerland; no listing in the N.Y. area or Grennwich, Ct. There is no prominent disc jockey in the N.Y. area with this name. Do not consider usage to conflict.

Ed(ward Andrew) McCall, p. 1   We find only one listing for this surname (all spellings) in Stamford, CT. See Opening Note. No listing in Greenwich for this name. HOWEVER, NOTE: there is a prominent listing in Manhattan for the advertising firm of ''McAffrey & McCall,'' and a listing in <u>Who's Who</u> for David McCall, President of that firm. Considering the duplication of surname, city and purview, we would advise a surname change. Mr. Shanks has requested the surname be retained. Research will be happy to clear an artistically acceptable alternative, if deemed advisable.

Katherine McCall, p. 1   See above. Also, we find only one possible listing for this name in the N.Y. area: in Brooklyn; no listing in Greenwich. If surname is retained, Research will be happy to clear an artistically acceptable alternative given name, if deemed advisable.

Elizabeth McCall, p. 2   See above, re Ed McCall. We find no prominent person with this name; no listing in Greenwich.

Dr. Martin Purness, p. 4   We find no prominent person with this name: no listing in the N.Y. area. There is no listing for this exact name in the American Faculty Directory.

David McCall, p. 8   See above, re Ed McCall for comment concerning both surname, and prominent listing for this exact name. We find four possible listings for this name in the N.Y. area; none in Greenwich.

Producers make scores of contracts on one movie: a contract with the buyer or network, with unions, with cast members, with the director and other key production personnel, with municipalities, location owners, and studio facilities, with a deficit financier and/or a distributor.

All subsequent contracts must conform to the applicable provisions of the network contract and the union contracts, and grant use of the film in perpetuity in other uses and markets.

The network contract is called an agreement. Its full terms and conditions are established when a network decides to go to script, even though the project may be abandoned after the script stage. At each network the agreements are negotiated and prepared by a department called business affairs.

The agreement states that the network has the right to license exclusively a picture of, say, two hours in length to be shot in 35mm color film, at 2.3 million dollars—the license fee—for two runs over four years. If there is a pickup, typically, the agreement calls for paying the producer one-third of the gross license fee twenty days before principal photography begins, one-third within twenty days following completion of principal photography, and the final one-third within twenty days after delivery of the completed film. The payments may be in quarter allotments and the days may be ten or fifteen instead of twenty.

There is a "play or pay" provision, which means a network must make all agreed upon payments whether it chooses to air the movie or not.

There is a time schedule of delivery dates—script, script revisions, pre-production, production, editing, rough cut, scoring and effects, and final print.

The license area is defined: the United States, its territories and possessions (excepting Spanish-language television in Puerto Rico), and sometimes Bermuda, Tijuana, Mexico, and the Bahamas. Restrictions are sometimes placed on certain Canadian sales the producer may be able to make because many U.S. and Canadian markets receive the television signals of both nations.

The agreement spells out the network's rights of approval over all creative elements—the cast, the director, the on-line producer, the writer(s), art director, director of photography, composer, and so on. The producer must agree to make "dailies" or film "rushes" available to the network as well as picture assemblies, rough cuts, and final cuts.

The final film must be delivered according to a list of technical specifications.

The network will seek property exclusivity or first negotiation/first refusal on sequels and series spinoffs.

The agreement stipulates that the producer must adhere to all applicable union contracts and federal, state, and local laws.

The agreement requires the producer to furnish the network with music cue sheets, including titles, kind and length of use, names of composers, lyricists, publishers, copyright owners, performing rights licensers, and synchronization rights licensers.

The network is granted the right to broadcast the film on any day of the week in primetime and to include any commercial sponsor. (The only exception to this latter, as far as I know, is Herman Wouk, who got the right from ABC to veto sponsors in *The Winds of War*.)

The producer promises "best efforts" to assure that his movie will contain no "objectionable material" and that all material will be subject to approval by the network's department of broadcast standards and practices.

The network gets the right to alter, loop, dub, and otherwise edit the movie as it sees fit.

The producer must include copyright notice in the movie and maintain copyright during the license period (and longer, of course, for his own protection).

The network gets the right to use any and all portions of the movie for advertising, promotion, sales presentations, and audience testing.

The producer grants specific and general indemnities that hold the network and its affiliated stations harmless in claims, damages, liabilities, suits, costs, and expenses in connection with the movie.

The producer affirms that he and the network are arm's-length contractors and that nothing in the agreement unites them in association, partnership, joint venture, or otherwise regarding the project.

There is a "name and likeness" provision. This grants the network permission to use and to allow others to use the names, likenesses, and voices of all creative personnel in the picture.

The producer warrants to provide the insurance coverage I have explained.

There are specific provisions setting forth how and where notices are to be furnished and how and where disputes are to be resolved. A network has the right to assign the contract to any third parties.

The producer promises to use his "best efforts" in seeing that his employees and subcontractors abide by the provisions of the Federal Communications Commission regulations, with particular heed to Sections 317 and 508. These define the rules for making it illegal to take money, gifts, services, or sundry considerations in return for favors in the movie, without disclosing the facts.

A lot of these items in a network contract are negotiable.

A network cannot share in ownership of your movie, though stars and studios will seek their pieces.

The contracts a producer makes with a deficit financier, principal cast members, and other creative personnel are similar in their provisions to the contract between the producer and the network. Withal, you must have an experienced television lawyer or agent.

Contracts for lesser cast members are normally handled by the casting specialist. Here is a sample of such a deal memorandum, with personal information blanked out. Following it are two pages of the motion picture–television permit from the City of New York and a specific location agreement, again suitably blanked out.

THE PRIMAL SCREEN

PROD. #

PRODUCER Ann & Bob Shanks

DIRECTOR Don Taylor

ARTIST

ROLE   Jose   START 1/7/82

SALARY $350.00/day.

BILLING   End titles, placement at Producer's discretion.

RESIDUALS   At SAG minimum requirements

THEATRICALS   At SAG minimum requirements

TRANSPORTATION   Not applicable

PER DIEM, MISC. EXP. Not applicable

AGENT   PHONE

LOAN-OUT

ARTIST'S ADDRESS

PHONE   SERVICE none

S.S.#

SPECIAL CONDITIONS

SCRIPT   REVISIONS

SAG   WARDROBE

DISTRIBUTION: CONTRACT STATUS

                                         NEGOTIATOR

338

MOTION PICTURE – TELEVISION PERMIT   CITY OF NEW YORK   *ann* 020

MAYOR'S OFFICE FOR FILM, THEATRE AND BROADCASTING
110 WEST 57TH STREET NEW YORK N.Y. 10019

This permit is issued to the applicant to film or televise on streets or property subject to the jurisdiction of the City of New York at the times and locations designated below. The permit must be in the possession of the applicant at all times while on location. For additional assistance call the Permit Division: 489-6714. Police Unit: 592-6226.

APPLICATION NOT ACCEPTED UNLESS TYPED.

Date_____ December 31, 1981 _____

1. Company: __CBS ENTERTAINMENT__   Production Contact: _G. Manasse/Nancy Wood_

2. Address: __1290 Sixth Avenue, Rm 250, NYC 10019__   Tel. No. __975-3345__

3. Locations: (If more than 2 use Schedule "A") __See Schedule A__

4. Dates of filming: __Jan 6-8, 1982__   Approx. times: __7A-7P__

5. Scene to be filmed must be described accurately: __See Schedule A__

6. Animals, firearms, special effects or unusual scenes: __None__

7. List production equipment: __Normal 35__   # in cast & crew __40__

    No. of Trucks & plate #s __1 Cine: 72139L-CA 1 Erie Truck: 4205HB-NY__

    No. of Autos & plate #s __(6+ cars/wagons/vans)__ 139RS-NJ/774-NXT-NJ/ 82YUY-NY/486XQE-NY/645-UGJ-NY/189-AUG-NY/

    Other vehicles & plate #s __1 Bus:__   3 Campers: 535TRS-NJ/386-MCY-NJ/525TUV-NJ

8. Feature Film: [X] TV Movie or Special: ☐ TV Series: ☐ Other: ☐ (Give title, producer, director and identify celebrities) __"Drop Out__ __Father", Producer Gottlieb & Bob/Ann Shanks, Dir: Don Taylor, Star: Dick Van Dyke__

    Asst. Director: __Jerram Swartz/Henry Bronchtein__ Prod. Mgr. __George Manasse__

9. If TV commercial name product: _____

10. Public Liability Insurance Company, Policy # and Agent: CONTINENTAL INSURACNE COMPANY __Schiff Terhune, #S RL363093, XXX__

    Amount: __1 million__   Expiration date: __1/1/84__

The applicant agrees to indemnify The City of New York and to be solely and absolutely liable upon any and all claims, suits and judgments against the City and/or the applicant for personal injuries and property damages arising out of or occurring during the activities of the applicant, his (its) employees or otherwise. The applicant further agrees to comply with all pertinent provisions of New York laws, rules and regulations. This permit may be revoked at any time.

VEHICLES LISTED ABOVE ARE PERMITTED TO PARK IN ANY AVAILABLE PARKING SPACES IN THE IMMEDIATE VICINITY OF THE ABOVE LISTED FILM LOCATIONS. EXCEPT: FIRE HYDRANTS.

__1/4/82__   *Nancy Wood*   *PC*
Date   Signature of Representative   Title

DO NOT WRITE BELOW THIS LINE
The Mayor's Office Seal must be embossed on original copy.

Dated _1/4_ 19 _82_   Film Coordinator, Mayor's Office of Film, Theatre and Broadcasting

THE PRIMAL SCREEN

SCHEDULE "A" — MOTION PICTURE — TELEVISION PERMIT

NAME OF FEATURE _____ DROP OUT FATHER _____ TEL. NO _975-3345_ PERMIT NO. _020_

LOCATION	DATE	TIME	DESCRIBE SCENE IN DETAIL
1. EXTERIOR TUDOR CITY PLAZA 1st Avenue & 42nd Street	FRIDAY 1/8/82	7A-9:30A	Dick Van Dyke & girl walk & look at United Nations.
REQUEST NO PARKING EAST SIDE OF TUDOR CITY PLAZA BELOW 42nd STREET. REQUEST T.P.F. ASSISTANCE.			
2. EXT. THE METROPOLITAN MUSEUM OF ART 82nd Street & Fifth Avenue	FRIDAY 1/8/82	9:15A-11A	Dick Van Dyke & girl on Met. Museum steps. **will not blockaccess**
REQUEST NO PARKING NORTH OF 82ND STREET ON WEST SIDE OF 5TH AVENUE. REQUEST T.P.F. ASSISTANCE.			
3. EXT. THE GUGGENHEIM MUSEUM 89TH Street & Fifth Avenue	FRI. 1/8/82	10A-12N	Dick Van Dyke and girl leave Guggenheim.
REQUEST NO PARKING NORTH OF 89TH STREET ON WEST SIDE OF FIFTH AVENUE. REQUEST T.P.F. ASSISTANCE.			
4. EXT. SAKS FIFTH AVENUE 50th Street & Fifth Avenue	FRI. 1/8/82	11A-1P	Dick Van Dyke & girl shop.
NO PARKING AS BELOW. CAMERA WILL BE IN VAN. REQUEST NO PARKING RESTRICTIONS FOR THIS SHOT.			
5. EXT. PULITZER FOUNTAIN Near Plaza Hotel @ 59th Street & Fifth Avenue	FRI. 1/8/82	12N-7PM 2-4p	Dick Van Dyke & girl enter hansom cab. Cab moves across Central Park South and up into park Against Traffic
REQUEST NO PARKING AROUND THE (PULITZER) FOUNTAIN, SPECIFICALLY THE SIDE FACING THE PLAZA HOTEL. REQUEST NO PARKING on 58TH STREET BETWEEN 5TH AVENUE AND END OF PLAZA HOTEL ON NORTH SIDE OF STREET.			
6. REQUEST T.P.F ASSISTANCE. EXT. SHERMAN STATUE PROMENADE (Central Park South, North side, near Fifth Avenue)	FRI 1/8/82	12-7PM	Dick Van Dyke & girl buy a hot dog.
REQUEST NO PARKING AS ABOVE. REQUEST T.P.F. ASSISTANCE.			
7. EXT. THEATRE DISTRICT 45th Street & 8TH Avenue	FRI. 1/8/82	5P-7P	Dick Van Dyke & girl go to theatre.
REQUEST NO PARKING AS ABOVE. CAMERA WILL BE IN VAN. NO PARKING RESTRICTIONS REQUESTED FOR THEATRE SHOT.			

1/4/82

A Division of CBS, Inc.
4024 Radford Avenue
North Hollywood, California 91604

LOCATION AGREEMENT

Gentlemen:

This agreement relates to the real property (herein referred to as the "Premises"), located at

In consideration of your promise to pay us the sum of $ 1,000.00 , we hereby grant you and your agents, employees and other persons connected with the television or theatrical film entitled: "DROP OUT FATHER" the following rights with respect to the Premises:

The right to enter and remain upon the Premises with personnel and equipment for the sole and express purpose of photographing scenes on said Premises on Jan 7, 1982 , weather permitting. If weather is not favorable, the date(s) shall be postponed to Jan. 8, 1982 .
The right to photograph the Premises on motion picture film and to take exterior and interior shots of any buildings or other improvements located on said Premises and to photograph any animals on the Premises. The irrevocable right to use photographs taken by you in any manner and to such extent that you may desire. The irrevocable right to photograph any name connected with the Premises and to use the name in and in connection with such television or theatrical film. You acknowledge that we have described generally to you any unusual or unlikely manner in which the Premises, the name of the Premises and/or your name may be intended to be used in the film.

Any or all of the rights granted herein may be exercised by you, your employer, agents, licensees, successors and assigns. You agree to indemnify and hold us harmless from all injuries to persons and properties (ordinary wear and tear excepted) as a direct result of your activities on the Premises. We hereby warrant and represent that we have full right and authority to execute this instrument to grant the rights herein contained.

Your signature together with ours hereunder will constitute this a valid and binding agreement.

C.B.S. agrees to leave premises by 1PM of the day on which shooting occurs.

Accepted and Agreed:

Yours very truly,

CBS TELEVISION NETWORK
A Division of CBS, Inc.

By: _____

By: _____

Consent to Enter and Photograph Real Property R-22H 7/70-6

Social Security #: _____

-145-

341

As with a script, production has its three acts: pre-production, production or principal photography, and post-production.

Ordinarily, a two-hour movie for television will be budgeted for four to six weeks of pre-production. This is set when there is a pickup and a shooting start date is determined. In the case of *Drop-Out Father* we had only three weeks. That is very tight, but it helped enormously that we already had Dick Van Dyke and Mariette Hartley signed to do the film. Since Van Dyke had a limited "window" of availability we had to shoot when he could in January, which cut down on the pre-production schedule. As I recall, Hartley had a similar problem after we signed her. She had to be in London by early February. It was either do it quickly or wait months until they were again available. A tight pre-production schedule was also eased by CBS having done some of the preliminary work, such as the budget and a location and cast breakdown and a preliminary continuity breakdown. Here is one page of each of these latter two items:

"DROP OUT FATHER"

Location/Cast Breakdown

INT. EXT.	PAGE NO.	PARA. NO.	SCENE	CHARACTERS	LOC
ACT I					
I	1	1	MCCALL HOUSE - BEDROOM	Ed / Katherine	CA
I	2	3	- BATHROOM	Ed	
I	2-6	4	- KITCHEN	Elizabeth / Ed	
I	6-8	5	- DAVIDS RM DOOR	Ed / David /	
I	8-15	6	- KITCHEN	Elizabeth / Ed / Peggy / Muhatna / David / Katherine	
I	15	7	MCCALL GARAGE	Ed	
E	15	8	SUBURBAN HOUSE FACADE #1	Doug / Ed	
E	15-16	9	" " " #2	Doug / Ed / Harry	
E	16	10	" " " #3	Doug / Ed / Harry / Warren	
E	16	11	TRAIN STATION - Stamford	Ed / Doug / Harry / Warren	
E	16-17	12	TRAIN CAR	Ed / Commuter #1 / Commuter #2 / Commuter #3/ Commuter #4	
I	17-18	13	TRAIN PLATFORM BETWEEN CARS	Ed / Conductor / Man	
ACT II					
I	18-20	14-20	STYLISH BATHROOM & BEDROOM	Handsome Man/ Beautiful Woman	
I	21-25	21	SCREENING ROOM	Cannon Rush / Tony Mosconi / Draper Wright / Ben Brown / Gloria Levine / Ed McCall	
I	25	22	OFFICE HALLWAY by elevators	Ed / Tony / Old Man Messenger	
I	25-27	23	ELEVATOR INT.	Ed / Tony / Woman Prude	
I	27-30	24	STYLISH CORRIDOR	Ed / Tony / Workers / Betsy / Laura / Yolande / Tiffany	
I	30	25	ED MCCALLS CORNER OFFICE	Ed / Tawney	

Date	BREAKDOWN PG.	11	12	13		6	8	9	31	10		50	54	59	62		47	48	44
Day or Nite		D	D	D		D	D	D	D	D		D	D	D			D/N	N	N
Period												NY	NY	NY	NY		NY		
Sequence																			
Prod. No.	125		1	6/8		2/8	7/8	7/8	4/8	5/8		1	7/8	1 3/8	1/8		7/8	7/8	1/8

"DROP-OUT FATHER"

Title

Director

Producer

Asst. Dir.

Script Dated

Column scene headings (top, reading down):
EXT: TRAIN STA. (STAFFORD CONN.) / INT: TRAIN CAR / INT: TRAIN-PLATFORM "THRU" CARS / EXT: DODDS' HOUSE / EXT: HARRY'S HOME / EXT: HARRY'S HOUSE / EXT: WARDEN'S HOUSE / EXT: WARDEN'S HOUSE / EXT: FACADE OF OLD SOHO BLDG / EXT: SOHO STREET / EXT: RESTAURANT-SOHO ST. / EXT: PARK - MONTAGE / EXT: N.Y. CITY / EXT: PLAZA HOTEL - FRONT FOUNTAIN SIDE / INT: MADISON SQ. GARDEN

Character	Artist	No.																	
ED. McCALL		1	1	1	1		1		1		1		V.O. 1	1	1		1	1	1
KATHERINE		2																		
ELIZABETH (MINOR)		3												3	3	3		3	3	3
DAVID (MINOR)		4	(NO BEARD)																	
PEGGY		5	(NO BEARD)																	
BUD		6																		
MUHATMA		7																		
CANNON RUTH	3 HOUSEWIVES	8																	
TONY MASCONI	4 COMMUTERS	9	9																	
DRAPER WRIGHT	CONDUCTOR	10		10																
RON BROWN	PICKPOCKET	11			11															
GLORIA LEVINE	KID/TIC DRIVER	12																		
DOUG	CAPT. O'MALLEY	13	13				13	17	13	15	15									
HARRY	RACE MASTER	14	14				14	14	14	14										
WARDEN	STEWARDESS	15	15						15	15										
TAWNY SHAPIRO	AUSTIN McGOV	16																		
Dr. LEFKOWITZ	ANGELO	17																		
Dr. HAROLD SHON	JOSE (MINOR)	18																		
MARTY ZIMMERMAN	WILLIE (MINOR)	19																		
MAN (N SHOW)	EMCEE (V.O.)	20																		
YOUNG WOMAN (LIFTED)	TOM BOSLEY	21																		
WOMAN PRUDE	DR. FURNAS	22																		
GRANDPA	BOX ANN #1 (VC)	23																		
HOUSE KEEPER	BOX ANN #2 (VC)	24																		
MALE HAIRDRESSER	T.V. ANN (V.O.)	25																		
	T.V. ANN (VC)	26																		
	OFFICE CUTIES	27																		
		28																		
		29																		
	ATMOS	30	30	30									30	30	30		30		
	VEHICLE	31					31	31	31	31	31		31				31		
	WEAT. INSR	32											32				32	32	
	EFX	33	33	33	33		33	33	33	33	33								
		34																		
		35																		
		36																		
		37																		
		38																		
	SCENE NO.	39	11	12	13		36	9	57	10		51	65	68	71		56	57	58
		40																		
		41																		

Don't panic. Specialists do the continuity breakdown and similar complex procedures to come. They have served long apprenticeships in these areas and do this arcanam quickly and ably. I have never known a producer who did this complicated work, though the producer will be familiar with the contents and terms and will usually make adjustments in the continuity breakdown.

We had our leads, our budget, our sanitized script, and our continuity breakdown. Now, it was time to perform the other myriad tasks of pre-production. These tasks do not necessarily take place sequentially but rather in mixed pursuit.

First, we established a production office on the CBS/Fox lot in Studio City. We hired an experienced production secretary, who has specialized film knowledge, as legal and medical secretaries do in their fields. We sent scripts to all the important agents for actors and directors, and other creative personnel.

We submitted our director preferences to the network for approval. Our first choice was Gene Saks, who, through his agent, read and liked the script and agreed to negotiate to do the film. Before we could get network approval and begin negotiations, Saks got a Broadway play offer, which he took. (Saks was our first choice on *He's Fired, She's Hired* and again he agreed to do it, subject to negotiation. The network balked at his price and the deal fell through.) After not agreeing on other choices, the network recommended Don Taylor, who had done good work previously for CBS and who the network knew was available. We did not know Taylor but looked at films he had directed and agreed to consider him.

We sent Taylor the script. After reading it overnight, he agreed to meet with us to discuss the possibility of taking the assignment. We met for a Sunday breakfast at the Bel Air Hotel.

Don Taylor is a large, affable man who as a young actor played the groom opposite Elizabeth Taylor's bride in *Father of the Bride*. Spencer Tracy played the father. Taylor recounts his excitement in playing his first scene with Tracy, who, after a couple of takes, stopped the action and said to Taylor, "What're you doin', kid—tryin' to win an award? Relax and listen. Don't act—*react*."

Taylor right away had several helpful thoughts about the script. It was his idea to bring Grandpa in at the end, which gave a good lift out. I had written it to end with David's line, "What *is* myrrh?" This snapper was considerably more fragile than Taylor's suggestion.

Ann and I got a good impression of Taylor and decided we could work with him. We informed the network. Taylor agreed to do the picture, subject to negotiation and to rearranging a holiday ski trip to St. Moritz that he had planned previously. (He went but cut it short.) Typically, directors get from 65 to 100 thousand dollars per two-hour television film (sometimes more these days). Taylor was signed.

We hired an excellent casting specialist—Barbara Claman of BCI (now heading her own company), which had offices in Hollywood and New York. These offices have small videotaping rooms—for testing actors on screen and taping them. Claman, like most casting directors, is quintessentially a fan, albiet a knowledgeable and experienced fan. Casting directors constantly see films and television, go to theaters—from Broadway to neighborhood garages—monitor acting classes and readings, staying abreast of the talent pool in Hollywood, New York, key regional centers, and London even. They know not only who is appropriate for roles but who is available and affordable, and how and where to reach them. Casting directors do not dictate casting choices. That power is reserved for the director, who defers to the producer, who defers to the network.

Claman immediately began submitting lists of casting suggestions for every part, based on her reading of the script. Interviews and auditions were set up for Ann and me and Don Taylor on both coasts. The three of us flew to New York twice for this purpose. Several candidates were taped.

Our choices had to be approved by the CBS casting department under the direction of Jean Guest. This department is independent of the movie programming department. If CBS was not familiar with some of the actors we wanted for smaller parts, these actors had to audition a second time for the network. We were fortunate. Guest's good taste and ours coincided. CBS approved all of our choices.

We were extremely fortunate in casting the key supporting roles. It is pure dumb luck to be able to get on such short notice William Daniels, Monte Markham, George Coe, Rhea Perlman, Arthur Rosenberg, and George Wyner, all seasoned and much-sought pros.

The only casting difficulty we encountered was on the critical role of the daughter Elizabeth. It was a star part, and there were no twelve-year-old stars. We saw at least forty girls on both coasts. The California girls were too programmed and plastic, the New York girls, while better-trained and more "real," had accents or the wrong looks and coloring to be the upper-middle-class Connecticut daughter of Dick Van Dyke and Mariette Hartley. I began to despair, which is one of the things I do best, and vowed that I would never write another lead part for a child. We went back to New York. This time we found Martha Byrne. From suburban New Jersey. Her look and manner were perfect. Her reading was a bit shaky, as she had little experience. Taylor opted for a less suitable, but more experienced, California girl, and I was about to yield, but Ann was resolute. She held out. Confronted by Ann's vigorous and sincere arguments on Byrne's behalf, Taylor and I did the only thing real men can do. We caved in. How grateful I am that we did. Martha was wonderful—shining—and got special positive attention from all the reviewers. (She is developing into a splendid young woman and actress and played a smaller role in *He's Fired, She's Hired.* We joke that we will keep writing her in and working with her until she is an old woman. A note for actors and aspiring human beings: She sends Ann cards at every holiday and on her birthday.)

By this point, Ann was performing all of the producer chores alone, as

I had to be off producing a special I had committed myself to before we got the CBS pickup on *Drop-Out*. She put on a production manager, Donald C. Klune, who met with Taylor's approval, as well as with CBS's executive in charge of production, Bernard Oseransky. Taylor recommended Gerald Perry Finnerman to be director of photography. Ann screened his work. She and the network (Oseransky) agreed that he should be hired. Taylor, Klune, and Finnerman began to hire the creative production personnel (with producer approval) and the crew for California. Klune, subject to the same approval, hired like personnel for the two days of shooting scheduled in New York.

Drop-Out was written with Connecticut and New York City locales. As most of you know, for various reasons, among them budget, weather, and politics, pictures are not always shot where they are allegedly taking place. In *Drop-Out*, a suburb of Los Angeles stood in for Connecticut, a constructed set on a soundstage at the CBS/Fox lot subbed for a SoHo loft, and an office complex in Century City, from the windows of which you could see two highrises, became Ed's Manhattan ad agency and, redressed, doctor's and accountant's offices. New York City—mostly exteriors and identifying landmarks—showed as itself for only the two days out of a total of nineteen shooting days. The script said it was April in New York. In the shoot it was January and twenty degrees. Neither Van Dyke nor Martha Byrne complained as they worked in spring wardrobe while the crew off-camera wore arctic gear.

Ann hired a location manager, Bruce F. Lawhead, for the California shoot, and Klune hired a counterpart in New York. Location managing is a full-time career, and professionals in the field are as expert about sites as casting directors are about talent. Lawhead gave Ann four or five choices for each of the major sites. He showed her Polaroids of each interior and exterior. She, Taylor, Klune, and the art director, Albert Heschong, visited all the locations, and, working with the team, Ann made the final decisions. A fully furnished, two-story, frame colonial house in a town in California became the McCall residence. The production worked in the house for seven days. The family who lived in the house was paid a handsome fee for the location and lived in a motel, which the production also paid for until the shoot there was completed. Lots of families in southern California make extra money renting their houses to the movies. I was watching *The Devlin Connection* one night on "The Late Show" and recognized a neighbor's house across the street. Then, Rock Hudson came out of the house, the camera panned, and there he stood, with the Shanks manse in the background. (Lawhead, by the way, was astute at keeping the neighbors happy during production with gifts and good-will.)

With casting completed and locations selected, Don Klune, using the continuity breakdown as a guide, did the "day for day" board. The board is a triptych construction about four feet wide by three feet high that is easily portable when closed and can rest on almost any surface, including the ground, when open. Its interior face has some permanently labeled information and is otherwise slotted to allow the insertion of paper strips that contain pertinent but fluid information. These strips are color-coded to represent various kinds of information. While the board is called in industry shorthand "day for days," its official designation is "Day out of Days," which means that at a glance you can see each day's production routine as well as the routines for all the production days. The information displayed on the board finally represents an organization of each scene matched with each player into shooting days and becomes the basis for preparing the "shooting schedule" and eventually, with real-world modifications, the daily "call sheet," both of which we will come to.

Scenes and players are matched according to cast and location availabilities; efficiency of movement from one location to another; readiness and economical use of personnel, equipment, sets, furnishings, and props. The difficulty of scenes, both physically and emotionally, is taken into account. You may want compatible scenes shot day after day to sustain a performance. On the other hand, you may want to spread out difficult scenes to allow actors or the crew to refuel or catch their breath. Days should be scheduled to get big scenes with lots of extras or added equipment done early so these can be released as soon as possible rather than kept waiting while a more intimate two-person scene is being shot that might run longer than anticipated.

Every department head is consulted about the Day out of Days schedule. Will scenery be ready—props, costumes, cars, horses?

The production manager will usually make several different arrangements on the board (and work paper versions as well) before he is satisfied that he has organized the best schedule. The director and producer may or may not be involved during the embryonic stages. At the end, however, the production manager will meet the producer and director to go over the board in detail. Each can make changes. When all are in agreement, the board is officially signed by the producer and the director to indicate that they believe they can realize in actual shooting days what is indicated on the board. The board information is then transferred to written paper form, photocopied or mimeographed, and distributed to key creative personnel and department heads so that they know what is expected of their areas and can plan their efforts accordingly. Too, the budget controllers get their copies.

Keep in mind, even after the director and the producer have signed-off on the board, it remains a living animal. Suppose an actor gets sick or is otherwise suddenly unavailable. A set is not ready when you thought it would be. A location burns down or electricity is shut off. It rains or snows. There is an earthquake. Or its equivalent—a director running behind schedule. Any of these and lesser production glitches send you back to the board, which guides and haunts a production until principal photography is completed.

Here is a reproduction of the paper version of the Day out of Days board for *Drop-Out Father*, as revised on the first day of shooting:

DAY OUT OF DAYS
ABC ENTERTAINMENT

SCRIPT DATED	1/5/82
SCRIPT TITLE	DROP-OUT FATHER
PRODUCTION #	1310-3211 0805
Initial Date Issued	12/16/81
Revision #	4
PRODUCER	ANN & BOB SHANKS / ANDREW GOTTLIEB
Date Revised	1/7/8
DIRECTOR	DON TAYLOR

MONTH → JANUARY → FEBRUARY

N.Y. → L.A. →

#	NAME	CHARACTER
1	Dick Van Dyke	Ed McCall
2	Mariette Hartley	Katherine
3	Martha Byrne (m)	Elizabeth N.Y.
4	Charles Bloom	David
5		Peggy
6	Michael Cummins	Bud
7	Terry Hard	Muhatma
8	Georges Coe	Kahlon Rush
9	Monte Markham	Tony Malerado
10	William Daniels	Draper Wright
11		Ben Brown
12	Shelly Batt	Gloria Levin
13	Roy Singer	Doug
14	Jeff	Harry
15	Todd Susman	Warren
16	Rhea Perman	Tammey Shapiro
17	George Wyner ##	Dr Lefkowitz
18		Dr Harold Simon
19	Arthur Rosenberg	Marty Zimmerman
20	Paul Coccioletti	Handsome Man
21		Beautiful Woman
22	Susan Ruttman	Woman Prude
23	Bill Erwin	Grandpa
23A		Song Lee
24	Sly Abergs	Housekeeper - Hilda
25	Xander Berkley	Male Hairdresser
26	Ned Wilson	"Tom Brokaw"
27	William Litngold	Dr Furness

* ## Gould work cover set 1/11

DAY OU.. OF DAYS
BC ENTERTAINMENT

CRIPT DATED: 1/5/82

SCRIPT TITLE: DROP-OUT FATHER

Initial Date Issued

● Revision # 4

Date Revised 1/7/8

PRODUCER: Anne & Bob Shanks / Andrew Gottlieb

DIRECTOR: Don Taylor

PRODUCTION #: 13x0-3211 0805

MONTH

DAY OF MONTH

DAY OF WEEK

SHOOTING DAYS

NAME	CHARACTER	
Sandy Barry	Maffy	28A
Marianne McAndrew	Diane	28B
Celia Wellman	Bethman	28C
Terry Wills	Commuter 1	29A
Richard Penn	Commuter 3	29C
Dallas Alinder	Commuter 4	29D
Ernie Brown	Conductor	30
O.M.T.	Pick Pocket	31
Ed Call	Capt O'Malley	33
Lynn Londos	Stewardess #1	34
Terri Berland	Stewardess #2	35
Bruce Gray	Austin Morrow	36
Frank Rozlo	Angelo	37
Jose Aleman (N)	Negro Kid N.Y.	37A
Israel Juarbe(N)	Jose N.Y.	38
Bobby Duncan	Willie N.Y.	39
David Boyle	T.V. Annc #1	43

JANUARY

FEBRUARY

In the day boxes across from "Name" and "Character" you will see various letters: S, T, W, H, and F—for stand-by, travel, work, hold, and finish. You will note that even with shooting begun, three parts were as yet uncast. This happens often. I have known of movies beginning on a Monday in which the lead—the star—was not cast until the Friday before or even over the weekend. This is not the way to do it, but sometimes, given the necessary approvals, negotiations, talent availabilities, and so on, it is the way it is.

Look now at reproductions of samples of the shooting schedule for *Drop-Out Father*. I have given you shooting days 1 and 7 as examples. I have blanked out the name, address, and phone number of the family whose house we were using in day 7. This shooting schedule grows out of the Day out of Days board and is prepared by the production manager in consultation with the producer, director, and key behind-the-camera personnel. It is not published daily during the shoot but only when revisions are required. Revised copies or pages are published in different colors, usually, in order, blue, pink, yellow, green. All revised copies carry a legend in the upper right corner of every page that says "Revised such-and-such-a-date."

DAY/DATE	SET/SCENE/DESCRIPTION	CAST/ATMOS	NOTES

DAY 1
Thursday
1/7/82
Continued
 	
New York
	EXT. NEW YORK SCHOOL (D)
	
	Sc. 76, 77,
	3 2/8 pg.
	
	David is nervous about
	NY school.
	
	Opening of Act. VI.
		3 ELIZABETH
		   (minor)
		4 DAVID
		37A MEAN KID
		   (minor)
		38 JOSE (minor)
		39 WILLIE
		
		Extras:
		10 kids
		20 teachers,
		etc.
		
		Atmos:
		2 Willie's
		friends
		STUDIO TEACHER
			Props:
			   David's guitar.
			   Book, etc.
			
			Grips:
			   Western dolly

	EXT. SOHO (D)
	
	Sc. 62,
	2/8 pg.
	
	Establish loft.
		1 ED
		3 ELIZABETH
		   (minor)
		
		Atmos.:
		As discussed.
		
		STUDIO TEACHER
			Art Dept.:
			   Windows match
			   Sc. 62

	INT. MUSIC CLUB (N)
	
	Sc. 78, 78A
	3/8 pg.
	
	David and co. play.
		3 ELIZABETH
		   (minor)
		4 DAVID
		39 WILLIE
		
		40 EMCEE (V.O.)
		
		Atmos:
		2 Willie's
		friends
		28 Audience
		
		STUDIO TEACHER
			Props:
			   Drinks, etc.
			   David's guitar
			   Drums
			   Keyboard
			   Bass
			
			Sound:
			   Live Recording

END DAY 1   TOTAL PAGES 6 3/8

CBS STUDIO CITY   December 29, 1981

SHOOTING SCHEDULE

DROP OUT FATHER

CBS STUDIO CITY # 1310-3211-0805   PRODUCERS: Ann Shanks/Bob Shanks
START DATE: January 7, 1982   SUPERVISING PRODUCER:
CLOSE: February 2, 1932   Andy Gottlieb
CAMERA DAYS: 19-1st Unit;   DIRECTOR: Don Taylor
  1-2nd Unit;   PROD. MGR.: Donald C. Klune
TRAVEL DAYS: 2   NY PROD. MGR.: George Manasse
Production Office # 760-5811   ASST. DIR.: Jerram Swartz
NY Production Office # (212) 975-3345

DAY/DATE	SET/SCENE/DESCRIPTION	CAST/ATMOS	NOTES
2ND UNIT Wednesday 1/6/82	**EXT. TRAIN STAT.** (D) Sc. 11, 1/8 pg. SECOND UNIT	Photodoubles: Ed Doug Harry Warren	Props: Briefcases License plates Ward: Coats Vehicles: Train Stationwagon (match to L.A.)
DAY 1 Thursday 1/7/82 New York	**EXT. SOHO ST.** (D) Sc. 66, 6/8 pg. Discussing NY cuisine.	1 ED 3 ELIZABETH (minor) Extras: 20 as discussed STUDIO TEACHER	Props: Interesting things for atmosphere. Grips: Western dolly.
	EXT. ARTISTIC REST. (D) Sc. 70, 1 6/8 pg. They walk from rest., see Angelo's photo studio.	1 ED 3 ELIZABETH (minor) Extras: 20 atmos. as discussed STUDIO TEACHER	Art: Angelo's signs Note: Consider obscuring windows with displays or curtains to avoid matching problems. Grips: Dolly track.

DAY 1 CONTINUED

"DROP OUT FATHER"   12/29/81
1310-3211-0805   Page 13

DAY/DATE	SET/SCENE/DESCRIPTION	CAST/ATMOS	NOTES

Day 7
Friday
1/15/82
 	
The
Residence
 	
LCanada
	INT. FRONT DOOR (D)
	
	Sc. 53
	2 2/8 page
	
	O'Malley arrives - as
	does everybody else.
	Everyone troops upstairs.
		2 KATHERINE
		3 ELIZABETH
		   (minor)
		4 DAVID
		5 PEGGY
		6 BUD
		7 MUHATMA
		8 KANNON RUSH
		9 TONY MOSCONI
		18 DR. SIMON
		33 FIREMAN O'MALLEY
		
		Atmos.:
		Firemen (4)
		4 neighbors
		
		STUDIO TEACHER
			Props:
			  David's guitar;
			  Fireman's
			  clipboard;
			  Axe - 1 real,
			  1 fake;
			
			Vehicle:
			  Firetruck

	INT. ED'S BEDROOM(D)
	
	Sc. 54
	2 7/8 page
	
	Ed unlocks door,
	reveals his plans.
		1 ED
		2 KATHERINE
		3 ELIZABETH
		   (minor)
		4 DAVID
		5 PEGGY
		6 BUD
		7 MUHATMA
		8 KANNON
		9 TONY
		33 O'MALLEY
		18 DR. SIMON
		
		STUDIO TEACHER
			Props:
			  "War and Peace"
			  Lists
			  Axe (fake one)
			  Broken TV
			
			Make-up:
			  Beard (11 days)
			
			Ward:
			  Ed's clothes
			  grungy.
			
			Set dressing:
			  Room's a mess.

	EXT. MC CALL DRIVEWAY (N)
	
	Sc. 29
	1/8 page
	
	Ed arrives home.
		1 ED	Props:
			  Briefcase
			Set dressing:
			  Peggy's furniture
			  is in garage
			Vehicles:
			  Station wagon
			  Continental
			  (in garage)
			  White VW
			  David's Datsun
			Make-up:
			  Ed's shaving cuts
			Loc.:
			  Automatic garage
			  door works.

END DAY 7   TOTAL PAGES 5 5/8

"DROP OUT FATHER"   12/29/81
1310-3211-0805   Page 12

DAY/DATE	SET/SCENE/DESCRIPTION	CAST/ATMOS	NOTES

Day 7,
Friday,
1/15/82
 	
The
Residence
 	
    LaCanada,
CA
	EXT. MC CALL HOUSE (Dawn)
	
	Sc. 1
	2/8 page
	
	Establish.
		41 RADIO
		    ANNOUNCER
		    #1 (V.O.)
		
		Atmos.:
		Moped Newsboy
			Props:
			  Moped
			  Newpaper
			
			Set dressing:
			  Birdbath
			
			Vehicles:
			  Datsun
			  Stationwagon

	EXT. MC CALL GARAGE (D)
	
	Sc. 7,
	1/8 page
	
	Ed starts his car.
		1 ED
		
		Atmos.:
		1 w/car
			Props:
			  Briefcase
			
			Vehicles:
			  Katherine's
			  Continental;
			  Ed's stationwgn.;
			  VW convertible
			  David's Datsun
			
			Special Effects:
			  Smoke from car.
			
			Make-up:
			  Ed's shaving cuts
			Art:
			  Greens to
			  camouflage
			  Spanish house.
			
			Note: Greensman

DAY 7 CONTINUED

Script page changes are likewise printed on different-color pages—blue, pink, yellow, green—and carry the revised date on each revised page.

The shooting schedule is a critical road map. It contains not merely the locations and cast members scheduling but information as to equipment, vehicles, props, wardrobe, makeup, hair, and time frame lighting match-ups. Look, for instance, under notes on page 2 of day 7 at the notation "Beard (11 days)." Ed McCall's beard has been growing eleven days in the story and today has to look it.

Next, a preproduction of the daily call sheet. It is printed on one page front and back, legal size, though here it is reduced and set forth as two pages. The call sheet is prepared daily by the second assistant director, based on information provided by the director and production manager. It is published at the end of each shooting day and distributed to everyone immediately connected with the shoot. You will note that at the bottom of the call sheet are quick glimpses of the three shooting days ahead. "Call" in call sheet means the time each person and activity is to begin the following day, as in "What's the call?" or "What's my call?"

STUDIO CENTER
CALL SHEET

1st UNIT
3RD DAY OF SHOOTING

7:00 A CREW CALL REPORT TO BUS AT EMPLOYEE PARKING LOT

PROD. OFC. 760-5811

PICT. DROP-OUT FATHER   NO. 1310-3211-0805

Producer   ANN & BOB SHANKS
Supervising PRODUCER   ANDY GOTTLIEB
DATE   MONDAY -- JAN. 11, 1982
DIRECTOR   DON TAYLOR

SET #	SCENES	CAST	D/N	PAGES	LOCATION
EXT DOUG'S HOUSE	8 ED PICKS UP DOUG	1, 13	D	7/8	AGNES ST AT VALLEY
EXT HARRY'S HOUSE	9 HARRY JOINS ED & DOUG	1, 13, 14	D	3/8	HEART STUDIO CITY
	36 DOUG PICKS UP HARRY	13, 14	D	3/8	
EXT WARREN'S HOUSE	10 WARREN JOINS BOYS	1, 13, 14, 15	D	4/8	
	37 BOYS PICK UP WARREN	13, 14, 15	D	4/8	
INT TRAIN	12 ANGST RIDDEN RIDERS	1, 13, 14, 15, 29A, C, D	D	1 5/8	UNION STATION TRACK 5
EXT TRAIN BETWEEN CARS	13 - PICK POCKET	1, 30	D	4/8	800 N ALAMEDA DOWNTOWN L.A.
COVER SET INT. DR. LEFKOVITZ OFC STAGE 3			TOTAL PAGES	4 7/8	

CAST AND DAY PLAYERS	PART OF	MAKEUP	SET CALL	REMARKS
1. DICK VAN DYKE	ED MC CALL	7:00A		REPORT TO STUDIO
3. MARTHA BYRNE (M)	ELIZABETH	TRAVEL		
4. CHARLES BLOOM	DAVID	HOLD		
13. RAY SINGER (NEW)	DOUG	6:30A		REPORT TO STUDIO
14. JEFF ALTMAN (NEW)	HARRY	6:30A		EMPLOYEE PARKING LOT
15. TODD SUSMAN (NEW)	WARREN	6:30A		
29A. TERRY WILLS (NEW)	COMMUTER #1	1:00P		REPORT TO UNION STATION
29C. RICHARD PENN (NEW)	COMMUTER #3			TRACK 5
29D. DALLAS ALINDER (NEW)	COMMUTER #4			800 N. ALAMEDA
30. ERNIE BROWN (NEW)	CONDUCTER			DOWNTOWN L.A.
				PARK IN ALL RIGHT PARKING

ATMOSPHERE AND STANDINS		REPORT:		
3 STAND-INS		7:30A		REPORT TO STUDIO
5 MEN COMMUTERS W/ N.D CARS	3 PIECE SUITS W/	7:30A		
25 MEN COMMUTERS	OVERCOATS AND HATS	1:30P HAVING HAD LUNCH		REPORT TO UNION STATION TRACK 5
10 WOMEN COMMUTERS	AND UMBRELLAS			PARK IN ALL RIGHT PARKING BRING TICKET TO LOC. MGR.

ADVANCE SCHEDULE OR CHANGES		
TUESDAY -- JAN 12 -- DAY 4	WEDNESDAY -- JAN 13 -- DAY 5	THURSDAY -- JAN 14 -- DAY 6
Sc 24 INT OFC. CORRIDOR	Sc 28 INT EXEC DININGROOM	Sc 69 INT AUSTIN'S OFC
Sc 25 INT ED'S OFC.	Sc 27 INT ACCT'S OFC.	Sc 74E INT AUSTIN'S OFC.
Sc 39 INT ED'S OFC.	Sc 23 INT ELEVATOR	Sc 21 INT SCREENING ROOM
Sc 4PT INT TODAY SHOW		Sc 22 INT OFC. HALLWAY COMPLETE Sc 23

STEADICAM Sc 24

ASST. DIR.   JERRAM SWARTZ/ANDERSON HOUSE   PROD. MGR. DONALD C. KLUNE

PRODUCTION REQUIREMENTS

REPORT TO BUS AT EMPLOYEE PARKING LOT.

PICTURE **DROP-OUT FATHER**   NO. **0805**   DATE **MONDAY JANUARY 11, 1980**

NO.	ITEM	TIME		NO.	ITEM	TIME		NO.	ITEM	TIME
1	DIRECTOR	7:00A		1	MIXER	7:00A		1	DRIVER CAPTAIN -	2
1	UNIT MANAGER				RECORDER			14	DRIVERS	
2	ASSISTANT DIRECTORS			1	MIKE BOOM MAN					
1	SCRIPT SUPERVISOR	↓		1	CABLE MAN	↓			CAMERA/INSERT CAR	
	DIALOGUE DIRECTOR		SOUND	X	10 WALKIE TALKIES	ON TRK		X	CAMERA TRUCK	
								Y	PICTURE CARS 2	
					PLAYBACK OPERATOR				ED'S STATION WAGON	
					PLAYBACK MACHINE				DOUG'S MERCURY	
1	DIRECTOR OF PHOTOGRAPHY	7:00A							MISC. CARS	
1	CAMERA OPERATOR			1	PROPERTY MASTER	7:00A				
1	1ST ASSISTANT CAMERAMAN			1	ASST. PROPERTY MASTER	↓				
1	2ND ASSISTANT CAMERAMAN	↓							STANDBY CARS	
	EXTRA OPERATOR		PROPERTY							
				1	SET DECORATOR	O/C				
	EXTRA ASSISTANTS			1	LEADMAN			X	2 STATION WAGON	
				2	SWING GANG	↓				
X	CAMERAS: PANAFLEX	ON TRK						X	2 STRETCHOUT	
				1	MAKEUP ARTIST	6:12A		X	1 MOTORHOME	
								X	1 BUSSES	
			MAKEUP		HAIR STYLIST			X	1 CREW CAB	
	STILLMAN							X	1 UTILITY P.U.	
1	ART DIRECTOR	O/C			BODY MAKEUP WOMAN				GOOSE WITH SOUND	
1	CONST COORDINATOR	↓							SOUND TRUCK	
1	KEY GRIP	7:00A							ELECTRICAL TRUCK	
1	2ND CO. GRIP			1	COSTUMER (MEN)	7:00 A				
1	DOLLY GRIP			1	XTRA	↓		X	PROP TRUCK	
2	EXTRA GRIPS	↓	COSTUME				TRANSPORTATION	X	GRIP TRUCK/PROP VAN	
									HORSE WAGON TRUCK	
X	CRAB DOLLY STDNT	ON TRK		1	COSTUMER (WOMEN)	7:00A				
X	ELEMACK DOLLY	↓							WATER TRUCK	
	HYSTER FOR HIGH SHOT				MUSIC REPRESENTATIVE			X	HONEY WAGON 7 RMS	
					SIDELINE MUSICIANS					
1	CRAFT SERVICE MAN	7:00A	MUSIC		SINGERS				DRESSING ROOM TRAILER	
								X	5 TON SET DRESS	
	GREENSMAN				PROCESS PROJECTIONIST			X	STATION WAGON SET DRESS	
			PROCESS		PROCESS GRIPS					
					PROCESS EQUIPMENT					
	PAINTER									
	SPECIAL EFFECTS				STUDIO POLICE				RAMROD	
					WHISTLEMAN				HORSE TRAINER	
	PORTABLE DRESSING RMS.		POLICE/FIRE/MED.	2	MOTORCYCLE POLICE	6:0R/7:00A			ANIMAL HANDLER	
					FIRE WARDEN				WRANGLERS	
					FIREMAN				WAGONS	
	SCHOOL ROOMS				FLAGMAN				COACHES	
					WATCHMAN				HORSES	
1	GAFFER	7:00A		1	FIRST AID	7:0			CATTLE	
1	BEST BOY			2	UNION STATION SECURITY	12.0			OTHER ANIMALS	
	GENERATOR OPERATOR									
4	LAMP OPERATORS	↓		X	BREAKFASTS RDY	6:30				
					BOX LUNCHES					
	GENERATOR		MEALS	73	HOT LUNCHES RDY	1:00				
	WIND MACHINE				DINNERS					
				X	CATERING TRK					
				X	COOK					
				X	HELPER					

DEPARTMENT	SPECIAL INSTRUCTIONS
ALL DEPT'S (CASTING → DEPT →)	BE PREPARED TO WORK ON COVER SET Int DR LEFKOWITZ'S OFC. STG 3 AFTER WORK COMPLETED AT UNION STATION
CAMERA DEPT	200' MAGAZINES FOR PANAFLEX & 200 FT LOADS FOR HANDHELD IN CAR
CAMERA DEPT	SPEC. EQPT. FOR TUESDAY -- STEADICAM -- F. MURPHY

ST. DIR. **JERRAM SWARTZ / ANDERSON HOUSE**   UNIT PROD. MGR. **DON KLUNE**

CREW SHOULD NOTE: ON LOCATION.. THE CATERER WILL ALWAYS BE READY TO SERVE WALKING BREAKFASTS 15 MINUTES BEFORE THE CREW CALL. IF YOU EAT BREAKFAST OFF THE TRUCK PLEASE DO SO BEFORE YOUR CALL.

Following is a one-page example of the staff and crew list, addresses and phone numbers eliminated here. You can see from the date and the blanks that this is an early edition of the list, printed before everyone was hired. These lists run eventually to twenty or thirty pages. A similar list would be prepared for the cast and for network and studio executives as applicable. All of these lists contain the names, addresses, and phone numbers for everyone—*everyone*—who has anything at all to do with the production, from senior network executive to the insurance broker, equipment houses, and labs; from the nearest hospital and fire and police stations to the caterer and to the lowliest gofer. If this seems excessive to you now, you will understand it one day when a star walks off the set and you have to reach his agent and the network, or scenery falls on a grip, or a faulty lamp ignites the set, or lunch does not arrive on time or you need a midnight errand from the gofer to fetch a whatsit in order to get the whichit right before you can shoot in the morning. These lists are widely distributed, as various people must be able to contact the various other people at a moment's notice twenty-four hours a day. These lists are called contact sheets.

THE PRIMAL SCREEN

CBS INC., CBS STUDIO CENTER   DECEMBER 15, 1981

PRODUCTION #: 1310-3211-0805

DROP-OUT FATHER

STAFF AND CREW LIST

POSITION	NAME	EXT.	PHONE
PRODUCERS/ WRITER	ANN SHANKS BOB SHANKS	5811	(213)
SUPERVISING PRODUCER	ANDREW GOTTLIEB	5811	(213)
DIRECTOR	DON TAYLOR	5811	(213)
PRODUCTION MANAGER	DONALD C. KLUNE	5811	(213)
PRODUCTION COORDINATOR	PAGE S. WHIDDEN	5811	(213)
1ST ASSISTANT DIRECTOR	JERRAM SWARTZ	5811	(213)
2nd ASSISTANT DIRECTOR	ANDERSON G. HOUSE	5811	(213)
ART DIRECTOR	E. ALBERT HESCHONG	5375	(213)

SCRIPT
SUPERVISOR

DIRECTOR OF
PHOTOGRAPHY

CAMERA OPERATOR

The next form is called the daily production report. It tells what has been done on each day of shooting; what time the cast and crew began and ended each day; how much film was used and printed; how many setups were accomplished; how many pages and minutes of script were shot. This is an additional means of controlling the budget and the schedule and is a guide to what changes may be necessary to keep to these. The report is one page, legal size, printed on both sides. Here again it is reduced and shown as two pages. This report is the responsibility of the production manager, who gathers the information from camera reports, sound reports, continuity reports, assistant director, and department head reports.

PAPER CASTLES
DAILY PRODUCTION REPORT

	REH	TRAVEL	HOLI-DAYS	IDLE	RETAKES & ADD.SCHS.	WORK	TOTAL	AHEAD
No. of Days on Picture Including Today								
								BEHIND

Director _____

Working Title   Paper Castles

Picture No. _____

Set _____

Set No. _____ Location _____

Call _____ Leave _____ Arrive Location _____ 1st Shot: AM _____ PM _____ Wrap _____ Arrive Studio/Hotels _____

Crew Lunch _____ To _____ Crew Supper _____ To _____ 1st Shot _____

Camera Call _____ Camera Wrap _____ Sound Call _____ Sound Wrap _____

Date _____

Date Started   June 2, 1984

Estimated Finish Date   June 28, 1984

SCRIPT	SCENES	PAGES	MINUTES	SETUPS	ADDED SCENES	RETAKES	Scenes completed today:
Scenes In Script	194	104					
Taken Prev.							
Taken Today							
Total To Date							

FILM USE	GOOD	WASTE	N.G.	TOTAL	SOUND	ROLLS	
Prev.					Prev.		
Today					Today		
To Date					To Date		
2nd Unit To Date					2nd Unit To Date		

CAST	W H S F R TR	MAKEUP WDBE.	WORK TIME		MEALS		TRAVEL TIME			
			ON SET	DIS. STUDIO	1ST MEAL IN	1ST MEAL OUT	LEAVE FOR LOCATION	ARRIVE LOCATION	DIS. LOC.	ARRIVE STUDIO

EXTRA TALENT — MUSICIANS, ETC.

NO.	RATE	ADJ. TO	O.T.	T.T.	WARD.	MPV	NO.	RATE	ADJ. TO	O.T.	T.T.	WARD.	MPV

Assistant Dir. _____ Unit Mgr. _____

Picture _____

Report ABSENCES on Account of Illness of Any Member of the Cast or Staff

NAMES	REMARKS

Remarks and Explanation of Delays _____

PROD.	DIRECTOR	**SOUND**	MIXER	**TRANSPORTATION**	DRIVER CAPTAIN	
	UNIT MANAGER		RECORDER		DRIVERS	
	ASSISTANT DIRECTORS		MIKE BOOM MAN		CAMERA INSERT CAR	
	SCRIPT SUPERVISOR		CABLE MAN		CAMERA TRUCK	
	DIALOGUE DIRECTOR		PLAYBACK OPERATOR		PICTURE CARS	
			PLAYBACK MACHINE		MISC CARS	
CAMERA	DIRECTOR OF PHOTOGRAPHY				STATION WAGON	
	CAMERA OPERATOR				STRETCHOUT	
	ASSISTANT CAMERMAN	**PROPERTY**	PROPERTY MASTER		BUSSES	
	STILLMAN		ASST. PROP. MASTER		BLUE GOOSE W SOUND	
	CAMERAS BNC NC ARRI		SET DECORATOR		SOUND TRUCK	
			LEADMAN		ELECTRICAL TRUCK	
			SWING GANG		PROP TRUCK	
					GRIP TRUCK	
					HORSE WAGON TRUCK	
OPERATIONS	ART DIRECTOR	**MAKEUP**	MAKEUP ARTIST		WATER TRUCK	
	CONST COORDINATOR		HAIR STYLIST		HONEY WAGON	
	KEY GRIP		BODY MAKEUP WOMAN		DRESSING RM TRAILER	
	2ND GRIP					
	DOLLY GRIP					
	EXTRA GRIPS	**COSTUME**	COSTUMER (MEN)			
	CRAB DOLLY		COSTUMER (WOMEN)			
	CRANE					
	HYSTER FOR HIGH SHOT					
		MUSIC	MUSIC REPRESENTATIVE			
			SIDELINE MUSICIANS			
	CRAFT SERVICE MAN		SINGERS			
	GREENSMAN					
	PAINTER					
	SPECIAL EFFECTS MAN	**PROCESS**	PROCESS PROJECTIONIST			
	PORTABLE DRESSING ROOMS		PROCESS GRIPS		RAMROD	
	SCHOOL ROOMS		PROCESS EQUIPMENT		HORSE TRAINER	
					ANIMAL HANDLER	
		POLICE, FIRE, MED.	STUDIO POLICE		WRANGLERS	
			WHISTLEMAN		WAGONS	
			MOTORCYCLE POLICE		COACHES	
ELECTRICAL	GAFFER		FIREMAN		HORSES	
	BEST BOY		FIRE WARDEN		CATTLE	
	LAMP OPERATORS		FLAGMAN		OTHER ANIMALS	
	GENERATOR OPERATOR		WATCHMAN			
	WIND MACHINE OPERATOR		FIRST AID			
	GENERATOR					
	WIND MACHINE					
		MEALS	BREAKFAST			
			BOX LUNCHES			
			HOT LUNCHES			
			DINNERS			

ADVANCE SCHEDULE

Date _____ Time Called _____ Location _____

Set _____

Remarks _____

Assistant Director

Pre-production is the period in which the art director and costume designer work up and then show ideas, sketches, models, amd color and fabric swatches to the director and producer for approval. There are agreements, disagreements, changes, reapprovals. During pre-production, principal cast members must be available for wardrobe consultation and fittings and for tests of special makeups and hairstyles or hairpieces. Wardrobe gets the sizes for all cast members and begins to assemble the goods. There may be film test shoots in pre-production if special lenses, lighting, or color are called for, or miniature sets and special effects. Full-scale sets must be constructed. Equipment, vehicles, transportation, trucking, housing, and food service must be arranged. Everything that can be planned for and decided upon *is* during pre-production. When the production is assembled and the camera begins to roll nothing must make these wait or, hell of hells, stop. Pre-production is a time of intense and piebald activity, effervescent hope, and the anxiety that abides like fever, born of the fear that you have forgotten something. Then, suddenly, it is time to shoot.

I know a lot of producers who spend very little time on the set when principal photography has begun. They may confer early in the day in-person or on the phone with the director to go over that day's plan, then spend the rest of the day working to sell or prepare future productions—or shop and play tennis—before returning to the present production by viewing the rushes at lunchtime or in the evening.

While Ann and I are seldom on the set together as producers because it is better to have one voice and presence there and because one of us can use the time to work on other projects, one of us, for sure, is on the set every minute. We think of ourselves as creative producers first and as salesmen-executives second. We support the director and stay out of his way as much as possible, since the director has to have command of the action. But we must be involved in and reserve the ultimate decision-making role. I am mostly concerned with script and story nuances. Ann is a demon on performance, on taste and aptness of wardrobe, hair, makeup, lighting, and décor. Television directors on a nineteen-day shooting schedule do not have time to oversee these details and welcome a producer's concern.

Each specialty is nearly always myopic about everything but its own area and may not be cognizant of how that specialty must be integrated with the whole. The producer has to be the one keeping this larger vision in mind at all times. There are so many disparate views at work on a film and so much is happening quickly and simultaneously that not even the director can catch all of these sometimes irreconcilable differences or lapses in detail. Or, from our point of view, it may even *be* the director who has ordered or is committing the transgression.

These deviations are frequently judged to be small, but they are large to us. One might allow one or two to go by—and there are times when this is necessary to accommodate even larger necessities—but when the offenses multiply they do irrevocable damage to the look of a film and to the truth of the characters and story.

Some examples: In *Drop-Out Father* the daughter Peggy is going through a religious-ascetic phase. No jewelry, no makeup, and so on. This is how the actress had been prepared, but when she arrived on the set ready to shoot, the fine young actress who was playing Peggy, Claudia Lonow, on her own, and who can blame her for wanting to look pretty, had added blue eye-shadow, lipstick, and chic earrings. No one but Ann noticed. She went to tell Don Taylor who stopped rehearsing the scene and got Claudia back "in character."

(This last is an important point. We do all of this kind of thing through the director—and only the director—and quietly. No shouting, no cast members or production people involved. Even as the producer-writer, we will look to the director for permission to respond to an actor if the actor calls out with a question about a particular line. This kind of respect for protocol—and human feelings—prevents tension and conflict on the set.)

Ann questioned a scene before another shooting began in which the set decorator had gone overboard in his interpretation of a character's office toys. He had included a huge display of female pinups on one wall and some ghastly kitsch on the desk. None of these items was to be featured in the shot but would have been seen and would have led to a misunderstanding of the character. Ann pointed this out to the director, who, surprisingly, disagreed with her. She overrode his opinion. It took half an hour to remove the offending items, but it was worth it. Remember that, relatively, a film is forever and so is the wrong in it.

On another occasion, I was on the set, replacing Ann, who was off directing and producing a second film. I was intensely involved in the scene at hand and had not checked out a set to be shot later in the day. It was for a short scene placed in the hat bar of an elegant New York department store. The chief hairdresser on the picture, who knew our taste by that time, or at least Ann's, came and whispered to me, "Have you seen the set for the discount store?"

"Discount store?" I said. "We don't have a discount store in the script."

"Exactly."

"Oh. You mean—?"

"Exactly. *Ann's going to hate it.*"

I went quickly to look at the "elegant" department store set. It did not look much like a New York department store. *Something* can always be done in these cases, and when it is not I find that the reason is always more a failure of imagination than a lack of money. I looked around. The area, of course, was littered with film paraphernalia. I remembered seeing decorations in New York stores that carried out themes from Hollywood. I ordered a sign painted saying "Hats Inspired By Hollywood" and got the set decorator to redress the setup with film cans, ends of film, klieg lights, clapsticks, grip stands, and a ladder. The redressed set was ready by the time the director came to the scene later in the day, and no shooting time was lost. It was not perfect but at least had some style and passed on camera for elegant. I am grateful to the hairdresser for looking beyond his specialty and having a producer's eye.

Ann and I both have removed cardboard coffee cups, errant clothing, light stands, and other unwanted but overlooked debris from sets just before a take. In the press to get the shot, these can easily go unnoticed—until you see them glaring forth in the dailies.

I will never forget one giant anachronism in a European film about the Trojan Wars. There stood Helen of Troy, in her bare-arm, flowing, white Grecian gown, looking beautiful enough to have launched indeed a thousand ships, but all of it sank when you saw on screen, big as the side of a house, her arm with a twentieth-century small pox vaccination mark on it.

Movies, especially television movies, are filled with these sins. Audiences do not always see them, but, truly, "God lives in the details," and Ann and I try to be His chief disciples in this regard. It is the producer's job. We do not always endear ourselves to the director or others in these situations, but filming is not a lawn party or a run for office.

By noon or evening of the second day, the rushes or dailies are ready to be viewed; and so on until the day after principal photography has ended. Rushes are the one-light prints made by the lab overnight of the previous day's shoot—the footage that was ordered printed. A director does not print every take, only those he deems worthwhile. Usually, the director will print at least two or three takes of each setup to make sure he has coverage for each of them and has foiled the million invisible gremlins that can inhabit any single take.

A fine director-friend, Robert Ellis Miller (*Reuben, Reuben; Any Wednesday; The Heart Is a Lonely Hunter*, etc.), is a warm and supportive but meticulous director. One cast and crew gave him a T-shirt that said on the front, "IF IT WAS SO WONDERFUL—" and on the back, "WHY DOES HE WANT ANOTHER TAKE?"

One views dailies for adequacy of performances and scores of technical details. In attendance at the screenings are the director, the editor and assistant, the director of photography, the continuity person, the art director, the production manager, sometimes the cast members involved (though some actors prefer not to see the rushes and some directors forbid actors to see them), and, certainly, the producer. A separate screening of the dailies is set up each day for the appropriate network personnel. The network executive supervising the movie will relay the network's notes to the producer.

In detail, the rushes are enormously instructive and can trigger midcourse corrections or reshoots before it is too late. As to overall realization of a film, rushes can be misleading. For security regarding the latter, one must look at the ongoing assembly, which I will come to. Before we leave the rushes, however, I want to tell you an educational story.

Pharaoh's daughter brought the baby Moses to her father in the palace, praising and cooing about the baby's beauty. The father took the baby, pushed back the enveloping wrappings, looked, and said, "You're joking. This is the ugliest baby I've ever seen." "That's funny," the daughter replied, "He looked great in the rushes."

I know how she felt. When I was with ABC in New York, one of my associates in California would phone with glowing reports about our shoots on the coast; then the footage would arrive in New York. It was no longer so glowing. Once I called and said, "Why was the shoot so great in Los Angeles and so dull in New York?" There was a long pause and then my associate said, "A lot of shows die over Denver."

If the film editor is cutting in the proximity of the production, near to the studio or to the location, he will sit with the director during each screening of the rushes. If the editor is at a home base away from the shoot location, the director will view dailies at the location, indicate his "preferred" or "starred takes" for each setup to the continuity person, who will include this information along with any special technical notes and the camera and sound reports that will be shipped with the film to the editor. (Negative film and original ¼-inch sound tapes are shipped separately.) Guided by the director's instructions, the editor will begin to cut scenes together immediately, even while the film is still being shot.

This ongoing assembly of footage, with black leader inserted for missing sequences, will be shipped back to the director for his appraisal. It is here that one begins to get a truer sense of whether and how scenes are playing. The director can give recutting notes to the editor; or, if, in conferring with the editor, he realizes that the coverage is insufficient to get what he wants in a cut, he can reshoot.

In one film of ours a scene played very well in the rushes. But in the rough assembly it was clear that an actor was delivering a key line of dialogue as he was walking out of the picture. It was the only take we had of this line. We printed up another take. Same problem, plus a weaker performance. We could not go back to the set, which was a location—a working office space that had been made available for one shooting day only. Fortunately, we did not need the actor to stand or walk out of the scene at all. (The actor had been booked for a standby day.) Originally, he had been seated on a couch against a closed Venetian blind. This had been covered in a wideshot and a medium shot for earlier lines.

We rented a duplicate Venetian blind, hung it from two grip stands, and poured heavy light through it from behind in order to match the sunlight of the original. Since we did not have the office, we did not have the couch either. Marc Daniels, the director, sat the actor on the floor, made an eye-line-of-sight position with the camera, and shot the actor close-up. He got the key line of dialogue, which played well, and the picture matched perfectly the wide and medium shots from the original day's shoot. This quick correction would not have been possible—nor the problem even discovered until too late—without a viewing of the ongoing or rough daily assembly.

Earlier, I mentioned a snag Ann hit with Dick Van Dyke. As the producer on the set that day she had to handle it, but the fault was mine.

When Van Dyke's agent at William Morris, Sol Leon, called to say that Dick would play the part, he added that Dick had some little script changes in mind and that there was one scene in particular that bothered him more than a little. Would I be willing to rewrite? Of course, I said. When CBS gave us the pickup, Ann and I and Don Taylor met Van Dyke and his manager, Byron Paul, for lunch at Ma Maison. Van Dyke is a gentle, self-effacing man, soft-spoken and shy. While Ma Maison is a primo sanctuary for celebrity wildlife, Van Dyke, a major star, seemed uncomfortable there. He commented that the restaurant was maybe too grand a place to meet. He smiled and chatted easily, though one could not help feeling that this took some energy with strangers, which we were. None of these Van Dyke characteristics is uncommon in people of the Middle West, where Dick was raised (Bloomington, Illinois). I should know; I was born (Sullivan, Illinois) and raised (Lebanon, Indiana) there and have some of them myself.

We went over Dick's script notes. Most concerned small problems easily fixed. Dick did make it clear, however, though he said it very quietly and nicely, that he had a major problem with shot 79. Here is the scene as it was written in the draft Dick had read.

DISSOLVE TO:

79   INT. THE LOFT – DAY   79

We see as CAMERA PANS the loft that the furniture is now half thrift shop and half Early American from the Connecticut house. Katherine's influence is everywhere. The CAMERA PICKS UP Ed leaving kitchen area carrying a tray which bears two compotes of fresh fruit, glasses and a bottle of champagne. The CAMERA FOLLOWS him into the bedroom area. Katherine is in bed, sitting up, reading the Sunday New York Times. She is wearing an ''I Love New York'' tee-shirt (the kind where for love is a heart). Also, glasses. Ed is in jeans, no shirt nor socks. Ed pours the champagne.

                    KATHERINE
          Champagne? For breakfast?

                        ED
          To Katherine--den mother of the huddled masses.

                                        (CONTINUED)

79   CONTINUED: 79

> KATHERINE
> To an original photographic talent
> --witty, powerful, humane.

> ED
> Aw, shucks, Ma'am.

They drink.

> KATHERINE
> I didn't say it. The New York
> Times did.
> (reading from paper)
> 'The current exhibition of work by
> Ed McCall at the Victor Jonas
> Gallery marks the debut of an
> original photographic talent--
> witty, powerful and humane.'

> ED
> (getting back in bed)
> That's me, folks.
> (Pretending to
> answer phone)
> 'Good morning, witty, powerful
> and humane.' We got to get up
> soon. Go buy a Christmas tree.

> KATHERINE
> (still reading the paper)
> We will, we will.

> ED
> Have a strawberry.

Ed puts one in her mouth.

> ED
> (continuing)
> Do you really have to go to City
> Hall this afternoon--on Sunday?

> KATHERINE
> You ought to march with me. You
> know how important those funds are
> to the center--they're cutting
> off everybody.

> ED
> Run for President.

> KATHERINE
> Maybe I will.

(CONTINUED)

79   CONTINUED: (2)   79

                          ED
          You're marvelous. I love you.
          I can't believe the change.
          You're wonderful with those kids.

                       KATHERINE
          You can't be all those years in
          therapy and not learn something.
          But, Ed, I've got to go back to
          school--real school. I don't
          want to just assist. I want to
          be a full-fledged therapist. I
          can be a damned good one.

                          ED
          You are now. Who else could show
          Tito Lopez there's more to self-
          expression than trying to assault
          your English teacher?

Katherine picks up a beautiful, ornate, red Spanish fan
from her end table.

                       KATHERINE
          I don't believe he gave me a
          Christmas present.

                          ED
          You saved his life, Katherine.

                       KATHERINE
          I cried like a baby--in front
          of the whole group. Ed--thank
          you for these past eight months.
          I feel so alive again--and
          useful.

He starts to kiss Katherine. She resists.

                       KATHERINE
                     (continuing)
          You never did tell me what happened
          at that New Year's Eve party with
          Diane.

                          ED
                     (taking her in
                      his arms)
          Nothing to spreak of, my darling.

                       KATHERINE
                     (responding)
          I'll bet, she said.
                          (MORE)

                              (CONTINUED

79   CONTINUED: 79

> KATHERINE (CONT'D)
> Wiping that stupid grin off her
> husband's face.
> (she does)
> Don't be smug. I could still
> take 'em up on their offer.

> ED
> Baby--you'd of made a fortune.

> KATHERINE
> (turned on by
> the idea)
> You think so? I'm still not too
> bad looking, am I?

> ED
> Mon Dieu. C'est sie bon. C'est
> magnifique.

Katherine works the Spanish fan and begins coming on to Ed.

> KATHERINE
> Ees better for free, no? Eh,
> Senor?

She begins to kiss him. Big kiss. Ed breaks kiss.

> ED
> Damn.

> KATHERINE
> What?

> ED
> Everything's so great--almost
> perfect. Except for Peggy and
> Bud. I wish they'd--just talk to me even.

> KATHERINE
> (grabs him,
> kissing)
> Could we discuss that later--
> okay, Gringo?

                                        FADE OUT.

<u>END OF ACT SIX</u>

Dick thought the scene was still a bit sentimental and not funny enough—his original criticisms. Also, it bothered him as being unbelievable that Ed had gotten a one-man exhibition of his photographs at a gallery—and such a good review in the *Times*—so quickly. I heard via Ann a couple of times early in the shoot that he was wondering when he would get another rewrite. In response, I tried a couple of more passes at the scene. I thought these versions were worse and did not submit them.

At that point the production was back in California, and in general everything was going smoothly. More than smoothly. Network, cast, director, crew, Ann believed they were getting something special. From looking at the rushes, so did I. I heard nothing further about shot 79, even when I visited the set one day and chatted with Van Dyke. Stupidly, I assumed that Van Dyke now trusted the scene and was willing to go with it as written.

Day 17. Only three more days to shoot. The day was to begin with shot 79. Since the production had settled into a finely tuned harmony of pros, Ann, expecting another happy and fretless day, decided she could arrive at the set at 8:30 A.M. instead of 7:00 A.M., which was still a half-hour before anything would get shot.

But when she walked in, the soundstage was curiously quiet. Nothing was happening. Before she could inquire, one of her favorite grips, a fresh-talking, I've-seen-it-all veteran came up and said, "Today's the day you earn your money, honey. You better talk to the director."

Ann found Don Taylor, who told her Van Dyke was "in his trailer"—an ominous phrase in the movie business—and was refusing to get made up or to shoot until shot 79 got fixed. Taylor added, "I've tried—this one's your baby."

Ann went to the trailer and knocked. Van Dyke let her in. Stars do not always, not always right away. He was polite but reiterated his problem with the scene and said he just could not do it as written. Ann knew that she would not be able to reach me, so she had to deal with the problem without the writer, and deal with it quickly. The meter was running, nearly a hundred people were waiting. Ann did not confront Van Dyke, which would have been a mistake.

(She never directly confronted our children either, which always amazed me. She would, instead, hear them out, sincerely weighing if whatever their need of the moment was could be satisfied. Usually, either the need would be forgotten in talk or, being unreasonable, would soon collapse of its own weight. I guess that is successful conflict management. My technique centered around "no" and "because.")

Ann agreed with Van Dyke that the scene could be better. She suggested that they send for Mariette Hartley so that she and Dick could read through the scene together, line by line, looking for changes. Mariette, a gifted comedienne and actress, is also a *mensch* or a *menschess*—a builder, not a destroyer. She knew a pickle when she saw one. She said she too was having trouble with the scene but knew they could fix it. She worked with Ann to keep the atmosphere light and constructive.

Ann dealt first with the one-man exhibition burr. She changed it so that only five of Ed McCall's photos were being shown in a *group* show. As a former New York photo journalist whose work is in the permanent collection of the Museum of Modern Art, The Museum of the City of New York, and others, Ann was able to convince Van Dyke that a group show participation for a new photographer was not unrealistic. Furthermore, she reasoned, Ed McCall, despite dropping out, remained a creative and achieving man. Having been exposed to photographs and good graphics in advertising all those years, it was not incredible that he would be a good photographer.

A former actress, Ann pulled out a technique from that experience. She said, "What's the scene about really? That you're back together and Mariette's a new woman. She's accepting the new life—thriving on it. You're both going to make it. Now, she can really forgive Ed for what he did— even thank him for it. They celebrate their new relationship by making love. Dick—why don't you and Mariette improvise that and let's see what we get." Van Dyke agreed and so did Mariette. They soon arrived at what you read as the scene in chapter 4, except for the last line. In the repeated improvs, they kept getting to Dick's last line and kept getting stuck for a way out. Finally, time was really running out. The set had been dark now for almost an hour. Ann suggested they "get it on its feet," try it on the set as far as they had improvised and established the dialogue. Mariette and Dick agreed, and Don Taylor began to rehearse them with the full crew, choreographing the camera moves. As they filmed the first take and beginning of the scene, Don whispered to Ann, "You better have a tag for this one, honey, and soon."

Ann waited off to the side, again they reached Dick's last line, and, following the idea that humor comes out of character, Ann ad-libbed: "It would put us in a higher tax bracket." Both Dick and Mariette laughed and the scene got shot.

Annie—"You earned your money, honey." The rest of the day and the rest of the shoot went off without a hitch.

The danger here is that I had turned a deaf ear to Van Dyke's quiet, gentlemanly plea for help on a scene. I should not have forced him to balk at playing the scene before it could be made right. I learned an enduring lesson.

This is some of how it goes during principal photography. The days are liquid, intense, crowded with activity, and long—5, 6, 7 o'clock in the morning to 8, 9, 10 and midnight—all of which require immense emotional discipline and physical and mental stamina. A film shoot is a microuniverse. As in wartime, deep and intimate friendships are made quickly, especially on location. There are uproarious laughs, fights, denouncements, private revelations, romances, and soaring moments of exhilaration when "it" works. There are lonely and impersonal hotel and motel rooms. The flotsam of room service. The waking to the electric fry and snow of a television set after a station has gone off the air and you have fallen asleep in front of it a few hours before watching a program you did not like. When it is all over, there is a wrap party for cast and crew, and at least one person who all along has been quiet, modest, perhaps unnoticed, gets drunk now and shows an entirely different personality. Bullies become lambs, lambs become lions, puritans become studs, and mice are made into sirens. Someone is a surprising dancer. There are effulgent thank yous, hugs, kisses, tearful goodbyes, and earnest vows to stay in touch. Vows that mostly evaporate in the scatter of personal lives and in the rekindling heat of a next shoot with differing personas. But, while you are in it, production is a sustained moment of human and logistical magic. As wondrous as a surprised deer frozen in the headlights of a car. A grand illusion of a reality that only shatters when the director finally says after the last shot of the last day, "Ladies and gentlemen, that is a wrap for today and a wrap for this production."

Then comes post. Post-production.

Some producers and directors work together right away on the editing of a film, but Ann and I think this is unfair to a director, rather like looking over the shoulder of a painter, writer, or composer in the midst of his work. For three weeks then, for us, there is little for the producer to do creatively. As the DGA rules and justice dictates, the director now gets that time to make his cut of the film. He sequesters himself in some usually grungy little cubicle called the cutting room, along with the editor and the assistant editor.

Here are miles of footage. The walls are crowded with spartan metal racks weighted with stacks of boxes and cans of film and sound tracks, all carefully labeled and numbered. Felt-lined bins on wheels are filled with the black spaghetti of film and the brown linguini of magnetic sound tracks that are kept from total chaos by their head-ends being raised to hang from a super structure aluminum frame on the bin that is teethed along the cross-bar on both sides by tiny pins, and variously attached to these pins by their sprocket holes.

Working with the completed rough assembly, the director and editor begin at the beginning of the picture, cutting, trimming, extending, replacing shots and scenes, as they move forward through the reels. Wide shots, mediums, close ups, P.O.V.s, inserts, reversals, stock or library shots. They may use the last part of a first take and the first part of a last take and the middle part of a middle take of a shot in order to make it work. They choose takes and cuts of takes to tell the story with the best possible rhythms and performances available. They weigh these against the takes with the best picture compositions, lighting, sound, and camera moves. The take finally selected may not represent the best of any of these items but is instead the best compromise.

The basic tool is an upright or flatbed editing machine—Moviola, Kem, or Steenbeck. On the uprights, the picture image is either four inches by three or eight by six; on the flatbeds, twelve high by sixteen inches wide. The film and sound track(s) are run "double system"—that is, they are separate elements at this point, and run through the editing machines in synchronous lock. The editor marks the film with yellow crayon pencils for fade ins and fade outs and dissolves and other indicated optical effects. Commercial blacks are slugged in where commercials and station breaks and promo blanks are called for by the written format provided by the network.

The assistant editor keeps all the footage and takes organized and works with labs and sound transfer and optical houses. He may, using the yellow crayon pencil, mark or "spot" the film for opening and closing credits, subject to approval by the director. He will order graphics, based on the director's selection of a typeface, style, and color. He will keep notes as to where the director and editor want to "loop" sound. This means that the natural sound in some takes is not usable or does not match in other takes of the same scene. Actors may have squashed or mispronounced lines and words. Maybe a dog barked or a truck ground its gears in the background of one take and not in another. Wind may have been a problem in exteriors, or car horns or chain saws or motorcycles and airplanes or a hundred other noise pollutions. All of this sound must be replaced and smoothed. The process is called looping and we will come to it.

Certain lines of dialogue may not work now, or a certain cut will have made it necessary to add new lines. Sometimes the director himself will write these lines, but most likely he will call in the writer. (I added seven new voiceover jokes during the editing phase of *He's Fired, She's Hired.*) The director may record these lines in his own voice and lay them into the picture as scratch tracks.

Then, when the rough cut is ready, the director calls in the producer. They look at the film together, usually with the editor, either in a screening room or on the editing machine. (When watching a complete run-through, I prefer to view the film in a screening room, since picture problems may go unseen on the small or flickering screen of the editing machine, and the sound of the machine itself can mask sound problems in the track.)

After viewing the film, the producer and director confer and minor changes are negotiated and made back in the cutting room. Major changes are another consideration. Though, fortunately, we have never experienced it, huge fights can take place between producer and director about the cut of a film.

Now the movie is shown to the supervising executives at the network with the producer, director, and probably the editor and assistant in attendance. In an after-meeting, the network executive(s) gives notes. Again, pointing out problems, maybe minor, maybe major. There are disagreements, explanations, clarifications, negotiations; and always the residual power of the network to have its way.

Sometimes the director and the producer will work together on a second cut. As I have said, Ann and I prefer to edit without the director on this producer's cut. We go through the same process with the editor that the director has been through, only in less time as a rule—a week to ten days—since we have the director's "draft," or cut, to work from. When we have finished our cut, a screening is set up again for the network, with appropriate executives, the producer, the director, the editor, and the assistant in the room.

Steve Mills at CBS usually sits in a row forward of all the others in the room, or at least he did for *Drop-Out*. I will never forget, when the picture ended and the lights went up—not unlike the scene in the advertising agency in the movie—everyone waiting silently for him to speak first. He turned, faced the group, and said, *"Now* we've got a movie. It's terrific. Congratulations, everybody." He asked for only a few minor fixes and said he would not have to see it again until we had the music and effects and an answer print.

Immediately following the screening, Ann and the editor made the minor fixes and had a finished cut. That same afternoon we screened the picture for broadcast standards and for Peter Matz, whom we had signed to compose the musical score. He and Ann and I discussed the kinds of music we wanted for the film.

Andy Gottlieb, our fine, efficient supervising producer, booked for Ann, the director, Matz, the editor, and the music editor what is called a "spotting session," in which the picture is screened, start-and-stop, from beginning to end, to discuss and decide where music shall be "spotted," or begin and end, in the various scenes of the film.

As they go through the movie, the music editor prepares a "cue sheet breakdown," which lists by frame and footage count where every musical cue comes in the film. Thirty-five millimeter film projects at 90 feet a minute and 24 frames a second. This can be put also as 1.5 feet a second or 1,440 frames a minute. These speeds are constants for all tracks that will accompany the picture. If you wanted a music cue, for instance, at three minutes and fourteen seconds into a scene, the footage counter would read 291. (Or, in fact, the accumulated count of the reel that scene is in.) The cue sheet breakdown would be marked accordingly for this scene. Musical changes within the scene, after the initial cue, would be marked in accumulated running footage count and frame count from the first cue.

The composer goes off with these cue sheets and begins to write. He may have a script that is marked with footage counts next to scenes and next to dialogue or action descriptions within the scenes, and, these days, he may have a video cassette copy of the actual picture cut. Most composers, however, still write music against the cue sheets from the spotting session without reference to the script or picture. They use a click track, which is a fancy metronome with audible, adjustable-speed clicks that can vary from 40 to 208 beats a minute. This allows the composer to maintain steady tempos against the footage count as he is writing, or scoring, as it is also called. This set of tempos is literally punched into a track that can run in synchronous time with the picture and voice tracks so that music cues can hit down to the exact frame.

While Matz was off composing, Ann and the editor set up a "looping" session and a "Foley" session with the sound editor. The term "looping" came into use in the earlier days of film when certain sound effects—say, a bird whistle—were put on separate pieces of recording tape, the ends of which were spliced together to form loops. These loops of individual sounds wound continuously over the individual sound heads, allowing the separate tapes of sound to be mixed through a console into a single soundtrack of a scene for as long as necessary without having to re-cue tapes constantly. If you listen carefully to tracks in a scene that lasts long enough, you can hear the same birdy tweet repeating at intervals—or a New York traffic horn or a dog bark and so on. Audiences rarely notice these background repetitions. The looping technique is still in use, though the loops are now in cartridges.

Looping's acquired secondary meaning has become the primary one: the lip-sync rerecording of voice sound. Actors are called into a session (no extra charge, as this work is part of what they get paid for) where they face a large screen with themselves in the various scenes of the movie. They wear headphones that feed them the original natural track at a low-decibel level. Then, looking at the picture of themselves on the screen and listening to their original voice performances, they speak into a microphone and record new voice tracks, trying to match the newly spoken words to the lip movements on the screen. They also try to match voice production to the body and face gestures, moves, and emotions on the screen.

Though most experienced film actors get good at lip syncing it is tedious work at best and always imperfect sound (or too perfect), since acoustics at the looping session studio differ from those at the original location or studio, which is why at the original site the director and sound man always ask for "wild sound" or "room tone." This means the general background sound of the location without movement or voice. It is recorded for each separate scene, usually a minute's worth; this is later looped and can play as long as needed. This room tone is mixed with the actors' looped tracks to make the actors sound as though they are talking at the original sites. You may have just finished a scene outdoors in the Grand Canyon and the sound man will call out—"Quiet, everybody. I need some "room tone." It is an expression used for exteriors as well as interiors.

There is another looping session for voice replacements and "walla walla." Suppose an actor who looks right on the screen has a flat-out terrible voice. You can hire specialists to come in and loop—lip sync—-the actor's lines. This is done frequently in commercials, where a model may be beautiful but cannot talk.

Or, suppose an original actor is not available for his own lip syncing. It may be only one or two lines that you need, and the actor is off in Morocco doing another shoot. There are actor-mimics who specialize in lip syncing and imitating the first actor's voice and speech.

"Walla walla" means crowd sounds. (I played a lot of walla walla parts when I was an actor.) Suppose you have a scene in a restaurant with an intimate conversation taking place between your two leads in the foreground. In the background are other people—they are called "atmosphere." In the shoot—in the picture—you have to have the atmosphere moving its lips and behaving naturally as people in a restaurant, but you do not want them to utter a sound, because you want clean sound from your two leads. At the looping session you add the atmosphere people's human hums and background talk—"walla, walla, walla, walla, walla, walla."

In a Foley session—a Mr. Foley invented the system—you record live or prerecorded sound effects to match actions and sounds on the screen. For instance, a car or room door slamming shut or opening. High-heel footsteps walking on concrete or parquet flooring. Gun shots. Punches. Explosions. Silver and china sounds in a dinner scene. Say we have two people toasting champagne glasses, and one is talking at the "clink." The clink may have covered the line of dialogue. You will have had the actress rerecord the line, you will have the room tone, but you have no clink. You put in the clink at the Foley session.

When I was doing the *Omnibus* shows I spoke of earlier, I was at the looping session (sometimes called the pre-lay in tape production) on the first of the two hours when Billy Foster, who would be directing the second hour, came by to visit. I had hit a snag before he got there. I had a sequence in which Gene Kelly and the former all-pro receiver of the Pittsburgh Steelers, Lynn Swann, were doing a short time-step dance together. In editing the piece, it had never occurred to me that when I had added the prerecorded music in post-production—which I had now just done—it would be impossible to hear them dancing. As I looked at the sequence—listened to it—it seemed a disaster. The sound editor had no time-step dance sound cartridges and if he had had, we would have been up all night trying to sync them first for Kelly and then for Swann. I was cursing myself for not having seen this problem ahead of time and having been prepared for it.

Foster saw my gloom and said, "Hey, what's wrong?" I told him. "No problem," he said, "I was a hoofer as a kid. Didn't you know that? I used to foot-sync at M-G-M for Kelly all the time. You got a piece of plywood?"

We found a piece of plywood, put it on the floor of a small audio booth used for announcers' and actors' lip-syncs, put Foster in the room, and played back the picture to him. He did a time-step sync, expertly for Kelly and, on a second pass for Swann, a little less certainly, perfectly matching the action in the picture. I was able to mix these tracks in balance with the music. I call that Foley to Foster to Chance. Dumb good luck.

For *Drop-Out Father,* the Foley tracks, the actors' lip-sync loops, and the walla-wallas were ready.

Ann and I went to Peter Matz's studio. He played for us on the piano--and humming as he went—against a video cassette of the picture—the themes and incidental music cues he had composed. These were fine, especially the main theme. He talked about how the music would be orchestrated. With our approval of the music, Peter next booked the recording session and the musicians. He arranged and orchestrated the score and hired a copyist to make the charts for the twenty-seven players in the orchestra. A librarian is hired to keep track of the charts. A three-hour session was booked and Peter finished in two.

Now comes the "dubbing" session. It can also be called "the mix." In videotape production it is called "the sweetening." In every case, it is the process by which all of the prerecorded elements—the Foleys, the natural tracks, the actors' loops, the walla wallas, and the music are brought together into a single balanced soundtrack. There may be as many as forty-eight channels of sound feeding through the console, feeding into a final, single piece of tape, or magnetic-striped track.

Only now is the original negative of the film cut to match the final cut of the work print. This is possible because in its initial printing the negative and all work prints have been given precisely the same "edge numbers." Edge numbers are tiny sequential digits printed on to the film itself and spaced every foot in 35mm. Following the edge numbers on the finished work print, the negative cutter cuts the negative to conform. It is precise, arid labor. As a producer, I went once to see this procedure and have never returned again.

When you have the cut negative, it is sent to the lab and a first answer print is "struck," or made, with optical effects and titles integrated. You view the answer print at the lab at this stage, without sound. Color values and light timings are sure to be off. So may be dissolves and titles. You make notes, retime, and redo opticals. You get a second corrected answer print or maybe a third and so on. When an answer print is finally acceptable, you arrange another network screening, in which the picture and sound still play double-system, separately, but in sync.

With *Drop-Out,* the network continued to be amused. Mills, for this screening, had invited all the executives in his department, even those who had not been directly involved. This is standard procedure when a picture is at this point. He had no notes and no changes to request. The film went back to the lab and a composite print was struck. This is the print that combines picture and optical soundtrack. The optical soundtrack is a picture of sound that can be transformed by a light (the exciter bulb) into electrical impulses that recreate sounds. It runs on one-tenth inch of one side of the film for the entire length of the film and is hidden from audience view by an aperture mask.

We had a good composite print, made some video cassette copies, and delivered the finished film to CBS. That is a day of high good feeling.

The movie was completed, but the producer's job was not finished. I do not mean the administrative chores, which do have to be cleaned up as well. I mean it was now time to lobby for a good air date and to go about promoting the film. Both of these tasks were made easy on *Drop-Out Father* after Harvey Shephard—the senior V.P. of CBS Entertainment—had seen the film. He decided to make it a special and scheduled it to open the season. He gave it a saturation on-air promotion campaign. Dick Van Dyke did "Entertainment Tonight" and the Griffin show. Hartley went on "The Tonight Show." Both did "phoners." These are long-distance phone interviews with television newspaper editors all around the country. They are set up by the picture's publicist, and as many as twenty may be done in a single day. Ann and I did additional phoners, as did Don Taylor, and we placed day-of-air ads in the trades. We made sure review casettes were sent to critics around the country and *TV Guide* for a "Close-Up," which we got. We hosted a pre-air industry screening of the film in Hollywood. You have to cater these, not a full dinner, but wine and cheese, etc.

We had in mind to get local CBS stations to do minidocs in their newscasts on the phenomenon of adult drop-outs in their respective communities and tie these stories to our film, but since we had only three weeks' notice of the air date, we could not get this in motion. We also missed out on Sunday color covers in newspaper supplements because of the short lead time. On *He's Fired, She's Hired,* we did get "Over 40" Clubs interested in the picture as a tie-in to their concern about aging executives confronting hiring bias. This gave "Entertainment Tonight" and local newscasts a legitimate angle and got us mentions of the picture. It is important to give the media news-slants or pegs to which your picture can tie in. While a lot of papers, magazines, and television talk and information shows will do straight coverage on your film—or out-and-out "plugs" to get a star—you enhance your chances for coverage with a news or story hook.The promotion for NBC's *A.D.* began a full year before air-time and included, in addition to the usual electronic and print coverage, special brochures and study guides to educational and religious groups. A glossy color insert in *Reader's Digest* magazine, paid for by the sponsor, Procter & Gamble, reached their circulation of seventy million people. A book version of the film made the best-seller list. Celebrity interviews via satellite were a more recent technique used by the network. This spared stars the long, cross-country tours and permitted them to be interviewed in one studio, in one city, the results to be transmitted to stations all over the country for insertion in local news, talk, and information shows.

The difficulty in all of this, beyond having good promotional ideas, is in getting an air date far enough in advance to be able to take advantage of the promotional possibilities. Except in the case of a clearly anticipated blockbuster such as *The Winds of War* and *The Day After,* networks, for competitive scheduling reasons, are loathe to commit air dates much in advance of the three-week minimum required to get listed in *TV Guide.* Or, you may get one air date, only to have it quickly changed in a network's response to what the competition has scheduled.

I mentioned lobbying for a "good" air date. What is that? Generally, it means from the season opening in mid- to late September; October (except to be opposite the baseball playoffs and the World Series, which is death), the highly desirable ratings sweep month of November; December up to the twentieth; January after the tenth; February—another desirable sweep month; early March; or May—another sweep month, though the number of sets-in-use is down in May, and while you can get a good audience share, your audience rating is likely to be lower.

From December 20 to January 10 is not so good, as the audience is preoccupied with the holidays or sated from them and views less; and advertising budgets are anemic. Mid-March through April is series rerun time, so your picture gets little program-flow help. While season-opening, November, February, and May air dates say to the business that the network regards your picture highly, you do run the risk of being scheduled against the toughest competition. Late December–early January and mid-March through April air dates signal to business insiders that the network has doubts about either the quality of your film or its ratings chances.

CBS, with a history of being number one, takes May less seriously than do the other two networks, since there is industry consensus that the "season" ends in mid-April. Indeed, General Electric wanted fully to sponsor *Drop-Out Father* as a special in May, a time of the year that served its corporate needs well, but CBS did not want to "waste" strong product there.

None of this, of course, is a pure science, but all of us take it seriously, as though it were, and fight for what we perceive to be the optimal air date.

I have told you a lot about producing movies for television. There is a lot more I am sure I have skimmed in detail or left out. Much of the role is imbedded in your brain cells and can only be summoned under the stimulus of the moment. Everything technical and procedural can be learned, or you can rely on the talented specialists who abound at every step. I do advise you to learn as much as you can as it will increase the weaponry of your creativity—knowing what is possible to do in situations—and will protect you from specialists who, when they get tired or bored—human—may withhold or forget certain "tricks," in order to rush the job and get finished with it. On the other hand, when you do not know, do not try to fake it. Ask for help and information. For the most part, all the specialists take enormous pride in their crafts and skills and are eager to contribute generously to the making of a film. Knowing or not, a producer should have as his greatest gift the ability to be a good audience. Would I pay five bucks to see this thing? Or sit through it for two hours of television time? How can I—how can *we*—make it better?

I hope you know now what a producer does, at least as it can be reduced partially to a list of specific functions. As to the "feel" you must also bring to the role, I will tell you one more story that may be instructive.

When I was producing "The Merv Griffin Show" from Broadway's Little Theatre, located on west Forty-fourth Street, next to Sardi's on the east and the St. James Theatre on the west, *Hello, Dolly* was *the* smash hit in town and was playing at the St. James. Ann and I had become friends with *Hello, Dolly*'s producer, David Merrick, and with its original star, Carol Channing, and her husband, Charles Lowe. When Carol decided to leave the show, Merrick gave a small dinner party for her and for the incoming star, Ginger Rogers, at the St. Regis Roof. We were invited. Also included were Ginger Rogers's mother and the musical's director, Gower Champion.

That same season the hottest club in New York was a disco called Arthur's, located on East Fifty-fourth Street. It generated the same heat and snobbism and drew the same status-starved crowds as Studio 54 and Xenon did in their day.

The club was named Arthur's because of John Lennon's remark once to a reporter who asked him hostilely about his long hair, "What do you call that haircut?" Lennon said, "I call it 'Arthur.' " Arthur's was run by Sybil Burton (Richard's ex-) and her new husband, Jordan Christopher, at the time a burgeoning rock star and actor.

As the dinner party was ending, Merrick said he had never been to Arthur's but would like to go. Carol Channing got excited. She too had never been, she said, but would like to see it. "But it's impossible to get in," Merrick said, and Carol agreed.

I heard myself saying, "I can get you in."

Ann looked at me as though I were crazy. "Can you?" she whispered. "Do you know someone?"

"Not there," I said, "but you'll see."

On my assurance of getting us in, Merrick and Channing agreed to go to Arthur's. The street in front of the club was so crowded with traffic that the limousine we were in could not get to the front of Arthur's, which was in the middle of the block. As we got out of the cars and began to move toward the entrance, I said to Ann, "I'm just going to walk ahead."

I made my way through a throng that looked like the last scene of Nathaneal West's *The Day of the Locust* and stood finally before a humanoid behemoth who was blocking the entrance door and who had arms and chest made of rum kegs. I was sure that he ate people of my size for snacks and had never won any prizes for congeniality.

"Hi," I said, "I'm here with David Merrick, Carol Channing, and Gower Champion—a party of six."

Grunt, he did, and said, "Where?"

I turned and coming through the crowd behind me were the people I had named. "Right behind me," I said.

Instantly, the behemoth cleared a path and our party entered without hesitation. Burton found a table for us. Through the din—I do hate those places—Merrick said to me, "I'm very impressed, Bob. You must know everybody." He referred to this incident more than once over the years of our acquaintanceship. That night, I shrugged and nodded, modestly. I felt modest. All I had done was use Merrick's name and Channing's and Champion's to get us in, which I knew would work. My God, they were stars, even if it did not occur to them that night. All I had done was "produce."

Summary

Don't

Oh, it's a good idea, lovely, fresh, original, should be done,
but I know it will never be, take it from me, not practical; you
don't know the problems; they won't let you; you don't have
the background, foreground, foreskin; the talent; I had the
same idea, but ran into endless obstacles; you have no idea,
no concept, don't even try, don't be silly, absolutely no; are
you out of your mind? You'll never finish it. Sorry, I must
forbid you and if you try, I'll stop you if it's the last thing I
do. (Trust me.)

—Ed Spitzer

That is what it feels like most of the time, having an idea, a vision, trying
in television's boisterous bazaar to keep a little stall open to trade in the
trinkets of art and entertainment. Any level of human creation begins as
an imposition on others. An impertinence. Does the world need another
book or poem or play or movie for television? Who needs *you?* Who wants
what *you* want to say and show and create? Can you companion what you
want to say and show and create with the sophist imperatives of the network buyer?

The answer, the act, is always paradoxical, like jogging in smog or
smoking and eating carrots.

Still, the screen is never blank now and must not be. Because millions
of people have made television the primal screen, a peristaltic necessity,
the buyer must buy *something* and the viewer must view *something*. People
need art, even bad art, because they cannot live without story and fantasy
and representation. Humans must have metaphor. You know it from the

prehistoric drawings on the walls of a cave at Altamira to the parboiled trash-for-cash of "Hollywood Wives"; and they need it reinterpreted, renamed, redressed, rearranged, and told anew for their times. Odysseus becomes *Road Warrior;* and Jesus, *E.T.;* and *King Lear, Cat on a Hot Tin Roof.* We sent in J. R. Ewing for Iago-Macbeth and Bill Cosby in his day for Clarence Day.

The need is perpetual. Although we seem a conceited, conniving, competing mob of carnivores to each other, it is only a few thousand writers (and producers and directors and actors and designers and technicians) who spend the days of their lives trying to fill it. Maybe, just maybe, we and the audience will have to have your help. If you cannot resist your own impertinence and your passionate need to say, it is probable that you can find your way to a home in television. If you have these, there will, in any case, be no stopping you from trying. I believe in that. The whole point of this book has been to counter "Don't" with "Do." To urge you to, as Lord Byron said, "make journies" and, as Elizabeth in *Drop-Out Father* said, to "have a tremendous adventure."

That is what my own life in television has been about, and I hope this book can be a realistic road map for the travels now that you must make. Alone. I do beseech you on the way to try to make it something honest. Something saying true. Treasure your lightning bugs, but strive, as you are able, to hurl us down some lightning. Go on now, if you must: write (and produce) and be damned if anybody can stop you. As the man said, "If it ain't on the page, it ain't on the stage."

Ladies and gentlemen, thank you—that is a wrap for today and a wrap for this production.

FADE OUT.

THE END

Appendix

The Writers Guild of America is a group of radio, television, and motion picture organizations representing writers. It has roughly 7,900 members. As a labor union it represents the membership through collective bargaining agreements with the commercial networks, PBS, major studios and independent producers, and local stations. (See chapter 2 for more details.)

Following are a list of the Guild's functions and services; its code of working rules; and a few of the key forms and information it provides to members.

Guild Functions and Services

1. Contracts
   a. Negotiation of Basic Agreements in screen, television (both live and film), radio and staff agreements (news and continuity writers).

   One (1) free copy is available to Guild members.

   b. Administration of same:
      (1) Handling of writer claims.
      (2) Checking of individual writer contracts for violations of the MBA.
      (3) Enforcement of Working Rules.
      (4) Distribution of Unfair Lists and Strike Lists.
      (5) Processing of Grievances.
      (6) Arbitrations under the MBA.
      (7) Collection and processing of television and motion picture residuals.
      (8) Pension Plan.
      (9) Health Fund.
      (10) Signatory Lists.

2. Credits
   a. Receipt of tentative notices.
   b. Arbitration of protests.
   c. Maintenance of Credit records.
   d. Distribution of Credits Manual.
   e. Credit information to members and to producers and agents.

3. Original Material
   a. Registration.
   b. Collaboration Agreements (television).
   c. Settlement of disputes (Committee on Original Material).
   d. Copyright information and legislation.

4. Agents
   a. Negotiation of Basic Agreement with Agents.
   b. Recording, filing and administration of individual agreements between writers and agents.
   c. Distribution of lists of authorized agents.
   d. Arbitration function in disputes between writers and agents.

5. Employment
   a. Compilation and distribution of TV Market Lists to members (included in the Newsletter).
   b. Compilation and circulation of motion picture and TV credit lists to producers and agents.

  c. Compilation and circulation of statistical data re members where requested.

  d. Compilation and distribution of Directory.

6. Information

  a. Inquiries by producers re member credits and contract provisions and agents.

  b. Inquiries by members and non-members re production date and contract provisions.

7. Affiliation and Cooperation

  a. The Writers Guild of Great Britain

  b. The Australian Writers Guild

  c. Association of Canadian Television and Radio Artists

  d. Writers Guild of America, East

  e. Inter-Guild Council

  f. Hollywood Broadcast Labor Council

  g. Motion Picture and Television Fund

  h. Permanent Charities Committee

  i. American Film Institute

  j. Other industry functions and services

8. Public Relations

  a. Publications-Newsletter Fade-In

  b. Trade press

  c. TV forums—Seminars

  d. Annual Awards Event

9. Credit Union

  a. Loans

  b. Investments

  c. Life Insurance

10. Group Insurance

  a. Life Insurance

  b. Disability; Hospitalization; Major Medical

11. Legislation

  a. Copyright

  b. Censorship

  c. Taxation

  d. Unemployment Compensation

12. Film Society

13. Workshop Programs

14. Support of Freedom of Expression

  a. Litigation

  b. Press

  c. Other

15. Directory

16. Committees
    a. Affirmative Action
    b. Screen and Television Awards
    c. Copyright
    d. Screen and Television Credits
    e. Cultural Exchange
    f. Freedom of Expression and Censorship
    g. Guild Study
    h. Industrial Films
    i. Original Material
    j. Publications
    k. Social
    l. Welcoming
    m. Women's
    n. Writers' Workshop
    o. Writers' Conference (and others)

17. Writers Guild Theatre
    a. Screenings (See Film Society)
    b. Rental

18. Blood Bank

19. CPR

Code of Working Rules

Operating:
1. Under the Constitution, The Guild may from time to time, adopt Working Rules, as set forth below, governing the working relationship of members with employers, agents and others with whom writers have professional dealings in connection with writing services and literary properties. Any proposed working rule must be approved by the Board of Directors before submission to the membership for approval but shall not be effective or operative if, in the discretion of the Board of Directors, it is contrary to the provisions of the Constitution or causes a breach of any contract entered into by the Guild. A VIOLATION OF ANY WORKING RULE SHALL BE CONSIDERED GROUNDS FOR DISCIPLINARY ACTION.

2. Each member shall comply with these Rules in spirit as well as in the letter.

Employment:
3. (A) All agreements and contracts between writers and producers must be in writing.
   (B) Each member must promptly file with the Guild office a copy of his contract of employment (whether such agreement provides for leasing of material, participation in profits, residuals or otherwise) in no case later than one week after the receipt of the con-

tract. *In addition to any other disciplinary action which may be deemed proper, an automatic fine shall be levied upon a member who fails to file his contract within two weeks after written notice that there is no contract on record.*

4. No member shall do any work, including reviewing stock film, before the commencement of a definite assignment under contract.

5. Each member shall comply with the terms of the Minimum Basic Agreement in spirit as well as in letter, and shall not accept any employment, sign any contract or make any arrangement for employment which violates such Minimum Basic Agreement.

6. No member shall contract for employment with any producer upon terms less favorable than those set forth in the applicable Minimum Basic Agreement.

   Violation of this rule shall subject the member to disciplinary action and a fine of up to $2,000, or on flat deals where the amount of money involved exceeds $2,000, a fine of not more than 100% of the amount received for such writing.

NOTE: If you are working at the minimum on any assignment, check with the Guild office for further particulars as to the applicable provisions of the Minimum Basic Agreements.

7. No member shall make or enter into any contract or participate in any venture requiring the writing of any literary material by such writer whereby writer's initial compensation for the writing of such material shall be less than the minimum set forth in the applicable MBA except with the specific written approval of the Guild, which approval may be granted only under unusual circumstances. In the case of joint ventures or other similar engagements or deals involving participation in profits, a waiver may be granted only where the writer's participation is substantial.

8. No member shall accept employment with, or sell literary material to any person, firm or corporation who is not a signatory to the applicable MBA.

   Violation of this Rule shall automatically subject the member to a fine, the maximum amount of which shall not exceed 100% of the remuneration received from such non-signatory.

9. It shall be the responsibility of every member to report, in confidence to the Guild office, for appropriate action, any violation or abuses of the terms and working standards established by the current Minimum Basic Agreement and Code of Working Rules, including any 'offers' of employment which violate the current Minimum Basic Agreements.

10. No member may enter into a contract for the rendition of writing services with any producer whose name is contained in the then current Guild unfair list unless such producer shall have first posted a bond

with the Guild guaranteeing the full amount of the writer's proposed compensation pursuant to such contract.

Violation of this Rule shall automatically subject the member to a fine, the maximum amount of which may not exceed 100% of his remuneration pursuant to such contract and the minimum amount of which shall be $250 or the applicable minimum, whichever is lower.

11. No member shall participate in any arrangement for ghost writing.

    Violation of this Rule shall subject the member to disciplinary action and a fine of up to $2,000.

12. Each member upon being assigned under an employment contract is required to ascertain from the proper authorities in the production company the name or names of any other writers currently assigned to the same material. It will be the obligation of the member to notify the other writer or writers on the property of the fact that he has been assigned to it.

13. Each member shall report to the Guild any engagement as a producer, director or executive, or any activities which involve the hiring and firing of writers.

Speculative Writings:

14. No member shall work for a producer on speculation or under any arrangement in which payment is contingent on approval or ability to pay. Members may, however, discuss their thoughts and reactions regarding material owned by the producer; it is recommended, however, that in such cases the writer should make a written memorandum of any suggestions made by him and register this material at the Guild office.

    Violation of this Rule shall subject the member to disciplinary action and a fine of up to $2,000.

Credits and Arbitration:

15. No member shall accept credit which misrepresents the member's contribution to a picture or program.

16. Members shall accept, abide by and contract for credit only in accordance with the terms and provisions of the applicable Minimum Basic Agreement; and members shall cooperate fully with the Guild Credits Committee in order that all credits shall properly reflect the writer's contribution to the final script.

17. Each member shall promptly report to the Guild all writing credits received on pictures or programs produced by non-signatory producers.

18. If a writer performing duties as a production executive intends to claim collaboration credit, he must, at the time he starts to work as a writer, signify such intention in writing to the Guild and to any other writer

or writers assigned to the script. *Failure to comply will subject the member to disciplinary action.* In order to be entitled to credit, such production executive must be able to furnish the Guild with written material of his own, which can be identified as his contribution to the finished script.

Pseudonym:

19. A writer must use his own name in all writing credits unless he has already established a pseudonym or registers one at the Guild office *before commencement of employment* on a writing assignment, or *before disposition of any rights* to literary material on which he wishes to use such pseudonym.

Original Stories, Series and Program Ideas:
Original Radio, Screen and Teleplays:

20. For the purposes only of these Rules, original stories, series and program ideas and original radio, screen and teleplays shall be defined as material which is the sole creation of the member or members and which is written by the member or members on his or their own time.

21. Each member shall promptly file with the Guild office a copy of his original story, series or program idea, and/or original radio, screen or teleplay sales or leasing contract, which filing shall in no event be later than one week after receipt of such contract.

NOTE: Members are strongly urged to register all literary material which they own with the Registration Service maintained at the Guild offices prior to offering such material for sale or other exploitation. While such registration is not a substitute for the statutory copyright which must be obtained on publication of the work, it is extremely helpful if suit is brought for any copyright infringement or plagiarism of the material.

Advertising:

22. The Writers Guild of America, west, Inc. has adopted and approved the agreement between the Screen Writers' Guild and the consenting trade publications condemning the following practices as unfair:

1. Slanting reviews on account of advertising, or retaliating against a writer for failure to advertise.

2. Using pressure from a writer's employer to get advertising.

3. Engaging in any harrassing practices, such as making repeated solicitation, asking for chain advertising, or soliciting an advertisement in connection with a particular picture before the picture has been previewed (or a particular show or series before the program has been broadcast).

The consenting trade publications have instructed their staffs to refrain from engaging in any of the above practices.

Members should immediately notify the Guild of any violation of the Code of Fair Practices.

Agents:

23. No writer shall enter into a representation agreement whether oral or written, with any agent who has not entered into an agreement with the Guild covering minimum terms and conditions between agents and their writer clients.

Addresses:

24. Each member shall inform the Guild of his residence address and agent and will immediately advise the Guild of any changes thereof.

    A member whose address is outside the United States shall inform the Guild immediately upon his entry into the United States.

    The Guild must be able to contact a member whenever necessary.

Standard Form
Freelance Television Writer's Employment Contract

Agreement entered into at _____,
this _____ day of _____ 19__ between _____,
hereinafter called "Company" and _____,
hereinafter called "Writer".

WITNESSETH:

1. Company hereby employs the Writer to render services in the writing, composition, preparation and revision of the literary material described in Paragraph 2 hereof, hereinafter for convenience referred to as "work". The Writer accepts such employment and agrees to render his services hereunder and devote his best talents, efforts and abilities in accordance with the instructions, control and directions of the Company.

2. *Description of Work*

    (a) IDENTIFICATION
       Series Title: _____
       Program Title: _____
       Based on _____

    (b) FORM

( ) Story	( ) Option for Teleplay
( ) Teleplay	( ) Plot
( ) Rewrite	( ) Polish
( ) Sketch	( ) Narration
( ) Non-Commercial Openings and Closings	
( ) Plot Outline—Narrative Synopsis of Story	

    (c) TYPE OF PROGRAM
       ( ) Episodic Series   ( ) Unit Series   ( ) Single Unit

    (d) PROGRAM LENGTH: _____ minutes

(e) METHODS OF PRODUCTION & DISTRIBUTION

( ) Film   ( ) Videotape   ( ) Live

( ) Network   ( ) Syndication

3. (a) The Writer represents that (s)he is a member in good standing of the Writers Guild of America (West or East), Inc., and warrants that he will maintain such membership in good standing during the term of his employment.

(b) The Company warrants it is a party to the WGA 1985 Theatrical and Television Basic Agreement (which agreement is herein designated MBA).

(c) Should any of the terms hereof be less advantageous to the Writer than the minimums provided in said MBA, then the terms of the MBA shall supersede such terms hereof; and in the event this Agreement shall fail to provide benefits for the Writer which are provided by the MBA, then such benefits for the Writer provided by the terms of the MBA are deemed incorporated herein. Without limiting the generality of the foregoing, it is agreed that screen credits for authorship shall be determined pursuant to the provisions of Schedule A of the MBA in accordance with its terms at the time of such determination.

4. Delivery

If the Writer has agreed to complete and deliver the work, and/or any changes and revisions, within a certain period or periods of time, then such agreement will be expressed in this paragraph as follows:

5. Compensation

As full compensation for all services to be rendered hereunder, the rights granted to the Company with respect to the work, and the undertakings and agreements assumed by the Writers, and upon condition that the Writer shall fully perform such undertakings and agreements, Company will pay the Writer the following amount:

(a) Compensation for services $_____

(b) Advance for television reruns $_____

(c) Advance for theatrical use $_____

No amounts may be inserted in (b) or (c) above unless the amount set forth in (a) above is at least twice the applicable minimum compensation set forth in the MBA for the type of services to be rendered hereunder.

If the assignment is for story and teleplay, story with option for teleplay or teleplay, the following amounts of the compensation set forth in (a) above will be paid in accordance with the provisions of the MBA:

(i) $_____ following delivery of story.

(ii) $_____ following delivery of first draft teleplay.

(iii) $_____ following delivery of final draft teleplay.

6. Right to Offset

With respect to Writer's warranties and indemnification agreement, the Company and the Writer agree that upon the presentation of any claim or the institution of any action involving a breach of warranty, the party receiving notice thereof will promptly notify the other party in regard thereto. Company agrees that the pendency of any such claim or action shall not relieve the Company of its obligation to pay the Writer any monies until it has sustained a loss or suffered an adverse judgement or decree by reason of such claim or action.

IN WITNESS WHEREOF, the parties hereto have duly executed this agreement on the day and year first above written.

(Writer)	(Company)

Address _____ By _____
_____ Title _____
_____ Address _____

Writer's Flat Deal Contract

(Short Form; complete screenplay, no options)

EMPLOYMENT AGREEMENT between _____
(hereinafter sometimes referred to as "Company") and _____
_____ (hereinafter sometimes referred to as "Writer"),
dated this _____ day of _____, 19___.

1. The Company employs the Writer to write a complete and finished screenplay for a proposed motion picture to be budgeted at $_____, and presently entitled or designated _____ and including the following:

   ( ) Treatment   ( ) First draft screenplay
   ( ) Original Treatment   ( ) Final draft screenplay
   ( ) Story   ( ) Rewrite of screenplay
                              ( ) Polish of screenplay

   based upon (describe form of material & title) _____
   _____

   written by _____

2. (a) The Writer represents that (s)he is a member in good standing of the Writers Guild of America, (West or East), Inc., and warrants that he/she will maintain his/her membership in the Writers Guild of America, (West or East), Inc., in good standing during the term of this employment.

(b) The Company warrants it is a party to the WGA 1981 Theatrical and Television Basic Agreement (which agreement is herein designated MBA).

(c) Should any of the terms hereof be less advantageous to the Writer than the minimums provided in said MBA, then the terms of the MBA shall supersede such terms hereof; and in the event this agreement shall fail to provide for the Writer the benefits which are provided by the MBA, then benefits for the Writer provided by the terms of the MBA are deemed incorporated herein. Without limiting the generality of the foregoing, it is agreed that screen credits for authorship shall be determined pursuant to the provisions of Schedule A of the MBA in accordance with its terms at the time of such determination.

3. The Company will pay to the Writer as full compensation for his services hereunder the sum of _____ DOLLARS ($_____), payable as follows:

(a) Not less than _____ DOLLARS ($_____) shall be paid not later than the first regular weekly pay day of the Company following the expiration of the first week of the Writer's employment.

(b) _____ DOLLARS ($_____) shall be paid within forty-eight (48) hours after delivery of the TREATMENT, ORIGINAL TREATMENT or STORY, whichever is appropriate, to the Company.

(c) _____ DOLLARS ($_____) shall be paid within forty-eight (48) hours after delivery of the FIRST DRAFT SCREENPLAY to the Company; and

(d) _____ DOLLARS ($_____) shall be paid within forty-eight (48) hours after delivery of the FINAL DRAFT SCREENPLAY.

(e) _____ DOLLARS ($_____) shall be paid within forty-eight (48) hours after delivery of the REWRITE.

4. The Writer will immediately on the execution hereof diligently proceed to render services hereunder and will so continue until such services are completed.

5. This contract is entire, that is, the services contemplated hereunder include all of the writing necessary to complete the final screenplay above described, and this Agreement contemplates payment of the entire agreed upon compensation.

_____	_____
(Writer)	(Company)
Address_____	By _____
_____	Title _____
_____	Address _____
_____	_____

Writer's Week-To-Week Contract
for Motion Pictures

(Short Form Approved by WGA/w)

EMPLOYMENT AGREEMENT between _____
(hereinafter sometimes referred to as "Company") and _____
_____ (hereinafter sometimes referred to as "Writer").
dated this _____ day of _____, 19__.

1. The Company employs the Writer to write, compose and prepare:

   ( ) Story   ( ) Polish
   ( ) Treatment   ( ) Rewrite
   ( ) Original Treatment   ( ) Other (Describe)
   ( ) Screenplay

   based upon _____
                    (describe form of material and list title)
   written by _____
   for use in the production of a theatrical motion picture photoplay
   presently designated _____
                              (title of property)
   The Writer accepts such employment.

2. (a) The Writer represents that (s)he is a member in good standing of
       the Writers Guild of America, (West or East), Inc., and warrants
       that (s)he will maintain his/her membcrhsip in the Writers Guild
       of America, (West or East), Inc., in good standing during the term
       of his/her employment.

   (b) The Company warrants it is a party to the WGA 1977 Theatrical
       and Television Basic Agreement (which agreement is herein des-
       ignated MBA).

   (c) Should any of the terms hereof be less advantageous to the Writer
       than the minimums provided in said MBA, then the terms of the
       MBA shall supersede such terms hereof; and in the event this
       Agreement shall fail to provide for the Writer the benefits which
       are provided by MBA, then such benefits for the Writer provided
       by the terms of the MBA are deemed incorporated herein. With-
       out limiting the generality of the foregoing, it is agreed that screen
       credits for authorship shall be determined pursuant to the provi-
       sions of Schedule A of the MBA in accordance with its terms at
       the time of such determination.

3. The term hereof shall commence on the _____ day of _____,
   19__ and shall continue for not less than _____ weeks and for a
   number of whole weeks thereafter until notice of termination hereof
   shall have been given as provided by the MBA.

4. The salary shall be _____ Dollars
   ($_____) per week and such weekly rate shall be prorated on the
   basis of one-fifth (1/5) of the weekly rate for each day worked after
   expiration of the guaranteed period.

_____   _____
          (Writer)   (Company)

                                         By _____
Address: _____   Title _____
_____   Address: _____
                                         _____

Notice of Tentative Writing Credits—
For Theatrical Motion Pictures

Before the writing credits are finally determined, the Company is required
to file with the Guild Credits Department (within three days after completion of principal photography) a copy of the attached NOTICE OF TEN-
TATIVE WRITING CREDITS. The notice should state the company's choice
of credit on a tentative basis. Copies should be sent to the Guild and to all
participating writers along with a copy of the final shooting script.
Please retain this blank form, running off copies as you need them.

Notice of Tentative Writing Credits—
Theatrical

                                         Date _____

TO: Writers Guild of America, West, Inc., 8955 Beverly Bl., Los Angeles,
      Ca. 90048
         AND
      Participating Writers
Names of Participating Writers   *Address*

_____   _____
_____   _____
_____   _____
_____   _____

Title of Photoplay _____
Executive Producer _____
Producer _____
Director _____

Other Production Executives, if
  Participating Writers _____

According to the provisions of Schedule A of the Writers Guild of America
Theatrical and Television Basic Agreement of 1981 credits are now being
determined on the above entitled production.

ON SCREEN, the tentative writing credits are as follows:

ON SCREEN, Source Material credit, if any:

ON SCREEN and / or in ADVERTISING, Presentation Credit, if any:

The above tentative writing credits will become final unless a protest, or
request to read the final script is communicated to the undersigned not
later than 6:00 P.M. on _____.

                                      _____
                                              (Company)
                              By _____

WRITERS GUILD OF AMERICA, west, INC.
8955 Beverly Boulevard, Los Angeles, CA 90048

September 1, 1984
AGENCY LIST

We suggest that the individual first write or telephone the agency, detail his
professional and / or academic credentials and briefly describe the nature of the
material he desires to submit. The agency will then advise the individual whether
it is interested in receiving the material with a view toward representing it.

Most agencies, as a courtesy to writers, will return material sent to them if a
self-addressed stamped envelope accompanies the submission. However, should a
submission not be returned for any reason, the individual should be aware that the
agency is under no obligation to return literary material to a writer seeking representation. The Guild cannot assist in seeking the return of material.

We regret we can offer no assistance in finding, selecting or recommending an
agent.

(*) This agency has indicated that it will consider unsolicited material from
     writers.
(**) This agency has indicated that it will consider unsolicited material from writ-
     ers only as a result of references from persons known to it.
(P) Indicates packaging agency.
(S) Society of Authors Representatives—signed thru WGAE only.

The following agencies have subscribed to the Writers Guild of America Artists' Manager
Basic Agreement to 1976:

 *Act 48 Mgmt., 1501 Broadway #1713,NY (10036), 212 / 354–4250
  Adams Limited, Bret, 448 W. 44th St., NY (10036), 212 / 765†5630
**Adams, Ray & Rosenberg, (P) 9200 Sunset Blvd, PH 25, LA (90069), 278–3000
**Agency For The Performing Arts, (P), 9000 Sunset Bl., #1200, LA (90069), 273–0744

Agency For The Performing Arts (P), 888 7th Ave., NY (10016), 212 / 582–1500
*All Talent Agency, 2437 E. Washington Bl., Pasadena (91104), 797–2422
*Allan Agency, Lee, 4571 N. 62th St. Milwaukee, WI (53218), 414 / 463–7441
**Altonl, Buddy, PO Box 1022, Newport Beach, CA (92663), 714 / 851–1711
Amsel & Assoc., Fred, 291 S. LaCienega Blvd., #307, BH (90211), 855–1200
**Animal Crackers Entertainment, 215 Riverside Dr., Newport Beach (92663), 714 / 645–4726 or 435–0255
Artists Agency, The (P), 10000 Santa Monica Bl., #305, LA (90067), 277–7779
**Artists Career Mgmt, 8295 Sunset Blvd., LA (90046), 654–6650
Artists' Entertainment Agency (P), 10100 Santa Monica Blvd., #34B, LA (90067), 557–1507
Artists Group, The, LTD., 1930 Century Park W., #303, LA (90067), 552–1100
Associated Artists Mgmt., 1501 Broadway, #1808A NY (10036), 212 / 398–0460
**Associated Talent Agency, 8816 Burton Way, BH (90211), 271–4662

Ballard Talent Agency, Mark, 1915 W. Glenoaks Blvd. #200 Glendale (91201), 841–8305
Barskin Agency, The, 11240 Magnolia Bl #201, NII (91601), 985–2992
*Barnett Agency, Gary Jay, Box 333 Bay Station, Brooklyn, NY (11235) 212 / 332–2894
**Bauer Agency, Martin, 9255 Sunset Bl., #710, LA (90069), 275–2421
**Bauman & Hiller 271–5601
Beakel & Jennings Agency. 427 N. Canon Dr. #205, BH (90210), 274–5418
**Beaty Agency, Mike, 1350 Manufacturing St., #217, Dallas, TX (75207), 214 / 747–8880
**Bennett Agency, The, 150 S. Barrington, #1, LA (90049), 471–2251
Berger Associates, Bill (S), 444 E. 58th St., NY (10022), 212 / 485–9588
**Berkeley Square Literary Agency, P.O. Box 25324, LA (90025), 207–3704
Berman, Lois, 240 W. 44th St., NY (10036)
Bernstein, Ron, 119 W. 57th St., NY (10019), 212 / 265–0750
Big Red Talent Ent. 8330 Third St., LA (90048), 463–4982
Blassingame, McCauley & Wood (S), 60 E. 42nd St., NY (10017)
**Bloom, Levy, Shorr & Assoc., 800 S. Robertson Blvd., LA (90035), 659–6160
Bloom, Harry, 8833 Sunset Blvd. #202, LA (90069), 659–5985
Bloom, J. Michael, 400 Madison Ave. 20th FL, NY (10017), 212 / 832–6900
Bloom, J. Michael, 9200 Sunset Bl., #1210, LA (90069), 275–6800
Blue Star Agency, PO Box 2754, Arlington, VA (22202)
*Braintree Prod., 422 E. 81st St., NY (10028), 212 / 472–2451
Brandon & Assoc., Paul. 9046 Sunset Bl., LA (90069), 273–6173
Breltner Literary Assoc., Susan. 1650 Broadway #501. NY (10019)
Brewis Agency, Alex, 8721 Sunset Bl., LA (90069), 274–9874
Broder / Kurland Agency, The (P), 9046 Sunset Bl. #202, LA (90059), 274–8921
*Brody, Howard T., P.O. Box 291423, Davie, FL (33329), 305 / 587–2863
Brooke-Dunn-Oliver, 9165 Sunset Blvd., #202, LA (90059), 859–1405
Brown Agency, J., 8733 Sunset Blvd. #102, LA (90069), 550–0296
Brown, Ltd., Curtis (S), 575 Madison Ave., NY (10022), 212 / 755–4200
Brown, Ned, 407 N. Maple Dr., BH (90210), 276–1131
*BTV Ltd., PO Box 460, NY (10016), 212 / 696–5469
Buchwald & Assoc., Don, 10 E 44th St., NY (10017), 212 / 857–1070
*Butler, Ruth, 8622 Reseda Bl. #211, Northridge (91324), 886–8440

*Calder Agency, 4150 Riverside Dr. Burbank, (91505), 845–7434
Career Mgmt., 435 S. La Clenega Blvd., #108, LA (90048), 657–1020
*Carpenter Co., 1434 6th Ave., San Diego (92101), 619 / 235–8482
Carroll Agency, William, 448 N. Golden Hall, Burbank (91502), 848–9948
Carvanis Agency, Maria, 235 West End Ave., NY (10023), 212 / 580–1559
**Case, Bertha, 345 W. 58th St., NY (10019), 212 / 541–9451
Catalytic Agent, The, 685 West End Ave., NY (10025), 212 / 666–3991
**Cavaleri & Associates, 6405 Hollywood Blvd. #220, Hwd. (90028), 461–2940
Charter Mgmt., 9000 Sunset Blvd. #1112, LA (90069), 278–1690
Chasler Park Citron Agency, 9255 Sunset Bl., LA (90069), 273–7190
Chasman & Stick, Assoc. 6725 Sunset Bl., #506, Hwd. (90028), 463–1115
*Cinema Talent Agency, 7906 Santa Monica Bl. #209, LA (90046), 655–1937
**Clients' Agency, The, 2029 Century Park East, #1330, LA (90067), 277–8492

*Cloud City Agency, P.O. Box 3009, Roosevelt Field Station, Garden City, NY (11530), 212 / 570–7297

CNA & Associates, 8721 Sunset Blvd., #102, LA (90069), 657–2063

Cotton, Kingsley & Assoc., 16561 Ventura Bl., #400, Encino (91436), 818 / 788–6043

Connell & Assoc., Polly, 4605 Lankershim Bl., NH (91602), 985–6266

Contemporary-Korman Artists, 132 Lasky Dr., BH (90212), 278–8250

**Conway & Assoc., Ben, 999 N. Doheny Dr., LA (90069), 271–8133

*Cooper Agency, The (P), 1900 Ave. of the Starts, # 2535, LA (90067), 277–8422

**Coppage Co., The, 9046 Sunset Bl., #201, LA (90069), 273–6173

Creative Artists Agency (P), 1888 Century Pk.E, LA (90067), 277–4545

*Cumber Attractions, Ul, 6515 Sunset Bl., Hwd. (90028), 469–1919

*C.W.A. Chateau of Talent, 1633 Vista Del Mar, Hwd. (90028), 461–2727

**D, H, K, P, R, 7319 Beverly Bl., LA (90036). 857–1234

*D..J Enterprises, 339 S. Franklin St., Allentown, PA (18102), 215 / 437–0723

Dade / Rosen Assoc, 9172 Sunset Bl. #2, LA (90069), 278–7077

*Dalmler Artists Agency, 2007 Wilshire Blvd., #808, LA (90057), 483–9783

**Davis Agency, Dona Lee, 3518 W. Cahuenga Blvd., Hwd. (90058), 850–1205

Dellwood Enterprises, 409 N. Camden Dr., #206, BH (90210) 271–7847

DeMille Talent Agency, Diana, 12457 Ventura Blvd., #104, SC (91604), 761–7171

Dennis, Karg, Dennis and Co., 470 S. San Vicente Blvd., LA (90048), 651–1700

Diamant, Anita (S), 51 E. 42nd St., NY (10017)

**Diamond Artists, 9200 Sunset Bl. #909, LA (90069), 278–8146

Donadio & Associates, Candida (S), 111 W. 57th St., NY (10019), 212 / 757–7076

**Dorese Agency, Alyss Barlow, 41 W. 82nd St., NY (10024), 212 / 580–2855

Eisenbach-Green (P). 760 N. La Cienega Bl., LA (90069). 659–3420

Elmo Agency, Ann (S), 60 E. 42nd St., NY (10165), 212 / 661–2880

Exclusive Artists Agency, 4040 Vineland Blvd., #225, SC (91604) 761–1154

*Ferguson & Berry Talent Agency, 1090 S. LaBrea Ave., #201, LA (90019), 857–0519

Ferrell Agency, Carol, 708–7773

Film Artists Mgmt. Enterprises, 8278 Sunset Bl., LA (90046). 556–8071

Fischer Co., Sy, (P), 1 E 57th St., NY (10022), 212 / 486–0426

Fischer Co., Sy (P), 10960 Wilshire Blvd. #922, LA (90024), 557–0388

Fox Chase Agency (S), 419 E. 57th St., NY (10022), 212 / 752–8211

Freeman-Wyckoff & Assoc., 6331 Hollywood Bl. #1122, LA (90028), 454–4866

Friedman Dramatic Agency, Robert A., 1501 Broadway, NY (10036), 212 / 840–5760

Frings Agency, Kurt, 415 S. Crescent Dr., #320, BH (90210), 274–8881

*Garrick Int'l Agency, Dale, 8831 Sunset Blvd., LA (90069), 657–2661

Geddes Agency, 8749 Holloway Dr., LA (90069), 657–3392

**Gerard, Paul, 2918 Alta Vista, Newport Bch, CA (92660), 714 / 644–7950

**Gerritsen International, 8721 Sunset Blvd., #203, LA (90069), 659–8414

Gersh Agency Inc., The, 222 N. Canon Dr., BH (90210), 274–6611

Gibson Agency, J. Carter, 9000 Sunset Blvd., #811, LA (90069), 274–8813

**GMA, 1741 N. Ivar St., #221, Hwd. (90028), 466–7161

Goldman & Novell Agency, The, 6383 Wilshire Blvd., #115, LA (90048), 651–4578

Goldstein & Assoc., Allen, 9000 Sunset Bl., #1105, LA (90069), 278–5005

Grashin Agency, Mauri, 8170 Beverly Bl. #109, LA (90048), 651–1828

**Gray Agency, Stephen, 9025 Wilshire Bl., #309, BH (90211), 550–7000

Green Agency, Ivan, The, 9911 W. Pico Bl., #1490, LA (90035), 277–1541

Groffsky Literary Agency, Maxine, 2 Fifth Ave., NY (10011), 212 / 677–2720

Grossman & Assoc., Larry, 211 S. Beverly Dr. #206, BH (90212), 550–8127

**Halsey Agency, Rucce, 8733 Sunset Bl., LA (90069), 652–2409

Hamllburg Agency, Mitchell, 292 S. La Cienega Bl., BH (90211), 857–1501

**Hannaway-We-Go, 1741 N. Ivar St., #102, Hwd. (90028). 854–3999

Harvey, Helen (S), 410 W. 24th St., NY (10011), 212 / 675–7445

**Heacock Literary Agency, Inc., 1523 6th St., SM (90401), 393–6227

**Henderson / Hogan Agency, 247 S. Beverly Dr., BH (90212), 274–7815

Henderson / Hogan Agency, 200 W. 57th Str., NY (10019), 212 / 765–5190
**Henry, Devin Jon, 7301 Westwood Blvd., LA (90064), 475–9737
**Hesseltine / Baker Associates, 165 W. 40th St., #409, NY (10036), 212 / 921–4460 Letters Only
*Hollywood Talent Agency, 213 Brock Ave., Toronto, Ont., Canada M6K 2LB 414 / 531–3180
*Hostetter, Esq. J. Ross, 8300 Douglas Ave. #800, Dallas, TX (75225), 214 / 363–6684
**Hunt Mgmt., Diana, 44 W. 44th St., #1414, NY (10036), 212 / 391–4971
Hunt & Associates, George, 8350 Santa Monica Bl., LA (90069), 654–6600
**Hussong Agency, Robert, 721 N. La Brea Ave., #201, Hwd. (90038), 655–2534
*Hyman, Ansley Q., 3123 Cahuenga Bl W., LA (90068), 851–9198

International Creative Mgmt. (P), 8899 Beverly Bl, LA (90048), 550–4000
International Creative Mgmt. (P), 40 W. 57th St., NY (10019), 212 / 556–5600
International Literary Agents, 9000 Sunset Blvd., #1115, LA (90069) 874–2563
*Ippolto, Andrew, 4 E. 46th St., NY (10017), 212 / 687–0404

*Jaffe Representatives, 140 7th Ave. #2L, NY (10011), 212 / 741–1359
**Joseph / Knight Agency 6331 Hollywood Blvd., #924, Hwd (90028), 465–5474

Kane Agency, Merrily, 9171 Wilshire Bl. #310, BH (90210), 550–8874
**Kaplan-Stahler Agency, 8383 Wilshire Bl., #923, BH (90211–2408), 653–4483
Karlan Agency, Patricia, 12345 Ventura Blvd., #T, SC (91604), 506–5666
**Karlin Agency, Larry, 10850 Wilshire Bl. #600, LA (90024), 475–4828
*Kerwin Agency, Wm., 1605 N. Cahuenga BL #202, Hwd (90028), 469–5155
**Keynan–Goff Assoc., 2049 Century Park East, #4370, LA (90057), 556–0339
*Kimberly Agency, 3950 W. 6th St. #203, LA (90020), 738–5087
*King, Ltd, Archer, 1440 Broadway #2100, NY (10018), 212 / 754–3505
*Kingsley Corp., 112 Barnsbee Ln., Coventry, CT (05238), 203 / 742–9575
**Kohner Agency, Paul, (P), 9159 Sunset Bl., LA (90069), 550–1060
**Kopaloff Company, The, 9046 Sunset Blvd. #201, LA (90069), 273–6173
*Kozak, Otto R., 33 Bay St., E. Atlantic Beach, NY (11561), 516 / 889–4370
Kroll Agency, Lucy (S), 390 West End Ave., NY (10024), 212 / 577–0527

**Lake Office, Candace, 1103 Glendon Ave., LA (90024), 824–9706
Lantz Office, The, 888 Seventh Ave., NY (10106), 212 / 586–0200
Lantz Office, The 9255 Sunset Bl. #505, LA (90069), 858–1144
Lazar, Irving Paul, 211 S. Beverly Dr., BH (90212), 275–6153
**Leading Artists, Inc., 445 N. Bedford Dr., Penthouse, BH (90210), 858–1999
*Lee Literary Agency, L. Harry, Box 203, Rocky Point, NY (11778), Letters Only 516 / 744–1188
Lenny Assoc, Jack, 9701 Wilshire Bl., BH (90212), 271–2174
Lenny Assoc., Jack, 140 W. 58th St., NY (10019), 212 / 582–0272
Light Co., The, 113 N. Robertson Bl., LA (90048), 273–9602
Light Co., The, 1443 Wazee St., 3rd Fl., Denver, CO (80202), 303 / 572–8363
Literary Artists Mgmt., P.O. Box 1604, Monterey, CA (93940), 408 / 899–7145
*London Star Promotions, 7131 Owensmouth Ave., #C116, Canoga Park (91303), 709–0447
Loo, Bessie, 8235 Santa Monica Bl., LA (90046), 650–1300
Lund Agency, The, 6515 Sunset Blvd., #304, Hwd (90028), 465–8280
Lynne & Reiily Agency, 6290 Sunset Bl. #1002, Hwd. (90028), 451–2828
Lyons Agency, Grace, 204 S. Beverly Dr., #102, BH (90212), 652–5290

Major Talent Agency (P), 11812 San Vicente Bl., #510, LA (90049), 820–5841
*Management One, Talent Agency, 6464 Sunst. Bl.m #590, Hwd (90028), 461–7515
*Mann Agency, Sheri, 11601 Dunstan Way #309, LA (90049), 476–0177
Maris Agency, 17620 Sherman Way, #8 Van Nuys, CA (91406), 708–2493
Markson Lit. Agency, Elaine, 44 Greenwich Ave., NY (10011), 212 / 243–8480
**Markson Literary Agency, Raya, 6015 Santa Monica Blvd., Hwd (90038), 552–2083
**Marshall Agency, The, 2330 Westwood Bl., #204, LA (90025), 650–1628
**Matson Co., Harold, 276 5th Ave., NY (10001), 212 / 679–4490

McCartt, Oreck, Earrett, 9200 Sunset Bl. #531, Hwd. (90059), 278–5243
McIntosh & Otis (S), 475 5th Ave., NY (10017), 212 / 689–1050
Merit Agency, The, 12926 Riverside Dr. #C, SO (91423). 986–3017
Merrill, Helen (S), 337 W. 22nd St., NY (10011), 212 / 924–6314
Messenger Agency, Fred, 8235 Sante Monica Bl., LA (90046), 554–3800
Miller, Lee, 1680 N. Vine St., #417, Hwd (90028), 469–0077
**Miller Agency, Peter, The, P.O. Box 764, Midtown Station, NY (10018), 212 / 221–8329
**Mills, Ltd., Robert P., 333 5th Ave., NY (10016), 212 / 685–6575
Morris Agency, William (P), 151 E. Camino Dr., BH (90212), 274–7451
Morris Agency, William (P), 1350 Ave / Americas, NY (10019), 212 / 586–5100
Morton Agency, 1105 Glendon Ave., LA (90024), 824–4089
**Moss, Marvin, (P), 9200 Sunset Bl., LA (90069), 274–8483
*Munsen Agency, Chris, 1680 N. Vine St. #721, LA (90028), 460–4461

**Nachtigall Agency, The, 1885 Lombard St., SF (94123), 415 / 346–1115
Neighbors, Charles, 240 Waverly PL, NY (10014), 212 / 924–8296

Ober & Associates, Harold (S), 40 E. 49th St., NY (10017), 212 / 759–8500
Oscard Assoc., Fifi, 19 W. 44th St., NY (10022), 212 / 764–1100

*Panda Agency, 3721 Hoen Ave., Santa Rosa, CA (95405), 707 / 544–3671
Paramuse Artists Associates, 1414 Avenue of the Americas, NY (10019), 212 / 758–5055
Phoenix Literary Agency, 150 E. 74th St., NY (10021), 212 / 838–4060
**Pleshette Agency, Lynn, 2700 N. Beachwood Dr., Hwd. (90068), 465–0428
**Preminger Agency, Jim (P), 1650 Westwood Bl. #201, LA (90024), 475–9491
Prescott Agency, Guy, The, 8920 Wonderland Ave., LA (90046), 656–1963
*Professional Authors Literary Services, 4237-2 Keanu St. Honolulu HI (96816), 808, 734–
5469
Progressive Artists Agency, 400 S. Beverly Dr., BH (90212), 553–8561

Raines & Raines (S), 475 5th Ave., NY (10017), 212 / 684–5160
Raper Enterprises Agency, 9441 Wilshire Bl. #620D, BH (90210), 273–7704
Rappa Agency, Ray, 7471 Melrose Ave., #11, LA (90046), 650–1190
**Regency Artists Ltd., 9200 Sunset Blvd., #, LA (90069). 273–7103
*Rhodes Literary Agency, 140 West End Ave., NY (10023), 212 / 580–1300 Letters Only
**Richland Agency, The, 1888 Century Park East, #1107, LA (90067), 553–1257
**R.L.M. Enterprises, 5816 Lankershim Bl., #3, NH (91601), 818 / 506–1124
**Roberts Co., The, 427 N. Canon Dr., BH (90210), 275–9384
*Roberts, Flora, 157 W. 57th St., NY (10019), 212 / 355–4165
Robinson-Luttrell & Assoc., 141 El Camino Dr. #110, BH (90212), 275–6114
**Rogers & Assoc., Stephanie, 9100 Sunset Bl., #340, LA (90059), 278–2015
Rose Agency, Jack, 6430 Sunset Blvd., #1203, Hwd (90028), 463–7300
**Ross Assoc., Eric, 50 E. 42nd St. #426, NY (10017), 212 / 687–9797

Sackhalm Agency, The, 9301 Willshire Bl., BH (90210), 858–0606
Safier, Gloria (S), 667 Madison Ave., NY (10021), 212 / 838–4868
**Sanders' Agency, Honey, 229 W. 42nd St. #404, NY (10036), 212 / 947–5555
**Sanders Agency, Norah, 1100 Glendon Ave., PH, LA (90024), 824–2264
**S.F. Agency, 595 Mission, #403, SF (94105), 415 / 495–5945
**Sanford-Becket Agency, 1015 Gayley Ave., LA (90024), 208–2100
*SBK Assoc., 11 Chamberlain, Waltham, MA (02154), 617 / 894–4037
**Schecter, Irv (P), 9300 Wilshire Blvd., #410, BH (90212), 278–8070
*Schuster-Dowdell Org., The, PO Box 2, Valhalla, NY (10595), 914 / 761–3106
*Selected Artists Agency, 12711 Ventura Bl. #460, SC (91604), 763–9731 Quary Letters
Only
*Selman, Edythea Ginis, Ltit. Agent., 14 Washington Pl., NY (10003), 212 / 473–1874
Shapira & Assoc., David, 15301 Ventura Blvd. #345, SC (91403), 906–0322
*Shapiro-Lichman, Inc., (P), 1800 Ave. of the Stars, #433, LA (90067), 557–2244
**Shaw Agency, Glenn, 3330 Barham Bl., Hwd. (90058), 851–6262
Shedd Agency, Jacqueline, 9701 Willshire Blvd., BH (90212), 274–0978
Sherrell Agency, Lew, 7060 Hollywood Bl., Hwd. (90028), 461–9955

**Shumaker Talent Agency, The, 10850 Riverside Dr., #410, NH (91609), 877–3370 Letters Only

Segel Assoc., Jerome, 8733 Sunset Bl., LA (90069), 652–6033

Smith, Gerald K., PO Box 7430, Burbank, CA (91510), 849–5388

**Smith-Freedman & Assoc., 123 N. San Vicente Bl., BH (90211), 852–4777

**Starbrite, 409 Alberto Way #C, Los Gatos, CA (95030), 408 / 253–1991

Starkman Agency, The, 1501 Broadway, #301 A, NY (10036), 212 / 921–9191

**Steele & Assoc., Elien Lively, P.O. Box 188, Organ, (NM) (88052), 505 / 382–5863

*Stereo Management. 70–29 174th St., NY (11365), 212 / 959–0722. 212 / 591–8824

Stone-Masser Agency, 1052 Carol Dr., LA (90069), 275–9599

**Swanson, H.N., 8523 Sunet Bl., LA (90069), 652–5385

Talent Mgmt. International 6380 Wilshire Bl., #910, LA (90048), 273–4000

**Talent Network Intern., 9000 Sunset Bl., #807, LA (90069), 550–0397

Targ Literary Agency, Roslyn (S), 250 W. 57th St., NY (10107), 212/582–4210

**Tel–Screen Artists, 7965 SW 146th St., Miami, FL (33158)

**Thompson, Willie, 3902 6th St., #213, LA (90020), 380–0676

Tobias & Assoc., Herb, 1901 Ave. of the Stars #840, LA (90067), 277–6211

*A Total Acting Experience, 6736 Laurel Canyon Bl. #323, N. Hollywood (91606), 818/785–7244

Twentieth Century Artists, 13273 Ventura Bl., Studio City (91604), 990–8580

**Universal Artists Agency, 9465 Wilshire Blvd., #616, BH (90212), 278–2425

*Under Agency, 6298 Salem Rd., Cincinnatti, OH (45230), 513/231–7385

*Vamp Talent Agency, 713 E. La Loma Vee. #1, Somis, CA (93066), 805/485–2001

**Vannerson Agency, Ione, 10810 Bloomfield, SC (91602), 818/985–8725

*Vass Talent Agency, 6404 Hollywood Bl., #428, LA (90028), 481–0263

*Wain Agency, Erika, 1418 N. Highland Ave. #102, Hwd. (90028), 460–4224

Wallace & Shell Agency (S), 177 E. 70th St., NY (10021), 212/570–9090

*Waugh Agency, Ann, 4731 Laurel Cyn. Blvd., #5, NH (91607), 980–0141

Wax & Associates, Elliott (P), 273–8217

Weiner & Assoc., Barry, 8200 Bi. East #10G, N. Bergen, NJ (07047), 201/859–6015

Weitzman & Assoc., Lew, (P), 14144 Ventura Blvd., #200, SO (91423), 995–4400

**Wilder Agency, The, 8721 Sunset Bl., #101, LA (90069), 854–3521

**William Jeffreys Agency, 8455 Beverly Blvd., #408, LA (90048), 651–3193

Williams Talent Agency, Frances, 3518 Cahuenga Bl., W.H. (90068), 876–2989

**Wingate Management, 8383 Willshire Bl., #644, BH (90211), 659–3207

**Witzer Agency, Ted, 1900 Ave. of the Stars #2850, LA (90067), 552–9521

World Class Talent Agency, 8530 Wilshire Bl. #203-A, BH (90211), 655–9326

Wormser, Heldfond & Joseph, 1717 N. Highland Ave., Hwd. (90028), 466–9111

Wosk Agency, Sylvia, 439 S. La Cienega Bl., LA (90048), 274–8063

*Wright Assoc., Ann, 8422 Melrose Pl., LA (90069), 655–5040 Letters Only

**Wright, Marion A., 4317 Bluebell, SC (91604), 818/765–7307

Wright Rep., Ann. 136 E. 57th St., NY (10022), 212/632–0110

**Wright Talent Agency, Carter, 6533 Hollywood Bl. #201, Hwd (90028), 469–0944

Writers & Artists Agency (P), 11726 San Vincente Blvd., #300, LA (90049). 820–2240

Writers & Artists Agency (P), 162 W. 56th St., NY (10019), 212/246–9029

**Wunsch Agency, The, 9200 Sunset Blvd., #808, LA (90069), 278–1955

Ziegler Associates, Inc. (P), 9255 Sunset Bl, LA (90069), 278–0070

**Zeltman, Jerome, 6380 Wilshire Bl. #910, LA (90048), 273–4000

LA-Los Angeles	NH-North Hollywood
BH-Beverly Hills	NY-New York, New York
Hwd-Hollywood	SM-Santa Monica
SC-Studio City	SF-San Francisco
SO-Sherman Oaks	WH-West Hollywood

All telephone numbers are Area Code 213 unless otherwise noted.

Index

ABC
  Drop-Out Father, interest in, 178
  mini-series on, 24
  movie department, 66
  movies on, 19, 20–21
  see also: Roots
"ABC's Tuesday Movie of the Week," 21
above-the-line costs, 328
accordian scenes, 96
actor-mimics, 378
actors in television, 39–40, 305–7
adaptations, 161–62
  base material, dealing with, 162
  character modification, 163–65
  dialogue in, 163
  exposition in, 165–76
  getting started on, 176
  He's Fired, She's Hired, 163–76
Adler, Stella, 57
Adventures in the Screen Trade (Goldman),
  152
advertisers, 45, 47–48
aerial shots, 119
agencies, listing of, 401–6
agents:
  importance of, 58–59
  obtaining representation of, 60–61
  package deals, 59
  reputations of, 57–58
  working relationships with, 60
Alexander, Pat, 27
American Federation of Musicians (AMF),
  306, 307

Amlen, Sy, 45
answer prints, 64*n*–65*n*, 379
art directors, 364
Asner, Ed, 36, 77, 78
Authors Guild, 61
Authors League, 61
Autry, James, 11

Baby Boom generation, 21–23, 154
backdoor pilots for series, 85
Barber, Ed, 160
Barkley, Deanne, 178–79
Beatty, Warren, 57
Bein, Nancy, 182–83, 184, 304–5
Bellin, Katherine, 37
below-the-line costs, 328
Berg, Dick, 28, 59
Beverly Hills Cop, 145, 154
"bibles," 32–34
blackouts, 121
blacks in television, 38–39
Blau, Lou, 27
Blinn, Bill, 33–34
Blue Knight, The, 23–24
Brian's Song, 21
budget forms, 309–27
budgets, 308–9, 328
Burton, LaVar, 36–37
buyers, 78–81
Byrne, Martha, 346

cable television services, 46–47
call sheets, 356, 357–58

camera directions, 112–13, 115–22
camera positions, left and right, 121–22
Carsey, John, 56
Carson, Johnny, 127–28
Carter, Jimmy, 158
casting:
  of *Drop-Out Father*, 182, 183–84, 345–46
  of *Roots*, 36–37
  star casting, 37, 76
  stunting, 36
  unknowns, use of, 36–37
casting directors, 345–46
cast insurance, 308
CBS:
  Drop-Out Father, involvement in, 182–84
  executives of, 304–5
  movie department, 63–64, 65–66
  movies on, 19
censors, network, 328–29
Changing, aborted production of, 30–31
Channing, Carol, 382
character names, 126–27, 131, 132, 158
  conflict research re, 334–35
characters, empathetic, 34
Chayefsky, Paddy, 157
Chomsky, Marvin J., 37
Cinemax, 47
Claman, Barbara, 345–46
click tracks, 376–77
cliff-hangers, 128–29
Close Encounters of the Third Kind, 154
closeups, 116, 119
Coe, George, 346
Coe, Robert, 57
Cohen, Mark, 45
Cohen, Max, 33
collage, 120
comedy, *see* humor
commercials, 128
composite prints, 64*n*, 379–80
concept testing, 124
conflict management, 372
contact sheets, 359, 360
continuity breakdowns, 342, 344, 345
contracts, 335–36
  deal memoranda, 337, 338
  location permits, 337, 339–41
  network contracts, 336–37
  writers contracts, 395–401
control over the work, 13
copyright laws, 67, 68
Corry, John, 55
costume designers, 364
coverage, 54–55

crane shots, 117–18
credits, 97–98
Curry, Jack, 45
cut (camera direction), 116–17

dailies, 366–68
Daniels, Marc, 94–95, 367
Daniels, William, 346
Davis, Martin, 85
Day After, The, 91–92
day for day boards, 347–48, 349–50
day for night, 119
Dayton, Arlene, 183–84
deal letters, 31–32
Death of a Salesman, 158
Dee, Ruby, 26
deficit financiers, 64
deForest Research, 334–35
Deknatel, Jane, 179
detail in writing, 157–58, 160–61
development budgets, 30–31
dialogue:
  in adaptations, 163
  counterpoint, 155
  cultural and ethnic variations, 148, 151
  essential dialogue, 152–53, 156, 157
  exercises to improve, 147–48, 150–51
  in exposition, 143–44
  humor through, 153, 155–56
  individuality in, 146, 149–50
  mechanistic writing of, 146–47
  misunderstandings, use of, 148–49
  originality in, 147–48
  scene bridging with, 151
  self-putdowns, 153
  speech patterns, 148
  surprise, use of, 155–56
Diller, Barry, 21, 27, 29, 34, 85
directing television movies:
  coverage of the scene, 115–16
  shot breakdowns, 115–16
director executives, 65
directors, 37–38
  editing by, 97, 374
  responsibilities of, 39
  selection of, 345
Directors Guild of America (GDA), 306, 307
dissolves, 117
dolly shots, 118
Don't (Spitzer), 384
Doubleday and Company, 43
Dramatists Guild, 61
Drop-Out Father:
  act endings, 129–30

budget for, 325, 328
call sheets, 356, 357–58
casting of, 182, 183–84, 345–46
contact sheets, 359, 360
day for day board, 348, 349–50
deForest Research examination of, 334–35
detail in, 160–61
dialogue in, 148–50, 151, 152–53, 155, 157
editing of, 376
incident in, 158–60
internal status report, 73–74
musical soundtrack, 379
network dealings re, 179–83
opening scenes, 96
pitch meetings re, 178–79
pre-production, 342–61
presentation for, 68, 69–73, 75
principle photography, 365–66, 368–73
promotion of, 380–81
scene rewrites, 368–73
script, 186–300
shooting schedule, 351, 352–55, 356
staff and crew lists, 358, 359
standards notes, 329, 330–33, 334
success of, 184
title decision, 125
writing of, 180
dubbing sessions, 379
Duffy, Jim, 45

E.T., 154
editing:
assistant editors, tasks of, 375
dialogue, additional, 375
by directors, 97, 374
equipment for, 375
network input, 375–76
during principle photography, 367
rights re, 97
second cut, 376
sound editing, 377–79
Eisner, Michael, 85
Eleanor and Franklin, 24
elevated shots, 119
entertainment divisions of networks, 50
Erman, John, 37
errors and ommissions insurance (E&O), 308
establishing shots, 11
executive producers, 302
exposition:
in adaptations, 165–76

briefing technique, 142
dialogue in, 143–44
improper, 141
newspapers, use of, 143
preparation, use of, 144–45
symbols, use of, 142–43
voiceover narrators, 142

fade in and fade out, 111, 116
Fame Is the Name of the Game, 20
Finnerman, Gerald Perry, 347
Fitzgerald, F. Scott, 94
Fixx, James, 160
Flanders, Ed, 37
flash-forward, 166
Foley sessions, 378
foot-sync rerecordings, 378–79
Foster, Billy, 378–79
freeze frames, 121
front-loading, 128

Ghostbusters, 154
Goizueta, Roberto C., 85
Goldman, William, 152
Gone with the Wind, 118
"Good Morning America," 35, 123, 156
Gordy, Barry, 39
Gottlieb, Andy, 302, 376
Greene, David, 37
grid frames, 120
Griffin, Merv, 66, 128
Guest, Jean, 346

Haley, Alex, 31, 33, 40, 43
Harris, Jean, 25
Harris, Robert, 179
Hart, Gary, 154
Hartley, Mariette, 183–84, 342, 372–73, 380
Hartman, David, 156
"Hart to Hart," 124
He's Fired, She's Hired:
adaptation process, 163–76
budget for, 326–27, 328
production reports, 361, 362–63
title decision, 123–25
Hellman, Lillian, 54
Heschong, Albert, 347
high concepts, 59
Hill, Leon, 178
Hollywood Reporter Studio Blu-book Directory, The, 67
Holmes, Oliver, 329
Homebox Office (HBO), 47, 66

home video original movie, 47–48
humor, 133, 176–77
  dialogue used to achieve, 153, 155–56
  powerlessness motif, 153–54
hyphenate-producers, 302

incident in writing, 158–60
independent producers, selling to, 81–82,
  84, 85
insurance, 307–8
internal status reports of projects, 73–74
International Association of Theatrical and
  Stage Employees and Technicians
  (IATSE), 306

jump cuts, 121
jump sound, 121

Kanin, Garson, 82–83
Kazan, Elia, 303
Kennedy, John F., 158
Kinoy, Ernest, 33
Kirgo, George, 56
Klein, Paul, 179
Klune, Donald C., 347

Landsburg, Alan, 55
Larner, Steve, 37
Laster, Owen, 60
Lawhead, Bruce E., 347
lawyers, 62–63
Lee, James, 33
Leon, Sol, 368
licensed movies, 64
lip flap, 122
lip sync, 122
lip-sync rerecording, 377–78
location / cost breakdown, 342, 343
location managers, 347
location permits, 337, 339–41
log lines, 42, 70, 79
Lonow, Claudia, 365
looping sessions, 377
Los Angeles, life in, 52–54
Love Is Not Enough, 125

McGannon, Don, 86
malaprops, 148
Mancini, Al, 47
Mankiewicz, Joseph L., 54, 116
Manulis, Martin, 28
Margulies, Stan, 33, 40
Markham, Monte, 346
Mars, Janice, 55–56

Martini, Roland, 57
"Masterpiece Theater," 23
match dissolves, 117
Matz, Peter, 376, 379
Merrick, David, 382–83
Michener, James, 28, 59
Miller, Arthur, 158
Miller, Robert Ellis, 366
Mills, Steve, 182, 183, 184, 305, 376, 379
mini-series:
  current status of, 48
  initial appearance of, 23–24
  see also: Roots
Mobil Oil, 23n
montage, 120
William Morris Agency, 59
Moses, Gilber, 37
Moss, Irwin, 179
movie departments of networks, 50
  ABC, 66
  CBS, 63–64, 65–66
  Homebox Office, 66
  NBC, 66
  personnel in, 65–66
  Showtime-Movie Channel, 66
  whitelists of, 75–76
movie studios, selling to, 81–82, 84–86
Mueller, Joseph, 14
multiple projects, importance of, 27, 73–74,
  79–80, 184–85
Murphy, Brianne, 39
musical soundtracks, 376, 379
musicians, 306, 307

National Academy of Television Arts &
  Sciences, 62
NBC:
Drop-Out Father, interest in, 178–81
  mini-series on, 23–24
  movie department, 66
  movies on, 19, 20
negative cutting, 379
negative insurance, 308
Nelson, Novella, 165
network contracts, 336–37
network executives, 29–30, 40, 304–5
New York City, life in, 50–52, 55–57

O'Connor, John, 125
off-camera voices (o.c.), 112, 121
Once Upon a Beverly Hills:
  characterizations, 130–32
  character names in, 126–27
  dialogue in, 151

exposition in, 142–45
script, 99–110
story line development, 133–38
story outline, 138–40
title decision, 125
on-line producers, 302
Operation Prime Time (O.P.T.), 47
optical shots, 122
options on properties, 26–27
prices, 28–29
two-tier structure, 28
Oseransky, Bernard, 347

package deals, 59
pan (camera directions), 117
Parks, Gordon, 39
Paul, Byron, 368
PBS, 23
Perlman, Rhea, 346
photography directors, 37–38
responsibilities of, 39
Pierce, Fred, 34, 35, 45
pitch meetings, 65–66, 67–68, 77–81, 178–79
point of view shots (p.o.v.), 120
post-production:
answer prints, 64*n*–65*n*, 379
composite prints, 64*n*, 379–80
dubbing sessions, 379
editing, 374–76
musical soundtracks, 376, 379
negative cutting, 379
sound editing, 377–79
powerlessness theme, appeal of, 153–54
pre-production:
call sheets, 356, 357–58
casting decisions, 345–46
contact sheets, 359, 360
continuity breakdowns, 342, 344, 345
day for day boards, 347–48, 349–50
director, selection of, 345
location / cost breakdowns, 342, 343
production office, establishment of, 345
production reports, 361, 362–63
shooting schedules, 351, 352–55, 356
staff and crew lists, 358, 359
presentations, 68, 69–73, 75, 95
principle photography, 364–65
dailies, screening of, 366–68
editing during, 367
location shooting, 347
protocol on the set, 365
reshoots, 367–68
scene rewrites, 368–73

producers:
backgrounds of, 301–2
categories of, 302
entry-level jobs, 53–54
fees of, 85, 306
tasks of, 303
Producers Guild of America, 307
producing television movies:
actors, dealing with, 305–6
budget forms, 309–25
budget formulation, 308–9, 328
censors, dealing with, 328–29
contracts, dealing with, 335–41
controversial material, 329
creative personnel, dealing with, 305–6
deceit, use of, 31
details, concerns re, 366
insurance concerns, 307–8
multiple projects, importance of, 27, 73–74, 184–85
network executives, dealing with, 304–5
production control status reports, 326–27
promotional activities, 380–81
scheduling concerns, 381
script work, 304
standards departments, dealing with, 328–29, 334
unions, dealing with, 306–7
writers, designation of, 75
see also post-production; pre-production; principle photography
production control status reports, 326–27
production managers, 309, 348
production reports, 361, 362–63
programming executives, 29
promotion of movies, 380–81
network executives, wooing of, 40
newspaper and magazine ads, 41
on-air spots, 40–41
O & O markets, 41
press representatives, 42
saturation campaigns, 41
talk shows and interviews, 42–43
in *TV Guide*, 41–42
properties, 28–29, 31

QB VII, 24
quad split, 120

rack focus, 119
Radnitz, Robert, 37
Raid at Entebee, 24, 25*n*
Rand, Judy, 164
ratings, 43–44

Rayfiel, David, 55, 56
Rayfiel, Howard, 55–56
reading reports, 54–55
Reagan, Ronald, 154
rebellion theme, appeal of, 154–55
rejection, dealing with, 82–83
reshoots, 367–68
reverse shots, 120–21
Rich Man, Poor Man, 24, 44
ripple dissolves, 117
Robinson, Cynthia, 27
room tone, 377
Roots, 24
    ABC's interest in, 29
    advertisers for, 45
    casting of, 36–37
    directors for, 37
    option on, 26–27
    popular success of, 46
    promotion of, 40, 41, 42–43
    property rights, purchase of, 31
    scheduling of, 36, 43–46
    scripting of, 33–34
    step deal for, 31
Rosemont, Norman, 86
Rosenberg, Arthur, 346
Rosenwald, Julius, 83
Rudolph, Lou, 29, 33
rumors in television business, 34
Rush, Al, 178, 179, 180
rushes, 366–68

Saks, Gene, 345
Scarface, 11
scene rewrites, 368–73
scheduling, 381
    of *Roots*, 36, 43–46
Schneider, Al, 45
Schulman, John, 180, 183
Screen Actors Guild (SAG), 306–7
Screen Extras Guild (SEG), 306
script pickup, 183
scripts:
    actor directions, 115, 116
    camera directions, 112–13, 115–22
    character descriptions, 114
    credits, allowing for, 97–98
    descriptions in, 111–12, 114
    length concerns, 96–97
    opening shots, 111–14
    page structure, 95, 98–99
    physical descriptions of star parts, 114
    presentation of, 95

producer's involvement in, 304
    specificity in props and action, 114–15
    terminology, 95, 112–13, 116–22
    titles in, 112
script turnaround, 182
selling television movies:
    agents, importance of, 57–61
    buyers, concerns re, 78–80
    finished work, submission of, 82
    ideas to pitch, 86–87
    independent producers, 81–82, 84, 85
    interests of the networks, awareness of,
        67–68
    in Los Angeles, 52–54
    movie studios, 81–82, 84–86
    multiple projects, importance of, 27, 73–
        74, 79–80, 184–85
    in New York City, 50–52
    original material, 79
    payment and royalty concerns, 83–84
    phone calling, 82
    pitch meetings, 65–66, 67–68, 77–81,
        178–79
    presentations, 68, 69–73, 75, 95
    production personnel decisions, 75–76
    rejection, dealing with, 82–83
    star casting, 76
    talking the idea, 77–78
    unowned properties, ethics re, 27
sets-in-use numbers, 43
Shanks, Ann:
    casting decisions, 165, 345
    Drop-Out Father scene rewrite, 368,
        372–73
    Mobil Oil campaign, 23*n*
    pitch meetings, 77–78
    title decisions by, 125
    working relationships, 304
Shanks, Bob:
    career of, 13–14
    Changing project, 30–31
    commercials, dealing with, 128
    early days in New York City, 55–57
    "Good Morning America," involvement
        with, 35, 123, 156
    "Mary White" production, 37
    pitch meetings, 77–78
    rejection, dealing with, 82–83
    table at Arthur's, 382–83
    titles of programs and movies, 123–25
    working relationships, 304
Shaw, Jim, 45
Shephard, Harvey, 30, 380

shooting schedules, 351, 352–55, 356
Showtime / Movie Channel, 47, 66
Sidel, Ellie, 305
Silberling, Bob, 305
Silverman, Fred:
  personality of, 34–35
  Roots project, 36, 41, 45–46
Simon, Niel, 126
Simpson, O. J., 36
Six Wives of Henry VIII, 23
soft property, 182
sound editing, 377–79
soundtracks, 122
Space, 28
Spitzer, Ed, 89, 384
split screen, 120
spotting sessions, 376
staff and crew lists, 358, 359
stage positions, 122
standards departments of networks, 328–
  29, 330–33, 334
standards notes, 329, 330–33, 334
Starger, Martin, 31, 34
step deals, 31, 32
Sting, The, 145
Stoddard, Brandon, 29, 33, 66
story line development, 132–34
story outlines, 138–40
supervising producers, 302
sweep periods, 43–44
swish pan (camera direction), 117

Tartikoff, Brandon, 67
Taylor, Don, 345, 346, 347, 365, 368, 372,
  373, 380
television movies:
  audience for, 25–26
  Baby Boom generation, influence of, 22–
    23
  on cable, 47
  current status of, 48
  financing of, 64
  gestation periods, 24–25
  home video original movies, 47–48
  initial appearance of, 19–21
  length requirements, 97
  licensed movies, 64
  popularity of, 21
  production approval for, 29–31
  profits from, 84, 85
  quality productions, 26, 49
  topicality in, 24–25
  see also: Roots

television series, profits from, 84–85
television viewing:
  household averages, 12
  as primal need, 11–12
Tesich, Steve, 87
theatrical movies:
  on cable television, 46–47
  on network television, 19–20
  teen audience for, 23
Thomopoulos, Tony, 45
Thompson, Tommy, 55
tilt shots, 117
titles, copyright of, 67
title sequences, 122
titles of movies, 122–26
  familiar phrases in, 126
  place names in, 126
  puns in, 125
  straightforward titles, 125–26
title testing, 124
To Be or Not to Be, 156
track record problem, 38–39
Tracy, Spencer, 345
trade papers, importance of, 76
trauma drama, 67
truck shots, 118–19
TV Guide, 41–42
Twentieth Century Fox, 19
2-shot, 119
Tyson, Cicely, 36

umbrella deals, 83–84, 86
Universal Studios, 20

Van Dyke, Dick, 157, 183, 342, 368, 372–
  73, 380
Vane, Ed, 45
vice-presidents, network, 29–30
voiceovers, 113, 121, 142

Waite, Ralph, 36
walla-walla sounds, 378
weather insurance, 308
Week-End, 118–19
White, Steve, 67
whitelists, 75–76
wide angle shots, 119
Wilcots, Joseph, 37, 39
Wildmon, Donald, 11, 12
Wilson, Irv, 180–81
wipes, 120
Wizard of Oz, The, 19, 21

Wolper, David, 24
  personality of, 25–26
  see also: Roots
Women in Film, 62
women in television, 38–39, 94
work prints, 65*n*
workshops for writers and producers, 62
Wouk, Herman, 337
writers:
  attitudes toward, 33, 55, 94–95
  career-boosting activities, 62
  connections, use of, 55–57
  entry-level jobs, 53–54
  getting started, 55–57
  loneliness of, 53
  psychological survival, 54–55
writers contracts, 395–401
Writers Guild of America (WGA), 60–61,
  387
  admission to, 61–62
  agency list, 401–6
  Code of Working Rules, 62, 391–95
  coverage by, 62
  flat deal contract, 397–99
  functions and services, 389–91
  headquarters of, 61
  as labor union, 61, 306, 307
  Manuscript Registration Service, 68
  membership of, 61
  Minimum Basic Agreement, 62
  week-to-week contract for motion pic-
    tures, 399–400
  writer's employment contract, 395–97
  writing credits, notice of, 400–1
writing television movies:
  accordion scenes, 96
  act endings, 128–30
  act lengths, 127–28
  act one, importance of, 127–28
  "bibles," 32–33
  characterization, 95–96, 130–32
  character motivations, 140–41
  character names, 126–27, 131, 132, 158
  characters, empathetic, 34
  cliff-hangers, 128–29
  commercials, allowing for, 128
  competition re, 53
  compression of words and pictures,
    156–57
  creation aspect of, 93–94
  cutting scenes and characters, 140
  death, use of, 159–60
  detail, 157–58, 160–61
  fame, from, 88
  humor, 133, 153–54, 176–77
  ideas to write about, 86–87
  incident, 158–60
  influence through, 91–92
  inspiration / perspiration ratio, 177
  legal protection of writings, 68
  logic within the script, 145
  milieu, 130
  motivation for, 88–94
  opening scenes, importance of, 95–96,
    127–28
  outlines, 138–40
  personal mark through, 89–91
  producers, involvement of, 304
  riches from, 89
  self-expression through, 89
  selling and producing, relation to, 12–13
  story line development, 132–34
  story outlines, 138–40
  theme, 130–31
  titles of movies, 122–26
  two drafts and a polish rule, 32
  visuals, emphasis on, 163
  see also adaptations; dialogue; exposition;
    scripts
Wyner, George, 346

zoom shots, 119